ESSAYS ON HUMAN RIGHTS

Contemporary Issues and Jewish Perspectives

Salo W. Baron • Herbert Chanan Brichto • David Daube
Yoram Dinstein • Leonard Garment • S. D. Goitein
Leslie C. Green • Ben Halpern • Rita Hauser • Louis Henkin
Jacob Katz • Mitchell Knisbacher • Walter Laqueur
Sidney Liskofsky • Pavel Litvinov • Michael Meerson-Aksenov
Daniel P. Moynihan • Jerome J. Shestack • Shimon Shetreet
David Sidorsky • Jacob L. Talmon

The Jewish Publication Society of America

PHILADELPHIA · 5739 – 1979

WITHDRAWN

ESSAYS ON HUMAN RIGHTS

Contemporary Issues and Jewish Perspectives

EDITED BY DAVID SIDORSKY

In collaboration with SIDNEY LISKOFSKY
and JEROME J. SHESTACK

Copyright © 1979
by The Jewish Publication Society of America
All rights reserved
First edition
ISBN 0-8276-0107-7
Library of Congress catalog card number 78-1170
Manufactured in the United States of America

Designed by Adrianne Onderdonk Dudden

Burgess

DS
143
.E76

c. 2

In memory of
JACOB BLAUSTEIN
and
RENÉ CASSIN

1981 FEB 2.3.

CONTRIBUTORS

SALO W. BARON is professor emeritus of Jewish history, literature, and institutions at Columbia University and director emeritus of Columbia's Center of Israel and Jewish Studies. He has served as president of the American Academy for Jewish Research and the American Jewish Historical Society. Among his many works is the multivolume classic *Social and Religious History of the Jews*.

HERBERT CHANAN BRICHTO is professor of Bible at Hebrew Union College–Jewish Institute of Religion in Cincinnati. He is a member of the Society of Biblical Literature and the American Oriental Society, and the author of numerous articles on philological and conceptual issues in biblical criticism.

DAVID DAUBE was Regius Professor of Civil Law and Fellow of All Souls College, Oxford from 1955 to 1970. Since then he has been professor of law at the University of California at Berkeley and director of the Robbins Collection. A Fellow of the British Academy and of the American Academy for Arts and Sciences, he has served as president of the Classical Association of Great Britain. His publications include *Collaboration with Tyranny in Rabbinic Law*.

YORAM DINSTEIN, dean of the Faculty of Law of Tel Aviv University, is a professor of international law and editor of the *Israel Yearbook on Human Rights,* and has taught at the University of Toronto. A member of the Israel Permanent Mission to the United Nations, he has also represented Israel on the Commission on Human Rights and the Sub-Commission on Prevention of Discrimination and Protection of Minorities. He is chairman of the Israel Section of Amnesty International. His books include *International Claims* and *International Law and the State.*

LEONARD GARMENT was the United States representative to the UN Commission on Human Rights in 1975. He has served in the White House as special consultant and acting counsel to President Nixon and as an assistant to President Ford.

S. D. GOITEIN is a member of the Institute of Advanced Studies at Princeton. He is director emeritus of the School for Oriental Studies of the Hebrew University, Jerusalem and was professor of Arabic there and at the University of Pennsylvania. His books include *Introduction to Muslim Law* and *A Mediterranean Society: The Jewish Communities of the Arab World.*

LESLIE C. GREEN has been professor of international law at the University of Alberta since 1965 and is the director of studies of the Canadian Council on International Law. He has taught international law in Singapore and India, in several European countries and in South America. He is the author of *Law and Society* and *Superior Orders in National and International Law.*

BEN HALPERN, Richard Coret Professor of Near Eastern Studies at Brandeis University since 1968, was research associate at the Harvard Center for Middle East Studies. He is the author of *The American Jew: A Zionist Analysis* and *The Idea of a Jewish State.*

RITA HAUSER was United States representative to the UN Commission on Human Rights from 1969 to 1972, and a delegate to the Twenty-fourth General Assembly. A member of the State Department's Advisory Panel on International Law, she has lectured at the Naval War College and the U.S. Army War College, and in universities in Australia, New Zealand, Egypt, and India.

LOUIS HENKIN is Harlan Fiske Stone Professor of Constitutional Law at Columbia University and a director of the Columbia Center for Human Rights. He is president of the United States Institute of Human Rights and a member of the board of editors of the *American Journal of International Law.* Among his many books and articles is *How Nations Behave.*

JACOB KATZ is professor of Jewish history at the Hebrew University in Israel and has been a visiting professor at Columbia, Harvard, and the University of California. His books include *Tradition and Crisis: Jewish Society at the End of the Middle Ages* and *Exclusiveness and Tolerance.*

MITCHELL KNISBACHER is an attorney with the office of the General Counsel, U.S. Postal Service. His published works include articles on the protection of the right of emigration under international law in the *Harvard International Law Journal* and a legal analysis of the Entebbe operation in the *Journal of International Law and Economics.*

WALTER LAQUEUR is chairman of the research council of the Center for Strategic and International Studies of Georgetown University. He has taught at Johns Hopkins, Chicago, and Brandeis universities. He is coeditor of the *Journal of Contemporary History,* and his publications include *Communism and Nationalism in the Middle East, Young Germany,* and *A History of Zionism.*

SIDNEY LISKOFSKY is director of the Division of International Organizations of the American Jewish Committee and program consultant to the Jacob Blaustein Institute for the Advancement of Human Rights. A UN representative of the International League for Human Rights, he was also an adviser to the U.S. delegation of the Twentieth General Congress of UNESCO. He is the author of numerous articles on international human rights and coeditor of *The Right to Leave and the Right to Return.*

PAVEL LITVINOV, a grandson of former Soviet Foreign Minister Maxim Litvinov, was a leader of the Moscow democratic dissident community and was arrested for human-rights activities, including leading public protests against the Soviet invasion of Czechoslovakia in 1968. An editor of *A Chronicle of Human Rights Events in the USSR* and author of *The Demonstration in Pushkin Square,* he teaches physics at the Hackley School in Tarrytown, New York.

MICHAEL MEERSON-AKSENOV, a graduate of Moscow University in history, taught Russian history in Moscow and worked in the Institute of World History of the Academy of Science in the USSR from 1968 to 1971. After leaving Russia in 1972, he studied theology in Paris, New York, and Jerusalem. He is coeditor (with Boris Shragin) of the anthology *The Political, Social, and Religious Thought of Russian* Samizdat.

DANIEL P. MOYNIHAN, senator from New York, served as the U.S. Permanent Representative to the United Nations, Ambassador to India, and presidential assistant for urban affairs. Senator

Moynihan has been professor of government at Harvard and director of the Joint Center for Urban Studies of Harvard and the Massachusetts Institute of Technology. His books include *Maximum Feasible Understanding* and *The Politics of a Guaranteed Income.*

JEROME J. SHESTACK is president of the International League for Human Rights. He has lectured in law at the University of Pennsylvania and Rutgers University and has served as chairman of the Section of Individual Rights and Responsibilities of the American Bar Association.

SHIMON SHETREET, a lecturer in law at the Hebrew University of Jerusalem, has taught law at the University of London, University of Manitoba, and the University of Oklahoma. Born in Morocco, he studied law at the Hebrew University in Jerusalem and received his doctorate of civil law from the University of Chicago. He has published widely on Israeli legal issues.

DAVID SIDORSKY is professor of philosophy at Columbia University where he teaches ethical theory and political philosophy. His publications include a study of the works of John Dewey, essays on the liberal tradition in modern European thought, and *The Nature of Disagreement in Social Philosophy.*

JACOB L. TALMON is a professor of modern history at the Hebrew University, Jerusalem. A member of the Israel Academy of Sciences and Humanities, he has also been a member of the Institute for Advanced Studies in Princeton and of the Netherlands Institute in Wassenar. He has been a visiting professor at Oxford, Columbia, and M.I.T. Among his books are *The Origins of Totalitarian Democracy, Political Messianism—The Romantic Phase, Israel Among The Nations,* and *The Myth of the Nation and the Vision of Revolution—The Origins of Ideological Polarization in the Twentieth Century.*

ACKNOWLEDGMENTS

Several of the essays in this volume were first presented at the McGill International Colloquium on Judaism and Human Rights, sponsored by the Jacob Blaustein Institute for the Advancement of Human Rights of the American Jewish Committee, the Canadian Jewish Congress, the Consultative Council of Jewish Organizations, and the International Institute for Human Rights (Cassin Foundation). The colloquium was initially proposed by Karel Vasak, then secretary-general of the International Institute for Human Rights in Strasbourg, and currently director of UNESCO activities in human rights. This book had its origin in that colloquium. We are grateful to the Jacob Blaustein Institute for the grant that made this book possible and express our thanks to the members of the Administrative Council of the Institute for their understanding and encouragement.

We thank Secker and Warburg Ltd. for permission to reprint "Mission and Testimony: The Universal Significance of Modern Antisemitism" from its collection of Jacob L. Talmon's essays *The Unique and the Universal* (London, 1965). The present essay, a shorter version of the original, contains additional material written for this volume by Professor Talmon.

Two essays in this book have appeared in differing forms (under different titles) in Israel. We are grateful to the *Israel Yearbook on Human Rights* for permission to use "The International Human

Rights of Soviet Jews" by Yoram Dinstein and "Some Reflections on Freedom and Conscience in Israel" by Shimon Shetreet from volume 4 of the *Yearbook*. Mitchell Knisbacher's essay "The Jews of Iraq and the International Protection of the Rights of Minorities (1856–1976)," written for this volume, has also appeared in the *Israel Yearbook on Human Rights,* volume 6.

We should also like to thank *Commentary* magazine for permission to reprint Walter Laqueur's article "The Issue of Human Rights" from their number of May 1977.

Finally, it is a pleasure to acknowledge the major debts we have incurred in the preparation of this volume.

Maier Deshell, editor of The Jewish Publication Society of America, has provided firm guidance in the shaping of this book.

Morris Fine offered wise counsel and strong support, reflecting his own sensitivity to the themes of this work.

Judith Roberts has been extraordinarily generous and helpful in the myriad secretarial and organizational tasks that were required throughout the gestation of the book. The demands made on her time and energy were always met with enthusiasm and grace.

This volume benefited greatly from the linguistic skills and literary sensibility of its copy editor, Cyrille White.

We deeply appreciate these contributions.

D. S.

CONTENTS

ONE CONTEMPORARY CONCERNS

HUMAN-RIGHTS ISSUES IN THEIR NATIONAL CONTEXTS

TWO THE HISTORICAL DEVELOPMENT IN
JEWISH THOUGHT AND EXPERIENCE

CLASSICAL SOURCES

Contents | xv

MODERN MOVEMENTS

DAVID SIDORSKY

Introduction

I

This collection of essays on the topic of human rights reflects the broad range and diversity of recent writings on the theme and exhibits the coherence and convergence that emerge in current discussion of the relevant issues. As the title of the book indicates, all the essays revolve around two focal points—contemporary issues and Jewish perspectives.

The concern with contemporary problems is expressed in a group of essays, written primarily by persons who have been protagonists in the forums of the United Nations, on the role and direction of the United Nations in the international protection of human rights. There is also an examination of the special responsibilities and new initiatives of American policy in the area of human rights. In addition to the topical analysis of the issues, there is a regional approach to the current status of human rights with case studies of the Soviet Union, Iraq, and Israel.

The concern with Jewish perspectives is asserted through a series of essays that investigate the significance of the classical Jewish sources of the biblical, rabbinic, and medieval periods for the development of human rights. There is also a number of interpretations of the relevance for human rights of crucial aspects of Jewish experience in modern times: Jewish emancipation and liberalism, national self-determination and Zionism, contemporary totalitarianism and new forms of anti-Semitism.

While the two themes that are brought together in this book have autonomous subject matter and are capable of independent treatment, they are related in many different ways and on many levels. Historically, this relationship can be traced back to the earliest phases of the idea of human rights since the concept has roots in both Hebraic and Hellenic thought. In modern times, the interaction between the Jewish community and movements for human rights has been intense and complex. That interaction is a recurring theme throughout the volume.

Thus, in his essay "The United Nations and Human Rights: 'Alternative Approaches,' " Sidney Liskofsky is primarily concerned with safeguarding the traditions of freedom within the spectrum of human rights at the United Nations. In the course of his analysis, he reviews the origin of the UN human-rights institutions in the early postwar planning of the international organization's structure. He shows that a major motive for their founding was the recognition by the Allied nations of the need for some response to the belated revelation of the Nazi policies directed against European civilian populations—epitomized by the acts of genocide carried out primarily against the Jewish population of occupied Europe.

Daniel P. Moynihan stresses the importance of an American position in the United Nations forums which would confront the efforts of the Soviet Union and its collaborators to exploit the human-rights machinery of the United Nations for their political advantage. Yet the climax of that confrontation, as Senator Moynihan shows in his essay "The Significance of the Zionism-as-Racism Resolution for Human Rights," involves the UN's adoption of a resolution that would distort the goals of a proposed international decade of activity against racism by defining Zionism as a form of racism.

Similarly, Leonard Garment's essay "Majoritarianism at the United Nations and Human Rights," which derives from his experience as American delegate to the UN Human Rights Commission, is an argument for an American policy that would counter what he believes to be the conspiratorial actions of the totalitarian nations in using UN programs in human rights to harm the interests of the Western democracies. Garment shows that a primary goal of these actions has been the delegitimization of Israel as a member of the international community.

The human-rights programs and activities of the UN symbolize and reflect, often in mirrored distortion, the state of human rights in various countries of the world. In assessing the progress of human rights it is important to examine national developments in human rights. An event of paramount importance is the emergence of a human-rights movement in the Soviet Union and some other countries of Eastern Europe.

Pavel Litvinov, an early leader of the Soviet human-rights movement, recounts its origins and first aspirations and struggles in his essay "The Human-Rights Movement in the Soviet Union." For Litvinov, the critical factor was the awareness by a small group of courageous activists of the significance of the rule of law and of democratic "traditions of practice" for societal reform. In the aftermath of the partial thaw of the Stalinist regime, this awareness generated a movement that would stress respect for the legally recognized human rights of Soviet citizens rather than for an ideologically oriented revolutionary transformation of Soviet social structure.

The Soviet human-rights movement relates to Soviet society independent of the Jewish community but it has had particular significance for that community which suffers a unique deprivation of rights in that society. Yoram Dinstein has indicated that significance by enumerating in his essay "Soviet Jewry and International Human Rights" the list of rights that Soviet Jews would be able to exercise if only the Soviet Union would permit the practice of rights that it has already explicitly recognized in its international agreements. Dinstein demonstrates that the Jews of the Soviet Union, both as a collective group and as individuals, are denied cultural and religious freedom as well as freedom of educational choice, rights which are granted to all other minority groups in that country. Interestingly, he suggests that were it not for this singular discrimination, the claim of Soviet Jews for the right of emigration would represent a form of preferential treatment since other citizens of the Soviet Union are not permitted to emigrate. In Dinstein's view, since the injustice to the Jewish community of the Soviet Union is unique, their claim for remedy can also be distinctive, that is, a right to emigrate.

There is an instructive contrast between the theses of Pavel Litvinov and Yoram Dinstein. Litvinov stresses the common fate of all Soviet citizens who are denied some fundamental human rights. Dinstein stresses the special fate of the Soviet Jewish community that is denied some human rights recognized in the Soviet system. Yet in the context of the Soviet human-rights movement, these two approaches may not be too divergent.

Thus Michael Meerson-Aksenov, in his essay "The Influence of the Jewish Exodus on the Democratization of Soviet Society," shows how often the self-consciousness of each of the two forms of dissident activity—request for the right to emigrate or efforts to achieve human rights within Soviet society—is heightened by the other. In fact, as Meerson-Aksenov notes, the impact of the more concrete process of receiving an exit visa through personal petition and protest is much greater upon the proverbial Soviet man-in-the-street. It provides a readily understandable model of the "thinkability" and even "doability" of individual assertion of rights against the totalitarian system. Taken together the three essays by Litvinov, Dinstein, and Meerson-Aksenov present a spectrum of the contemporary human-rights issues in the Soviet Union. They also indicate the measure of courage and resourcefulness that is required in the effort to assert human rights within an established totalitarian system.

There are few parallels between the human-rights situation in the Soviet Union and in Iraq. An important difference from the point of view of the Jewish polity is that the fate of the Iraqi community has been sealed, while the outcome of the struggle of Soviet Jews remains undecided. It is only in terms of the drama of its history and, perhaps, also its significance for helping to shape the agenda of human rights that the case of the Iraqi Jewish community compares with that of the Soviet Union.

As Mitchell Knisbacher points out in his article "The Jews of Iraq and International Protection of the Rights of Minorities (1856–1976)," the Jewish community of Iraq may properly be considered the oldest community of the Diaspora. It traces its history back (though not in a virtually unbroken chain of residential continuity like Rome) to the biblical exile of Babylon. There is an appropriate eschatological tremor in the thought that the community whose final days are being recounted had its great creative moments, inter alia, in the prophetic works of Ezekiel under Nebuchadnezzar, the debates of the talmudic rabbis under the Sassanids, and the philosophical writings of Saadia Gaon in the period of the early Islamic caliphate.

Knisbacher's point of departure, however, is not the unique historical aspects of the Jews of Iraq but their paradigmatic legal and moral status as a minority community. In that country, there was a significant attempt to apply all of the major systems of international protection of the rights of a minority devised in the past century: from bilateral treaty arrangements among great powers through the League of Nations mandate system in the age of declining colonialism to the present proto-system of international covenants for the new nation states of the Third World. Knisbacher's reading of the record, both in its partial success and ultimate failure, is instructive for a range of comparable situations.

The record in Iraq has policy implications, though not unambiguous directives, for Jewish communities residing in other Arabic or even Islamic countries from Morocco and Tunisia to Syria and Iran. It has even more relevant implications for other minority populations in the Middle East, including the Armenians, and particularly the Kurds in Iraq and the Maronite Christians in Lebanon.

Finally, Knisbacher's account raises the most challenging and disturbing questions regarding the intolerant attitude toward the human rights of minorities by ruling groups in countries that have only recently liberated themselves from the subjugation of colonial status and are driven by the perceived need for national and social unification. An alphabetical listing of such countries would begin with Afghanistan, Bangladesh, Burma, Burundi, and Cambodia, and would conclude with Uganda, Vietnam, and Zaire.

There is a special poignancy and force to this question if it is turned toward the Israeli record on human rights. Israel represents not only a new nation in Asia that has recently achieved sovereign status but also an historic people with a considerable body of experience in suffering deprivations of human rights, as well as a major religious tradition in which high standards of treatment for minorities have been asserted. Against that background, Shimon Shetreet explores the adequacy of the legal protection of religious freedom in Israel. In his essay "Freedom of Conscience and Religion in Israel," Shetreet suggests some of the complexities involved in the adjustment of a millennial tradition

of religious law to the requirements of a secular society undergoing rapid technological and social change. Although he recognizes the distinctiveness of Jewish legal tradition and the political
complexity posed by legislation on religious issues in Israel, Shetreet argues the case for the application to Israel of the general
norms of religious freedom as interpreted in contemporary Western
societies. In doing so, he probes recent Israeli court decisions on
religious freedom and recommends directions for reform.

Much more central to the character of Israel's stand toward
human rights in the light of its own past is Israel's treatment of
minority groups. A particularly challenging case is the Israeli administration of the West Bank and the Gaza Strip since this involves the governing of a large Arab population in a territory that
was captured during a war that has not been ended by the terms
of a peace treaty. The challenge is compounded by the fact that
the territory is claimed by an organized and potentially violent
terrorist movement based in neighboring and belligerent countries.

Since the spotlight of UN investigation of human rights focuses
so selectively on a handful of politically determined targets, of
which Israel is one, there is more difficulty than usual in determining even the appropriate basis for evaluation of the human-rights
performance of the Israeli administration. However, the recognition of the bias of those organs of the UN that are influenced by
the Soviet or Arab blocs, does not in itself disprove alleged abuses
of human rights just as the selective morality of those organs does
not legitimate a double standard. Jerome J. Shestack examines
the relevant and applicable legal and moral standards in his essay
"Human-Rights Issues in Israel's Rule of the West Bank and
Gaza." Using those standards, he surveys the record of the decade
of Israeli rule in the administered territories. An interesting consequence of this kind of inquiry is its demonstration of the thesis
that even the most difficult and contested issues of contemporary
political conflict can be examined in their human-rights aspects by
a fact-finding and judicial procedure. It is a thesis whose implementation in specified geographic areas or with reference to specified human-rights abuses has great significance for contemporary
progress in human rights.

The turn from the examination of contemporary issues to the
interpretation of the classic sources for Jewish perspectives of

human rights confirms a remarkable fact about present-day use of moral concepts. That fact is the translatability of moral terms from the idiom of one society or the vocabulary of one language into those of another. It is evident, as the case in point, that the contemporary phraseology of human rights had not been used in the formulation and the expression of the moral ideas of many earlier and different societies, including biblical, rabbinic, and medieval Judaism. Yet the explication of the terms that were employed for moral expression in similar contexts and the careful transposition of the appropriate frame of reference point to the relevance of the ideals and values of these earlier societies for the analysis of human rights in our own times.

In general, the attempt to understand another culture always requires the interpretation of its own unique moral vocabulary and its distinctive way of framing ethical attitudes. Accordingly, the student of any culture that is different in time or place—whether anthropologist, historian, linguist—or simply a person in search of what T.S. Eliot has termed the "usable tradition," inevitably translates the terms of another moral vocabulary, which have been embedded in their own context, into the more familiar contemporary idiom.

As Herbert Chanan Brichto points out in his essay "The Hebrew Bible on Human Rights," there is no term in biblical Hebrew that can be translated as human rights. Even though the moral concepts of biblical literature were characteristically formulated in language that preferred reference to concrete things and persons rather than to abstract entities like rights, it is possible to identify and delineate biblical attitudes to issues that today would be understood as human rights. Indeed, most often the Bible is cited as a source for moral judgment or human rights through acontextual exegesis, without any consideration of the ways in which the very meaning of its moral concepts were developed in the institutional framework of ancient Near Eastern culture. Since Brichto makes use of the comparative historical and literary evidence, his characterization of the moral attitudes of biblical literature is often novel and challenging. On the basis of this characterization, Brichto examines how and why those attitudes resemble or differ from contemporary human-rights standards.

Analogously, in his essay "The Rabbis and Philo on Human Rights," David Daube begins by investigating the meaning of a number of terms in the literature of the Talmud that were used to perform a function similar to that of the appeal to human rights in contemporary moral discourse. Daube's method is to trace the use of a particular term in a series of linked contexts so as to delineate the trend or thread of the rabbinic argument on a specific theme. By the use of this method, Daube is able to present the texture and pattern of the attitudes of the Talmud on some areas of human rights. Since these attitudes are expressed in discussion of numerous legal cases—both actual cases decided by rabbinic courts and hypothetical cases in which inferences are drawn as to the appropriate legal and moral standards consistent with rabbinic decision and precedent—Daube's approach enables him to characterize the moral values of the Rabbis without claiming to adduce the governing dictum from the variety of competing opinions and arguments. Particularly given the idiosyncratic character of this body of materials, it is instructive to note how claims of human rights can be formulated in a different frame of discourse.

Along these lines, S.D. Goitein shows that for medieval Jewish philosophers (just as for their Muslim and Christian counterparts) the thesis of human freedom and dignity was not asserted by derivation of the rights of man qua man but by the determination of the duties of man qua creature of God. Still, when Goitein turns to the substantive issues of what would now be termed the protection of the human rights of individuals, in his essay "Human Rights in Jewish Thought and Life in the Middle Ages," he is able to chart the considerations that entered into the treatment of such diverse groups as slaves, women, children, strangers, or the poor. These considerations and the arguments advanced in support or in criticism of legal or moral procedures relating to these classes of persons are intelligible to us, even though there have been many changes in belief, outlook, and institutional context since the medieval period. Accordingly, there is no necessarily illegitimate anachronism in evaluating the achievement of human rights in a different historical tradition.

This point has some relevance for current discussion as well. So often the debate over human rights in many international forums, particularly as it relates to the application of political or civil liberties in economically underdeveloped countries, turns upon the question of moral universalism versus moral skepticism or relativism. It is noteworthy that contemporary human-rights standards can be transposed and understood, to a degree, in moral traditions that antedate the specific idiom or frame of reference of the modern human-rights movement.

The three essays of Professors Brichto, Daube, and Goitein are, each in its own way, responses to the challenge of a comparative approach in which the standards developed in the literature of human rights are compared and contrasted with the sources of Jewish tradition. Yet in carrying out this comparison, there is, inevitably, some sketching of the indigenous moral landscape of these works. The moral vision that is present in these works is only partially related to issues of human rights and requires interpretation in its own terms. In the process of examining their relevance for human rights, an interpretation is advanced that illumines the moral assertions of these classics in their own historical and cultural frame of reference.

It is also noteworthy that all three bodies of literature under review—the Bible, the literature of the rabbinic period, and the writings of the medieval Jewish philosophers—had an important formative influence in the development of moral thought and attitudes outside their own historical societies. The moral themes and theses of the Bible have transcended—whether in transmission, interpretation, exegesis, or distortion—both ancient Near Eastern and Jewish cultures to become part of the substance of the moral heritage of Western society. The rabbinic discussions provided the background and were the intellectual context for the emergence of Christianity. Indeed, the writings of both Josephus and Philo, that were contemporaneous with rabbinic literature, became accepted to a far greater degree in Christian circles than they ever were in Jewish tradition. The medieval Jewish philosophers, most of whom wrote in Arabic, were deeply influenced by Islam and contributed reciprocally to its development. These writings, through diverse and sundry channels, subsequently became part of the common heritage of Western culture.

These works had a role in shaping the religious traditions of Western society. Those traditions, in turn, had an important influence on the standards embodied in the doctrines of human rights. At the same time, the characteristic and major formulations of doctrines of human rights in the modern period have often been directed against the religious presuppositions of the moral traditions of Western culture. Thus, the ancient or medieval thesis that all

men ought to be treated with equality of consideration was re-
formulated in the secular thesis that all men have natural rights.
The change in formulation marked a shift in political and social
policies and attitudes. Many efforts to realize the political, civil, or
social rights of excluded and deprived groups and individuals were
launched under the banner of natural rights. It is in the context of
those efforts that the struggle of Jewish communities for civil rights
took place and that the relationships between Jewish groups and
movements for human rights were formed.

Thus, as Salo W. Baron points out in his essay "The Evolution
of Equal Rights: Civil and Political," the emancipation of the
Jews of Western Europe was related to the emergence of a social
order in which all citizens would have equal rights. The supporters
of the new or modern social order proposed eliminating certain
forms of discrimination against Jews as part of the ending of a
system that assigned special status to a variety of religious, occupational, or hereditary groups. Baron also suggests that in the course
of the process of emancipation there took place a significant
transformation in the attitudes of the Jewish communities of
Europe.

The nature of that transformation is, in part, the theme of Jacob
Katz's essay "Post-Emancipation Development of Rights: Liberalism and Universalism." As a result of that transformation,
there developed different forms of Jewish religious self-identifica-
tion in Western Europe. Further, Jewish groups and individuals
often became part of the vanguard of European liberalism. Katz
raises some interesting considerations about the degree to which
these liberal attitudes of emancipated Jews can be traced back to
the Jewish past, even to the influence of prophetic religion. In any
event, new patterns of involvement of the Jewish community with
the cause of universal human rights were developed.

Interaction between the new forces of modernity and the traditional factors of Jewish religious belief and ethnic identity forms
the theme of Ben Halpern's essay "Jewish Nationalism: Self-
Determination as a Human Right." Jewish traditionalists in the
pre-modern period related to Zion as a "sacred space" or as a
locus of messianic redemption; they were not interested in the
project of nation-building or in the founding of a political state.
Secularized Jews were influenced by European nationalist move-

ments of the nineteenth century and many saw in liberal nationalism or in the idea of a national cultural renaissance a model for the revitalization of the Jewish community. In a symbiosis between selected aspects of Jewish tradition and liberal or even socialist thought, the various ideologies of Jewish auto-emancipation, Jewish nationalism, or Zionism were formulated. In the context of human rights, these ideologies reflected the belief that individuals have human rights, as members of linguistic, ethnic, or even religious groups, to collective self-determination.

The emergence of self-determination as a human right is examined in Leslie C. Green's essay "Jewish Issues on the Human-Rights Agenda in the First Half of the Twentieth Century." As Green shows, the recognition of this right was a major factor in the deliberations of the Versailles Peace Conference and was used in the redrawing of the map of Europe after the First World War. He indicates that the Zionist movement represented a pioneering effort in the assertion of the human right of self-determination for an oppressed minority. Accordingly, Green reviews the movement's legal history in the context of an experiment in the implementation of such a human right.

The view that human rights also includes the needs that individuals have as members of a group did not only affect the issue of Zionism in Jewish history of the recent past. In the protection of the minority groups of Eastern Europe as in the concern for the rights of minorities in mandated territories, international recognition was accorded to minority rights. Here too, as Green relates for several East European countries (and Knisbacher has documented for Iraq), the Jewish community was involved in a pioneering effort to define and maintain rights of minority cultural and communal self-expression.

It is a mark of the retrogressive character of the twentieth century that one of the final pioneering efforts on which Green reports in his survey of the human-rights record refers to the achievement of Raphael Lemkin. That achievement is the introduction and acceptance in international law of the concept of genocide, defined to include the destruction of a nation through "mass killings" or through forced disintegration of national or cultural identity. Lemkin first unsuccessfully initiated his proposal—which ultimately led to the adoption of the Genocide Convention by the

UN General Assembly in 1948—at an international legal conference in 1933.

The catastrophic impact of the rise of contemporary totalitarianism for universal human rights is the point of departure of Jacob Talmon's essay "Mission and Testimony: The Universal Significance of Modern Anti-Semitism." Talmon traces the roots of modern totalitarianism, particularly Nazism, and shows how anti-Semitism was intrinsically connected with its own ideological self-definition. This connection involved, in Talmon's account, a repudiation of the two most powerful moral traditions of Western civilization: Christian humanitarianism and secular rationalism. Christianity, which affirmed the contributing role of the Jewish people in its own development, was repudiated through a number of extremist interpretations of the entire religious and cultural history of the West. Secular rationalism, which asserted the equality of all persons, including Jews, was repudiated through an appeal to new and often pseudo-scientific or pseudo-historic theories of racism. In consequence, the struggle of the Jews against their totalitarian oppressors became inseparable from the effort of the West to maintain the integrity of its own moral heritage. Thus, in Talmon's reading of the record of the past century, the Jews have been cast (and not for the first time) in the role of symbol, victim, witness, and even champion in the battle for human rights.

The study of history relates of course to the past. It requires going beyond the historical record to decide what are the implications of history for action or what commitments and policies a community should adopt in the light of its history. The interpretation of the historical record in human rights, however, can bring an enhanced perception to the challenging task of policy-making in this field.

II

"Books have their own histories." This volume had its genesis in a series of papers prepared for an international conference on human rights held at McGill University in April 1974. From that conference it derived its dual focus since several sessions at McGill discussed the relationship between Judaism and human rights while others concentrated on the place of the United Nations in the international protection of human rights.

The extraordinary career of the idea of human rights in the past five years gave new impetus and direction to the present collection. Since 1974, we have witnessed great expectations for the realization of human-rights goals in American foreign policy and the perversion of the ideal of human rights in resolutions adopted in the most universal forums of the international community. An important task set for this volume is to interpret and to examine the record of the vicissitudes and achievements of human rights in this period.

Many of the topics discussed in this volume—whether they are theoretical concerns or issues of practical policy, whether they raise problems that relate to scholarship in history and morals or involve the strategies and tactics of contemporary powers—have become the subject of intense and ongoing controversy. Although this volume was conceived as a set of independent essays on human rights and not a record of such debate—for that reason it does not include the many comments on these themes advanced at McGill both extemporaneously and in prepared comments by respondents —it is important to call attention to the range of the discussion on at least some of these topics of controversy.

RELIGION AND HUMAN RIGHTS

One theme deriving from the essays that interpret the place of human rights in Jewish tradition is the relationship between religion and human rights. At McGill Madame M.P. Herzog, former director of the human-rights activities of UNESCO, articulated the ambivalence she had discovered in human-rights activities in the course of directing international social and educational agencies in many developing countries. On the one hand, the religious traditions of the country usually comprised a series of moral aspirations, ideals, or principles which were the major stimulus in that environment for the realization of human rights. On the other hand, strongly cherished religious institutions and traditions often formed the main obstacles to the specific social changes that would result in progress for groups deprived of human rights.

Justice Haim Cohn of the Israeli Supreme Court advanced a

somewhat analogous view on Jewish religious law. Thus, in his view, Jewish religious law had been a major source of the ideal of equality of all men and had supplied a reservoir of precedents against any principle of the inequality of persons on the grounds of race, religion, or sex. Yet Justice Cohn also argued that traditional Jewish religious law, if only because it reflected the society of earlier times, contains instances of justification of discrimination on grounds of sex or religious views that are contrary to contemporary egalitarian ideals. Accordingly, the realization of human rights would require criticism and change of religious traditions.

An interesting comment on this argument was suggested by Simon Greenberg of the Jewish Theological Seminary of America. It is Dr. Greenberg's belief that the moral standards projected or exemplified in the historic religions, including Judaism, have fallen short in some instances of ideal standards recognized by contemporary moral sensibility, particularly on issues of liberty or equality. These failures, in his view, inevitably generate tension within the religion, for they stand in contradiction, explicitly or tacitly, to the primary values that the religion affirms. Therefore, any major historic religion bears within itself the seeds of its own reformation in any domain of human rights through an appeal to its own best moral insight.

An important aspect of any investigation of the relationship between religion and human rights is the parallel consideration of secular values and human rights. Thus, in the course of the McGill deliberations, Milton Himmelfarb argued that the confidence of eighteenth-century revolutionaries in the universal acceptance of natural rights like liberty presupposed a tradition of civility and moral discourse which had been brought into being by the institutions of the historic religions. Consequently, with the erosion of religious belief in contemporary secular society, the result may be a moral skepticism or nihilism which would relegate human rights, in theory and in practice, to ideological fashion or arbitrary life-style.

The thesis of the risk secularism bears for human rights, one might note, is a recurrent theme in the thought of the world's most authentic hero of the struggle for human rights, Aleksandr Solzhenitsyn, who asserts that it is an error to trace the denial of human rights in Soviet totalitarianism to Stalin's perversion of the

Leninist model, to Lenin's adaptation of the Marxist ideal, or even to Marx's socialist and historicist transformation of Western utopianism. The atrocities of totalitarianism, Solzhenitsyn avers, stem from the development of a secular and materialist cultural tradition which has been cut off from its own religious sources.

To be sure, Solzhenitsyn's thesis (which gains partial support from any interpretation of Nazism as a post-Christian phenomenon) has encountered diverse criticism. The controversy will not easily be reconciled since there is evidence of violations of human rights within institutional religions, just as there is evidence of erosion of moral character in some secular societies. At the same time, there can be no doubt that the "usable tradition" of human rights includes the reservoirs of human thought and experience that found expression in the great historic religions, and that compelling and cogent justifications of human rights have been found in the works of humanists, secularists, utilitarians, or pragmatists without any appeal to theological or metaphysical presuppositions. In the pluralistic international environment in which the movement for universal human rights operates, an ongoing examination of the relationships among secular traditions, religion, and human rights may be a good way to further progress in the clarification of human rights.

UNIVERSALISM AND PARTICULARISM IN
JEWISH PERSPECTIVES OF HUMAN RIGHTS

A perennial controversy in any consideration of Jewish communal policy on human-rights issues, and one which recurs in several of the essays in this volume, both historical and contemporary, is the relationship between activities that defend group or communal interests and those that promote universal human rights. This controversy is itself, in many ways, a particular illustration of the general tension in any foreign policy between the defense of the national interest and the realization of moral ideals.

In modern Jewish history, as Professors Baron, Green, and Katz here demonstrate, there has been a high degree of convergence between movements that supported the civil rights of all minority groups and movements that supported Jewish emancipation. It is not surprising, therefore, that major segments of the Jewish community have concluded that the optimal policy for Jews would be a universalist policy in support of human rights under which the legitimate interests of individual Jews would benefit as a matter of course.

At McGill Milton Konvitz sought to identify three different phases in Jewish communal policy on human rights. The first is characterized by an emphasis of direct-action support of the immediate needs of the Jewish community as a persecuted minority. As a paradigm, Konvitz cited the recruitment and organization by Jews of their own self-defense units during the breakdown of governmental protection in the period of the Russian pogroms at the turn of the century.

A second phase is marked by the founding of Jewish communal organizations in several countries of Western Europe and the United States whose primary purpose was the protection of the rights of Jewish individuals and groups subjected to discrimination or persecution in other countries. The activities of these organizations ranged from seeking guarantees of religious freedom for Jewish communities within the Ottoman empire or assisting the development of a primary Jewish school system in the ghettos of North Africa to facilitating the emigration of Jews from Romania or Russia. There would appear to be a semantic option to describe these programs as supporting particularistic communal interests or as advancing the universal human rights of persecuted individuals and deprived minority groups.

A third phase is distinguished by the adoption of the thesis of the indivisibility of human rights. In Konvitz's view the agenda of the major Jewish communal organizations since the Second World War has stressed the advancement of universal human rights as the practicable means for attaining a political and social environment in which the interests of the Jewish community, like other minorities, are appropriately safeguarded.

The two emphases—the universal and the particular—reflect a fundamental dichotomy of perspective and attitude, even though formulas for reconciling them can be developed. After all, particular interests cannot be protected in a general community in which fundamental human rights are frequently and casually violated, while the ideal of universal human rights, as of any common good, has no point if it is not realized in the welfare of special groups and particular communities. In practice, the disagreement hinges upon the appropriate balance between actions which are perceived as satisfying legitimate and usually immediate group interests and those which are perceived as directed toward a more inclusive and usually more remote social goal.

One major criticism of the universalist approach is directed against the psychological origins of universalism. The criticism is that the universalist approach reflects the cultivated moral sensibilities of the more protected and insulated Jewish groups rather than the more pressing needs and interests of deprived and threatened Jewish communities. In a variant of this argument, the Jewish assertion of moral universalism is itself seen as the product of the rejection of the ghetto by Jews who have only recently left the ghetto behind them and bear a kind of "trauma of ghettoization." As a result, they constantly seek to demonstrate their transcendence of their ghetto background by identifying with universalist causes. There are abundant examples of such identification, usually characterized by an almost obsessive hostility to the assertion of any Jewish interest as legitimate. Historically, Marx's singling out of Judaism for special opprobrium as a reactionary religion is an apt illustration. A contemporary recurrence of this phenomenon is the declaration by some Jewish members of the left that the State of Israel, alone among the many sovereign states that have arisen in response to modern nationalist movements, is illegitimate.

These are extreme cases, though from the perspective of the psychological argument they are typical. Just as there is a natural and widespread tendency to abandon ghetto customs and practices, so there would seem to be a parallel drive to assert an inverse of the ghetto attitudes of in-group solidarity. The more controversial instances are to be found where Jews have supported the priority of universal movements aimed at achieving liberty and equality for all groups at the price of some degree of weakening of Jewish interests. Examples range from the tragic activity (in retrospect) of Jewish civil libertarians who advocated the rights of the banned Nazi movement to participate in elections in Bavaria in the 1920s, to the much less significant insistence by some American Jewish defenders of free speech on the rights of the American Nazi party to hold public rallies.

The issue of general civil rights and particular Jewish communal interests has also been raised in some discussion of affirmative-action policies, reverse-discrimination justification, or the adoption of "benign" group quotas. To a greater or lesser degree, some have suggested that there is a conflict between the vanguard civil-libertarian position and the interests of the Jewish community in open access of its members to employment and educational opportunities.

The issue does not hinge, of course, upon the validity of the psychological argument. Universalists can claim that prudent pursuit of Jewish group interests requires some degree of sacrifice of short-term advantages for the common good. Critics of this view respond that the pursuit of an image of moral universalism becomes immoral when it calls for a sacrifice of the legitimate needs and interests of the relatively disadvantaged or deprived within the Jewish community, especially in a political framework where the decision-making process is structured as a negotiation of compromise among competing assertions of group interests.

In wider historical terms, the most pervasive ideological debate on Jewish particularism and universalism took place in the first three decades of this century between the Jewish socialist and Zionist movements. The socialists (and many liberals) argued that Jewish interests and aspirations could best be realized by efforts toward the achievement of a just national polity and international order which would lead to the abolition of war and of all manifestations of racial and religious prejudice. The Zionists argued that Jews should try to achieve a Jewish national homeland both as a potential residence for refugees and as a base for political advocacy in a world in which racial and religious discrimination seemed to be constant.

Though this debate was often polarized, there were also many activities and programs that sought to compromise, reconcile, or synthesize these two movements. As Leslie C. Green indicates in his essay in this volume, the Zionist cause was formulated in terms of the universal human right to national self-determination and many socialists, even in the Soviet Union, argued the case for the human rights of minorities to ethnic and linguistic self-expression. One interesting formula of reconciliation was advanced by Sigmund Freud in a letter to Theodor Herzl, in which, among other matters (the letter dealt mainly with the possibility of Herzl reviewing Freud's book on the interpretation of dreams), the founder of psychoanalysis hailed the founder of political Zionism as a champion of the "human rights of the Jewish people."

In any event, by the 1940s Nazism had cut the knot of polemics and stilled the ideological controversy. There emerged a broad and deep consensus in favor of Zionism as a recognition of the special needs of the Jewish people who had uniquely suffered genocide and also in support of new international instrumentalities to strengthen universal human rights. The adoption in 1948 by the UN General Assembly of three major instruments—the United Nations report on the partition of Palestine that led to the founding of the State of Israel, the Universal Declaration of Human Rights, and the Convention on Genocide—was a confirmation of this consensus.

Since the controversy identified by the phraseology of particularism and universalism reflects, as previously noted, a fundamental dichotomy of attitudes, it is not surprising that it should recur in new contexts. Thus, in some measure, the expectation that the State of Israel should undertake unilateral and extraordinary risks to its national security for the sake of peace and the rights of Arabs derives from the tradition of Jewish universalism. The contrary view, that Jews should liberate themselves from an internalized double standard and recognize the appropriateness of policies that assert the national interest within the conventions of international diplomacy, usually derives its support from the tradition of Jewish particularism. Although this controversy is only one aspect of a fundamental and complex policy decision, it is an important conditioning factor.

Another current expression of this dichotomy is the controversy within the Soviet Jewish community between a strategy which emphasizes the achievement of human rights for all Soviet citizens, including Jews, and one which focuses on the right of Soviet Jews to emigrate to Israel.

Some of the leading Soviet Jewish activists have urged the separation of the emigration movement from the general human-rights movement. Their argument is straightforward. The recognition by the Soviet authorities of civic, political, or cultural rights requires a revolutionary transformation of the Soviet system; consequently, its realization is difficult and improbable. No great structural reform is required, however, for the Soviet authorities to permit and increase Jewish emigration. Under the formula, often the fiction, of reunification with relatives abroad, or in the guise of repatriation, emigration has been sanctioned by the Soviet system. (Indeed, the government has sometimes made use of this means to expel dissidents who were not Jewish and had explicitly denied any intention of emigrating to Israel.) It follows that Jewish emigration can be achieved in substantial numbers, even beyond the record figures attained in the first six months of 1974, if this goal is pursued independently of other kinds of confrontation on human-rights questions with the Soviet Union.

There are many variants and alternatives to this thesis. As previously noted, Yoram Dinstein suggests in his essay that it is possible to develop a rationale for the human rights of Soviet Jews that might strengthen the justification for Soviet Jewish emigration. Reference has also been made to Michael Meerson-Aksenov's report of the ways in which the activities of potential emigrants impact in practice upon the movement for human rights. Moreover, there is the argument that since emigration of the Jewish community under a simple projection of Soviet Jewish population and optimal rate of emigration would go on for several decades, there is no practical option other than also to support the human rights of Soviet Jews who will continue to live in the Soviet Union. Indeed, a significant degree of interaction is to be discerned between the leadership of the Soviet human-rights movement and of the emigration movement.

The most dramatic evidence of this is afforded by the case of Anatoly Shcharansky, a leading figure in the Soviet dissident movement, whose trial and sentence in July 1978 received worldwide attention. Shcharansky's original act of dissidence within the Soviet system derived from the discovery of his self-consciousness as a Jew. This resulted in an application for emigration to Israel. The denial of his application and his enforced separation from his wife Avital catalyzed his activity as a leader in the Soviet movement for human rights. Shcharansky became a leading spokesman for the group that aimed to monitor Soviet implementation of the Helsinki Accords under which the Soviet Union committed itself to observance of human rights of its own citizens. With the Soviet effort to imprison or exile virtually all of these monitors, Shcharansky was singled out to be tried for treason and sentenced to thirteen years. His statement to the Soviet court, just before the sentence was pronounced, places its stress upon emigration to Israel:

Five years ago, I applied to emigrate to Israel. Now, as never before, I am far from my dreams.

One would think I would be sorry, but I am not. I am happy because I have lived at peace with my conscience and I have never betrayed my conscience even when threatened with death. I am happy that I helped people, and I am proud to have met and worked with such honest and courageous people as Sakharov, Orlov, and Ginzberg. I am happy to have witnessed the process of liberating Soviet Jewry.

Those close to me know that I wanted to exchange the life of an activist in the Jewish emigration movement here for a reunion with Avital in Israel. For more than 2,000 years, my people have been dispersed. Wherever Jews were, they would repeat every year: "Next year in Jerusalem." At present I am as far as ever from my people, from Avital, and many hard years of exile are in store for me.

To my wife and my people, I can only say, "Next year in Jerusalem." To this court, which decided my fate in advance, I say nothing.

Shcharansky's statement, with its reference to both the cause of human rights and his wish for reunion with his wife in Jerusalem, is testimony to the complex and unpredictable ways in which the universal and the particular factors become fused in practice.

THE ROLE OF THE UNITED NATIONS IN HUMAN RIGHTS

The shift in position on human rights by the majority within the United Nations has brought into focus a sharp disagreement over the future role of the UN in the realization of human rights. Here, too, the formulation of the polar positions can serve to clarify the continuum of policy options.

At one extreme, there is a willingness to face up to the reality that the human-rights agencies and programs of the UN have been subverted from their original purposes. Increasingly, they have become instruments for Soviet or Arab policy directed toward the weakening of vulnerable and targeted governments aligned with the Western democracies. Consequently, it has been urged that the United States and allied governments withdraw from the offending UN agencies and programs until they are restored to authentic support of human rights. The recent U.S. withholding of dues from UNESCO and the American withdrawal from the International Labor Organization were two such responses to the extraordinarily biased behavior of UN agencies.

The proponents of this approach assert that their policy need not be a negative one. It may generate changes which will lead to their return and participation in UN human-rights programs. In any event, there are numerous opportunities for national policy to demonstrate accomplishment in human rights outside the UN. In particular, regional groups such as the European or inter-American councils for human rights provide effective mechanisms for pioneering in international protection of rights without the necessity of participating in the processes by which human-rights goals are politicized in the UN institutions.

The contrary position is that any strategy which abandons the field of human rights to the current majority at the UN, with all the moral symbolism and resonance in public opinion that the international organization still maintains throughout the world, would be a signal disservice to the ideal of human rights.

According to this view, a negative perception of the UN is inaccurate. The Western democracies still have an important voice and vote in the organization. There are many ongoing programs in human rights which have significant promise. The majority coalition is, after all, a temporary one that comprises the totalitarian nations, the Arab bloc, and many developing nations in a brittle alliance. Many of the developing nations have a strong commitment to social and economic rights which merits a response from the democratic West, not a withdrawal. Other Third World states are prepared to assert the importance of political and civil liberties and their position would be gravely weakened by an American withdrawal from UN forums. Accordingly, the proper American policy is increased participation in the UN and reiteration of its own human-rights policy in every appropriate forum.

The debate that swirls around these options shows signs of convergence. Severe critics of the United Nations performance in the area of human rights—Rita Hauser, for example, as expressed here in her essay "International Human-Rights Protection: The Dream and the Deceptions"—have argued for American readiness to confront abuses within the UN human-rights agencies. Similarly, both Leonard Garment and Daniel Moynihan have advanced American initiatives within the UN, like the proposed office of the Commissioner for Human Rights, as a response to the politicization of human-rights issues. At the McGill conference Philip Hoffman reported on his tenure as the American representative to the UN Commission on Human Rights. He stressed the ability of the Western democracies to counter the negative tendencies within the organization. Even in carrying out this defensive task, in Mr. Hoffman's view, there was a real possibility of progress toward the continuing realization of enforceable UN legal mechanisms in selected and important areas of human rights.

It is noteworthy that a founder of the United Nations human-rights system, the late René Cassin, suggested at McGill that there was an important place for human-rights activity outside the UN at the present time. His colleague David Ruzie pointed out how French anti-discrimination laws were amended in the light of activities undertaken by the UN in combating racism. And Thomas Buergenthal, at the same occasion, documented the reciprocally beneficial influences that have taken place between some UN programs in human rights and the several regional commissions dedicated to human-rights investigation and enforcement.

Still, one familiar consolation seems to have been eroded. Since La Rochefoucauld it has been customary to note that the violators of human rights at least pay lip service to the ideal. One of the disturbing facts of recent history, as illustrated in my own essay below, "Contemporary Reinterpretations of the Concept of Human Rights," is the success of the totalitarian nations in gaining acceptance, especially within the UN, of redefinitions of the human-rights vocabulary. As in *1984,* verbal obeisance is then demanded on moral grounds to the denial of human rights; hence the importance of continued semantic clarification of the idea of human rights.

The most important decisions are not semantic, however, but those of intelligence and will. The charting of an appropriate policy on the role of the UN within a framework and history delineated in this volume by the essays of Louis Henkin and Sidney Liskofsky remains a continuing challenge.

AMERICAN FOREIGN POLICY AND HUMAN RIGHTS

Most recently, new American initiatives declaring the priority of human rights in the pursuit of foreign policy have stimulated popular interest in human-rights issues. These initiatives form the topic of the opening essay in this volume, "The Issue of Human Rights," by Walter Laqueur. As Laqueur shows, new ventures in human rights necessarily entail challenging problems for the conduct of foreign policy.

There are three readily identifiable approaches within governmental human-rights policy. These are, first, the procedures of traditional diplomacy; second, the congressional initiative in human-rights legislation; and third, presidential leadership including public statements on human rights. A review in brief of some of the main claims and criticisms of each approach can illuminate the fundamental challenges to be met in designing an effective human-rights policy.

For traditional diplomacy, it has been axiomatic that national security is the primary goal of any country's foreign policy. It is recognized that support of human rights in a foreign country may be an intrinsic and legitimate national interest, particularly when there is evidence of a connection between acts of internal repression and external aggression. Thus, it is clear in retrospect that the Nazi German government's violation of human rights of its own citizens provided an early warning signal, which was tragically ignored, of its designs for expansion and aggression.

Yet, human rights can seldom be a primary and publicly pursued priority for traditional diplomacy in the contemporary world. It is an issue that tends to complicate relationships with powerful military states such as the Soviet Union and China with whom the primary task of the United States is to negotiate a structure of international stability. Human-rights goals must usually be pursued quietly in traditional diplomacy since no significant sovereign power, whether antagonistic or friendly, could permit open criticism of its internal arrangements without resort to counter-pressure. Within this realistic framework, however, traditional diplomacy permits a variety of policies both innovative and pragmatic in support of human rights of individuals in foreign countries.

A prerequisite for any governmental success in human-rights policy is its having a situation of strength in a functioning international security system. The British actions in the nineteenth century that led to the abolition of the slave trade and to the protection of religious minorities in the Ottoman Empire presupposed British naval strength. Conversely, to cite a contemporary example, there can be little point in cutting off arms aid to Ethiopia on the grounds of human-rights violations if the immediate Ethiopian governmental response is to invite mass shipments of Soviet arms and

Cuban troops. From this perspective, American foreign policy between 1968 and 1974 was able to generate significant movement in several areas of human rights. The United States was then able to use its nuclear sufficiency to negotiate mutual arms-limitations agreements with the Soviet Union and was also capable of responding extremely forcefully to deter Soviet efforts to achieve regional advantages through limited wars by proxy in Southeast Asia and the Middle East. In consequence, American policy was in a position to offer the Soviets economic credits, wheat sales, and technology transfers in return for a degree of change in Soviet policies in human-rights areas. The formerly unthinkable idea of emigration from the Soviet Union became a reality during this period and, in fact, the number of emigrants increased each year. While Soviet policies fluctuated, there was a number of effective incentives for the elements of leadership in Soviet society that wished to heighten educational and cultural ties with the West and to move the Soviet system in the direction of greater moderation.

Yet, as Richard Maass pointed out at McGill, the procedures of traditional diplomacy were augmented throughout this period by concerned public opinion and public pressure in support of the right of emigration of Soviet Jews. This pressure, Maass argued, served as a prod to diplomacy and also made credible the view that progress in human rights was a prerequisite for any improved relationships between the United States and the Soviet Union.

In the approach of traditional diplomacy there is little overt pressure on countries that are allied with the United States, whether democratic or authoritarian, to improve their domestic human-rights performance under penalty of loss of American support. Yet to the degree to which the most extreme abuses that occur in authoritarian regimes become counterproductive of their own security interests or generate public reaction against the American alliance, there is a foreign-policy interest to seek some mitigation of these abuses. Such efforts have a long and noble tradition in American diplomatic history. The recent record includes American involvement with such issues as improved treatment of prisoners in South Vietnam, reducing torture of prisoners in Iran, and lessening the more repugnant aspects of apartheid in South Africa. Supporters of this approach argue that within the framework of maintaining a structure of international stability for national security, a series of important, marginal improvements in human rights can be carried out through the leverage and the methods available within the tradition of quiet diplomacy.

A second approach to human rights has been developed by leading congressional spokesmen in this area. The congressional activists are themselves divided, however, between those like Senators Henry Jackson and Daniel Moynihan who advocate greater public support of human-rights dissidents primarily in the Soviet Union or other totalitarian countries, and those like former Congressman Donald Fraser who took the lead in legislation conditioning U.S. aid upon the human-rights performance of its allies.

Both groups advance two criticisms of traditional diplomacy. First, the critics maintain that the United States deprives itself of the important image and symbol of moral leadership in its conduct of foreign policy by muffling its overt and public pressure in support of human rights. They concede that such an image may risk being charged with the stereotype of moral missionary to the world and could even lead to a distortion of the primacy of security interests in national foreign policy. Yet more important in their view is that such a moral image is the necessary condition for providing leadership in an international security structure which requires the support of public opinion in order to be effective.

Their second criticism is that the pursuit of human rights through traditional diplomacy is excessively subordinated to considerations of military and geopolitical strategy. In their view, the United States can exercise great leverage on the domestic policies of authoritarian regimes; the risk that any weakening of strategic alliances might ensue from greater American insistence on human-rights standards in allied nations has been highly exaggerated.

There have been few tests of the efficacy of the congressional approach. The Jackson-Vanik amendment that tied increased Soviet trade to an increase in the number of emigrants from the Soviet Union is a notable example of congressional initiative, and there is no consensus on whether it can yet prove useful or has been counterproductive. In general, Senators Jackson and Moynihan advocate a stronger human-rights policy even at the price of an increase of tensions between the United States and the Soviet Union. They hold that the reduction of tensions depends upon the overall American position including strategic and military strength, and not upon quiescence on human-rights issues.

It is also difficult to assess the degree to which recipients of American aid have moved to reform their domestic human-rights procedures under pressure from congressional sanction. There has been considerable public evidence that even countries that have long-standing mutual security arrangements with the United States are prepared to protest unilateral guidance from the U.S. Congress on how they should reorder their domestic affairs. At the same time, the Carter administration has sought to carry out the congressional mandate on human rights by linking, in selected cases, American aid to human-rights performance in several countries.

Supporters of the approach of the Carter administration on human rights point out that in asserting the significance of human rights in its foreign policy, the administration was able dramatically to reverse the posture of American defensiveness in the international community. They believe that in order to make its human-rights approach credible and universal, the administration risked confrontation with a number of traditional allies, particularly those whose governments are authoritarian. This risk is justified, in their view, since the United States cannot claim moral leadership if it does not criticize repressive regimes around the world. From their perspective, these regimes, ranging from Argentina or Chile to South Africa and South Korea, will undertake internal reforms if the United States perseveres in requiring such reform as a condition for its aid, friendship, and alliance.

The approach of the Carter administration has received its share of criticism. On the one hand, some critics have charged that it was provocative and led to an exacerbation of relationships with the Soviet Union. On the other hand, some critics have charged that human-rights policy was exploited by some of its protagonists within the administration to try to destabilize targeted governments like Chile, Iran, or Argentina. The most common criticism, however, has been that the Carter administration was not sufficiently aware of the unanticipated consequences of its new initiatives in human rights. On this view, there has been a pattern of strong rhetorical initiative that generates a predictable counter-response. At that point, the administration has no plan for linkage or leverage on human-rights questions, whether with potential antagonists such as the Soviet Union or traditional allies such as Brazil.

The Carter letter to Andrei Sakharov, for example, seemed to raise expectations for support of other Soviet dissident leaders like Yuri Orlov, Aleksandr Ginzburg, and Anatoly Shcharansky. It is arguable whether the American action may have provoked the Soviet Union to respond by counterpressure, resulting in the escalation of the 1978 treason trials for dissidents and libel trials for American journalists. In any event, following the harsh sentencing of Shcharansky and Ginzburg, official American reaction seemed merely verbal, vacillating, and ineffectual. Yet any weakening of the American human-rights posture with respect to strong totalitarian countries while the pressure continues on American allies who have traditionalist authoritarian regimes, would lend credence to the charge made in Solzhenitzyn's Harvard commencement address that the United States was practicing a double standard against its friends. According to Solzhenitzyn, the United States, lacking in the courage to confront the realities of totalitarianism, had turned instead to selective criticism of less formidable countries whose human-rights record, though incomparably better than that of the Soviet Union, was blemished.

Both supporters and critics of the Carter administration recognize that what is needed is an effective connection between the intentions of the new policies and their consequences in the current international polity. They also agree that the administration has been successful in heightening international self-consciousness on human rights. The test remains, as Walter Laqueur argues, to translate that awareness into realistic progress in human rights.

Each of the three approaches reviewed briefly—traditional diplomacy, congressional activism, and public presidential statements—provides important directives in the formulation of an adequate American policy in human rights. An analysis in depth of the arguments and evidence for each is a necessary step in the realization of this goal. And the development of an adequate human-rights policy is fundamental for a major democratic power, for it is nothing less than the touchstone of whether the country can conduct its foreign affairs in a manner which reconciles the requirements of strategic realism with moral idealism.

This survey of the debates about human rights that stimulated some of the essays in this collection has focused upon the practical aspects of contemporary human rights. It is again worth emphasizing that several of the essays in this volume also examine the idea of human rights in historical or theoretical perspective without orientation to contemporary policy problems. For it is the assumption of this book that the issue of human rights merits examination as an idea of intrinsic significance apart from the fact that human rights has become a phrase referring to a set of ideals whose realization is so important for the shaping of the future.

ONE

CONTEMPORARY CONCERNS

Human Rights on the International Agenda

WALTER LAQUEUR

->>>->>>->>>->>>->>>->>>->>>->>>->>>->>>->>>   <<<-<<<-<<<-<<<-<<<-<<<-<<<-<<<-<<<-<<<-<<<-<<<-

The Issue of Human Rights

I

Human rights as an idea, as an issue in religious, political, and moral philosophy, has an ancient and illustrious pedigree; the differences between the empirical and the normative foundations of human rights, between moral rights and legal rights, between group rights and individual rights—each of these topics has been the occasion of substantial intellectual disquisition. The English Bill of Rights, and more emphatically the American Declaration of Independence and the French Declaration of the Rights of Man, were all based on the idea of inalienable, indefeasible, and absolute rights. Later, Jeremy Bentham and others were to argue, to the contrary, that there were no such rights, that the idea of natural rights was rhetorical nonsense—"nonsense upon stilts." In our time some philosophers have gone even further, claiming that the whole idea of human rights is a recent invention, alien to most non-Western cultures, and that it has been foisted by the neo-colonialist West on a more or less unwilling world.

This last position is far-fetched. Even if there were no explicit covenants to that effect in ancient Chinese or Indian culture, the idea of freedom was hardly alien to those civilizations. And as for today, were it not for the concepts of individual and group rights, the countries of the non-Western world would still be colonies. Moreover, while the distinction between (positive) law and morality has its uses in philosophy, it is safe to say that neither Bentham nor his latter-day disciples would have preferred to live under arbitrary or tyrannical government, to be arrested and tried without due process, to be tortured, maimed, or killed, to be deprived of property or sold into slavery—even if such practices were in conformity with the law of the land.

Advocates of natural rights may admittedly have had a somewhat simplistic concept of human nature, and have failed to make due allowance for the fact that political and social conditions vary from age to age and from country to country, but even so it is difficult to make a convincing case for torture and slavery. Even those purists who once argued that international law is not concerned with personal liberty have had to confront the international conventions against slavery. It is, in fact, the theory of absolute nonintervention to protect human rights that is nonsense upon stilts. Cases of such intervention have been common ever since Gelon, Prince of Syracuse, having defeated Carthage in the year 480 B.C.E., made it a condition of peace that the Carthaginians abandon their time-honored custom of sacrificing their children to Saturn.

In recent decades there has been a palpable shift in interpretations of international law, a shift in favor of the idea of universal human rights; few still maintain that international law concerns states alone.* Though the Covenant of the League of Nations did not address itself to the issue of human rights (other than the protection of certain minorities) but rather to the pacific settlement of disputes, a new approach manifested itself in the Atlantic Charter of 1941, the Declaration of the United Nations the year after, and in countless speeches of wartime leaders. This new approach found expression in the United Nations Charter and more specifically in the Universal Declaration of Human Rights, approved without a dissenting voice in December 1948. The President of the General Assembly said at the time that this was the

---

*L. Oppenheim, writing his famous textbook on international law before World War I, still regarded the "right of mankind" as something more or less fictitious. The Lauterpacht edition of Oppenheim's book, published in the 1950s, took a far more positive view, noting the inauguration of a new and decisive departure with regard to human rights and freedoms transcending the laws of states.

first occasion on which the organized world community had recognized the existence of human rights and fundamental freedoms transcending the laws of sovereign states, and "millions of men, women, and children all over the world, many miles from Paris and New York, will turn to help, guidance, and inspiration to this document."

Three decades have now passed since these words were spoken, but while millions of men and women have indeed turned for inspiration to the Universal Declaration of Human Rights, they have received precious little guidance and no help from the organization that propagated it. In fact, the declaration was flawed from the very beginning: it did not include provisions for the rights of ethnic, linguistic, and religious minorities. More important, the stipulation made in the early drafts for the right of individuals to petition the UN was deleted later on at the insistence, among others, of the United States, which believed that such a right of petition would be abused by cranks. This was a giant step backward to the old idea that international law is concerned only with relations among states, and it has enabled the UN to refuse even to acknowledge receipt of complaints by persecuted individuals such as Soviet dissidents.

Another major problem with the declaration is the question of how its provisions are to be squared with Article 2, Paragraph 7 of the UN Charter, according to which the UN is enjoined from intervening in matters which are essentially within the domestic jurisdiction of individual states. Member states switch their views on this issue as it suits them from one day to the next. When, for instance, early in the history of the UN, India complained about racial discrimination in South Africa, the Russians argued that the issue was entirely within the competence of the UN to decide. But when Poland, Hungary, or the Soviet Union itself has been challenged for violation of human rights, it has naturally claimed that the Commission on Human Rights (established in 1946) has no power to take action.

Since the late 1950s the debates on human rights have been increasingly dominated by a stress on economic and social as opposed to civil and political rights. This reflects the changed composition of the United Nations itself. As the Communist and Third World countries have gradually become a majority, they have insisted that economic and social rights must be attained before any other rights can even be discussed. Some have contended that civil rights might even have to be sacrificed (temporarily, of course) in order to build the economic and social foundation on which they are allegedly based. The countries promoting such views have invariably been those with the worst record on human rights.

Political and civil rights defend the citizen against arbitrary action on the part of the state: economic and social rights, to the contrary, are based on positive state action. One illustration should suffice to point up the difference: Article 7 of the International Covenant on Civil and Political Rights states that "no one shall be subjected to torture or to cruel, inhuman, or degrading treatment or punishment." This is an absolute right which can and should be universally enforced today. Article 7 of the International Covenant on Economic, Social, and Cultural Rights, on the other hand, imposes on every country the duty to grant its citizens periodic holidays with pay and remuneration for public holidays. This right cannot be universally enforced at the present time since, among other reasons, many countries do not have the resources. Moral considerations aside, it is quite clear that a law that cannot be enforced is not a law but an aspiration. But in any event, the idea that remuneration for public holidays, however laudable per se, should take precedence over the ban of torture, makes nonsense of the whole concept of human rights.

It is true that in a wider perspective economic and social aspirations and civil and political rights are not mutually exclusive but interdependent and supportive of each other. But they are not in the same category, and the attempt to equate universal moral rights that need to be observed here and now with the introduction of social services is simply part of the endeavor to belittle the importance of human rights, to reduce them from the level of inalienable human requirements to the level of ideals that might, or might not, be achieved at some future date. Giving priority to economic and social rights does not reflect a different political outlook, but is usually merely an alibi for states that practice oppression at home, and whose record even in the economic and social field is anything but brilliant. Among the loudest proponents of the primacy of social and economic rights there is not a single one that permits the existence of free trade unions—a principle enshrined in Article 8 of the covenant.

This is not to say that there must be in every single respect one universal standard for the most developed countries and the most backward ones: the protection of human rights has to be judged in the cultural, social, and economic context of societies in different stages of development. But it is pernicious nonsense to argue that under a certain range of per capita income (say, $500), human rights have to be dispensed with because only tyrannical regimes will be in a position "to mobilize the masses in order to attain food, shelter, and health care" (to quote Charles Yost). This argument is not only morally wrong, it is historically wrong; the per capita income at the time of the French Revolution (not to mention the time of Magna Carta) was substantially lower than it is now in most countries whose governments claim that basic human rights can be dispensed with. Most of these dictatorships, furthermore, have not the slightest wish to "mobilize" their masses; nor is it readily obvious in what way torture and slavery will make for more effective health care. Except to the extent that slaves with a full stomach are better off than slaves with an empty stomach, the idea that full economic and social rights can be enjoyed by people who do not possess civil and political rights is a deliberate falsehood. Recent events in India have shown that illiterate peasants are better judges of what is good for them than some of their well-wishers in the West.

The real problem is that in most member states of the UN, elementary civil liberties do not exist, and, more important still, there has been little if any progress in that direction. In theory such states subscribe to principles of human freedom and civil liberties as outlined in the United Nations conventions and their own constitutions, but too often in reality the practice is oppression, persecution, and the violation of basic human rights. A new unholy alliance has come into being at the United Nations, one that has a vested interest in the denial, not the promotion, of human rights, and one that shows a great deal of solidarity in pursuit of that interest.

The meetings of the Human Rights Commission, for example, have become a farce: though appearances are still maintained, though lofty ideals are invoked, and though there is much talk about solemn obligations and human solidarity, in actual fact there is not the slightest chance of any resolution being passed that runs counter to the will of the anti-human-rights majority.

Western delegates continue to participate in this farce, and from time to time they even claim to discover some grounds for hope. Thus, commenting on the 1977 session, Allard K. Lowenstein, the U.S. delegate, said that it was "far more balanced" than previously and that "new ground was broken"—this, about a session which was not even willing to sponsor an international investigation into the situation in Uganda.

On top of everything else, the Human Rights Commission is a totally irrelevant institution. Its publications are not read, its resolutions are scarcely noticed, and it makes headlines only in the case of some specific outrageous statement or resolution. But it is unfortunately true that the continued presence of delegates from countries *cherishing* human rights conveys legitimacy to an institution which deserves to be regarded as a laughingstock and a public menace. Unless they use every opportunity to speak out in the strongest possible way against the dishonesty of the commission—to counterattack constantly, castigating mercilessly the prevailing mendacity, and holding up to ridicule the whole humbug—Western representatives become accessories to the general perversion. Yet to hope for such words and actions on the part of Western diplomats seems somewhat unrealistic. They are expected to react coolly and considerately, in measured and temperate language; when they stray from those canons, as Daniel P. Moynihan and Leonard Garment did, they are upbraided for eccentricity and breach of dignity.

The old League of Nations showed weakness and cowardice, but even in its worst moments it never reached the depths of degradation achieved by the United Nations. Western representatives on the Human Rights Commission and other such bodies say in mitigation that they have succeeded in preventing even worse outrages. This does not change the fact that by playing the evil game and adhering to the perverted rules, they confer respectability on institutions whose main function is to prevent the implementation of human rights, and to justify their suppression.

II

The failure of the United Nations to live up to early expectations and to become an effective instrument for the promotion of human rights has induced individual governments and non-governmental bodies to take fresh initiatives in the area. In 1948 the Organization of American States passed a declaration on the rights and duties of man which has, however, largely remained a dead letter. The Council of Europe agreed on a covenant for the protection of human rights and fundamental freedoms, and established a European Commission for Human Rights as well as a European Court of Human Rights in Strasbourg which has heard many cases since it first met in 1960. But these activities concern only Europe, meaning those societies least in need of human-rights protection. Various private bodies, such as the International League for Human Rights, Freedom House, and Amnesty International, have published reports about the condition of unfreedom in various parts of the world, drawing attention to particularly flagrant violations and on occasion mobilizing public support to bring pressure on the governments concerned. But the scope of these activities and their impact are by necessity limited.

It is only in recent months and years, when public opinion in the United States and elsewhere has begun to press for new initiatives, that human rights have become a major issue in international politics. That the Soviet-bloc nations and repressive regimes generally have reacted angrily to the new initiatives is not surprising, but there has been opposition also from other quarters that are disturbed by what they regard as the unwarranted intrusion of this issue into the normal political process.

To be sure, the concern shown in some quarters over the allegedly harmful effects of the emphasis on human rights was to some extent predictable. Although it has been quite fashionable in recent years to invoke human rights, enthusiasm for the cause has been rather selective in character. Some of those expressing unhappiness about conditions in the Soviet Union and Czechoslovakia or even Cuba have obviously regarded the situation in Uruguay, Chile, Iran, and South Korea as far more serious; they protest, from time to time, the arrest of a Soviet dissenter, but one feels their main passions lie elsewhere. Then there are the fair-weather protagonists of human rights, those who hold freedom's banner high so long as storms are not blowing. It is not that such people do not care about human rights, but they certainly do not like the risks involved and are bitterly opposed to any linking of this particular struggle with other political issues. There is less to be said in favor of a position of this kind—a position which reduces human rights to a matter of public relations—than for the candor of the neo-isolationists who, while they regret the violation of human rights in foreign parts, believe it is wrong to interfere in behalf of abstract ideas.

The arguments put forward against an aggressive stand on human rights have varied. There have been warnings that such initiatives will create new international tensions and perhaps a new "ice age" (as one commentator put it). It is said that the Carter administration in particular has gone too far and too fast, that quiet diplomacy can achieve more substantial results, and that speaking up will only cause greater repression in the countries singled out for attention. It is also claimed that since the United States does not have clean hands, it is not in any position to criticize others. The specter has been invoked of a new militant anti-Communism, precisely the sort of crusade that led the U.S. into disaster in the past. Above all, it is maintained that undue emphasis on human rights will adversely affect arms-control efforts, which are an overriding concern if the human race is to survive.

Most of these arguments are simply spurious. There is no danger that too strong an emphasis on human rights will "provoke international ideological warfare on a global scale"; the Soviet Union has never *stopped* conducting ideological warfare and has made it abundantly clear that it considers such warfare akin to a categorical imperative, détente or no détente. And if Brezhnev has not hesitated to receive Marchais, Berlinguer, and Gus Hall in Moscow, why should Western presidents refuse to see leading Soviet dissenters?

As to the dangers of causing greater repression by speaking out, Marshall Shulman, who now advises the Secretary of State on Soviet affairs, has written in *Foreign Affairs* that any easing of repression within Soviet society is more likely to result from internal evolutionary forces than from external demands for change. He does not deny individuals and groups in the West the right to express their repugnance for violations of human rights, but for governments to do so is, he contends, clearly counterproductive. Soviet dissenters, notably Andrei Sakharov, disagree with Professor Shulman. As Sakharov has said: "Resolute and ever-growing pressure by public and official bodies of the West—up to the highest—the defense of principles and of specific people can only bring positive results. Every case of human-rights violation must become a political problem for the leaders of the culprit countries."

Professor Shulman's notion of an "easing of repression" as the result of a relaxation of tension is, moreover, not borne out by the historical record. Surveying the history of détente and the democratic movement in the USSR, Frederick C. Barghoorn reaches the conclusion that the heyday of the democratic movement was in the 1960s, and, "with the blossoming of what was in the West hailed as détente Moscow was more than ever determined to crush dissent" *(Détente and the Democratic Movement in the USSR)*. Professor Shulman might counter that his own argument holds true over the long run, but this optimism is shared by few experts inside or outside the Soviet Union. Sakharov wrote in 1968, and again in 1975, that détente unaccompanied by increased trust and democratization was a danger, not a blessing, that rapprochement without democratization inside the USSR was worse than no rapprochement at all. The world, according to Sakharov, faced two alternatives: "either the gradual convergence of the two superpowers, accompanied by democratization inside the Soviet Union, or increased confrontation with a growing danger of thermonuclear war." He subsequently envisaged a third alternative—"the capitulation of the democratic principle in the face of blackmail, deceit, and violence." These are harsh words, bound to irritate Western diplomats trying not to make controversial or polemical statements. Perhaps Sakharov is not well informed about Soviet affairs; or has he too been corrupted by an excess of moral indignation?

A more weighty case against the emphasis on human rights in foreign policy has been made by the believers in realpolitik who argue that, given the global balance of power, the United States is simply no longer strong enough to promote human freedom among its chief adversaries and certainly cannot afford to antagonize its allies on this score. Sooner or later, this school holds, the human-rights campaign is bound to become muted or highly selective in its targets, or both. The exponents of realpolitik do not doubt the commitment of President Carter to the cause of human rights, but they know that this concern is by no means shared in equal measure by all his collaborators and advisers, and they reason that the administration's desire to reach an accommodation with the Russians will in the end prevail over other considerations (provided the Russians refrain from open provocations). In the face of Soviet

charges of interference, American denunciations of Soviet infringements of human rights will become more "tactful" (as proposed by
Brezhnev himself), and will focus on individual dissenters rather
than on the enforced silence of the great majority. Thus there will
be no sudden backdown by the Democratic administration but a
gradual "slump in idealism"—which will eventually affect the
American posture not only toward the Soviet Union but toward
other countries as well. Although human rights will still be invoked from time to time as an abstract and unfortunately distant
ideal, it will no longer be a consideration directly impinging on
foreign policy. This to all practical purposes will be the end of a
great departure announced with so much fanfare and accompanied
by so much enthusiasm.

While these fears may be quite real, it must be said that the
skepticism of the proponents of realpolitik is based at least in part
on a misconception. The struggle for human rights in present conditions is not a lofty and impractical endeavor, divorced from the
harsh realities of world affairs, but itself a kind of realpolitik, one
with a direct bearing on international security. This was clearly
recognized by Secretary of State George Marshall in a famous
speech at the opening of the UN General Assembly in Paris
in 1948:

> Systematic and deliberate denials of basic human rights lie at
> the root of most of our troubles and threaten the work of the
> United Nations. It is not only fundamentally wrong that mil-
> lions of men and women live in daily terror, subject to seizure,
> imprisonment, and forced labor without just cause and with-
> out fair trial, but these wrongs have repercussions in the
> community of nations. Governments which systematically dis-
> regard the rights of their own people are not likely to respect
> the rights of other nations and other people and are likely to
> seek their objectives by coercion and force in the international
> field.

These fears were amply justified at the time, and in the three
decades that have passed since they were first expressed, the
dilemma has become even more pressing. It is all very well to propose that countries with different political, social, and cultural systems should peacefully coexist, but the moment the attempt is
made to translate these sentiments into the language of reality,

insurmountable difficulties arise. Genuine détente has to be based on at least some degree of mutual trust.

It is in this context that the problem of arms control has to be seen. It is generally accepted that meaningful future agreements on both strategic and conventional arms have to be based on effective means of inspection. But such means do not exist, and they do not exist precisely because of the absence of democratic checks and balances in the Soviet Union and the unwillingness of the Soviet leaders to open up their country to foreign inspection and free, unlimited travel in general. Thus, the prospects for genuine progress in arms control are virtually nil unless and until the Soviet system becomes more open and democratic; the movement toward the protection of human rights is an essential part of such a process. The same applies, *mutatis mutandis,* to trade with the Soviet bloc, which at present is largely based on credits and loans. The indebtedness of the Soviet bloc now amounts to almost $50 billion; unless Soviet and East European society becomes freer and more open, the financial risk involved in such massive credits—according to some projections, the sum total might be $100 billion by the end of the decade—will become too great, and U.S.-Soviet trade may grind to a halt.

It is quite untrue to argue, as some Western critics have done, that the human-rights campaign aims at changing the Soviet social system; the question of whether Soviet factories and farms should remain nationalized is not for outsiders to decide. The purpose of the campaign is far more modest: it simply asks that the Soviet regime live up to its own constitution. Until it does, there will never develop that climate of trust and confidence, so often invoked by Soviet leaders, which is a precondition for effective arms control, for mutually beneficial trade, or indeed for any lasting understanding.

III

To be credible, the commitment to human rights must be consistent. Does this mean that the same standard ought to be applied to both Denmark and Afghanistan? Obviously not. The cultural and social context, the grade of development of each country, are factors that have to be taken into account; and what especially has to be taken into account is the general *trend* in a country: has there been a movement toward greater human rights or away from them? The various maps and surveys published by the State Department and private bodies do not provide a guide to political action because they do not take these considerations into account; nor do they make a clear differentiation between totalitarian regimes in which all aspects of society are controlled by the state, and authoritarian governments which nevertheless allow a measure of freedom. This elementary distinction is known to every student of politics, yet time and again it is blurred and obfuscated. In Professor Shulman's article, which bears the title "On Learning to Live with Authoritarian Regimes," all kinds of non-democratic governments are lumped together, despite the fact that the author is well aware that there exist "significant differences" among them.

These differences, however, are not just significant, they are crucial. In Spain, the death of the dictator constituted a decisive turning point; precisely because the regime was never quite totalitarian, a far-reaching democratization could rapidly take place. In a totalitarian regime such a development is clearly impossible, and this fact has deep implications for Western policies toward such countries. There are, admittedly, marked differences in the degree of repression inside the Communist camp as well—between countries like Hungary and Yugoslavia on the one hand, and those like North Korea on the other. But it is still true that the whole structure of all these regimes is based on the systematic denial of certain human rights, such as impartial tribunals, freedom of movement and open expression, and peaceful assembly and association (all of which, as it happens, are guaranteed in the constitutions of these countries themselves).

As for the Third World, each country has to be judged individually in the context of the considerations I have mentioned. Much depends on whether a regime respects at least *some* human rights, whether or not it is a relatively enlightened dictatorship working for political, economic, and cultural progress, whether or not it has aims other than the perpetuation of its own repressive rule. There is infinitely more freedom in Tanzania or Kenya than in Uganda, more in Iran and Egypt than in Iraq—even though all these are authoritarian regimes.

What standards, finally, are to be applied to countries that are members of the Western alliance or maintain friendly relations with the U.S.? Here again the political context has to be taken into account. To provide an example: it is quite possible that certain infringements on civil liberties have occurred at one stage or another in the British struggle against terrorism in Northern Ireland. Such cases are reprehensible wherever they occur, but a terrorist campaign on a substantial scale constitutes a warlike act, and the standards that prevail in war are not those of peacetime. Human rights are rooted in natural law, but natural law does not prohibit free people from defending themselves against enemies hostile to the values of a democratic society. In such situations, as in wartime, certain temporary restrictions on human rights may be necessary.* Terrorists are a menace not because they will ever seize power, but because they provoke massive counter-terrorism which frequently leads (as in Uruguay and Argentina) to the establishment of military dictatorships, and these, having seized power, seldom, if ever, feel inclined to restore democracy.

Once terrorism has been defeated, it is indefensible to perpetuate a state of siege, and a strong stand has to be taken against regimes that show no willingness to restore basic freedoms and human rights. This goes *a fortiori* for regimes which do not even have the excuse of defending themselves against the onslaught of anti-democratic forces. In the long run, the U.S. cannot be allied with governments flagrantly and massively violating human rights. But it is also true that the prospects of influencing such governments in the Western hemisphere or in the Far East by means of quiet diplomacy are far better than with Communist countries—if only because the former are more dependent on the U.S. and the other major countries in the Western alliance. Dealing with these countries, the United States will certainly face difficulties: a price will have to be paid for forcefulness, such as losing a military base; if, on the other hand, concessions are made, they

*President Carter, at the Clinton, Massachusetts, town meeting in March 1977, said that he would continue to speak out against violations of human rights whether they occurred in Northern Ireland or elsewhere. He did not appear to have in mind the atrocities committed by the two warring sides in the civil war, but the few infringements committed by the British forces trying to prevent a total breakdown of public order and mass slaughter. Yet it is precisely because of the almost unprecedented restraint of the British forces that terrorism still continues in Northern Ireland; terrorists do not persist against governments that react with equal ruthlessness.

will invite accusations of a double standard. But the fact that there will be obstacles does not mean that the policy is impracticable or that the nation should desist from pursuing it.

The U.S. and the other Western countries find themselves hopelessly outnumbered in the United Nations in the struggle for the promotion of human rights, but they have many millions of allies all over the world and above all in the countries in which human rights are trampled under foot. The idea of freedom has exercised a powerful attraction throughout history, and this attraction is probably stronger at present than at any time in the past. Hence the violent reaction of the Soviet Union to the Carter administration's initiatives and the nervousness shown by other repressive governments. These regimes are well aware that Western societies have a weapon that can be used to great effect in the ideological struggle to whose continuation the Soviet Union is committed. Attempts will be made to prevent the West from using this weapon—cajolery and threats. Obviously, the United States will have to take the lead for the West as a whole, for the Western European governments (with some notable exceptions) lack the self-confidence, the determination, the solidarity, and also the political weight to act on their own. But will such leadership be forthcoming from Washington?

The Carter administration has committed itself to the struggle for human rights on a global basis, but so far not much thought has been given to implications and to the proper strategy. Hence the confusing and contradictory statements that have been made: three steps forward and two steps back. Thus, President Carter declared in his inaugural address that "because we are free we can never be indifferent to the fate of freedom elsewhere"; then Cyrus Vance announced that the U.S. will speak out only from time to time, and that its comments will be neither strident nor polemical. Unfortunately, to press for human rights is by definition a provocative act even if the language used is neither shrill nor strident; to deny this, to create the impression that the aim can be achieved by platonic expressions of regret and sorrow, is to admit defeat even before the struggle has begun in earnest.

Even more detrimental is the attempt to be "evenhanded" at any cost, to establish a false symmetry. It is understandable when a private organization like Amnesty International, which does its work under exceedingly difficult conditions, "balances" denunciations of gross violation of human rights in an Eastern-bloc or Third World country with criticism of a Western government even when the cases are totally different in severity and magnitude. But a big power like the United States does not have to engage in such questionable practices in order to establish its legitimacy as a champion of human rights.

Spokesmen of the Carter administration have said they will place far greater emphasis on human rights than did their predecessors. But Henry Kissinger too, in his speech to the UN General Assembly in 1976, declared that human rights were of "central importance, one of the most compelling issues of our times," and the speeches made by Daniel P. Moynihan and Leonard Garment at the United Nations, as well as the private initiatives of Ambassador Laurence Silberman in Yugoslavia, were at least as forceful as any subsequent declarations. The real test is not speeches or even appointments, but deeds. President Carter has said that he "cannot go in with armed forces and try to change the internal mechanism of the Soviet government." No such proposal has been advanced. There are, however, a great many things that can be done besides cutting military aid to some Latin American countries. Domestically this would involve the ratification of the Convention on Genocide as well as the other conventions as yet unsigned (for the Elimination of Racial Discrimination, the Covenant on Economic, Social, and Cultural Rights, etc.). In foreign policy it would involve constant pressure for the protection of human rights through all possible channels, public statements on the highest level as well as the publicizing of gross infringements through the Voice of America and the U.S. radio stations in Europe.

Above all it means linkage—linkage, by whatever name. As El Cid said, *Lengua sin mános, cuemo osas fablar?* ("Tongue without arms, how do you dare to talk?") Resistance has been mounted to the use of U.S. resources for the promotion of human rights, and there will be more such resistance in the future. But it is perfectly obvious that unless the human-rights records of the most powerful countries are taken into account in U.S. foreign policy, fine sentiments will not have the slightest impact; they will be rightly considered by friend and foe alike as a public-relations exercise aimed at American domestic consumption. There are countless ways for linking the help sought from the United States by countries great and small to their record on human rights. Opportunities have never been lacking, only the will to make use of them.

The human-rights issue presents an immense challenge to any American administration. President Carter, having made it a cornerstone of his policy to restore the moral authority of American foreign policy, may stand or fall with his performance in this field. If it is mishandled, carried out without judgment and discrimination, or based on a false symmetry, a global campaign for human rights can lead to the further isolation of the United States and a further lowering of its prestige. Firmly and prudently pursued, it could give an enormous impetus to the cause of freedom all over the world and enhance American stature and influence. Excuses for inaction may be made by small countries whose capacity to influence the course of world politics is by necessity limited. But a great nation hesitant or afraid to speak up and to act on its beliefs and values at a crucial juncture of world history is forfeiting its international standing and embarking on a course of moral and political decline.

RITA HAUSER

International Human-Rights Protection: The Dream and the Deceptions

I

Judged by the perspective of more than twenty-five years of history, the immediate post-World War II days marked the zenith of belief in a collective world consensus as to protection of individual rights. The West had just destroyed the forces of fascism which, in themselves, were viewed then as no more than a massive deviation from accepted international rules and normative political behavior, the handiwork of madmen. The United States in particular was supremely confident that its liberal democratic values, nourished in a benign peacetime atmosphere, would prevail, and that parliamentary democracy would be adopted by most nations. Thus, Harry Truman could assure the nations gathered in San Francisco that an international bill of rights would be adopted which "will be as much part of international life as our own Bill of Rights is part of our Constitution."

It was in that very spirit that President Roosevelt envisioned the postwar world on the still cherished but unproven concept of collective security through an international structure. Despite the pragmatic skepticism of Winston Churchill, Roosevelt insisted on his dream and, albeit with some misgivings, agreed to pay a heavy price to gain the participation of the Soviet Union and the support of Stalin in the work of the United Nations. Moreover, from the days of the Atlantic Charter, he emphasized the Wilsonian ideal of "self-determination of peoples," and thus helped unleash the forces that destroyed the remains of the great British and French empires, yielding a multiple birth of new countries peopled primarily by non-whites.

The United Nations Charter, drafted largely by American hands and with the support of the Western majority which made up the organization at its birth, speaks in poetic terms of the brave new world to emerge from the scourge of world war (and atomic weaponry development). Mankind is dedicated to pursue peace, harmony, justice, and equality of peoples. All nations are elevated to sovereign egality. Disputes between them are to be resolved by parliamentary procedure, reasoned debate, and majority vote. And, for the first time in modern history, the Charter envisaged a system of universal protection of human rights of all people. Every member state is enjoined to promote universal respect for human rights and the fundamental freedoms of all. The sexes are, by fiat, pronounced equal in rights, and race, religion, nationality, and other forms of ethnic distinction are relegated to an irrelevance. The human individual everywhere is held to enjoy basic rights that inure to his very existence, inalienable and, without being so said, God-given and naturally endowed.

This universal approach, which looks beyond the boundaries of the sovereign state, was the result both of the horror of the Western world at the scope of Hitler's atrocities and the determined lobbying of interested organizations which made their views known long before San Francisco was selected as the Charter drafting site. Numerous Jewish groups, in particular, promoted the idea of an International Bill of Rights, believing, as they did, that Jews would be protected in the enjoyment of their rights to the extent the rights of others everywhere were similarly respected. Protection of minority groups, which had been the approach adopted after World War I through the mechanism of Minorities Treaties to be enforced by the League of Nations, was written off in favor of this universalistic tactic. The brave new world to come after the cessation of the fighting would presumably be free of narrow nationalistic considerations. And man, whatever his political, social, or economic condition, would be protected by the international institution to be created—the United Nations—and be a citizen of the world community in the largest sense of that concept.

Many dedicated Zionists, it should be noted, did not subscribe fully to this universal view as far as protection of Jews was concerned. Their energies were directed to fulfilling a national, not an international dream, and they worked toward creating a Jewish state where the rights of Jews, by definition, would be clearly protected and dependent on none but Jews.

That a universal vision was utopian, unrealistic, impossible of rapid attainment, indeed foolish in many respects, did not daunt the Charter drafters of those extraordinary men and women of similar dreams—Eleanor Roosevelt, René Cassin, Charles Malik —who went on to define with clarity and precision the rights granted to all mankind. Somehow they managed to paper over and compromise the nagging differences of ideology and possibility that marked the long and often acrimonious debates of the Human Rights Commission during the drafting of the Universal Declaration of Human Rights. For them, 1789 was still the benchmark year; for others, the focus of reference was 1917. And the millions of newcomers to nationhood were still dormant, arriving only after the fact in the late 1950s and 1960s, soon to argue that making nationhood a reality was more important than any individual's enjoyment of freedom and civic rights.

Even more amazing from a current vantage point was the ability of these singular people to pursue a goal in deliberate defiance of the unfolding reality of the post-1945 world. Not only had the Cold War commenced with a vengeance on the political and military fronts, but daily the brutality and utter ruthlessness of the Soviet Union was revealed both within Russia and in its expanded orbit in Eastern Europe. While the drafters of the Declaration proclaimed the right of each individual to liberty of person and political belief, literally scores of thousands of people were wiped out as one country after another was swept into the Soviet orbit. Torture, assassination, and repression were the hallmark of Stalin's policy; total concentration of state power in complete disregard for the individual was the goal.

And in virtually every area where the colonial powers withdrew, voluntarily or under duress, massive human degradation occurred. Communal massacres in India were unparalleled as

Hindu and Muslim unleashed centuries of mutual hatred. Palestine produced war and dispossession. Indochina was the scene of protracted civil discord, North Africa rebelled, and most of black Africa simmered. Who was there at the UN or elsewhere to assure the millions of hapless victims of these brutal events enjoyment of their human rights and fundamental freedoms? The answer, alas, was no one. Concern was manifest not for the individual, but rather for the political currents that underlay these gross violations of human rights.

II

Despite these stark realities, the people concerned with human rights set themselves the extraordinary task noted by President Truman: drafting an international bill of rights. Opposition existed, however, from the start. Few were the nations, including the United States, which did not shrink at the idea of placing protection of the human rights of its own citizens in the hands of an international group. As a compromise, the Human Rights Commission in late 1947 decided first to draft a non-binding declaration of human rights, then a binding covenant, and, finally, implementing machinery. The Declaration was completed one year later and adopted on December 10, 1948, as "a common standard of achievement for all peoples and nations," to be promoted by teaching and education.

The Declaration is largely conceived in terms of Western norms and principles intended to preserve individual liberty against the tyranny of the state and to eliminate racial and religious discrimination. Even the economic rights listed presupposed a certain state of industrial development. No one could be presumed to have contemplated in 1948 the world to be in 1960, when the majority of the UN members were from the less-developed nations enjoying few, if any, of the conditions assumed as the intellectual underpinning of the Declaration.

The Declaration established universal norms. Many countries born after 1948 copied its key provisions into their constitutions. Statutes and, in some instances, actual practices of nations changed under the pressure of public opinion and the desire of countries to be modern and achieve the standards laid out as the ideal. UN debates refer to the Declaration continually, and it has been a beacon of hope for many people still living under tyranny.

The next stage, that of drafting the two major covenants—one on economic, social, and cultural rights; the other on political and civil rights—took eighteen years to complete. But the implementing provisions of the latter covenant, through a complaint mechanism and the right of individuals to petition directly, was made optional. As of today, some twenty or so countries have ratified both covenants; but with a few exceptions, they have a long way to go toward achieving most of the key provisions in the treatment of their own citizens.*

During these eighteen years, conventions were drafted and adopted to deal with specific human-rights problems: prevention of the crime of genocide, protection of refugees and stateless persons, advancement of women's rights, abolition of slavery practices, and the elimination of racial discrimination. Other projects, such as a convention on freedom of information and one to eliminate religious intolerance, have languished under objections of various countries. The International Labor Organization (ILO) and the UN Educational, Scientific, and Cultural Organization (UNESCO) have adopted human-rights conventions in the fields of employment and education which are significant in scope.

The record since 1945 of establishing norms, principles, aims, and quantifying ideals is a good one. The nations of the world seem in intellectual accord on a great number of matters. But when it comes to enforcing these norms, or indeed to agreement on the legal nature of these provisions, the record of accomplishment drops sharply. Many countries refuse to accept the possibility that others might judge and find them wanting; even fewer are willing to accept binding human-rights enforcement machinery of any nature. The idea that a citizen of the Soviet Union might come to the UN, be heard on a violation of the Declaration or a convention, and cause the Soviet Union to be judged and condemned is beyond the tolerable limits of acceptance of almost

---

*In announcing its ratification on September 28, 1973, the Soviet Union cited the national security and other limitations clauses of the Covenant on Civil and Political Rights in justification of its restrictions on the rights to free speech, movement, and assembly.

any Soviet leader. This is true of many other national leaders, including a host in the U.S., and will probably always be the case for many whose vision stops at the national boundaries.

The earliest debates in the UN on human-rights questions, even at a time the West dominated the sessions, rapidly demonstrated that nationalism was far more significant and powerful a political force than the idealism of the Charter and the Universal Declaration. Almost every nation accused of deviation from the standards loftily proclaimed in these documents either denied the accusation or focused on a counter-attack as to the failures of other countries. And, before long, a juridical defense was postulated: Article 2(7) of the Charter was asserted to prevent interference in matters "essentially within the domestic jurisdiction of any state." By definition, concern with a state's treatment of its own subjects was deemed to be such an interference.

In the post-1950 years, the membership of the United Nations changed radically. Scores of new nations, largely poor, lacking in Western traditions and institutions, and fiercely anti-colonial in outlook, entered the UN. By 1960 the non-white countries made up the majority. Thereafter, members tended to group and vote in blocs, and regionalism emerged as the dominant political mechanism of the UN system. Countries aligned within a geographic region which, more often than not, coincided with a given state of political, economic, and social development, and sometimes with religion and race. Not only did the nations in each region tend to vote as a bloc but by 1970 it was clear that few nations were willing to point a finger of accusation against violators of human rights within their region, even when the violations were gross and systematic, to use the UN terminology. Nothing was sadder than the total silence of the UN members in the face of mass starvation during the Biafra war, the extermination of many thousands of Hutus in Burundi, and the utter disregard of basic rights of nationality and alienage in Uganda. The African countries declared these to be matters of local or African interest alone, to be resolved without interference by the rest of the world. Nor, for that matter, has any Western country chosen to voice concern in the world body regarding bloodshed and atrocities in Northern Ireland. And which among the Latin American nations has censured the gross violations of the Declaration's standards in Chile or in Brazil?

Any nation whose government is in serious violation of the internationally accepted norms is not likely to be deterred from its activities by accusations of others in the UN bodies, particularly if the accusers can be dismissed as prejudiced or antagonistic by the very nature of prevailing world politics. Thus, Rhodesia and South Africa ignore as worthless the hundreds of condemnatory resolutions pushed by black Africans and allied nations, for, after all, what else can be expected of those countries? What matters to South Africa and Rhodesia is the attitude of their political friends in the Western world, whose continued abstentions on key votes are proof enough to them that human matters are so much political noise. Reciprocally, the failure of the West to call black Africa to task for its egregious violations leads these countries to believe the West was and is completely cynical about individual rights unless whites are involved.

The only situation which has produced a positive response to accusation predicated on the Declaration's standards has been that of the Jews desiring to emigrate from the Soviet Union to Israel. This aberration from the UN pattern is due to a happy coincidence of external events (détente with the United States deriving from trade desires and fear of a Chinese-American combine) and concern that the contamination of dissent not spread from a small number of "troublemakers" to a much larger group of malcontents.

III

The record on international enforcement of human rights since 1945 has not been good and the dreams of the drafters of the Charter and the Declaration not well met. Of course, progress was achieved merely by the acceptance of these seminal documents and other conventions by the international community and the application of an external rule of law as to the manner in which a nation treats its own nationals. There are those who argue that perseverance will finally produce widespread observance of these rules. While this may be the result in certain cases, I, for one, conclude that the prospects for general international respect of human rights are dim.

The reason for pessimism derives from the fact that the basic premise of the drafters failed to take hold. Liberal democracy has declined everywhere as a model for governmental authority. Where it persists, largely in the Western world, respect for individual rights is the product of nineteenth-century history, little affected in essential aspects by the establishment of the United Nations. Only West Germany may be excepted from this general statement, for it never achieved true parliamentary rule from the time of the unification of Germany in 1871 to its crushing defeat in 1945 (save for the short-lived and virtually doomed Weimar Republic). The ingredients of liberal democracy are lacking almost everywhere outside the Western world, save for Japan which has its own unique authoritarianism and singularity of people and political consensus. In the less-developed world, which contributes the vast majority of the UN's members, poverty, illiteracy, failure of establishment of independent institutions of power outside the government, and backwardness in general make the question of respect for human rights seem a matter of high theology utterly removed from the realities of life. The individual has always counted for little in circumstances where governments are struggling to maintain the integrity of the nation itself.

And the tragic history of the Communist nations under Soviet domination gives testimony to the failure of the Allied leadership of 1945 to comprehend that totalitarianism could be a permanent form of government. While fascism was defeated in the Axis Nations, ruthless exercise of state power became a fact of postwar life in the Soviet Union. So, too, in Communist China, a nation which has escaped the close scrutiny of Western humanitarians largely because of its complete political isolation since 1949. How can respect for human rights seriously be imagined as a possible achievement where the regime in power contemplates no limitations whatsoever in its insistence that it remain unchallenged in its power? Aleksandr Solzhenitsyn recalls for us the tautology that total power is totally corrupting and that human values are absolutely eroded in the exercise of that totality of puissance.

Perhaps, to mute a pessimistic conclusion, it can still be hoped that marginal nations will respect to some degree the universal norms. Most of Latin America enjoys a Western tradition, although without benefits of a solid institutional apparatus to guarantee the tradition. So, too, countries like Greece. And, occasionally, even great Western nations deviate from the standard, especially in times of stress (one thinks here primarily of France), to be pulled back by the force of international opinion and internal dissent.

The UN Charter and the Universal Declaration stand as truly significant achievements. Whether they remain a living source of law and political restraint is not yet clear, but if the past thirty years is any guide, hope must be slim. Only now can it be seen that the century of individualism ushered in, in 1789 touched but a certain part of the world; the rest largely seems destined to backwardness or to modernity through authoritarian government, neither of which conditions are conducive to the enjoyment of individual rights.

Within the United Nations and in other forums, the United States and other free countries should nevertheless continue to assert their support for human-rights enforcement based on the universal standards which constitute the fundaments of the world we hope to see develop. To do anything less is to abandon hope. At the same time, I believe other effective pressures should be brought whenever possible to produce adherence to these standards by nations which deviate from them on a regular basis. Just as the Soviets for years used debate and pressure to prevent progress, the West must continue its effort to prevent erosion of standards.

The law-making period of the UN was extremely productive in the human-rights field; enforcement of the norms much less so. Perhaps enforcement will come not so much through debate and resolution but through practical political methods, including informal recourse to the Secretary General. The development of regional groupings of nations—as in the European Human Rights Court—similar in heritage and trusting enough of one another to permit criticism, is another avenue of hope.

The dream of protection of Jews, so long the victims of abuse, by universal schemes seems ill-fated. Jews thrive in free nations; in others, they can only hope for escape to the homeland in Israel. The Zionists of 1945 were probably right.

LEONARD GARMENT

Majoritarianism at the United Nations and Human Rights

Shortly after the Human Rights Commission ended one of its recent sessions, the *Manchester Guardian* commented on the work of the Commission in the following terms: "Once upon a time . . . the United States and others saw the United Nations as a champion of human rights. . . . Disillusionment has now reached such a level that the U.S. delegate at this year's annual session of the UN Human Rights Commission would call the Commission's work a 'travesty of human rights' and accuse the Commission of having become an 'instrument of evil.' " The *London Times,* in its report entitled "A Conspiracy to Oppress," said the Commission was "perhaps the most poignant and disgraceful of false international pretences that the governments of the world have yet had the temerity to devise." It asserted that the Commission is "an almost total lie"; and that it "plays a vital part in what Sean McBride, the 1974 Nobel Peace Prize winner, had described as a 'conspiracy of governments' to deprive people of their rights."

The use of the term "conspiracy" reflects the fact that there had been a pattern of concerted acts by many countries with varying primary motives and objectives that have had the result, in my view, of weakening the ideas and forms of the democratic West and strengthening the ideas and forms of totalitarianism.

The Warsaw Pact countries have been at the center of these activities but the alarming fact is that the Soviet Union and its satellites now provide mainly ideological and strategic inspiration. Most of the work is performed by Third World countries, ranging from Cuba and Yugoslavia to Tanzania. The common denominator of this group is their pervasive fear of the liberties—free speech, assembly, religion, regular elections, guarantees of due process— that exist in the industrial democracies. Tito's Yugoslavia is an interesting example. Stirred by concern over the possibility of conflict and disintegration when its leader finally passes from the scene, Yugoslavia has tightened the screw of totalitarian oppression, as in the recent arrest and condemnation of a prominent lawyer for having made too vigorous a defense of a client charged with a political crime. Yet it continues successfully to exploit its reputation in international forums for relatively enlightened policies.

My acceptance and use of the word "conspiracy" is not casual. I know the risks and resistances that word engenders. I know that the interplay among the participant nations at the United Nations and elsewhere is complex. But I also know there is no way to comprehend the nature of the contest in which the democratic nations find themselves and what their peril is, except by making clear that these activities are not the product of incidents and accidents. They result from coordinated international action, led and organized by nations who are consistently hostile to the West. They are hostile in significant measure because they rightly consider freedom the main threat to their long-term ability to exercise dictatorial power.

The characteristics of this conspiracy are classic. And as with any other conspiracy, the way to prevail against this one is through precise and complete exposure. One of the extraordinary things about this systematic and immensely successful attack on Western values is how rarely the West takes note of it. Even Aleksandr Solzhenitsyn, bearing witness out of a life of agony, meets with diffidence or skepticism—admired, yes, but also patronized and subtly discounted.

There is a large body of evidence and many detailed illustrations of the ways in which the forums and institutions of the United

Nations are being used to harm freedom. Consider freedom of religion. Starting over a decade ago, the United States and Western European governments urged the Human Rights Commission to adopt a Declaration on Religious Freedom. After ten years, the title and a handful of introductory paragraphs are agreed upon. It is not particularly significant that little progress had been made. What matters more is the direction the Declaration is taking. Its title is now "Draft declaration on the elimination of all forms of intolerance and of discrimination based on religion or belief." It is no longer a declaration clearly intended to protect the individual's religious belief from acts of official intolerance. Rather, it is slowly taking shape as a text designed to limit religious freedom and individual belief on the pretext that religion breeds intolerance, racism, and colonialism, causing threats to peace, and—this is a critical factor—endangering state security. Under Communist-bloc pressure, the draft Declaration is being transformed from a benign, if modest, affirmation of religious values into an instrument that can serve to undermine the legitimacy of religious organizations and religious practices, and that may even be used to legitimize religious repression in certain countries. The Declaration is years away from adoption but its direction is already obvious.

A second illustration is the issue of Israel's legitimacy. Thirty years ago the United Nations admitted the State of Israel to membership. In the interim, largely at Western initiative, the UN has adopted a series of resolutions that have the effect of denying legitimacy to governments that systematically violate human rights. Now we are seeing that structure being used by the UN majority—in the General Assembly, in the Human Rights Commission, and in other specialized agencies and bodies—to erode the legitimacy of the State of Israel. The syllogism of the approach has become familiar: racism is illegal; Zionism is racism; Israel is a Zionist state; Israel is therefore illegal. When the Israeli observer at a recent meeting of the Human Rights Commission raised the question of anti-Semitism in the Soviet Union, Ambassador Valery Zorin cut him off in these terms: "Of course I believe in freedom of speech and in the right of governments to speak here. But [Israel] is not an ordinary government. This is the representative of the Zionist regime. He has no right to speak on the subject of the violation of human rights."

So, step by step, resolution by resolution, in New York, Geneva, Nairobi, at a United Nations Conference on Trade and Development, at the World Health Organization, and so on, Israel is to be cast out of the international community. I have not the slightest doubt that the infamous UN resolution of 1975, equating Zionism with racism, played an instrumental role in subsequent incitement of Arab violence on the West Bank and in Israel itself. Consequences of this kind were calculated.

A third illustration is the advocacy of the "right to life" as the primary human right. Thirty years ago the UN Charter established the principle that violations of human rights in any country are a cause of international concern. The early work of the UN sought to assert this by building on the principle that human rights are inherent in the human personality and do not depend upon the state for their existence. This idea was crucial to the language of the Universal Declaration of Human Rights, which balanced concern for individual rights and for national security. It was also the philosophical basis for the West's insistence on some form of human-rights recognition at the Helsinki Conference whose main concern was the security of the states of Europe.

What action did the majority take on this issue in the Commission on Human Rights? The majority destroyed the balance by adopting a resolution based on a Soviet view that the "right to life" is the foundation for all human rights and takes absolute precedence. The meaning of that resolution is plain: if the state determines in some manner that it is not "secure," or if the state likewise determines that there is a "threat to peace," then it can, with the formal endorsement of the UN Human Rights Commission, suspend all other human rights, such as speech, religious exercise, assembly, emigration, until the threat to the supreme "right to life" passes. It is hard to imagine a more transparently cynical and counterfeit transaction by a so-called Human Rights Commission. By passing and publishing a resolution that affirms the primacy of the right to life, a foundation is laid for subsequent resolutions that may permit human-rights crimes to be committed in the name of peace and international security.

One other aspect of UN activity deserves special mention in demonstrating the pattern of activities: selective morality. It is universally known how narrow is the Commission's range of human-rights concerns—in recent years, repeatedly, exclusively, obsessively: Chile, South Africa, and Israel. There have been any number of well-documented cases against other well-known offenders, but never any action. In 1976, for example, the United States formally moved for studies or some form of action against three other countries. The Communist bloc and the so-called non-aligned states joined to vote overwhelmingly to drop these cases. This defeat, coming after a spurious debate, was preordained.

These illustrations document a thesis of a majority strategy in the forums of the United Nations. The strategy is to use the principles and procedures of the West in such a way as to undermine their legitimacy and ultimately to destroy them. The corollary of the majority's tilt to totalitarianism is their fear of freedom, particularly of the principle that no government is legitimate if it does not enjoy the regularly renewed consent of the governed.

There has been a certain elegance in the execution of this strategy in recent years. First, an initiative is taken with regard to one of the fundamental beliefs of democracy, such as the sanctity of life, tolerance, or the elimination of racism. Next, a numerical majority of the UN promulgates, in some world body, a new official definition of what exactly that belief means or how it is to be applied. On that redefinition, Zionism becomes racism, religion becomes intolerance, and so on. By this process the meaning of the concept is inverted, and this inversion is then used to condemn the West and to argue that the Western nations have betrayed their own ideals. Thus, the one state in the world that was established as a refuge from racism is attacked as the bastion of racism. Again, the right of an individual to life becomes the right of a state to impoverish life.

The tactics can be traced in detail. The distinguishing features are usually the same. The formal initiative is usually placed in the hands of the ex-colonial countries, to take advantage of Western guilt. The big moves are carried out in places like Geneva, Kampala, Lima, or Mexico City, where there is no active press corps and no spectator interest. The political precedents are achieved at meetings on the technical level in the hope that Western technicians will not put up too much fight. Then, with the small victories inscribed in six languages in UN documents, the General Assembly is to confirm the interpretation before the isolated and disarrayed Western democracies. An important device is to point out to Western nations that they can't win. Since they are permanently in the minority their best response is to seek to accommodate their own positions to the view of the majority. Further, to protect this majority, any non-aligned nation that openly votes against some new perversion of human rights is put on notice that it will suffer retaliation in future votes.

The role that Western nations and the United States are asked to play in this procedure is an extraordinary one: that of willing victim. What the free democracies have to do is transparently clear. The question is whether they have the will and the energy to do it.

First, all the intended victims—primarily the industrial democracies—must understand and accept the fact that in this process the life of the West is under attack.

Second, those who favor democracy have to be sure that this contest takes place in the open. The democratic strategy should be to respond in any UN forum on all issues of substance relating to human rights. The best defense is strong and clear language—to reassert the position of Western democracies on human-rights issues forthrightly without letting it be masked in the ambiguities of diplomatic jargon.

Third, the Western nations have to be sure that the enemies of freedom understand that there are no willing victims. Then they can persuade those, particularly among the newer countries, who join in the attack on freedom that freedom is in their own interest. The new elite groups of these nations will begin to realize that an oppressive society eventually makes everyone a victim, and that the protection of civil and political rights cannot be postponed indefinitely during the lengthy period of social and economic development.

The U.S. government must exercise leadership in this struggle. It must make clear, first of all to the American people themselves, that doubts about America's acts at home or her role in the world will not be permitted to degenerate into self-destructive guilt under the goading of societies whose main dynamic is fear and envy of the West.

The existence of free Western countries, alive with creative disorder, is anathema to the totalitarians. So long as free democratic nations exist, they demonstrate that there is an alternative, even a better way to achieve economic development and political freedom. After sixty years of tyranny, the Soviet Union, potentially one of the richest nations on the planet, cannot feed its own people. That so inefficient a government could have been taken as a model for emulation, in its techniques, forms, and practices (even where Communism itself has been scorned), must be one of the most astonishing occurrences of history. We must understand that what is important to the emulators has not been the economic failure or success of the model but the successful creation of a subservient, loyal, and incurious populace.

The Solzhenitsyns and Sakharovs, the dissenters from totalitarianism, and the lovers of freedom who live under tyrannies have often said—and it can never be said too often—that, like plants growing in barren soil, without the light that falls on them from the West, dissent cannot survive. The rulers of the unfree world believe that so long as the West continues united in freedom, their rule cannot be free from fear of criticism or dissent. The rulers of totalitarian nations recognize by the very necessity of expelling or repressing their own advocates of freedom some measure of the virtue of democratic principles and beliefs. These principles merit the commitment of American and Western diplomacy to their continuous defense, particularly in that unique forum which is the United Nations.

DANIEL P. MOYNIHAN

->>>->>>->>>->>>->>>->>>->>>->>>->>> 4 <<<-<<<-<<<-<<<-<<<-<<<-<<<-<<<-<<<-<<<

The Significance of the Zionism-as-Racism Resolution for International Human Rights

I

On October 17, 1975, the Social, Humanitarian, and Cultural Committee of the United Nations General Assembly adopted a resolution equating Zionism with racism. Specifically, in a one-sentence "operative paragraph," the committee adopted a resolution which states: "Zionism is a form of racism and racial discrimination."

The language is notable because it is a rare event in the political diction of the United Nations when a clear meaning is clearly stated. More commonly, its language is given over to the concealment of meaning, or its obfuscation, or its disguise according to the familiar Orwellian inversion, whereby peace means war and justice injustice. The Social, Humanitarian, and Cultural Committee demonstrates this abuse of language in its very name: it is not social; at most, it is asocial, conforming to few of the humanitarian standards in whose name it was established. But, most of all, it consistently directs itself to the destruction of cultural values as we would understand them. It is an event, then, when this committee, usually referred to in the UN as the Third Committee, issues something put plain.

James Joyce hit upon the term *epiphany* for such moments of showing through. "Its soul," he wrote, "its whatness leaps to us from the vestment of its appearance . . . the object achieves its epiphany." This happened in the Third Committee of the General Assembly of the United Nations when it adopted the resolution equating Zionism with racism.

Self-destruction is what first showed through. For some time now, the United Nations has been exhibiting a seemingly compulsive urge so to outrage those very principles on which it was founded as to suggest that a sinister transmutation has occurred in an organism that yet enough remembers its own beginnings as to be revulsed by what it has become and somehow to seek expiration in bringing on its own doom. How else to explain the incessant quest for yet new devices for scandalizing the good opinion on which the survival of the institution depends? I do not refer to the occasional onset of role reversal in which some of the newer nations in the world display a certain disrespect for some of the older ones. Some of the latter, the United States included, have a certain amount of disrespect coming, and occasional irreverence will do no one harm. Nor do I refer to the debates over the distribution of wealth among the nations of the world which have much occupied the United Nations in recent years. Centuries ago, Aristotle noted that the founding of any truly political forum is the signal for a struggle between rich and poor to commence. It is one of the redeeming qualities of the institution that that struggle has indeed begun at the United Nations.

The real problem is very different, and vastly ominous: the United Nations has become a locus of a general assault by the majority of the nations in the world on the principles of liberal democracy which are now found only in a minority—and a dwindling minority—of nations. Though this UN resolution was ostensibly a condemnation of Zionism, it was part of a concerted attack upon the State of Israel. And, significantly, Israel is one of the very few states, outside of Western Europe and North America and a few offshore islands, where Western democratic principles survive—and of all such places, currently the most exposed.

In its form and in its effect, the resolution was the very quintessence of the totalitarian mode. A total inversion of meaning, a total distortion of truth, was proposed. The moral force of the concept of racism was to be destroyed, making it nothing more than the epithet to be flung arbitrarily at one's adversary. The prior UN commitment to a Decade of Action to Combat Racism was now, through the ploy of defining Zionism-as-racism, to be rededicated to propagating anti-Semitism—one of the oldest and most virulent forms of racism.

This act was one of the most grievous errors in the thirty-year life of the United Nations. At risk was the moral authority of the UN. The UN cannot function, cannot even survive, unless it remains representative. You can have one-party states; you cannot have a one-party United Nations. In a representative institution which aspires to universality, no majority can arbitrarily limit the right of representation. When it permits a majority of its members to deny the legitimacy of a member state as was the intent of this resolution, the UN jeopardizes its only claim on the loyalty of all.

This obscene, reckless act was adopted in the Third Committee by 70 votes to 29, with 27 abstentions. The epiphany occurred in the wholesale decision of the despotisms of the Right to side with the despotisms of the Left, in common concert against the liberal democracies of the center. It was an awful occasion, but it had about it, most of all, the awfulness of truth. Yet it was in no sense an unrelieved disaster. To the contrary, there was a rallying of spirits on that occasion which may yet prove its greater significance. Reporting the event, the *Washington Post* noted, "A year ago, the Arabs had an 'automatic majority' of Communist, African, and Asian nations, and the nervous abstentions of most West Europeans." That majority disappeared in the committee vote; just possibly, it was broken. The resolution received only 70 votes, less than a majority of the membership. Many African nations either voted against the resolution or abstained, while earlier, many more had joined in a move to defer the whole question.

For a very long time the Western democracies could not find a common understanding of these issues. The inclusion of "Zionism" along with "racial discrimination" as a candidate for "elimination" first apeared in the Declaration of Mexico, adopted in July 1975, in connection with the International Women's Year. Only the United States and Israel voted outright against that declaration. On the "Zionism is racism" resolution, however, the democratic nations, with only a few exceptions, came individually to a common decision.

II

There is a need for some understanding about the kinds of encounters that are taking place in the forum of the United Nations. The UN is now much preoccupied with economic issues of a distributive nature, having to do with the relative condition of various classes of nations, much as the internal politics of many societies are preoccupied with similar issues having to do with classes of citizens. This ought not to surprise us, for by all the doctrinal lights of the twentieth century, this is what we are *supposed* to be preoccupied with. And yet, to the contrary, it is the ancient and supposedly recessive bonds of race and creed—so recently thought to be mere survivals from an earlier and rapidly vanishing era—which increasingly occupy the political forums of the world. As one goes about the business of the United Nations with cries of Athens, Damascus, Jerusalem ringing in one's ears, one wonders if we are not all caught up in some massive retrogression. Yet it is also true that most of the notions of race and ethnicity which we fling at one another with tribal passion draw on quintessentially modern ideas.

Indeed, the idea that Jews are a "race" was invented by such nineteenth-century anti-Semites as Houston Stewart Chamberlain and Edouard Drumont, who saw that in an increasingly secular age, which is to say an age which made for fewer distinctions between people, the old religious grounds for anti-Semitism were losing force. New justifications were needed for excluding and persecuting Jews, and so the new idea of Jews as a race was born.

With the passage of the resolution by the UN General Assembly on November 10, 1975, the abomination of anti-Semitism, as Nobel Peace Laureate Andrei Sakharov observed in Moscow, has been given the appearance of international sanction. The proposition sanctioned by the resolution stating that "Zionism is a form of racism and racial discrimination" is a lie. But as it is a lie which the UN has now declared to be a truth, the actual truth must be restated.

Historically, the word *racism* is a recent creation of the English language. The term derives from relatively new doctrines—all of them already discredited—concerning the human populations of the world, to the effect that there are significant biological differences among clearly identifiable groups; and that these differences establish, in effect, different levels of humanity. Racism, as defined by *Webster's Third New International Dictionary,* is "the assumption that . . . traits and capacities are determined by biological race and that races differ decisively from one another." It further involves "a belief in the inherent superiority of a particular race and its right to domination over others."

Clearly, this racial doctrine has always been altogether alien to the political and religious movement known as Zionism. As a strictly political movement, Zionism was established in 1897, although there is a legitimate sense in which its origins are indeed ancient. But the modern Zionist movement arose in Europe in the context of a general upsurge of national consciousness and aspiration that overtook most other peoples of Central and Eastern Europe after 1848, and that in time spread to all of Asia and Africa. It was a Jewish form of what today is called a national liberation movement. Thus, it was entirely appropriate for Soviet Foreign Minister Andrei Gromyko to deplore, as he did in 1948, in the 299th meeting of the Security Council, the action by Israel's neighbors of "sending their troops into Palestine and carrying out military operations aimed"—in Mr. Gromyko's words—"at the suppression of the National Liberation Movement in Palestine."

The State of Israel, which emerged from Zionist efforts, has drawn its citizenry from a wide range of peoples. In Israel one finds black Jews, brown Jews, white Jews; Jews from the Orient and Jews from the West. Most such persons could be said to have been "born" Jews, but it is critical in this context to observe that people of all ethnic and racial origins may become converts to Judaism—and once having done so are accorded equal status among Jews. Consistent with this religious factor, and in contradistinction to a racist position, a Jew who converts to another religion, as the Israeli courts have confirmed, is no longer a Jew. Of course, the population of Israel also includes large numbers of non-Jews, among them Arabs of both the Muslim and Christian faiths, and Christians of other national origins. Many of these persons are citizens of Israel, and those who are not can become citizens by legal procedures typically found in the nations of Western Europe. So, whatever else Zionism may be, it is not and cannot be a form of racism. In logic, the State of Israel could be, or could become, many things (theoretically including many things undesirable), but it could not be and could not become racist unless it ceased to be Zionist.

The United Nations has declared Zionism to be racism—without ever having defined racism. Lest I be unclear, the UN has in fact on several occasions defined *racial discrimination*. The definitions have been loose but recognizable. It is *racism*—incomparably the more serious charge—which has never been defined. Indeed, the term has only recently appeared in UN General Assembly documents. The one occasion on which we know its meaning to have been discussed was the 1,644th meeting of the Third Committee on December 16, 1968, in connection with the report of the Secretary-General on the status of the international convention on the elimination of all forms of racial discrimination. On that occasion (to give some feeling for the intellectual precision with which the matter was being treated), the question arose as to what should be the relative positioning of the terms *racism* and *Nazism* in a number of preambular paragraphs. The distinguished delegate from Tunisia argued that *racism* should go first, because "Nazism was merely a form of racism. . . ." Not so, said the no-less-distinguished delegate from the USSR. For, he explained, "Nazism contained the main elements of racism within its ambit and should be mentioned first." This is to say that racism was merely a form of Nazism.

The discussion wound to its weary and inconclusive end, and we are left with nothing to guide us, for even this one discussion of racism confined itself to word orders in preambular paragraphs, not touching at all on the meaning of the words as such. Still, one cannot but ponder the situation in the context of the Soviet statement on that not-so-distant occasion. *If,* as the distinguished delegate declared, racism is a form of Nazism, and *if,* as this resolution declares, Zionism is a form of racism, *then* we have, step by step, taken ourselves to the point of proclaiming that Zionism is a form of Nazism!

What we have here is a lie—a political lie of a variety well known to the twentieth century but scarcely exceeded in all the annals of untruth and outrage. The terrible lie that has been told will have terrible consequences. Not only will people begin to say—indeed, they have already begun to say—that the United Nations is a place where lies are told. Far more serious, and perhaps irreparable, harm will be done to the cause of human rights.

The harm will arise, first, because it will strip from racism the precise and abhorrent meaning that today it still precariously holds. How will the peoples of the world feel about racism, and about the need to struggle against it, when they are told that it is an idea so broad as to include the Jewish national liberation movement?

As this lie spreads, it will do harm in a second way. Many of the members of the UN owe their independence in no small part to the notion of human rights, as it has spread from the domestic sphere to the international arena and exercised its influence over the old colonial powers. We are now coming into a time when that independence is likely to be threatened again. There will be new forces, new prophets, and new despots who will justify their actions with the help of just such distortions of words. Today we have drained the word *racism* of its meaning. Tomorrow, terms like *national self-determination* will be perverted in the same way to serve the purposes of conquest and exploitation. And when these claims begin to be made—as they have already begun to be made—it is the small nations of the world whose integrity will suffer. And how will the small nations of the world defend themselves, on what grounds will others be moved to defend and protect them, when the language of human rights, the only language by which the small can be defended, is no longer believed and no longer has a power of its own?

What is at stake here is not merely the honor and the legitimacy of the State of Israel—although a challenge to the legitimacy of any member nation ought always to arouse the vigilance of all members of the United Nations. For a yet more important matter is at issue: the integrity of that whole body of moral and legal precepts which we know as human rights.

III

In any examination of the UN's record on human rights, universality of enforcement is of special concern. The first ground for concern is that the selective morality of the UN in matters of human rights threatens not only that organization's integrity but that of human rights themselves. Unless standards of human rights are applied uniformly and neutrally to all nations, regardless of the nature of their regimes or the strength of their military arsenals, it will quickly be seen that it is not human rights at all which are invoked when selective applications are called for, but simply arbitrary political standards dressed up in the guise of human rights. From this perception it is no great distance to the conclusion that, in truth, there are no human rights recognized by the international community.

Particularly disturbing are the processes by which the United Nations has come to be so concerned about human rights in some countries but not in others. We tend to know about violations of freedom—at the time they occur and in detail—only in those countries which permit *enough* freedom for internal opposition to make its voice heard when freedoms are violated. On the other hand, we have seen any number of regimes completely, or almost completely, seal off their countries, barring or expelling foreign newsmen, so that at most rumor reaches the outside world as to what is going on inside.

Simple justice requires that the United States, for one, acknowledge that, while it has supported General Assembly resolutions critical of repressive practices of the governments both of South Africa and of Chile, it has done so in the company of nations whose own internal conditions are as repressive, if not more so. Is it not also fair to say that much of the case being made against Israel by other nations today is made, in the first instance, by the fully legal opposition parties within Israel, including Arab-based parties, many of which have been quite successful in electing members to public office? And is not this opposition given notable expression in the Arab-language press in Israel, which has been described as the freest Arab-language press in the world?

More and more, the UN seems to know only of violations of human rights in countries where it is still possible to protest such violations. If this language can be turned against one democracy, why not against all democracies? Are democracies not singular in the degree to which at all times voices will be heard protesting this or that injustice? If the propensity to protest injustice is taken as equivalent to the probability that injustice does occur, then the democracies will fare poorly indeed. In 1971, for example, the World Social Report presented to the General Assembly a virtually totalitarian document. The fundamental premise on which the assessment of social conditions in respective countries had been made was the absence of public assertion of social wrong. Hence, without exception, the police states of the world were judged most in the right.

Americans, and those who have studied the history of the United States, will perhaps recall the memorable image which Abraham Lincoln once used in a speech which we have come to call his "Framing Timbers Speech." He was protesting, in 1858, what he judged to be the overall purpose being served by many seemingly unrelated legislative measures of the time—the purpose of extending slavery into our Western territories. Lincoln spoke of a "concert" of behavior:

> We cannot absolutely know that all these exact adaptations are the result of pre-concert. But when we see a lot of framed timbers, different times and places and by different workmen . . . and we see these timbers joined together, and see they exactly make the frame of a house or a mill, all the tenons and mortices exactly fitting, and all the lengths and proportions of the different pieces exactly adapted to their respective places, . . . in such a case, we find it impossible not to believe that . . . all understood one another from the beginning, and all worked upon a common plan or draft drawn up before the first blow was struck.

The question for us is whether there has indeed been a "plan or draft" involved in all the multifarious activities at the United Nations concerning human rights which, with nigh inhuman consistency, seem always to be directed toward nations at least somewhat more free than most UN members; and which now most recently have been directed toward Israel, a democratic society that is unquestionably free. The evidence suggests that there could be a design to use the issue of human rights to undermine the legitimacy of precisely those nations which still observe human rights, imperfect as that observance may be. It is precisely because of this background that it now becomes essential for the United Nations to undertake important initiatives that appeal to the classic notions of human rights in a universal manner.

SIDNEY LISKOFSKY

5

The United Nations and Human Rights: "Alternative Approaches"

During the closing days of the Second World War, civic groups in the Allied nations, especially in the United States, proposed diverse plans for a postwar world organization. Many of these plans called for the adoption of international standards for human rights and for mechanisms for safeguarding human rights. These proposals were motivated and given impetus by the realization that the Nazi regime was even then committing unprecedented acts of genocide. The development of these standards and mechanisms, it was hoped, would assure that crimes against human rights like those of the Nazi regime would never again be inflicted on any people.

The American Jewish community was actively involved in this effort. Several Jewish organizations had articulated formal proposals for a human-rights role for the intended international organization. They submitted these to the Dumbarton Oaks preparatory conference for the founding of the United Nations organization and at the Charter conference at San Francisco in 1945. The American Jewish Conference, then the comprehensive Jewish communal organization charged with postwar planning, also proposed that "anti-Semitism, as an instrument of internal and international policy be outlawed . . . by international conventions and national legislation." Together with other non-governmental consultants to the American delegation at the UN Charter conference at San Francisco, Judge Joseph Proskauer and Jacob Blaustein of the American Jewish Committee helped to ensure inclusion of the human-rights wording in the Charter, in particular the provision for a Commission on Human Rights. At the conclusion of the conference Blaustein stated: "The establishment of a Commission on Human Rights is a great step forward. . . . For the first time in history, the question of human rights and the treatment of individuals has been officially recognized as being of vital international concern."

But in the light of the often depressing human-rights record in many areas of the world and the current widespread skepticism about the UN's ability to deal with violations, the hopes and expectations expressed thirty years ago now have a hollow ring. The postwar world turned out to be more complex and less manageable than could have been predicted at the moment of the Allied victory.

The drafters of the Charter did not anticipate the Iron Curtain that was to wall off the Soviet bloc from the Western alliance nor the enlargement of the UN membership into an eventual majority of newly independent nations of Asia and Africa. These nations, which identify themselves as "non-aligned," "developing," or "Third World," have become effectively the majority in the United Nations. Nor did proponents of international human rights foresee the proliferation of issues that would be proposed for the international human-rights agenda. Social and economic rights were added at the outset to the traditional list of civil liberties, racial equality, and national self-determination. Since, there have been proposals for the recognition of new human rights reflecting emerging concerns, such as the right to a safe environment, the right to peace, and the right of protection from computer invasion of privacy or from genetic manipulation. Much less did they envisage the causes and claims that would be attached to the concepts of racial equality and self-determination, or that the idea of economic rights would be extended to include the concept of a new international economic order that would aim at restructuring economic relationships between the industrialized and the developing nations.

Certainly, the Jewish community that was active in the movement for international human rights did not imagine that a combination of Arab and Soviet states would be able to prevent the UN from condemning anti-Semitism in proposed conventions dealing with racial discrimination and religious intolerance in the 1960s and succeed in persuading the majority to condemn Zionism as a form of racism in the 1970s. They did not conceive that the human-rights bodies of the UN would serve after the 1967 war as a political platform for support of the Palestinian Arab cause.

In the thirty years since the founding of the United Nations, international human rights has become a battleground in the struggle between the authoritarian and democratic ideologies and forms of government. On the one hand, forces are at work within the UN itself to block the application of agreed human-rights norms to situations that require remedy and to apply them selectively in pursuit of political aims. There are continuing efforts to weaken or negate traditional concepts of human rights by reinterpretation and redefinition. On the other hand, there have been important elements of progress, including agreements on standards and on embryonic procedures for the protection of human rights. The goal of an international law of human rights to be implemented by international institutions has become a permanent item on the international agenda. In assessing both the achievements and the disappointments, it is fundamental that the interests of democracy and freedom require that the moral and political forces generated by the ideal of human rights—the symbolic as well as its institutional expression—should not be abandoned to the authoritarian and totalitarian states in the existing international forums.

Standard-Setting: The International Bill of Rights

At the San Francisco conference, some participants had hoped to include in the UN Charter an international bill of rights, but this proved impractical. Subsequently, in 1947, the Human Rights Commission undertook to draft such a bill in stages: first, a non-binding

Declaration to be followed by a legally binding Covenant and by measures of implementation. In 1948 the Universal Declaration of Human Rights was adopted by the UN General Assembly as a "common standard of achievement." Two decades later, at the 1968 UN-sponsored Teheran conference, the assembled nations proclaimed that the Declaration's thirty articles—covering a wide range of civil and political as well as economic, social, and cultural rights—constituted a "common understanding of the peoples of the world concerning the inalienable and inviolable rights of all members of the human family" and "an obligation for the members of the international community."

Although some experts have since viewed this proclamation as confirming the legally binding character of the Universal Declaration, it was not so viewed at the time of its acceptance in 1948. At that time, it was considered necessary to adopt its provisions, defined with more exactitude, in treaty form as binding covenants. Since all the provisions of the Declaration did not lend themselves to the same kind of implementation, the Assembly called for two separate Covenants, one dealing with civil and political rights, the other with economic, social, and cultural rights, each with its own measures of implementation. The Covenant on Economic, Social, and Cultural Rights was formulated in terms which rendered it binding in a different sense than political or civil rights. It was viewed as a statement of goals to be pursued "progressively" by "appropriate" means (especially legislation) to the maximum of "available resources." This formulation led some to consider it as more akin to a declaration than a convention.

These two Covenants, together with a separate protocol providing for a right of individual complaint in the case of the civil and political rights, were adopted by the General Assembly eighteen years later, in 1966. Another decade was to pass before the two Covenants and the Protocol received the number of ratifications required to bring them into force.* The goal set in 1947 for an international bill of rights that would include a declaration, binding covenants, and means of implementation was thus realized in 1976.

In addition to this international bill of rights, the UN under-

*By early 1978, the Covenant on Civil and Political Rights had forty-eight ratifications, the Covenant on Economic, Social, and Cultural Rights fifty, and the Optional Protocol, seventeen.

took in the early period the task of spelling out international standards in special areas, especially the preventing of discrimination in the areas of race, sex, and religion. The record is one of accomplishments in regard to race and sex, but not with regard to religion.

There is symbolic significance in the fact that the first result of this standard-setting activity was the Genocide Convention, which was adopted at the same time as the Universal Declaration of Human Rights, in December 1948. Over the next three decades the UN adopted a number of declarations dealing with the rights of particular groups—children, women, the disabled—and with the treatment of prisoners, torture, and the right to asylum. Binding conventions were adopted on the status of refugees and stateless persons, the political rights of women, and practices akin to slavery. The most important of the conventions was the Convention on the Elimination of All Forms of Racial Discrimination which embraces a wide range of governmental practices, provides for implementation, and has been ratified (as of early 1978) by 100 states. And standard-setting with a view to the adoption of new declarations or conventions, or both, is underway in regard to a variety of other issues, including migrant workers, elimination of torture, treatment of political prisoners, conduct of law-enforcement officials, impact of science and technology, and protection of minorities.

Sixteen UN conventions are now in force, though many important states have not yet ratified them.* The United States has ratified neither covenant, nor the Racial Convention, nor even the Genocide Convention. Paradoxically, the forty-eight states, parties (as of early 1978) to the Covenant on Civil and Political Rights, which more than any other convention reflects the Western civil-liberties tradition, include nearly all the East European states and most of the radical Arab states, but not such major Western constitutional democracies as France and the United States. This abstention prevents these democratic states from participating in the important early phase of the developing international jurisprudence of human rights.

---

*The sixteen conventions do not include the standard-setting agreements of ILO, UNESCO, and other UN specialized agencies, nor those of the regional organizations—the Council of Europe and the Organization of American States.

International Implementation

For the most part, intergovernmental processes are essentially mechanisms for organizing world opinion against perceived wrongdoers.* These mechanisms are based either on international conventions or on powers inherent in the Charter of the UN or the constitutions of the specialized agencies. Though the Charter empowers the Security Council to impose sanctions in any case of human-rights violations found to constitute a threat to international peace and security, in practice, the coercive powers of the Security Council have been invoked only in those rare instances where the permanent members have been able to agree, notably regarding Rhodesia and South Africa.†

The implementing measures of the main comprehensive binding agreements, the two Covenants and the Convention on the Elimination of Racial Discrimination, vary markedly in forcefulness. While the Covenant on Economic and Social Rights provides only for reporting by contracting states, the other Covenant and the Convention on Racial Discrimination also provide for grievance procedures. However, those procedures are markedly more rigorous in the Convention than they are in the Covenant, reflecting the UN majority's greater commitment to equality than to freedom. Thus, not only are the rights guaranteed in the Covenant circumscribed and weakened by extensive limitations and exceptions, but the Covenant renders optional the right of state-against-state complaint which the Convention makes obligatory. As for the right of private petition, which is optional in both, the Covenant limits this to individual victims of violations while in the Convention, this right is available also to non-governmental groups. The reporting procedure is also more meaningful in the Convention than in the Covenant.

But even the stronger procedures of the Convention are far from adequate. Thus, state-to-state complaints are not likely to be

---

*This argument is elaborated in a report by John Humphrey to the 1974 meeting of the International Law Association.

†In the case of South Africa, the express legal rationale was the existence of a threat to peace (warranting a mandatory arms embargo) stemming from its acquisition of arms and related material, but the Security Council avoided a determination—though this was the implication—that the human-rights situation in that country constituted of itself a threat to international peace.

invoked, since states are loath to invite reciprocal complaints or other forms of retaliation. The individual complaint mechanism has limited application, since the states which are most delinquent are precisely those which will not agree to this optional procedure. In the case of the reporting mechanism, governments are seldom inclined to engage in acts of public self-scrutiny. Despite these shortcomings, however, there are probable benefits in these procedures. Reporting, for example, can stimulate some constructive self-examination and occasional responsiveness to pressure from the examining bodies.

Frustration over delays in adopting and bringing the covenants and conventions into force, as well as dissatisfaction with the limited reach of their implementing procedures, motivated efforts to develop new mechanisms based on the Charter's implied powers. U.S. encouragement of this development was based in part on recognition of the unlikelihood of Senate consent to ratification of the pending agreements. For the black African states, additional pressures for accelerated change in southern Africa was the relevant factor. On condition that emphasis be placed on apartheid and racial discrimination in that region, these states were willing to agree to a procedure for dealing with human-rights violations elsewhere. The Western states, for their part, were willing to accept this quid pro quo.

The first step was taken in 1967 when the UN Economic and Social Council (ECOSOC) authorized the Human Rights Commission to study situations revealing a consistent pattern of gross human-rights violations, with special attention to apartheid policies and other racist practices in southern Africa. Three years later, ECOSOC resolution 1503 expanded the role of the Commission (and its Sub-Commission on Discrimination) by establishing a multi-stage, mainly secret, procedure for examining communications (i.e., complaints) from individuals and non-governmental organizations, and for identifying "situations" indicative of consistent and gross violations of human rights.

At first, Western governments and the non-governmental organizations recognized at the UN had high expectations of this procedure, but foot-dragging by Third World states and undisguised sabotage by the Soviet bloc—which now claims that resolution 1503 has been supplanted by the Covenants and is moot—have dissipated these hopes. Though working groups considered a number of cases, none of their reports to the Commission, including those relating to blatant situations of abuse like Uganda, have culminated in public study or investigations as envisaged in the resolution. Nevertheless, supporters of the 1503 initiative continue to look for strategies that will fulfill their hopes for it as implementing procedure for correction of human-rights violations.

At the same time, the Third World and Communist states, comprising the majority of the United Nations had other means under the UN Charter for dealing with human-rights situations of particular interest to them, while deflecting critical scrutiny of their own affairs. For example, they were able to focus attention on South Africa by a variety of means: special committees of the General Assembly (on apartheid and colonialism), an expert working group of the Human Rights Commission, a special convention on the crime of apartheid, special studies and reports (on the adverse consequences of continuing diplomatic, commercial, cultural, and other relationships with South Africa), special educational and promotional programs (global and regional conferences), and special condemnatory resolutions (on torture of political prisoners in South Africa). They could persuade the Security Council to order (November 4, 1977) a mandatory embargo on the supply of arms to South Africa and the General Assembly to recommend (May 3, 1978) that the Security Council impose mandatory economic sanctions against the country because of its continued occupation of Namibia (South-West Africa).

Special measures, less far-reaching, could be applied in the case of Chile. And in a case having nothing in common either with Chile or South Africa, Israel was the object of repeated reports by special investigatory committees and of innumerable condemnatory resolutions, even charged with war crimes on the ground that its policies in the occupied territories constituted "grave breaches" of the Fourth Geneva Convention relating to the treatment of civilians in occupied territory.

In this way, pressure in a variety of forms could be mustered against selected states without the initiators incurring the risk of being subjected to comparable investigation. Unlike the 1503 implementing procedure favored by the Western democracies, the ad-hoc approach insulated members of the majority. They were able to keep the UN occupied with investigations of alleged wrongdoing of a selected few while diverting attention from their own delinquencies. Even countries where killing on a vast scale and other massive human-rights violations occurred—as in Biafra, Bangladesh, Cambodia, Central African Republic, Indonesia, Uganda—could receive only minimum scrutiny, much less censure.

A High Commissioner for Human Rights

Dissatisfaction with the lack of a general system of human-rights implementation that would be equally applicable to all member states has led to a mainly Western-supported proposal to create an office of UN High Commissioner for Human Rights. The proposal, introduced in the General Assembly in 1965 by Costa Rica, was widely supported by the Western democracies and by the nongovernmental organizations. It envisaged an international ombudsman who could intercede discreetly on behalf of individuals or groups whose human rights appeared to be denied or violated. Though the description of the office varied in different versions of the proposal, the High Commissioner was generally depicted as an individual of a high degree of personal independence and prestige, who would serve under the authority of the Secretary-General with a mandate to render "assistance and services, including good offices" to UN member states (but only at the request of the state concerned), and to help coordinate the diverse UN human-rights activities and programs.

Notwithstanding prior approval by the Human Rights Commission, the proposal met with strong opposition from the Soviet bloc and from many Third World states when it finally came before the General Assembly in 1974. The tactic adopted by them was to request reexamination of the proposal under a more general agenda item of "Alternative approaches and ways and means within the United Nations system for improving the effective enjoyment of human rights"—a device designed to downgrade the proposed office of High Commissioner. The proposal was again sidetracked at the 1977 General Assembly even though its supporters redefined the terms of reference of the office to reflect some Third World priorities. Though it is to be studied anew by the Human Rights Commission, some of its advocates are concerned lest it emerge with so circumscribed a mandate as to prevent the High Commissioner from contributing usefully to human-rights protection except, of course, in cases that always receive extensive attention—namely, the selected targets of the UN majority.

"Alternative Approaches": *The General Assembly's 1977 Resolution*

The debate at the 1977 General Assembly was especially significant, since under the broad rubric of "Alternative Approaches" decisions were to be made which would establish the terms of the UN's future human-rights program. It brought into sharp focus views which regular UN observers had been hearing increasingly in recent years as the UN majority shifted from the industrial democracies of the West toward the less developed and predominantly authoritarian states of the Third World. The debate clearly revealed that the UN membership is now sharply dichotomized not only on the UN's role in implementation but also on the substantive questions of human rights.

The minority of democratic states, mostly in the West, continues to urge attention to civil and political rights, and to favor effective implementation processes applicable to all states, while the majority emphasizes governmental prerogatives in matters both of economics and security and remains wary of any UN implementation other than that directed against South Africa, Chile, Israel, or other unpopular targets. The Western democracies seek new agreement to cope with such issues as religious freedom, the right of free emigration, freedom of information, protection of political prisoners, the conduct of law-enforcement officials, the human-rights problems stemming from scientific and technological innovations, and other issues concerned with freedom of the individual. At the same time, they acknowledge (admittedly, however, partly in response to Third World pressure) the need to develop programs for economic and social rights.*

*The economic and social rights, mainly collective rather than individual, usually require positive governmental action—in contrast to the negative, classical Western type of rights which stress non-intrusion by government. However, the traditional division of rights into negative and positive has been criticized as simplistic by Henry Shue ("The Priority of Economic Rights," unpublished manuscript, 1978) and others, who point out that some civil and political rights are positive, in the sense that they require

The minority at the UN urges the establishment of an office of UN High Commissioner for Human Rights or, alternatively, assignment of the functions envisaged for that office either to the High Commissioner for Refugees or to the Secretary-General, with an appropriate extension of the scope of their offices. In addition, this group recommends the extension to Asia and Africa of the system of regional human-rights commissions already in effect in Europe and the Western Hemisphere.

Confronting the minority in this debate is a majority that comprises Communist and radical Third World governments as well as military and traditionalist authoritarian regimes, which formerly were routinely aligned with the West on such issues. Argentina and the Philippines, for example, have joined with the Left in justifying curtailment of civil and political rights on grounds of national security and other overriding requirements of national interest, and in characterizing these rights as merely derivative from West European and American political ideology. The Communist states show little or no interest in elaborating further norms in the area of individual rights. The Soviet Union, for example, has long filibustered against the proposed declaration on religious intolerance. The new norms its delegates propose are nearly always designed to uphold state power, with economic and social rights of the collectivity to be accorded priority over civil and political rights for the individual. The Soviet Union further urges priority for the right to peace, a seemingly uncontroversial notion that the Soviets intend to justify curtailing freedom in the name of security and order.

---

an active governmental role (e.g., right to a fair trial), while some economic and social rights are negative in the sense of entailing a governmental hands-off posture (e.g., right to form trade unions).

Many would limit the notion of "right" to claims which are justiciable in courts and therefore are uneasy about extending it to the economic and social area. But others say there is no reason for such a limitation, apart from the fact that the courts can be and are used to vindicate some economic rights. For economic claims, including those deriving from treaty obligations, can be asserted directly to the executive and the legislature. They can also be asserted by one government against another (on the basis of treaty or customary international law), without the complaining government having access to the courts of the defendant state.

Nevertheless, it is important not to blur the real distinctions between the two classes of rights, an important difference being the relative ease of establishing criteria for implementing the civil and political rights in contrast to the complexity of doing so in the case of economic and social rights. Nor should one minimize the difference between acts which require only governmental restraint as against active involvement.

With significant exceptions, most Third World—and all Communist—states oppose a High Commissioner for Human Rights on the ground that such an office would interfere in their internal affairs. The Soviet Union contends that the Commissioner could not possibly function impartially, but would be "the tool of a certain group of countries." The Soviet Union has traditionally preferred formal treaties, like the Covenants, which define precisely the limits of international action to flexible, Charter-based mechanisms—unless the latter were created ad hoc to deal with particular targets determined by majority vote. As mentioned above, the Soviet Union now maintains that the Covenants' implementing provisions have in fact rendered moot the procedure proposed under resolution 1503.

The operative paragraphs in the majority resolution on "Alternative Approaches" (that was overwhelmingly approved and on which only the Western democracies abstained) began by affirming the indivisibility, interdependence, and equal urgency of "all human rights and fundamental freedoms," including civil and political as well as economic, social, and cultural rights. Though an arguable proposition—for all rights and freedoms are clearly not equally urgent—this affirmation served a constructive purpose in emphasizing the need to give adequate attention in the UN program to the areas of both individual and collective rights. But the resolution then went on to tilt the balance by asserting that "the full realization of civil and political rights without the enjoyment of economic, social, and cultural rights is impossible"—*without adding the converse*. Though the imbalance was seemingly restored by a subsequent affirmation that "all human rights and fundamental freedoms of the human person and of peoples are inalienable," the succeeding paragraphs again weakened the commitment to the civil and political rights, by introducing an escape clause that calls for "taking into account . . . the overall context of the various societies in which [human-rights questions] present themselves. . . ."

This resolution has introduced a number of confusing priorities for the UN's future human-rights work by singling out, in addition to "apartheid and all forms of racial discrimination," "colonialism, foreign domination and occupation, aggression and threats against national sovereignty, national unity and territorial integrity." It also assigned priority, in "the search for solution to . . . mass and flagrant violations of human rights of peoples and persons," to "the fundamental right[s] of peoples to self-determination" and the right "of every nation to exercise full sovereignty over its wealth and natural resources." Finally, the resolution accorded priority to the New International Economic Order (NIEO) "as an essential element for the effective promotion of human rights and fundamental freedoms."

The Not-So-Hidden Agenda in the Resolution

The resolution is problematic not because these goals, values, or principles are of themselves undesirable; they are in fact agreed international moral or legal norms. The problematic element is their uses—and the intentions of their instigators in proposing them—as criteria for determining the nature and direction of the human-rights work of the UN.

Except for apartheid and racial discrimination, it is noteworthy that the priorities do not relate to the rights of the individual vis-à-vis his own government, but are essentially focused on the claims of the state vis-à-vis other states. Moreover, not only are they ambiguous and controversial but they blur the necessary distinction, however difficult to draw, between human rights and political issues. There is also the factor of their use as code-words. It is unlikely, therefore, that they were seriously intended other than to complicate efforts to deal with issues of civil and political rights and to narrow if not crowd out the space reserved for these rights in the human-rights program.

The NIEO is a case in point. To begin with, it is clearly not acceptable to equate with human rights all the claims of the NIEO—as articulated in UN-approved resolutions—which aim at reorienting or restructuring the economic relationships of the industrialized and the developing countries in favor of the latter. Doubtless, moral justification can be found for many of these claims (on grounds of a shared humanity if not of compensation for past exploitation). But, it is quite another matter to appear to give a blanket endorsement to all the claims and to insinuate them into the sphere of "rights." Not the least reason is that the industrialized countries, plagued by high unemployment and inflation—attributable in considerable part to the high cost of oil exacted by OPEC—are not without moral basis in trying to protect their own workers and consumers. That aside, to present interstate economic demands, however justified, in human-rights terms with a priority over the civil and political rights of the individual within his own society only compounds the ambiguities and other difficulties that already plague the UN's human-rights program. Surely, the practical implications of so far-reaching a development should be fully comprehended and not brought into UN normative statements in an ambiguous and roundabout way.

Moreover, several of the suggested priorities already enjoy extensive attention under other programs in other bodies and agencies of the UN system. For example, many of the issues involved in the NIEO are within the purview of the General Agreement on Tariffs and Trade (GATT). At its very session in 1977, the Assembly decided to hold a special global conference in 1980 to promote the NIEO, and it authorized establishment of a new top-level post within the UN Secretariat with a mandate to enhance the efficiency of the UN's economic and social programs.

To assign priorities to human-rights violations resulting from "aggression and threats against national sovereignty, national unity, and territorial integrity" can also only have an obstructionist purpose. For these are ambiguous concepts, replete with potential for controversy and confusion. Thus, "national sovereignty" is the usual defense of governments seeking to parry criticism of their human-rights practices, while "territorial integrity" was the Russian-Cuban justification for pouring massive amounts of arms into Ethiopia to help suppress the Somalia-assisted Ogaden secession, and was also the legal basis for the General Assembly's condemnation of Israel's Entebbe (Uganda) raid undertaken to rescue its hijacked citizens held hostage by Palestinian terrorists with Idi Amin's assistance.

"Self-determination" and "colonialism" have enjoyed long-standing priority in the UN, albeit without accepted general criteria and, in practice, with nearly exclusive focus on Western colonial rule and a corresponding lack of concern for the same issues in regions other than Africa and Asia. These issues would be assigned a priority in the human-rights program at the very time that the decolonization process has progressed so far that the Assembly's De-colonization (Fourth) Committee, like the Trusteeship Council, will soon be left with hardly any business to transact, unless a way is found to deal with the issues of self-determination in Eastern Europe (as in the Baltic region), Africa (as in Eritrea), or Asia (as in Sikkim and Tibet). "Self-determination" has also served as legal-political cover for legitimating the use of "all available means, including armed struggle" by liberation movements—with no criteria, except decisions of the Arab League and the Organization of African Unity—for determining which movements deserve to be recognized as such.

As for the priority proposed with respect to human-rights violations stemming from "foreign domination and occupation," this phrase has for years been a code-word for the Israeli-occupied territories. Next to southern Africa, this area has received more extensive and aggressive attention from the UN than any other human-rights situation. Indeed, the charge of human-rights violations in these territories has consistently been a major weapon in the Arabs' anti-Israel diplomatic arsenal. Apart from repeated attacks on Israeli policies and practices in nearly every UN organ (as well as at such UN special conferences as those on the International Women's Year and Habitat), these territories have been the subject of repeated investigations, debates, and resolutions. Even the Assembly's Special Committee on Apartheid has seen fit to single out Israel for condemnation on charges of military and economic collaboration with South Africa—notwithstanding the fact that Israel's trade with that nation is minimal in comparison to that of the U.S., Western Europe, and even black Africa. All of this anti-Israel activity is duplicated in the UN specialized agencies—WHO, ILO, and UNESCO—which monitor health, labor, educational, and cultural conditions of Arabs in the occupied territories.

The Challenges to Civil and Political Rights

It was to be expected that the Soviet Union would use the United Nations as a forum for its ideological crusade against the idea of personal freedom. Even in the earlier years of the world body, when it was dominated by the West, the Soviet Union could frustrate efforts to adopt agreements on freedom of information and the press, religious intolerance, and freedom of emigration.

Happily, it was not then in a position to block the major documents which affirmed the centrality of personal liberties to the concept of human rights, namely, the Universal Declaration and the Covenant on Civil and Political Rights.

These agreements are in grave danger today not only because they are so directly and blatantly violated, but also because their very philosophical assumptions are being challenged from several directions. Besides the persistent and skillfully orchestrated Soviet threat, the challenge comes increasingly from spokesmen for developing countries, including several extraordinarily wealthy ones. By identifying themselves as developing, these wealthy nations can rationalize their abuses of civil and political rights with the rhetoric of the priority of economic rights that is used by many of the poor countries. The threat, however, does not derive simply from malice or opportunism. It also comes from the well-intentioned sympathizers, some in the West, who would exempt developing countries from what they view as specifically "Western" human-rights standards, on the ground that their cultures, socioeconomic relationships, and political structures are different. And there is the danger from others who would broaden the concept of human rights to encompass all sorts of human needs and claims with too little attention to the effects the plethora of proposed new "rights" have on established and recognized personal freedoms. Echoes of the dangers from these varied sources were heard in the debate in the 1977 General Assembly under the "Alternative Approaches" agenda item.

While human-rights advocates must take into account cultural and sociopolitical differences, a completely relativist perspective is obviously not compatible with efforts to promote and protect universal standards of human rights. In any event, it is simply not true, as some Third World spokesmen and their Western sympathizers contend, that concern with political and personal freedom is just a Western ideological conviction. There is a great body of evidence that these freedoms have been widely recognized and deeply cherished by Third World peoples. It would be as gross a stereotype to neglect evidence of respect for individual, civil, and political rights in Asian and African traditions as it would be to believe that all Western societies remain wedded to a laissez-faire interpretation of economic and social development.

It is ironic that the most passionate opponents (like one Iranian representative) of "crucifying" the developing countries' "basic human needs" (read *economic* needs) on "the altar of abstract human rights," seem less concerned about sacrificing a felt human need for personal freedom to an "abstract" concept of "collective welfare." Indeed, as a delegate said in the 1977 Assembly debate: "If freedom is irrelevant on an empty stomach, so is a full stomach to a man on the rack." Without freedom of expression, assembly, and association, without forms of political participation and democracy, who will persuade rulers to reverse poorly conceived policies or practices, including those that perpetuate poverty? And as another delegate pointed out, the "exercise of individual rights and freedoms is the best safeguard for the group in protecting its rights as a collective."

It is relevant to the ideological or political motivation of the United Nations debate that human-rights relativists there tend to apply their relativist perspective exclusively to the personal liberties and seldom to issues of governmental prerogative. In the current human-rights exchanges in the UN there has been an interesting reversal: in the earlier years the view was that the civil and political rights could be immediately put into effect, while states would be expected to implement the economic rights, contingent as they were on development of resources, only gradually. Today the demand is for instant economic rights with the civil and political rights to be postponed to an unspecified future after the goal of economic development (vaguely defined) has been realized.

Moral relativism and almost exclusive concentration on economic rights are not the only strategies of those opposed to greater protection of civil and political liberties. Both the Right and the Left try to dilute the freedom principles in the UN agreements by stressing clauses which permit ratifying states to limit them on certain grounds—which means, in effect, giving the permissible limitation a higher standing than the right itself, or treating the right as the exception to the limitation. When the Soviet Union announced its ratification of the Covenant on Civil and Political Rights (whose clauses limiting the permissible exceptions it simply ignores), it openly declared that the national security and other exceptions in the agreement justified its restrictions on emigration, assembly, and other freedoms.

Yet another strategy, in which the Soviet Union excels, is to propose new and ambiguous rights that obfuscate issues and divert attention from individual freedoms. The endlessly reiterated, seemingly reasonable, request for priority attention to "the right to peace" is actually intended to justify curtailment of freedom in the name of security and order. Under this rubric and under the "right to life," the Soviet spokesmen would introduce an array of difficult issues like the arms race, the multinational companies, and others that are already being intensively studied in other international forums.

The "Alternative Approaches" resolution tentatively adopted by the 1977 Assembly (to be reviewed by the Human Rights Commission and then reconsidered by the Assembly) is hardly encouraging to those concerned to retain the value of freedom in the UN's human-rights program. Notwithstanding lip-service to the inalienability and equal urgency of the civil and political rights, the resolution clearly leans heavily in the direction of the requirements and prerogatives of the state. Though expressed in general terms abstractly applicable to all states, the code-word character of many of its concepts would orient the human-rights program mainly to Third World claims against the Western democracies. By a kind of Gresham's law, it would depreciate the coinage of traditional and generally understood human-rights principles with a plethora of ambiguous and controversial priorities, so that little room would be left for the non-priority area of individual rights.

The Assembly debate also confirms the authoritarian majority's continuing resistance to universally applicable implementation arrangements, except in the sharply limited and controlled contexts of the covenants and other conventions. The prospects of the existing 1503 procedure and of the proposed office of High Commissioner are not bright. Even if the High Commissioner's office is eventually established, its mandate may be so circumscribed as to be of doubtful efficacy.

Perhaps the threat of this "Alternative Approaches" resolution should not be exaggerated in that it contains within its own terms expressions that support personal freedom. Yet, supporters of human rights would be remiss if they failed to pay close attention to the current campaign within and outside the UN against the idea of universal and inalienable individual freedoms. For this campaign poses an undeniable threat to the international consensus on the values achieved in the Universal Declaration and other international agreements over the past thirty years.

The Positive Record

Others view the UN record and current situation more positively. Emphasizing the significant progress made in the formulation of norms, they point out that, largely as a result of this accomplishment, spokesmen of the democratic nations have been able to insist in international forums that a government's treatment of its own citizens is a legitimate international concern and that critical comments by one government about another's human-rights policies, including the way it interprets and applies international norms, is not illegal intervention in its internal affairs. Elevation of standard-setting to the universal scale—and institutionalization in the world organization—has made it possible to include human rights as a key item on the agendas of the international forums. It has enabled governments to focus attention inside and outside these forums on specific cases of human-rights violations, or on unsatisfactory general conditions in particular countries.

Thus, at its March 1978 session, the Human Rights Commission (reversing a long-standing policy) took the promising step of naming publicly countries being investigated under the confidential 1503 procedure and of initiating certain actions (unspecified) with regard to them. These countries included Uganda, on which the Western members failed the previous year to get any action at all, as well as Indonesia, Equatorial Guinea, Ethiopia, Bolivia, South Korea, Malawi, Uruguay, and Paraguay. While turning down a British proposal to undertake a "thorough study" of the situation in Cambodia, the Commission did ask its government "to send its comments" on statements made in the Commission about that situation. It offered to help the Organization of African Unity in its efforts to establish a regional human-rights commission and called for the creation of human-rights institutions in other regions where they do not yet exist. The U.S. delegate, in giving his impressions of the 1978 Commission session, considered that it had been more even-handed than in the past, at least in public debate although not in its formal procedures of investigation and censure.

The debate had not focused only on South Africa, Israel, and Chile. But, he noted:

> There were public statements about the American Indian, the Wilmington 10, about religious persecution, emigration restrictions, and the arrests of Helsinki monitors in the Soviet Union, about mass disappearances in Argentina, about political prisoners in Cuba. The door is now open, as never before. No nation, no continent is immune from criticism. We can no longer operate with the double standard. Selective morality is dissipating.

Though the statement was doubtless hyperbole to a degree, some observers shared some of the optimism it expressed.

The UN's norms have provided an ideological framework and an institutional focus for non-governmental human-rights efforts in many parts of the world, including those relating to the Helsinki Accord. Having been incorporated by reference into this East-West agreement, these UN norms provided human-rights activists and monitoring groups in the East and the West with a valuable legal, political, and educational handle. Not only the promulgated norms but the UN drafting process itself—with its study groups, opinion-gathering operations, and semantic debates—has inevitably enlarged the understanding of and appreciation for human rights on the part of both participants and observers. The cumulative impact of three decades of this worldwide dialogue should not be underestimated.

Since international instruments can be expected to play for a long time no more than a supplementary role to national guarantees for human rights, the main goal of international efforts should be to encourage member states to adopt higher domestic standards. Highest priority, therefore, should be given to obtaining ratification of human-rights conventions. For ratification is a commitment to incorporate international standards into domestic law, thereby providing aggrieved persons and groups with a legal basis for seeking remedies through institutions in their own countries. Ratification also puts the state in a position to "blow the whistle" on other contracting states which may be violating the standards. U.S. failure to ratify the major Conventions is therefore seriously regrettable.

Though painfully protracted and not always properly targeted, the international implementation processes can serve useful educational as well as political ends. Even "selectively-moral" implementing mechanisms may serve to inhibit repressive governments; on occasion, a government's criticism of the human-rights practices of another nation may encourage its own citizens to claim those same rights that are denied to them. Further standard-setting efforts—in such areas as protection of political prisoners, combating religious intolerance, threats to human rights from scientific and technological developments—provide important possibilities for new approaches. With appropriate care those who value freedom will be able to protect the integrity of the accumulated international human-rights law, even while they are open to its expansion to other human concerns and needs.

If the Assembly's recognition (in the "Alternative Approaches" resolution) of the inalienability of "all human rights and fundamental freedoms of the human person," including the civil and political rights, was reluctantly conceded by the majority, it can nonetheless be used to good advantage. Conversely, the sensitization of the West to economic concerns of the Third World, or of its own peoples, is a measure of progress, even though there are differences over how to narrow the gap between the older industrialized and the newer developing countries.

Finally, we live in a fluid world of changing political alignments and ideological allegiances. Given the recent turn toward democracy in Greece, India, Portugal, and Spain, it is conceivable that further easing of impacted internal situations—and it is to be hoped also in interstate relationships, as in the Middle East— may occur, opening up new vistas for the UN's human-rights role.

Conclusion

No one can predict with assurance the course of the United Nations in the human-rights field. While the UN as an institution is self-motivating to a degree, fundamentally it can only mirror the diverse and powerful forces—technological, sociopolitical, ideological—that move in different directions within countries as well as internationally. Unavoidably, the human-rights program will also reflect these forces, which include both the friends and the enemies of human rights. Those devoted to human rights must understand how these forces operate in the institution and, while supporting the ideals and goals of the Charter, respond critically to unwholesome developments. Rather than leaving the field because of disappointment with current tendencies, they should supplement the UN programs by encouraging additional approaches, including regional institutions—providing these do not serve merely as excuses for UN inaction—and even unilateral measures by the democracies.

But most important is the private sector. For it needs always to be remembered that the UN is an association of sovereign states which will usually place their "national interests" above considerations of human rights; that they will usually define these interests in terms of security—internal and external—and of economics, rather than of human rights; and that in their voice and vote, they will give priority to their alliances and other political requirements. This being the case, the searchlight of free inquiry and the committed idealism of the non-governmental organizations must be kept focused on those areas where the effective enjoyment of "all human rights and fundamental freedoms" remains an unfulfilled promise.

LOUIS HENKIN

6
Human Rights:
Reappraisal and Readjustment

The international human-rights movement that was born toward the end of the Second World War reflected three principal assumptions or hopes:

1. That there was, or would be, general consensus on the principle and the content of human rights.

2. That peoples and governments would give high priority to promoting human rights in their own countries, and would accept international scrutiny and intercession to protect those rights.

3. That peoples and governments would be concerned to promote and protect human rights in other countries, and would do so fairly and impartially.

None of these assumptions or expectations has yet come close to being realized. But some slight progress in the late 1970s toward their realization has given the human-rights movement renewed impetus and new hope.

Disappointed Expectations

THE QUEST FOR CONSENSUS

The human-rights ideology asserts that every individual enjoys specified fundamental rights vis-à-vis his society. During the first quarter-century of the international human-rights movement, however, there has been less-than-universal agreement on its principles, and even less on its content.

The Universal Declaration of Human Rights, whose creation and adoption without dissent are marvels of postwar international life, was conceived as the expression of such consensus, combining political-civil rights in the Western democratic, libertarian tradition, with the economic-social rights identified with socialism and the welfare state. But the Declaration was a product of the days when a much smaller United Nations was dominated by Western states and Western ideas. Unanimity, we know, was achieved in part by a high level of generality, and in part by repeated iteration that the Declaration was only an ideal, a moral standard, not a legal or even a political commitment. In the vote approving the Declaration, the Communist states abstained, as did South Africa and Saudi Arabia. Some states that voted for it in 1948 have since experienced political and ideological revolution—China, for one. Many of today's states did not exist at the time. Even states that have adhered to the Declaration have differed widely in their devotion to the various rights it proclaims.

Lack of universality in support of the Declaration reflects cleavage in the world at large. There has been a major division between the older, Western states, to whom human rights have meant primarily political and civil rights, and the Communist states, as well as most of the states in the Third World, which have emphasized the state rather than the individual, and economic and social development rather than political and civil rights. Some countries have been deeply committed to the traditional connotations of human rights: representative democracy, limited government, the rule of law, liberty and equality, fairness and privacy, limits on the sacrifice of the individual to the society, and of present to future generations; other countries do not pay even lip service to these. The rights to adequate diet, housing, and health care, to work and to equal economic opportunity, to minimum levels of education, while now commonly proclaimed, mean different things in different societies, and rarely are they enforceable rights of individuals. In new countries, of course, traditions of political democracy and individual freedom are absent, and in many countries there are no institutions to defend human rights against official violation. Countries struggling to build a nation and to develop the society and the economy sometimes assert that development cannot be achieved unless political and civil rights are postponed. One-party government, even one-man government, is sometimes deemed essential; and political freedom, even individual justice, is considered a luxury at best. In countries where there has been confrontation between terrorism and repression, there is little hope for individual rights.

RESISTANCE TO INTERNATIONAL SCRUTINY

Another assumption of the international human-rights program has been that human rights everywhere are everyone's business, and that nations can be induced to submit to international intercession in the interest of furthering those rights. In fact, except for limited regional efforts (notably in Western Europe and, to a lesser extent, in Latin America), few states to date have proved willing to accept such intercessions by other governments or by international organizations. Even states substantially committed to human rights resist having their behavior scrutinized by others who may have political or other ulterior motives for criticizing them.

The international human-rights program has placed particular hope in international standards adopted by international convention. It is remarkable evidence of the political significance of human rights in our day that, although no state is compelled to adhere to any UN-sponsored treaties on human rights, important states were reluctant to see draft conventions emerge, in the light of which their behavior might be deemed grossly deficient. They sought drafts which they might be able to live with, should they later feel impelled to adhere to them. Perhaps they feared that the UN drafts might become, for political or even for legal purposes, a standard of proper international behavior.

Only the Genocide Convention and the Convention on the

Elimination of All Forms of Racial Discrimination have been adhered to by a majority of states. States perhaps saw their adherence to the former as dissociating them from Hitler's unspeakable horrors. Wide adherence to the latter convention is a tribute to the success of the Asian-African bloc in rendering racial discrimination a major crime in contemporary international society, and to their ability to persuade or shame other powers, big and small, into adhering to this convention. Many states that have adhered doubtless believed that it would have no serious application for them, if only because, despite the convention's general language, its effective target is white discrimination against blacks. Other major conventions—notably the International Covenant on Civil and Political Rights and the Covenant on Economic, Social, and Cultural Rights—have far fewer adherences.

Even states willing to undertake international obligations to maintain human rights have not been prepared to submit to serious international enforcement of such obligations. Consider the largely hortatory character of the Covenant on Economic and Social Rights, and the decision to make the most promising enforcement methods of the Covenant on Political and Civil Rights largely optional. Of the states that have adhered to the latter by early 1978, only sixteen (out of forty-six) have also adhered to the Optional Protocol which would permit a committee to receive complaints from individuals; only six (the four Scandinavian states, Great Britain, and the Federal Republic of Germany) have agreed that the committee may receive complaints against them by other states.

States also continue to be reluctant to accept international scrutiny independent of legal commitment, as by an international human-rights commissioner or ombudsman, or even by an ad-hoc committee of inquiry or intercession. By great effort of a dedicated few in the face of powerful resistance, a procedure has been achieved whereby a working group of the Subcommission on Discrimination of the United Nations Human Rights Commission may receive private complaints of "a consistent pattern of gross violations," and begin a slow process of "quiet diplomacy" to investigate and end alleged violations. But few would say confidently that this procedure has a promising future and will deter or terminate many violations of human rights.

INADEQUACY OF INTERNATIONAL CONCERN

Another assumption of the international program has been that international society—states, governments, "elites," public opinion —is concerned for the welfare of individual human beings everywhere; that governments consider the state of human rights in other countries their legitimate and proper affair; that they will attend to that interest as to their other national interests, and pay a price if necessary to further it.

Like all international law, human-rights law reflects political forces in international society and depends on them for its survival. But states make international law generally as an element in their foreign policy, to promote national interests; human-rights law is fundamentally different. It is often said that international respect for human rights is essential to international peace and friendship. And it is true that some violations—e.g., apartheid in South Africa—engender grave international tensions, while others—e.g., slavery and submarginal labor conditions—might have important economic impact on other countries. In general, however, the interest in human rights in other countries tends to be idealistic, and their condition is not seen by other countries as of direct moment.

That nations have not perceived a serious national interest in how individuals are treated in other countries has substantially weakened the drive for extending human-rights law and, even more, the inducements to comply with such law. For international law is observed largely from fear of adverse consequences, principally the reaction of the victim of the violation and the desire to avoid damage to relations with that state. Human-rights violations, however, have no victim state: ordinarily, no other state is offended or prejudiced when a state abuses its own people; and no state, therefore, is particularly motivated to complain. A state tempted to champion the cause of Man would be seen as an officious meddler, and would risk its relations with and interests in the offending state. Charging others also makes a state vulnerable to charges in turn.

THE POLITICIZATION OF HUMAN RIGHTS

That many states do not rate human rights high in their own scheme of values; that they have been reluctant to undertake international legal commitments and to accept international political intervention as regards human rights in their own countries; that they have seen little reason to concern themselves for the rights of individuals in other countries; that, surely, they have been reluctant to expend goodwill and jeopardize friendly relations to intercede in behalf of foreign citizens against their own government—all these negative attitudes have seriously hampered the international effort to promote and protect human rights.

Lawyers have sometimes described what has happened as the politicization of human rights. Juridical bodies to consider complaints are not available; norms are not interpreted or applied as law; and legal processes are not invoked impartially but are subverted for political ends. In the principal political organs, like the UN General Assembly, and even in specialized human-rights bodies, larger political issues have often prevailed over human-rights concerns. States have tended to charge violations only by a few states, with which their relations are otherwise unfriendly. Political blocs have resisted airing of accusations against one of their members, or have united against a political enemy. Violations in many parts of the world have not even been discussed. Sometimes complaints have been fabricated, exaggerated, or otherwise distorted. On the other hand, even when the complaint is well-founded, the human-rights element in the controversy has often been subordinated, and the accused state has been unlikely to heed it. Some human-rights subjects—e.g., terrorism—have been politically too sensitive for honest discussion.

Politicization has also limited international concern to selected rights which particularly interested the majority: self-determination and freedom from racial discrimination. Even those interests have been narrower than they might be: self-determination has been applied less than impartially and has generally been limited to freedom from traditional-style white colonialism in Asia and Africa. The interest in freedom from racial discrimination has been acute where whites discriminate against blacks, as in South Africa; less concerned where Africans discriminate against Asians, as in Uganda; almost indifferent to discrimination against other kinds of groups, such as tribes, or ethnic and religious communities. Sometimes the label of human rights has been used for its opposite, as when states assert the right to deny information to their people ostensibly to safeguard their cultural identity and purity.

New Momentum for International Human Rights

The condition of human rights in most parts of the world has not markedly improved in recent years, yet the mood of disappointment and resignation that hung over the international human-rights movement has lifted, replaced by renewed determination and momentum. The reasons for the change in mood are several, and complicated.

Prospects for human rights improved in Spain and Portugal, where established autarchies were replaced by systems promising parliamentary democracy; in Greece, libertarian fortunes flourished again; India, the world's most populous democracy and a possible model for the democratic way in the Third World, voted out two years of repression. At Helsinki, when the Soviet Union sought political ratification of the status quo in Eastern Europe and increased East-West trade, Western states exacted human-rights commitments in exchange. Emboldened dissidents, particularly in Communist countries, invited and received support from Western governments. Communist parties and leaders in Western Europe spoke out for greater individual freedom. International human-rights efforts were given new hope and scope when the UN and the Organization of American States responded to charges of torture and repression on the part of some regimes that were otherwise unpopular (e.g., Chile). In 1977 the African states agreed to an investigation by the UN Human Rights Commission of alleged atrocities in Uganda. To the surprise of many, the International Covenant on Civil and Political Rights and its protocol, as well as the Covenant on Economic and Social Rights, came into effect, and the number of adherents has continued to grow, steadily if slowly. The Human Rights Committee established by the Civil and Political Rights Covenant was organized and began its work.

THE "UNIVERSALIZATION" OF HUMAN RIGHTS

The universality denied the Universal Declaration at birth was achieved in the 1970s with its acceptance by the Communist bloc. In 1973 the Soviet Union adhered to the two international covenants deriving from the Declaration; not only to the Covenant on Economic, Social, and Cultural Rights, which responds to socialist ideas, but also to the Covenant on Civil and Political Rights, which the West values. (Communist adherence, indeed, helped supply the number of adherences necessary to bring the two Covenants into effect.) In 1975 at Helsinki, in the Final Act of the Conference on Security and Cooperation in Europe, the Soviet Union and its allies accepted respect for human rights as a "principle guiding relations between participating states," and declared expressly that they "will act in conformity with" the Universal Declaration and will comply with human-rights agreements by which they may be bound, including specifically the international covenants.

Communist adherence to the norms and institutions of the international human-rights movement hardly reflects a sudden and radical conversion to Western ideas. There is no evidence that it ushered in any substantial change in the condition of human rights in the Communist countries; even the specific and limited commitments in "Basket Three" of the Final Act at Helsinki have received only modest and grudging implementation. They will doubtless justify their performance by insisting on their own interpretation of the documents, including the derogation clauses and loopholes, and on their versions of fact. But the Communist countries surely realized that by making these political and legal commitments they opened themselves to both domestic and international pressures to improve their human-rights performance. Whatever advantages they anticipated, whatever other reasons impelled them to make these commitments and invite these additional pressures, may well require also that they in fact ameliorate the condition of human rights in their countries and thereby substantially reduce the deficiencies in the human-rights consensus.

The Third World, including the many states that did not yet exist when the Universal Declaration was adopted, also has seen fit to come under its banner and, indeed, to assert its binding quality. The number of Third World states adhering to the international covenants is increasing slowly but steadily. Although, when acting together, they have the votes in international organizations to assert their own interpretations and priorities and to resist international criticism and pressure about human rights, they have joined the human-rights movement and responded to its appealing rhetoric. That, and the particular legal commitments by Third World states which have adhered to the covenants, also generate pressure on Third World countries to improve their own

performances at home, and to narrow the gap between their performance and the consensus reflected in the international documents.
The Third World also has its own human-rights priorities: to end
colonialism and white racism in southern Africa. And many Third
World states realize that the wide international support sought for
that struggle will be more forthcoming if the human-rights consensus generally is wider and stronger.

NEW U.S. ATTITUDES

Perhaps the strongest inspiration has come from developments in
the United States. Following a lead provided earlier by Congress,
the administration that took office in 1977 heralded a new activism
for human rights. President Carter, Secretary of State Cyrus Vance,
and other officials have spoken out vigorously against human-
rights violations and promised to consider human rights abroad an
important American concern in relations with particular countries
and in national policy generally. New attitudes, new personnel,
new initiatives offer hope that the U.S. might move into the mainstream of the international human-rights movement, and lend its
considerable weight, bilaterally as well as through international
bodies, to improving the human-rights conditions everywhere.

The new American preoccupation with human rights has not
been unanimously welcomed even in the West, nor yet in the
United States. Some have seen it as evangelistic, a moralistic intrusion into the domestic affairs of other states. Some have feared
that it would jeopardize alliances, trouble détente with the Soviet
Union, antagonize many other governments, disturb international
relations, and damage U.S. interests everywhere. Some have
thought it might encourage dissidence and build up false hopes
for U.S. intervention. Some have feared that it might make repressive regimes even more repressive.

Others, however, rose and responded to the new human-rights
activism. They thought that the United States should proclaim
its ideological commitment, speak out for freedom everywhere,
identify with and support those who share its values; and should
deny its alliance, its friendship, its largesse to those who reject
them. They have urged the U.S. to join the international human-
rights movement, adhere to international covenants, and participate
fully in human-rights agencies. They have stressed that the West,

having paid in valuable political coin for human-rights commitments by the Soviet Union and its bloc at Helsinki, ought now keep human rights as a central item on the East-West agenda. The whole world having made the commitment to civil and political rights (in the Universal Declaration and in the Covenant), the West ought now strive to assure that these authentic libertarian, humanitarian values are not distorted or diluted.

Building for the Future

The history of the international human-rights movement to date has shown that to advance human rights will be more difficult than some had believed or hoped. In retrospect, surely, there was never any reason to expect universal agreement on philosophical and political doctrine, or rapid radical conversion to human rights in countries where they were not embedded in the cultural consciousness and conscience. If there were ready, wide, and deep agreement on human rights, they would have been promoted and protected in every country through domestic institutions, and there would have been no need for an international human-rights movement. In fact, instead of despair, one might feel amazement and encouragement at even the modest progress in human rights and in international involvement, at the continuing vitality of the international human-rights program. It is instructive, and encouraging, that countries with different traditions and ideologies and different economic, social, and political situations should nonetheless accept a common code of human rights if only in principle and in aspiration, and devote resources and energies to their realization.

Much that I have described might change dramatically, even in the near future. With radical political change, respect for human rights might come to some countries and disappear from others. While a deep consensus on the content and value of human rights cannot come overnight, while attitudes that have politicized the human-rights movement cannot be quickly transformed, particular political motivations that have troubled the international program could disappear suddenly. A settlement in the Middle East, for a prime example, would make it easier for international organs to deal with human-rights issues on their merits in that area, and perhaps also with the human rights of Jews in Eastern Europe. By weakening the baneful influence of Soviet-Arab cooperation and other alignments hostile to international scrutiny, it would reduce the politicization of human rights generally. Resolutions in Namibia and Rhodesia and other changes in southern Africa might dilute the UN concentration on anti-black discrimination and encourage attention to other human-rights violations. Or, to the contrary, new tensions—among the big powers, in particular regions, or within countries—might set back human rights and the efforts to protect them.

Radical transformations, however, cannot be anticipated. Immediately, one must assume more of the same—in human rights around the world, in the UN, in international protection. One must assume that the original expectations and hopes will not fare dramatically better in the near future than they have until now. Obviously, then, those who care for human rights must readjust their sights and trim their expectations. The toilers in the vineyard must accept that authentic rights are not instant, and cannot be grown in some political hothouse; they must adjust to a culture requiring long gestation and maturation. Every new national constitution and bill of rights, every new institution to implement them, every particular advance and every victory in a particular case is to be fought for and applauded. The slowly increasing adherences to the Covenant on Civil and Political Rights, or the small, limited procedure for hearing some private complaints before a working group of a Subcommission of the Human Rights Commission, are to be seen not as meager accomplishments, and therefore grounds for despair, but as impressive cause for congratulation, and encouragement to push ahead—incrementally as well as by larger steps; if not by plan, then by seizing opportunities. The Human Rights Committee of the International Covenant on Civil and Political Rights has an important opportunity not only to strengthen the basic rights of the covenant against attempts to dilute or distort them, but also to establish new patterns of international enforcement, for example, by effective scrutiny of the national reports submitted by parties.

In any reappraisal of international human rights it is perhaps still necessary to emphasize that international protection of human rights is not a panacea, nor a specific and exclusive remedy, nor even an ideal. In a world of states, human rights depend initially, principally, and optimally on national laws and institutions. International protection was conceived because national protection failed so often in so many lands, but its object is to monitor, correct, and supplement national institutions so long as necessary; and its aim, at its best, should be to liquidate itself, to make active international protection unnecessary.

External, formal, legal, intergovernmental programs, with their uncertain assumptions and important obstacles, are not the only way to reform national law and institutions. Much—often more—can be done within societies, as the civil-rights experience of the past decades in the United States amply shows. Even—or especially—in states that resist international intervention, there is much to be done through the use of domestic law, domestic officials, domestic courts, domestic non-governmental bodies to implement both national and international human rights; indeed, officials must be made to recognize that only by improving national protection can they disarm and avoid international scrutiny.

While much has to be done from within national societies, outsiders—a UN Commissioner, UNESCO, transnational non-governmental organizations—can help build up national constituencies to care about and care for human rights. Friends of human rights outside a country, in cooperation with those within, can help promote better national laws and institutions, educate citizens in their use, create local bodies to assist victims. Whether on a universal or a regional basis, they might seek to persuade governments to enact into national law all or some of the Universal Declaration, or of some other model bill of rights to be developed. Academic centers for the critical study of national human-rights laws might, inter alia, assist governments as well as non-governmental organizations and individuals to prevent violations.

More might also be done to strengthen ad-hoc transnational monitoring by organizations and information media which can be effective particularly as regards occasional, dramatic violations. The recognition accorded to Amnesty International by the Nobel Peace Prize should help bring to that and other existing organizations the tremendous support they require. In addition, one might identify and create new groups that would promise successful ingress into various countries and effective influence there. More might be done, for example, through transnational professional links, such as organizations of trade unions, writers, scientists, lawyers.

A principal reason for past failures in the international human-rights movement has been inadequate leadership by those countries committed to human rights. Now, the new policy of the United States has put human rights at the top of every international agenda, weakened resistance to international human-rights activity, created opportunities for those most concerned. If active U.S. leadership might be resented and resisted, others can lead with United States support. Selected states from different parts of the world might be encouraged to form a human-rights bloc. Such a bloc might take the lead to defend, extend, and improve the procedure of the working group of the Subcommission on Discrimination for dealing with communications alleging a consistent pattern of gross violations of human rights. A human-rights bloc might assume leadership in the fight for a UN Human Rights Commissioner—still, I believe, the best hope for promoting respect for human rights everywhere on a continuing non-adversary basis, and for effective international intervention in support of human rights wherever the need arises. The often frustrated effort to create that office must go on. (Would many dare oppose a Commissioner if he began as only a Commissioner for the Elimination of Racial Discrimination?) Universal protection through the UN can be supplemented by encouraging additional regional programs where the conditions necessary for international protection are easier to achieve. Indeed, in instances where UN involvement frustrates international protection, or even condones violation, the cause of human rights—and the cause of the UN—should be served by preventing UN consideration.

No less necessary (or difficult) would be a concerted campaign by a human-rights bloc to depoliticize human rights. It should be possible to convince more states that politicization of human rights serves neither human rights nor the political causes for which human rights are subverted. Cannot the African states, for example, be persuaded that even the struggle against racial repression can only be served by neutral human-rights principles, applicable broadly, by impartial machinery operating universally, and by reciprocal support for human rights by all in each other's bailiwicks? Some depoliticization would lead to more, and states could then pursue the cause of human rights without jeopardy to their international relations, indeed with benefit to them. Then, the fundamental revolution in principle that made human rights everywhere everyone's business might be realized without jeopardy to other international business. Depoliticization will also contribute to the slow process of building consensus and making effective law.

All states have accepted the human-rights ideology. All states have accepted the internationalization of human rights and have supported international scrutiny and intercession, differing only—but sharply—as to which violations of which rights by which countries should activate international effort and what forms it should take. There is an opportunity and a need to explore, strengthen, and deepen this consensus on the substance of human rights, and an opportunity and a need to reason together about the future of the international preoccupation with human rights. Unilateral United States activism in support of human rights, and varying reactions to it, have also raised questions crying for reasoned deliberation. There is need to build human-rights bridges and extend human-rights dialogue, between West and East, with the Third World, among ourselves. (Dialogue, of course, is a two-way street and we must anticipate and be prepared to face our own human-rights deficiencies and our own failures to support international human rights; for example, our own dismal record of non-adherence to international human-rights conventions.)

The Communist states, having chosen to join the human-rights movement, and having made the deal at Helsinki, have given us the right to talk to them about human rights, officially and unofficially. They have asserted that human rights as reflected in the Universal Declaration and in the principal covenants are not inconsistent with Communism, and the Soviet Union has highlighted that consistency in its latest Constitution. Although we may not accept their view that the Communist system as established in the Soviet Union in fact satisfies the individual's human right "to take part in the government of his country through freely chosen representatives in genuine elections" (Universal Declaration Article 21, adapted), that difference is now doubtless unbridgeable and not "negotiable." Our own commitment to substantial freedom of enterprise, even if it inevitably entails some unemployment, may also be "systemic" and non-negotiable. But the Communists have asserted that the other specific rights—political freedom within the system, freedom of speech and other communication, emigration, apolitical justice, fair trial, freedom from torture and other mistreatment—are consistent with Communism. We should be prepared to exchange views on our respective understandings of these rights and our respective observance of them. Academics as well as officials might discuss the use (and abuse) of legitimate limitations on individual rights; for example, the concept of national security or public order. Our purpose in dialogue, it should be clear, is not to use human rights as a stick to beat the Russians with; we wish only to see the condition of human rights improved, everywhere. And we should be ready both to encourage and to respond to improvement by reenforcing détente, negotiating in good faith about arms, cooperating where our interests coincide (as in preventing nuclear proliferation), increasing trade, and carrying out the other forms of cooperation contemplated by the Helsinki Final Act.

We must press dialogue also with the Third World, particularly with Asian and African states. We must reject charges that our interest in human rights is "moral imperialism." Dialogue might begin with basic values. Accusations that our insistence on human rights is moral or cultural "imperialism" implies the view that the ideas of human rights are Western and European; in fact, many of the core ideas underlying human rights are common to the Eastern cultural tradition as well. Are the rejection of genocide, massacre, torture, detention without trial, faked trials, mass expulsion, and enslavement Western ideas and a Western monopoly? Can we agree at least on the importance of those rights and on programs to assure respect for them?

Both in the human-rights context and elsewhere (e.g., in the New International Economic Order), there is need to understand one another about human rights and development. Again, if, as some insist, the need for political development precludes Western-type representative democracy, and demands "strong government" and a single-party system, that issue may not be negotiable today. But what of other human rights in a single-party state? That some single-party states do show decent respect for other individual rights indicates that they are not essentially incompatible. In fact, might not respect for political-civil rights improve and accelerate nation-building?

One might explore, too, the alleged need to accord priority to economic-social rights, which the Third World had the UN General Assembly formally affirm in 1977. In what way is the improvement of economic-social conditions hampered by respect for political-civil rights? Is development really furthered by political repression? And how many people are fed, or how many industries built, by torture and detention? Is a particular kind of economic development program conducive even to economic-social rights, to meeting the basic human needs of today's population?

Human rights have not been imposed on the Third World. Its members have willingly proclaimed their acceptance of the Universal Declaration, and increasing numbers are adhering to the international covenants. The Third World insists that the condition of human rights is a legitimate matter of international concern, as in southern Africa, and they demand our support for ending violations there. But if in southern Africa, as we agree, why not elsewhere? If the abomination of racism, why not the abominations of torture, detention, perversion of justice? The difference between us and them is which rights and which countries the effort should include. We accept their preoccupations; we have a right to add our own items to the human-rights agenda.

The Third World, moreover, prefers multilateral "enforcement" and resists bilateral pressures like the linkages which the American Congress has established, barring U.S. aid or trade to gross violators of human rights. That, too, needs discussion. We are all agreed that human rights fare best when they are handled domestically between an individual and his country's government and institutions. International scrutiny, bilateral or multilateral, is invited only when national protection fails or falters, and the surest preventive of international intervention is for countries to improve their human-rights performance on their own, or under guidance and influence from regional neighbors. As regards international monitoring, it is clearly preferable that it be done by multilateral institutions that can provide expertise, impartiality, authoritative judgment. But so long as the multilateral agencies are ineffective or worse, perverting the cause of human rights and the process of vindicating them, bilateral reactions will be inevitable. The way to eliminate bilateral reactions is to depoliticize the international process and make it effective, even against Third World states (e.g., Cambodia, Uganda). The Third World has the votes, if they have the will to bring that about.

There is need, too, for dialogue between the United States and our allies. As parties to international agreements like Helsinki, we have a right to scrutinize others and call them to account; we are not in agreement, however, as to whether we should do so; and if so, by what means. It is necessary to make clear that the purpose of United States activism in human rights is not to wage ideological warfare but to improve human rights; that our means are wholly peaceful and legitimate. We might well discuss, however, which means are likely to help human rights, immediately or in the long run. Which efforts might be too costly to other Western interests? Can we afford to continue to press the East, or the Third World? Can we afford not to? The answers will not be easy to come by and we may not agree, but it is important that we ask these questions.

There is need for dialogue even among Americans. We are all in favor of human rights, abroad as well as at home, but we are not all agreed as to whether human rights abroad are our business, and what we may and should do about them. We are not agreed whether an active human-rights policy will cost us anything in terms of détente, disarmament, or trade; and, if so, whether we are prepared to pay the cost. Different groups and individuals among us identify with and respond to violations of some rights more than of others, and in some countries more than in others. We are divided, as is our government, about means: Congress is closer to the particular human-rights concerns of particular constituencies and to the popular mood generally, has more faith in its legislative weapons, and links human rights to aid and trade by legislative fiat; the President and the Executive branch are on the diplomatic firing line and are concerned to keep relations with all countries "friendly," preferring flexibility and "quiet diplomacy."

If it has done nothing else, the policy of the U.S. since 1977 has put human rights high on the international agenda, raised international awareness and sensitivity, intensified official and nonofficial preoccupation and activity, both national and international. Neither the United States nor any other country can now conduct its foreign relations without awareness of the issue. No country can commit consistent and gross violations of human rights without having that become an item in its international relations.

Human rights are both universal and international—the world cannot forget them.

Human Rights and Jewish Concerns

Disappointment in the international human-rights program has been strongest perhaps among Jews and Jewish organizations. Leaders in the effort to promote human rights, they have felt most keenly the lack of progress and, even more, its political abuses, particularly as a weapon with which to beat the State of Israel and to attack the Jewish non-governmental organizations. In the United States, domestic issues tending to range Jews in competition with less advantaged minorities have spilled over to trouble human-rights activities, including international human-rights programs. Some Jewish organizations have cut back their programs; some Jews have abandoned the field.

While reappraising and readjusting in the light of disappointments, Jews and Jewish organizations ought not, and will not, abandon the international human-rights effort. Even from a strictly ethnocentric viewpoint, they will recognize that Israel and the Zionist ideal cannot be the complete and exclusive support for Jewish rights. There will always be a Diaspora, and Jews who must live, or wish to live, in countries other than Israel must find security in national human-rights laws and institutions, supplemented by international programs. In the United States and Canada, and in other Western countries (despite political and economic unease, increasing Arab influence, and some anti-Semitism), Jews continue to participate freely in the larger society, and Jews and Jewish organizations will continue their active role in support of civic rights. In these countries, too, international human rights will shore up their national rights, if ever need be. Elsewhere, surely, Jews will have to rely even more on international protection. The campaign for Soviet Jews finds important support in the concepts, the documents, and the institutions developed in the international human-rights movement. (Despite abuse and distorting politicization, Soviet Jewry has been the subject of extensive discussion in UN forums, perhaps second only to problems of race in South Africa.) There may yet be need to resort to international protection for Jews in some countries in Latin America, where the increased political influence of Arab states aggravates Jewish insecurities due to political and economic instability.

Surely, protection for the Jews outside Israel should not be sacrificed from some misguided notion that international human rights must be scrapped lest they be used against the State of Israel. The answer to politicization in international forums is to fight it, not to abandon those who do and to leave the field to the enemies of human rights. Israel herself, though politically beleaguered and almost isolated, has not abandoned participation in the UN, or in its human-rights activities. Surely, if there is some kind of political settlement in the Middle East, Israel's political situation in international bodies will improve. And in an improved political climate, one can expect Israel would be shown to have a far better record than most in respect for the human rights of her inhabitants, and would herself become an active, energizing force in international human rights.

Jewish reappraisal of human-rights issues and activities, however, will not be without difficulty and dilemma. There will be at least the old, known dilemmas: how much effort to universal causes, how much to particular Jewish causes? How much to international effort, how much within national frameworks? How active should Israel and Diaspora Jewry be in opposition to racism in South Africa, in view of the status of the Jewish community in that country, and of black African support for the Arab position against Israel? In areas of major need—e.g., Soviet Russia—is the focus to be on emigration of the few, or on amelioration of conditions for the many who will stay behind?

Some of these, I believe, are non-issues. There is often no need to choose—say, between national and international approaches to Soviet Jewry—when both can be tried with some promise. The Jewish community can, and should, support both. Soviet laws and institutions which were once used with some success by Jews and dissidents have fallen into disuse; can they be reinvigorated? Can pressure be brought through other transnational bodies like Communist parties, associations of writers, scholars, lawyers, and trade unions?

On the other hand, there will continue to be some bona-fide disagreement on the effectiveness or desirability of different means. Every past "solution to the Jewish problem" continues to have its champions: world socialism or Zionism, assimilation or emigration, national or international protection. And is Israel only a refuge, or also a protector of Jews elsewhere? Since neither the desirability nor the effectiveness of some means can be proven or disproven, the issues will continue to be debated. One can only ask that they be debated in good faith. One can ask, too, that programs and pressures should be carefully tailored to assure greatest promise of success. To ask the Soviet Union, as one example, for specific concessions which they can plausibly grant is altogether appropriate; but to ask what they cannot possibly grant achieves nothing for the Jews, at best, and can plausibly be seen not as an effort for Jewish rights but as simply a weapon of opposition to détente.

Jewish interest in human rights, however, is not limited to specifically "Jewish" issues. Whether reflecting the Jewish ethos or the Western acculturation of Jewish communities, many Jews are identified with and committed to the liberal ideology which includes political and civil rights as well as the concept of welfare associated with economic and social rights. Like the Africans concerned with racial discrimination, like others with particular human-rights concerns, Jews must recognize that while they may and should pay particular attention to the rights of Jews, these can find protection, whether nationally or internationally, only in general principles, procedures, and institutions. As regards international protection, Diaspora Jews and Israelis share the necessary hope, if not confidence, that there are limits to the politicization of human rights; that the principle that human rights are of legitimate international concern can no longer be denied; that human-rights activities have acquired a life of their own that cannot be disowned, and a dynamic of activity that is slow, often imperceptible, but ineluctable. Jews will remain dedicated to human rights in principle and in program; they cannot do otherwise.

DAVID SIDORSKY

Contemporary Reinterpretations of the Concept of Human Rights

"The owl of Minerva takes flight only at dusk." With this metaphorical phrase Hegel suggested that the idea that dominates the history of an age, becomes widely understood and expressed only when its career is nearing its end. Hegel's metaphor captures some of the concern that has been focused on the idea of human rights in the past few years.

From the beginnings of the modern period fundamental social values, including political freedom and civil liberties, have often been asserted in the language of natural rights or of the rights of man. Recently, many human rights have received virtually universal assent in national, regional, or international documents of symbolic significance or legal force. Yet there is a pervasive apprehension of severe regression in the realization of even such minimal human rights as the right to live or freedom from arbitrary detention.

This apprehension may have its source in the much greater communication network now connecting all parts of the world, so that a much brighter light is cast upon longstanding abuses of human rights that were once ignored. It may reflect higher standards and rising expectations regarding the political and social behavior of nations.

Yet, this apprehension also stems from the knowledge that a disastrous regression in human rights took place at the center of Western culture in the past generation. And there have been recurrent and continuing acts of genocide, repression, and other major violations of human rights in a large number of countries without any effective response from the international community. These acts have been so extreme that they would seem to belong to a more remote and barbaric time than our own century, which has often been described as a progressive, enlightened, and democratic age.

In a context in which escalating rhetorical support for human rights as a cause célèbre coexists with systematic abuse of many of these rights, it is not surprising that the very meaning of human rights has become contested. Radically different definitions and interpretations of human rights have been proposed, each of which claims the banner of human rights. Thus, *human rights* has become the most recent of a series of terms over which semantic battles are waged in order to legitimate competing political and social attitudes.

Earlier, in the immediate aftermath of the Second World War, the term *democracy* had been much contested. The new governments of Eastern Europe in their route to single party states had defined themselves as popular democracies in contrast to the pluralist democracies of Western Europe. Several new authoritarian regimes of the post-colonial countries had labelled themselves directed or guided democracies to stress their sense of national unity under the guidance of a single leader or party. The Western model of democracy assumes pluralism of expression as its prerequisite so that any country with only one political party, no matter how progressive or attuned to popular will that party may be, could not be considered a democracy.

Similarly, in the United States in the past decade, there has been a deep division over the interpretation of the ideal of equality. Traditionally, equality is defined as non-discrimination among persons or groups on irrelevant grounds like sex, caste, religion, or race. Consequently, the goal of an egalitarian approach is to achieve equality of opportunity. In another view, however, equality means that there are no significant differences among individuals or groups in the distribution of benefits and burdens. Hence, the goal becomes a society in which there is an approximate equality of results among its major groups. In this view, policies that discriminate on grounds of race or sex may be adopted if they contribute ultimately to social equality.

In turning to the contemporary interpretations and the current uses of the concept of human rights, even before examining the ways in which the idea is contested, an appropriate starting point is the recognition that the term seems to be fulfilling two different, although consistent, functions. On the one hand, the phrase *universal human rights* is used to assert that universal norms or standards are applicable to all human societies. This assertion has its roots in ancient ideas of universal justice and in medieval notions of natural law. It is also found in early modern formulations of the conventions of international law which sought to bind all nations to outlaw some practices, like piracy or mistreatment of prisoners of war.

On the other hand, the idea of human rights is used to affirm that all individuals, solely by virtue of being human, have moral rights which no society or state should deny. This idea has its classic source in seventeenth- and eighteenth-century theories of natural rights. The language and form of the Universal Declaration of Human Rights adopted by the United Nations, for example, derives directly from the various declarations of rights of man or natural rights that flourished in the past two centuries in Europe and the United States. Thus, in many ways, the contemporary doctrine of human rights must be understood as a modification and reconstitution of the theory of natural rights.

Human Rights and Universal Norms

The idea of universal moral values is a broader concept than that of natural rights and the belief that all nations should recognize moral norms was present in ancient societies long before the theory, or even the language, of human rights came into being. The universality of moral values can be traced to ancient myth and poetry, where it is characteristically expressed in metaphors in which moral rules are identified with the processes of nature.

The theme that justice was immanent in nature was richly developed, for example, in early Greek philosophy. One striking illustration of the metaphorical mixing of natural regularities with moral rules in ancient Greek thought is the Heraclitean warning that the sun must keep to its courses, lest the deputies of justice pursue it and punish it. Werner Jaeger believed that the major achievement of early Greek thought was precisely the discovery that "creation is a cosmos—namely, a community of things under law."[1] The relevant implication of this discovery is that moral ideals are as universal as the order of nature. Hence they are to be observed by all cities and states, both in their domestic arrangements and in their international relationships.

The thesis of the universality of moral principles is also developed in the religious thought of the ancient world. Fundamental moral laws or ideals revealed or commanded by divine beings in early Hebraic texts are applicable to all nations. Perhaps the most dramatically relevant expression of this is found in the opening passages of the book of Amos, which are commonly believed to be the oldest of the preserved texts of biblical prophecy. In those passages Amos argues that the principle of justice holds in identical fashion for nations as diverse as Damascus, Gaza, Tyre, Edom, Ammon, Moab, and Israel. Their violations of justice, both in their own laws and in their treatment of foreign peoples, are an incursion upon the moral order that is present in nature and in history.

The idea of universal and international norms which is found in Greek scientific myth and Hebraic religious prophecy is distant from contemporary formulations of human rights. Yet it was the fusion of the mythopoeic view that moral values are built into the natural order of things with the doctrine of the immanent operation of divinely revealed moral laws that led to the theory of natural law. This theory of the existence of rationally discoverable norms regulating the diverse systems of positive law was used for centuries to assert universal standards in the international practices of independent political states. In the recent past, thinkers as different as Jacques Maritain and Walter Lippmann have argued for a revival of the doctrine of natural law as a philosophical prerequisite for international norms.[2]

The doctrine of natural law was displaced at the beginning of the modern period by the theory of natural rights. The shift from the term *law* to that of *rights* marked a change in political and social values. There was a lessened emphasis on confronting the new nation state with universal religious or moral norms and a heightened stress on confronting that state with the freedoms of the individual. In contemporary formulations of human rights, the protection of rights of individuals has become the goal. Yet, the achievement of this goal has not been viewed as the responsibility only of the nation state but, as in the doctrine of natural law, it is asserted as a norm of the international community.

The Theory of Natural Rights

The theory of natural rights had a major influence in the development of the political self-consciousness of modern Western society. The idea of natural rights as the sole justification for any political society was a challenge to all established political authority. From the perspective of the theory of natural rights, all the recognized theories of legitimacy—the divine rights of kings, the pragmatic necessity of stable political rule, conformity to divine or natural law or rootedness in historical and institutional traditions—were inadequate. A political regime was justified only if it satisfied the natural rights of its citizens.

The current function of the theory of human rights, unlike the doctrine of natural rights, is not primarily that of serving as a principle of legitimacy within a particular national state. It has become part of an effort to develop standards of achievement with respect to citizens' rights within an international community. Yet it is significant in this context to recognize the continuity between the traditional theory of natural rights and recent formulations of human rights. Six elements of that continuity merit special examination.

First, it was characteristic of theorists of natural rights to develop a list of specific rights. Although these rights allegedly derived from the universal and evident desires of all men, the content of various bills or declarations of rights differed. The appearance or omission of a specified right, like the right to property, was an index of the importance given in social policy to the defense or realization of that right. This tradition has been adopted in the theory of human rights and has resulted, for example, in the articulation of the more extended list of thirty rights that mark the Universal Declaration of Human Rights.

Second, in all traditional theories of natural rights, such rights were ascribed only to human beings. It was clearly recognized, of course, that other kinds of beings merit consideration and protection. Thus, works of art and creatures of nature, not just animals but forests or mountains, may possess transcendent value and justify great human effort and sacrifice on their behalf. Yet works of art or objects of nature do not possess rights. To possess a right assumes a context in which the holder of the right can assert a claim and carry out responsibilities related to this claim. Therefore, only the kind of being that exercises rational choice—traditionally, man as a rational animal—has rights. There are many different kinds of things—Rembrandt paintings, Stradivarius violins, the ruins of the Parthenon, California redwood forests, or Canadian whooping cranes—that ought to be preserved and protected. Yet it would not be correct to speak of their right to existence.

The further implication is that any human being, solely by virtue of his potential ability to exercise rational choice, had rights. It was in this sense that the theory of natural rights proposed the equality of all men. Since having natural rights was intrinsically connected to being a human being, there was a basis for the later transition from the phraseology of *natural rights* to that of *human rights.*

Third, a major characterization of natural rights derived from this belief that rights are the properties of persons capable of exercising rational choice. For, when men asserted their natural rights they were expressing their autonomy as individuals. Hence, the model or pattern for the exercise of natural rights became the protection of the sphere of the autonomous individual from arbitrary incursion by the state or other coercive association. The listing of the right to life, for example, did not involve a commitment to the extension or universalization of health care or to actions for shaping a safer environment but to a rule of law that would restrain arbitrary acts of violence, especially those of governmental authorities, against individuals. Similarly, the natural right to liberty did not refer to support of policies that would enhance self-realization through the universalization of education, but it did require the legal protection of individuals against arbitrary imprisonment.

Since the natural rights of men were bound intrinsically to their capacity to exercise rational choice as autonomous beings, the list of natural rights comprised what have been termed negative freedoms, rather than positive liberty, that is, the freedoms that protect the individual *from* the invasion of his domain of selfhood or privacy rather than the freedom of the individual or group *to* achieve its purposes or ideals. This stress is evident in the many detailed lists of the declarations or bills or rights that proliferated in the late eighteenth and early nineteenth centuries. The inclusion of a number of human rights that relate to social and economic development is a point of difference between the classic theory of natural rights and the theory that led to the Universal Declaration of Human Rights. That inclusion, and the priority to be assigned to social and economic rights, has become the single most contested item in discussions of contemporary theory of human rights.

Fourth, this account of natural rights suggests why these rights were held to be *inalienable* despite the continued criticism that limits to the absoluteness of any right are drawn in the circumstances and conflicts of social life. There are many rights that persons acquire or possess by virtue of their social status or achievement that they may renounce or transfer. No person, on pain of denying his own individuality or rationality, however, could decide to abrogate permanently his right to freedom of choice, for example. The alienation of the natural right to life or liberty is, according to the theory of natural rights, precisely such a permanent renunciation of individual autonomy. In that sense, natural rights can never be alienated.

Fifth, natural rights, as the adjective shows, derive from the order of *nature* or from the nature of "natural man" but not from society or history. Indeed, as truths of nature they were held to be rationally self-evident: that is, if the meaning of the term is understood, then all rational beings could intuitively know that men had natural rights. In this view, the recognition that the theory of natural rights had its genesis in the rise to power of the middle class no more shows the relativity of natural rights than the fact that the calculus was discovered in seventeenth-century Germany or England makes its truth relative to that place and time. While rational intuition is no longer relevant for the contemporary views of human rights, the belief that rights are universal, and not relative, to particular social or historical culture has become, if anything, even more important in their use as international norms.

Sixth, the frame of reference of the theory of natural rights was the secular sovereign state. In this theory, citizens of each nation were charged with realizing natural rights for their own domestic society. Consistent with this new frame of reference, in foreign affairs, the secular state was to be freed from the restraints imposed by supranational religious obligation or religious authority. The foreign policy of each secular state was to be guided only by the national interest. Yet the fact that natural rights provided the criterion for the legitimacy of any government anywhere in the world inevitably suggested that the behavior of a foreign sovereign state to the natural rights of its own citizens ought to be considered in the development of foreign relations. Thus, the classical theory of natural rights had given birth, in its own way, to the dilemma of reconciling the primacy of an express concern for natural rights with the recognized primacy of national interest as the basis for foreign policy.

The Criticism of the Theory of Natural Rights

The theory of natural rights during its emergence and ascendance in the seventeenth and eighteenth centuries helped to shape the legal and political institutions of modern democracy. It was central to the major documents of the English, French, and American revolutions of that period and was to become fundamental for the ideology of the liberal nationalist movements across Europe from Spain and Portugal to Greece, Turkey, and Russia in the nineteenth and early twentieth centuries.

The influence of the theory, moreover, was not limited to the West. Natural rights was one of the handful of doctrines that served to moderate the practice of colonial and imperialist governments in Africa and Asia. More strikingly, the theory of natural rights was often adopted by the native leadership of colonial countries in their struggle for national independence.

Yet throughout the history—from Bentham and Burke through Marx or Kelsen—the theory of natural rights has also been the subject of severe and continual criticism. The theory continued to have great impact upon world affairs through the time of the Wilsonian policies after the First World War, but its intellectual foundations had been weakened long before that. Major criticisms of the theory gained wide acceptance. These included philosophical criticisms of the meaning and derivation of natural rights, pragmatic criticisms of the application of these rights in social context, and historical criticisms of the origin and function of declarations of natural rights.

PHILOSOPHICAL CRITICISM

The philosophical criticism of the theory of natural rights has its starting point in the fact that *natural rights* is a term combining a descriptive fact of nature with a moral claim of right. Almost inevitably the question arises as to why the fact that all men are equal in nature should be identified with, or justify, the belief that all men ought to be treated equally. After all, if men were biologically or genetically unequal, it would not follow that they should be treated unequally. On the contrary, the recognition of natural inequality could intensify a commitment to egalitarian policies that would show equality of concern for all and seek to reduce differences among human beings. Similarly, a declaration of natural equality is logically compatible with social policies that would aim to enhance the acquired differences among human beings. So the philosophical critics asserted that the classic idea of rights derivable from the nature of things involved a semantic confusion.

Further, in the eighteenth century it was held that, in some sense, natural rights were self-evident truths intuited by all rational beings. Since then, claims of intuitively certain knowledge of any kind, but particularly of moral truth, have confronted pervasive skepticism. This skepticism has been continually reinforced by the apparent plurality of moral beliefs reported by the anthropologists. It has also been fostered by the critical attitude toward certainty of knowledge that seems to be part of the experimentalism and fallibilism associated with modern science. So philosophical critics of natural rights believed that the truth claimed for natural rights had no justification.

PRAGMATIC CRITICISM

Pragmatic criticisms of the theory of natural rights have focused most sharply on the belief that natural rights are inalienable. The point of that criticism is that the exercise of a right is limited in every social and legal context where conflicts of rights among persons and among different kinds of rights are inevitable. As early as 1776, commenting on the American Declaration of Independence, Jeremy Bentham wrote, "They see not . . . that nothing that was ever called Government ever was or ever could be exercised but at the expense of one or another of those rights, that . . . some one or other of those pretended inalienable rights is alienated. . . ." Accordingly, for utilitarians and pragmatists, freedom in any society depends upon the ways in which the rights of different parties in conflict are respected, weighed, and balanced, and upon the processes by which the consent of different persons and groups are negotiated; not upon the obeisance paid to the absoluteness of natural rights.

HISTORICIST CRITICISM

Apart from these philosophical and pragmatic criticisms, a third kind of criticism is that the historical institutions of particular societies, not the abstract rights or rational men in a state of nature, provide the relevant moral criteria for social ideals. For critics of the theory of natural rights, like Burke, Herder, or Oakeshott, every society in its historical tradition develops its own social values. It is within that tradition that the meaning of those values, even for universal ideals like *equality,* or *justice,* receives its relevant interpretation. Accordingly, any proposed list of natural rights reflects its historical context. Thus, the historicist critic argues that the universal prescription of natural rights to be applied to diverse historical institutions and traditions will tend to disrupt and distort the possibilities of development of the indigenous moral values that are latent in every society.

The Marxists advanced a special variant of this historicist criticism. In Marxism the theory of natural rights is interpreted as an ideology, that is, a doctrine that serves to express and to rationalize class interests. So, the Marxists held that natural rights were developed to provide an ideological basis for the new power of the middle classes in Europe and America. On their view, the theory of natural rights has been an effective ideology since it has masked these bourgeois interests with a universally appealing moral rhetoric. Accordingly, the task of Marxism was to unmask the moral cover afforded by natural rights theory and to reveal it as the ideology of an exploiting class.

As a consequence of this view, classical Marxists did not advance economic and social rights as a corrective or extension of the traditional natural rights that stress individual liberty. In their theory, any concept of rights was embedded in the ideological frame of reference of capitalist society. Only with the coming of a post-capitalist society would the language of rights be replaced by a new and more adequate set of moral concepts.

The cumulative impact of these three kinds of criticism of the theory of natural rights—philosophical, pragmatic, and historicist—was the erosion of belief in the theory. At the same time, most of these critics of the theory of natural rights had no desire to diminish in any way the civil liberties or political freedoms of any person.

The enormity of the totalitarian assault on the practice, as well as the theory, of natural rights came as a shock. It motivated a reappraisal of the doctrine of natural rights. To find logical faults in the theory of the equality of persons in a society where human worth is respected is one thing; to intellectually undermine the theory at a time when human dignity is systematically denied is another thing.

The Nazi denial of the right to life of millions of persons on the grounds of a racial theory suggested that the earlier thesis of natural equality was not a platitudinous piety. Similarly, the Soviet imprisonment of many millions with the justification that the prisoners were class enemies who, often unknown to themselves, represent reactionary interests in history, led to a new evaluation of the primacy of human nature and human rights, even in revolutionary contexts.

Consequently, there have been recurrent efforts to reinterpret and to reconstitute the theory of natural rights. The efforts that were carried out in the West, particularly in the aftermath of the Second World War and in Eastern Europe since the death of Stalin, have had results both of a theoretical and of a practical nature. In terms of theory there has emerged a reinterpretation of traditional natural-rights doctrine as human rights. With reference to practice, the main forum of activity has been the movement to establish human rights as recognized norms for the postwar international community.

Contemporary Reinterpretations of Human Rights

The task of contemporary interpretations of human rights has been to formulate the justification of these rights in ways which meet the recognized earlier criticisms of the theory of natural rights.

THE PHILOSOPHICAL REJOINDER

The change from the term *natural rights* to *human rights* indicates a change in the justification of such rights as life or liberty. It signifies the end of an effort to base the rights of man on the processes of nature. The nexus of universality of rights and the order of nature, which was so important in the ancient, medieval, and Enlightenment views, is broken.

The burden of philosophical discussion remains the clarification of how and why being human is connected to the right to life and liberty and how that right may be justified within an ethical theory that no longer claims intuitive proof of ultimate moral principles. Although the presentation of a philosophical basis for human rights goes beyond the scope of this essay, the sketch of proposed philosophical justifications can show the kind of rationale that is provided for human rights in contemporary thought.

In one philosophical formulation, whose explicit purpose was an examination of the theoretical basis of the Universal Declaration of Human Rights, Abraham I. Melden advanced the view that statements of human rights present what he termed the "significance conditions for moral discourse."[3]

In general, every human discourse presupposes some conditions for its significance. To take a colloquial example, there could be no discourse about baseball if there were no presupposed concepts of "games" or "actions" or "rules." As a matter of empirical fact, every human community, no matter how primitive or unusual, has some kind of moral vocabulary and some communication about moral issues. Yet, there could be no moral discourse whatsoever if men did not recognize the distinction between a human being and a non-human being, or between what it means to give a reason for behavior and to be completely arbitrary.

For Melden and for those who adopt similar kinds of justification for human rights, the function of the assertion of human rights is precisely the formulation of the presuppositions for any moral discourse. A person who would not be aware or could not understand that some reason must be given for the taking of human life—which is what the denial of a human right to life would mean—would have failed to grasp the presupposition of any moral vocabulary, including his own. Thus, to assert the human right to life is to formulate explicitly what are the significance conditions for the moral discourse that does take place in every human community.

Another interpretation of the thesis that all men have a human right to freedom has been advanced by the British legal philosopher, H.L.A. Hart.[4] The key to the argument, in compressed form, is the demonstration that any society which uses the idea of rights presupposes that some justification is always required in order to interfere with another person's freedom. To say that an employee has a right to his wages, for example, is to require a justification for allowing some other person to garnish, withhold, or interfere with his wages.

Societies in which the right to freedom of many persons has been violated are nonetheless societies which use the moral vocabulary of rights. For example, persons who may be employed as guards in an unjust prison system in such a society understand the meaning of the idea, as do their employers, that they have a moral right to extra pay for overtime if it had been promised them. To withhold such promised payment by those in power calls for a reason to be given. Even in such societies there is a recognition that some justification is required for interfering with another person's freedom.

Although it may seem a paradox, the claim that there is a human right to be free is essentially a recognition of the need for justification to interfere with a person's freedom. This can be seen when the human right to freedom is denied. What has happened then is that a person's freedom is interfered with in the absence of any valid reason like his prior violation of the law.

The behavior of men in societies that violate the human right of freedom but use a concept of rights in some contexts is implicitly inconsistent. It suggests that despite their own abuses in practice, they tacitly recognize that there is a universal right to freedom. So Hart has clarified how a minimal right to freedom is assumed in any society, even those that are dictatorial or totalitarian, if their institutions use the vocabulary of rights in significant ways.

THE PRAGMATIC RESPONSE

Contemporary interpretations of the theory of human rights also respond to the pragmatic criticism that absolute and inalienable rights to life or liberty are inevitably limited by conflict with other rights or claims in social situations. One line of response is that human rights represent initial or prima facie claims. Such claims to life or liberty are those that a person makes in the society solely on the basis of his being a human being, but that can be overridden by other kinds of compelling considerations.

That fundamental human rights were to be construed as prima facie claims was often recognized even in traditional versions of natural-rights theory. Founders of natural-rights doctrine did not argue that a natural right to freedom meant that if a person committed a crime he had a moral right to avoid going to prison. Rather, the point was that a person should never acquiesce in going to prison in any society in the absence of some rule or reason, like punishment for committing a crime, that is consistent with the prima facie right of all persons to freedom.

It might well be consistent with the universal right to life, for example, that a person participate in a military draft whose purpose is the protection of the lives of his family and other citizens. It would not be consistent, and would alienate his right to life, for a person to participate in a draft which was instituted at the whim of a ruler to provide human beings as game for the royal hunt. While the prima facie right to life may be overridden in both cases, only in the second case would it be appropriate to say that the right has been alienated. So, there is a process of resolution of conflict of prima facie rights that results in limits upon the effective implementation of absolute rights, without alienating human rights.

The challenge to an adequate theory of human rights is precisely the clarification of what are the relevant kinds of considerations that justify limitations of a prima facie human right. Generally speaking, advocates of theories of human or natural rights have urged that only reference to the rights of others and not considerations of utility or social convenience may be invoked as limiting or defeasible conditions for a fundamental human right.

THE REFUTATION OF HISTORICISM

Recent interpretations of the theory of human rights have also involved a response to the historicist criticism, which denied the universality of human-rights concepts on the ground that such concepts develop relative to the history of social institutions. Supporters of a theory of human rights argue that the degree of relativity or of universality of moral values are empirical questions. While there is evidence of the plurality of moral concepts and attitudes, there is also evidence for universality.

The common biological nature of the human species, for example, suggests that common patterns of response to similar circumstances are discoverable within diverse and dissimilar human societies. All human beings seem to recognize the distinction between the human and the non-human and to have shared in the evolutionary history of human rationality. Further consensus on universal rights may be the empirical result of a process of social communication and argument, not its prerequisite. There has been convergence and agreement among individuals whose origins are in extremely different cultures in the learning and the activities of mathematics and the sciences. While this example may not be decisive for the issue of universal moral values, it suggests the possibility of convergence of judgment among persons who are open to evidence and argument.

Finally, seemingly different forms of expression often embody common moral perceptions and values. The shared moral values are expressed in idiosyncratic ways in diverse cultures. Yet complex counterparts of characteristically Western concepts like freedom of speech and assembly exist in many other moral traditions. The phenomenon of translation provides an important index of the ability to communicate common values in different linguistic contexts. Even the most context-bound and value-laden works of a particular cultural heritage have lent themselves to translation. Thus, though there are many conflicts that relate to human-rights issues at the United Nations, it is difficult to find an instance where such conflicts derive from inability to understand the meaning of the rights or to translate their moral assumptions from one conceptual framework or language into another.

With special reference to Marxism as a variant of historicist criticism of natural rights, the shift within Marxist theory suggests that different social systems are no bar to communication on these issues. Although Marx had argued, as noted, that natural rights represent a bourgeois ideological concept, the Soviet Constitution of 1936 explicitly returned to the language of specific freedoms including those of speech, press, and assembly. It may be that this constitutional language reflected the concern of its supposed author, Nikolai Bukharin, with the breakdown of Soviet legality and the systematic violation of these freedoms at that time. In any event, the current Marxist view is that the values of social and economic development should be formulated as universal rights. The question of their existence and relative priority is sharply contested. Yet both parties to the argument assume mutually understood appreciation of human economic and social needs as well as of the language of universal human rights.

The record of human history suggests that there will be a gap between the recognition of moral values and their realization in practice that will never be bridged. Men will choose to perceive and interpret the relevant facts and concepts that relate to human rights in ways that rationalize their practices. Even so, it has not been proven that the human condition involves an ineradicable inability to recognize and understand moral terms like universal human rights.

The Content of Human Rights

The contemporary theory of human rights has led to a new examination of the scope of such rights. In several of the new interpretations of human rights, the list of human rights would comprise only a few fundamental rights. If these rights are interpreted as the conditions of significance for moral discourse, for example, a number of articles on such a list that express ideal aspirations for political, social, or economic development would not be included as human rights. For while every moral community must recognize a right to life or liberty, societies with moral standards have differed on many values that are present in extended lists of human rights. In this interpretation, conventions against genocide or slavery would be justified as would conventions against arbitrary use of detention and torture. The right to emigration belongs on such a short list if the rejection of an individual's desire to leave is a form of denial of his freedom. Beyond these, however, additional justification is needed to show why important individual and social ideals should be considered human rights.

Modern stress on civil liberties, for example, reflects to a degree the institutions and traditions of American and European political development. Yet many civil liberties such as the right to fair trial are not narrowly culture-bound and have been recognized in diverse societies. Their universalization as human rights involves an appreciation of their appropriateness and of their indigenous base in different political societies.

An analogous situation arises with political rights where these are understood as a universal human right to participate in the processes of government. On the one hand, political democracy has been the heritage of a small number of nations and reflects a rather special institutional and historical experience. On the other hand, at least since Aristotle, the desire to have a voice in political decision-making has been considered a natural and normal property of all men. For Aristotle, those societies in which there is no discussion or negotiation of consent between the ruler and ruled—as in despotism, oligarchy, or mob rule—deny the potentialities of human nature. Universalization of political rights as human rights assumes that all men would demand to participate in the political process if they were given a free choice to do so and understood the character of their own need and nature.

In what can be termed the minimalist view, a program of human rights should be limited to those fundamental human rights whose universality is most clearly recognized.[5] Whatever the practice, virtually no one argues in defense of genocide, slavery, or torture. On an alternative view, however, the cause of human rights would be frustrated if it did not include rule of law or growth in representative democracy, not as utopian ideals but as just demands, that is, rights, of all men in all societies.

In recent history the most severe confrontation on the question of the scope of human rights has been on their extension to social and economic rights.

Many supporters of the idea of social and economic rights justify a redefinition of the concept of rights so that the aspiration to achieve such goals as full employment, adequate health care, or satisfactory opportunities for education can be expressed in the rhetorically persuasive idiom of the rights of man. On one interpretation, human rights have been formulated as the minimal *conditions* that must be realized in order to achieve a society which may formatively be called human. Hence, a justification for identifying these conditions as human rights. Indeed, many advocates of this view argue that the realization of minimal standards in health, food, and education is a prior condition for the emergence of such rights as freedom of speech or freedom of press.

At the same time, it has been generally recognized, as previously noted, that the vocabulary of moral values is more inclusive than the vocabulary of rights. It may be extremely desirable, to vary the earlier example, that landmark buildings and true theorems be preserved, and there may be an obligation on all persons to help in their preservation. It does not follow that buildings or theorems have rights. The recognition that there are valid social ideals which do not justify the use of the language of human rights is the point of departure for critics of the inclusion of social and economic rights.

In the view of such critics, social and economic rights function not as claims of moral rights, but in support of policies which will maximize social and economic development. But to claim a right is to claim that some interference with one's freedom or actions should be halted. If a person has a right to freedom of the press, asserting this right has significance against some government, group, or individual interfering with his freedom to publish. A concept other than a right would be required to express the ideal of a society for the developing of persons of talent who would have something important to publish. Thus, it is a definitional or conceptual characteristic of claims of rights that they are the kind of entity possessed and asserted by individuals or groups to limit interference by others. Consequently, it was not a bias for laissez-faire over government intervention that led the traditional theorists of natural rights to cite freedom from interference, rather than freedom to realize ends and ideals as paradigmatically human rights. This is a feature of the distinctive vocabulary of rights, in contrast to a vocabulary of such moral values as progress or self-realization.

Another formulation of this view is that the language of rights can be used appropriately only when there is a correlative duty for some agency to provide or deliver the right. Rights that involve negative liberties, such as the right not to be tortured, not to be arbitrarily detained, not to be tried without due process can, in principle, be enforced against those who would torture, detain, or unfairly try a person. For most social and economic rights, however, it is extremely difficult to suggest how the right would be provided, and against whom the correlative duty of delivering the right is enforceable. Thus, Charles Frankel points to the case of a Third World country which proclaims the universal human right to elementary education and adequate health care. Yet it would take one-half of the gross national product of that country for twenty years to meet either one of these desirable goals. Frankel writes: "The uncontrolled and unharnessed expression or recognition of rights when the capacity to deliver is not present is philosophically unjustified and distorts the ordinary meaning of the term *right*. It is also cruel and impolitic; it turns loose aspirations that can't be fulfilled."[6]

Similarly, Maurice Cranston has criticized this aspect of social and economic rights by stating that "the effect of a Universal Declaration which is overloaded with affirmations of so-called human rights which are not human rights is to push *all* talk of human rights out of the clear realm of the morally compelling into the twilight world of utopian aspiration. However else one might choose to define moral rights, they are plainly *not* ideals or aspirations."[7]

In their rebuttal of these arguments, those who assert the validity of social and economic rights point out that at least some kinds of welfare rights—claims to minimal standards of health care, for example—have become legally enforceable rights in some societies.

In the main, most advocates of social and economic rights concede willingly that they are formulations of social ideals or human aspirations. In their view, it is justifiable to present these ideals as human rights, since they are fundamental for human self-realization and they represent conditions which must be met for any society to become human in the normative sense of that term. While many would grant that such ideals do not satisfy the conventions of language that govern the ordinary use of the term *right,* they believe that there are sufficient reasons to permit the redefinition of the term *human right* to include the idea of goals of social and economic welfare as a "common standard of achievement" for all human societies. Further, by using the language of social and economic rights, their advocates in the international community have hoped and planned to develop recognized international institutions which would begin to make the realization of such rights binding duties and even to enforce upon governments the requirements of affirmative action in response to the assertion of these rights.

Human-Rights Interpretations and the United Nations

In the context of this discussion, in international forums like the various bodies of the United Nations the theoretical arguments become entwined with political considerations. In the political debate champions of social and economic rights have contended that the stress on political freedom is a "neo-colonialist" device for criticizing the governments of developing countries and for evading the responsibilities of the industrialized nations to promote economic development and to effect measures of economic redistribution. Conversely, it has been argued that some Third World and socialist countries have used their emphasis on social and economic rights to ignore criticism of their own violations of human rights that relate to political freedom, even when these violations in no way conflict with, and may even impede, economic development.

Tactical considerations also enter the debate. Some of those who most prize political freedom and civil liberties, believe that they are threatened by the distortion of the concept of human rights. Accordingly, they argue for an interpretation of rights in a manner that will restrict them to civil and political liberties, so that human rights can be effectively used in the struggle for freedom. Other defenders of the ideal of freedom believe that this approach is counterproductive. Since the Third World nations who are in the majority are most deeply concerned about social and economic rights, it is unwise to place them in an alliance with the totalitarian nations. Rather, the Western strategy should be to stress the indivisibility of both kinds of rights.

The introduction of these considerations moves the argument to the forum of political practice. The politicization of human rights through the tactic of redefinition of concepts has proceeded rapidly in the past few years. Thus, within the United Nations, the classic idea of freedom of the press is currently undergoing redefinition to include as part of its meaning restrictions upon publication in order to protect national security.

One level of response to this process is the development of a coalition which asserts its interest in the significance of civil liberties and political freedom. Another important response, however, is the continual clarification of the history and use of human-rights terms to document the process of redefinition and demonstrate, where applicable, its logically illegitimate use of equivocation.

In the harsh political climate of the thirty years since the Universal Declaration of Human Rights was adopted, with perennial political instability and constant competition for power in so many parts of the world, it is surprising that universal human rights has remained a continual part of the political landscape. This is particularly true since the place that international human rights should have within the context of a foreign policy whose basic imperative is the defense of national interest has never been clarified even by those governments whose national interests most closely coincide with international human-rights programs. It is not surprising, on the other hand, that the idea of human rights has been reinterpreted, abused, and even subverted in that period. Men always contest for control of the definition of those concepts which they view as critical to the shaping of the future.

The vicissitudes that have accompanied the expression of human rights or closely related ideas from the ancient world to the present bear witness to its power to move men and to have a place in the formulation of social policies. The concept of human rights has had this power because it is one of those fundamental ideas in terms of which men have tried to understand and to justify political action. (Their relevant ornithological symbol would not be the Hegelian owl but the mythical phoenix.) Such ideas are not passing flights of the *Zeitgeist* but broad human ideals whose generality permits of their perennial reinterpretation in the light of new knowledge and new circumstances. The contemporary interpretations of the ideas of human rights represent efforts to express these ideals by integrating what we know about the deeply rooted desires of men in diverse societies with what we can responsibly say with special force in the appropriately relevant terminology of human rights.

NOTES

1. A summary statement of the position is found in Werner Jaeger, *Paideia: The Ideals of Greek Culture,* vol. 1, ch. 9, "Philosophical Speculation: The Discovery of the World-Order" (New York: Oxford University Press, 1939).

2. Of special relevance in this context is Jacques Maritain's formulation of his view in the introduction to the UNESCO symposium that antedated the adoption of the Universal Declaration of Human Rights. *Human Rights: A Symposium,* edited by UNESCO (New York: Columbia University Press, 1949).

3. Abraham I. Melden, "The Concept of Universal Human Rights" in *Science, Language, and Human Rights* (Philadelphia: University of Pennsylvania Press, 1952).

4. H.L.A. Hart, "Are There Any Natural Rights?" *The Philosophical Review* 64 (1955).

5. A concise formulation of the minimalist thesis is found in Irving Kristol, "The 'Human Rights' Muddle," *Wall Street Journal,* March 20, 1978.

6. Charles Frankel in "Human Rights and Imperialism," Proceedings of the Columbia University General Education Seminar, vol. 6, no. 1, University Committee on General Education, New York, 1977.

7. Maurice Cranston, *What Are Human Rights?* (New York: Taplinger Publishing Co., 1973).

Human-Rights Issues in Their National Contexts

PAVEL LITVINOV

The Human-Rights Movement
in the Soviet Union

I

It is well known that many fundamental rights are violated in the Soviet Union today: the right to freedom of speech, right of demonstrations and strikes, freedom of religious observance and formation of independent associations, the right to open and fair trial, and the right to freedom of emigration. Many other important violations or denials of human rights in the Soviet Union, however, are ignored or not well known. There is, for example, violation of the right of citizens to change their place of residence within their own country. The system of obligatory internal passports bearing a special, stamped entry for place of residence restricts a person's freedom of choice of residence, or abrogates it altogether. Anyone living without a passport or residence registration is subject to legal prosecution. The situation is aggravated by the fact that the law on residence registration has never been published in full; it has had only restricted distribution "for administrative use." Further, Soviet courts refuse to entertain arguments about residence registration.

The argument that has been developed as partial justification of these violations is that, although political rights are suppressed in the Soviet Union, economic and social rights have been fulfilled more than anywhere else. To this I would respond that any priority for social and economic rights over civil and political rights destroys in essence the very idea of rights. One need not search far for examples. In 1932–33 there was a widespread famine in the southern regions of the Soviet Union. Not only did the authorities make no attempt to relieve the emergency but they actually exacerbated it by forcibly preventing anyone from leaving the stricken region. The absence of free speech in the country enabled the government to conceal the fact of the famine from the entire world for many years. Yet had the world been informed, the famine could have been overcome, or at least alleviated, with the help of other countries, as happened during the famine along the Volga in the 1920s. This episode in Soviet history is only one of many supporting the contention that economic rights cannot be accorded priority over political rights.

Is there, then, justification for the reverse approach which considers economic and social rights as of secondary importance? Supporters of this approach suggest that economic and social rights are not human rights in the full sense of the term, that is, rights of man by virtue of his humanity, but rather goals and guidelines which are, in principle, applicable to all men. Developing countries, for example, because of their low economic level, may not be able to extend the right of education to all citizens.

In my view, it is pointless to speak of the preeminence of some rights over others. Their equal importance is confirmed by the continuity of development of social rights from political rights and their interdependence. Many emerging societies currently are succumbing to the temptation to sacrifice the political rights inherited from the West in favor of dictatorships which promise rapid economic and social advances. Paradoxically, it is often the dictatorship itself that compels these peoples, sooner or later, to start thinking about the problem of civil and political rights. As the primary case in point, it is becoming ever more apparent that the inadequacy of political and civil freedoms in the Soviet Union is exacting vengeance upon those who have denied these freedoms. In the absence of such freedoms, genuine development of the productive forces of the Soviet Union that would result in economic gains which could, in turn, promote social and cultural benefits, has not been realized.

Lack of faith in freedom—in the ability of man to make his own decisions and to determine his own course in life—is characteristic of totalitarian regimes, whether of the Left or of the Right. In the case of the Soviet Union, it has been suggested that its totalitarian potential was unleashed in reaction to the violence of the Russian Revolution. Yet it is not the case that totalitarian forces have inevitably triumphed after every revolution. Why, then, were they victorious in Russia?

One crucial response is the absence of a strong legal tradition in Russia. A sense of law was limited, if not lacking, both among the ordinary people and the educated segments of society. It is true that important changes were achieved by the judicial reforms of 1864, and that by the end of the nineteenth and the beginning of the twentieth century Russia had a galaxy of brilliant jurists and professors of law. Yet, on the whole, this aspect of life eluded the consciousness of the Russian intelligentsia. The Slavophiles, for example, actually considered the absence of a sense of law to be an advantage enjoyed by the Russian people over the Europeans. For the Slavophiles, the natural and organic social bonds were to be cultivated among the Russian people whose roots were in tradition rather than in legal forms and legal safeguards. Even the most enlightened among the Russian liberal and revolutionary thinkers, men like Herzen and Plekhanov, underestimated the importance of law. In the best of circumstances, law has traditionally been regarded in Russia as a value not of first priority; in the worst of circumstances, it has been considered a temporary, if inescapable, evil. Especially important here is the inadequate appreciation in Russia of the inseparable nature of law and freedom: if freedom is considered a synonym of anarchy, rather than setting the framework of opportunities and constraints within a legal system, then the consequences of a period of lawless freedom are likely to lead to a form of government which achieves order only by authoritarian repression.

The tragedy of Russia in the revolutionary and post-revolutionary period has often been ascribed to the Bolsheviks and their ideology. They claimed to be extreme advocates of the principles of equality and social and economic justice for the entire population. In order to seize power and to retain it, they had to proclaim themselves as the fulfillers of the old aspirations of the Russian intelligentsia, of its dreams about freedom and civil and

political rights. They therefore could not cast aside the revolutionary terminology and could not refrain from proclaiming the slogans of Marxism. But from the very beginning they modified these
slogans to meet their own needs. And once they had gained power,
they did everything possible to wipe out their liberal and revolutionary content. They transformed the ideas into a rigid ideology
which became the instrument of governmental repression, while
at the same time nationalizing to the maximum the international
content of Marxism, making its doctrines the instrument of Soviet
foreign policy. Through many years of terror and well-planned
ideological reeducation, they weaned the Russian people away
from any habit of trying to apply the critical sting of Marxism to
their own country.

Yet this undigested heritage of democratic ideals remained and
has forced the regime to improve its facade and to seek to assert
its legitimacy. Thus, at the height of the terror of the 1930s, the
first seriously drafted Russian Constitution was adopted. And in
the post-Stalin years a number of international covenants about
human rights were signed. Finally, in the 1960s, people surfaced
in the Soviet Union who had decided to read seriously what had
been written about freedom on the official banners. They pressed
to learn why these proclamations had not been put into effect in
their own country which was tirelessly propagating them abroad
and demanding freedom for all the peoples of the world. The
Soviet official ideology, ironically, had carried the concealed spirit
of freedom and justice across a half-century, thereby creating an
opportunity for its rebirth in the human-rights movement in the
Soviet Union.

This phenomenon has been given several names: "democratic
movement," "dissident movement," and even "movement of
inakomyslasch." The latter term sounds preposterous to the native
Russian ear, as does the Russian word *inakomyslyashchy* itself,
which is derived from the English word *dissident*. The word *dissident* has become common, but the phrase *dissident movement*
still has not taken root in Russian. The historical analogies in
Russian experience are too few and, when used literally, the phrase
in Russian has no meaning. The situation is more complicated with
the expression *democratic movement,* which is gaining popularity.
There are, however, several objections to this phrase. First, it exag-
gerates the scope and size of the movement. Further, it implies a

movement for democracy, that is, literally power by the people. In the twentieth century it has become unclear just what this means. Virtually every contemporary regime, no matter how opposed to the people, never ceases to call itself the most "democratic," accusing the traditional Western democracies of lacking popular democracy. The ambiguity of this term *democratic movement* is further aggravated by the fact that the Soviet regime has proposed an interpretation of the term *democracy* that has popular mass support. It seems to me to be of particular importance to emphasize the *non-political* character of this movement, which defends the right to express any opinion, including anti-democratic opinions. We therefore prefer the term *human-rights movement,* which does not have any political claims.

II

It is appropriate in this context to provide a short history of the emergence of the human-rights movement. In Moscow on December 5, 1965,* about fifty people gathered on Pushkin Square at the poet's monument. Some of them held banners reading "Respect the Constitution, the Basic Document of the USSR," and "Freedom for Sinyavsky and Daniel." The demonstration was broken up by "men in civilian clothes" pushing demonstrators with banners in their hands into waiting vehicles which drove them to militia stations and to headquarters of the people's *druzhina* (auxiliary police). On this occasion all those who had been detained were allowed to go home after listening to some moral admonitions.

The demonstrators had been protesting the arrest of the writers Andrei Sinyavsky and Yuli Daniel, accused of publishing their books abroad. The protest was of no avail. In February 1966 a trial was held, and Sinyavsky and Daniel were sentenced to seven and five years, respectively, in a labor camp with strict conditions. This conviction of writers for literary activity evoked a wave of indignation among intellectuals of the capital. Aleksandr Ginzburg, a Muscovite, compiled a "white book"—a collection of documents

* December 5 is Soviet Constitution Day.

about the trial, including a stenographic transcript of the proceedings, and Soviet and foreign reactions. His friend, the poet Yuri Galanskov, assembled the almanac *Phoenix* from various works of *samizdat* in which were included an article by Sinyavsky and his open letter to Sholokhov accusing the latter of joining the persecution of condemned colleagues. In a public speech, Sholokhov affirmed his view that the two writers had deserved to be shot. At the beginning of 1967, Ginzburg, Galanskov, Aleksei Dobrovolsky—who took part in compiling *Phoenix*—and Vera Lashkova, a typist, were arrested. They were tried in January 1968, and Galanskov was sentenced to seven years, Ginzburg to five years, Dobrovolsky to two years, and Lashkova to one year of detention in a camp with strict conditions.* Aside from the fact that these people were convicted for open expression of opinion, the trial itself involved many violations of Soviet legality: an excessive period of detention before trial, and more than a year before imposition of sentence; violation of the right to public trial since, although the trial was declared open, in reality entrance was restricted to relatives and specially selected spectators admitted to the courtroom with special passes; and failure to observe the defendants' right to legal defense.

Although trials of this kind were in no way new for Soviet society, the trial under discussion provoked an unexpectedly strong reaction inside the country and abroad. About a thousand people signed individual and collective petitions and letters of protest. There were several probable reasons for such mass public action, so extraordinary in the light of conditions under the Soviet regime. First, it was a response to the endeavors of the new leadership of the Soviet Communist party to wipe out even those fainthearted advances under Khrushchev toward liberalization that had given rise to so many hopes. Second, it coincided with the 1968 student demonstrations in Poland and the start of the "Czechoslovak Spring," in which many saw an example for possible future changes in the Soviet Union. Third, there was the link of continuity of the trial of the four to the affair of Sinyavsky and Daniel, which had already succeeded in arousing a massive neg-

---

* Yuri Galanskov was not destined to survive to the end of his term. Suffering from a stomach ulcer, he died in camp as a result of inadequate medical attention. Ginzburg, after his release, was rearrested. He was tried again, in July 1978, in the same week as Anatoly Shcharansky; both were given lengthy sentences.

ative reaction by the intelligentsia to a revival of Stalinist methods of suppressing free thought. Although the letters and petitions expressed loyalty to the Soviet Union and remained in the framework of Soviet legality, many of them contained a demand for a truly open trial. Not one letter or petition received an answer. Transcripts of the trial, as well as letters and petitions, began to appear in *samizdat,* made their way abroad and were published in the Western press, returning to the homeland in the form of books or broadcasts by Western radio stations.

The reaction of the authorities was immediate: they moved to crush the movement by selective acts of repression. The regime, relying on the population's long conditioning to intimidation, still expected to reap a harvest from the fear sown in many decades of mass terror. This time, however, the customary mechanism proved only partially effective. A campaign was launched against the *podpisanty** (signers of protests) in the press and at their places of employment, where they were confronted with demands for repentance and renunciation of their signatures. Some signers were dismissed from their jobs. Repression was not limited, however, to dismissal. The most active participants in the protest campaign were summoned to the offices of the KGB and the procurator, where they were subjected to blackmail and threats. A. Yesenin-Volpin, the mathematician, and the poetess, N. Gorbanyevskaya, were forcibly committed to psychiatric hospitals. The *podpisanty* were subjected to a humiliating working-over at meetings, to public condemnation, and to outright threats. Only a few "repented," however. The attempt to stop the protest movement was not successful; it became a regular feature of Soviet life that is continuing to this day.

The year 1968 remains the time of the greatest mass growth of the human-rights movement in the USSR. It was then that the form of the movement developed—solidly based letters and documents, restrained in language and always public. (Inasmuch as the Soviet press did not print these materials, what is meant by "public" is their distribution in *samizdat* and publication in the foreign press.) Every instance of persecution for political reasons

---

* The word *podpisant* was one of the joking neologisms that appeared in the 1960s to represent something not in the least amusing to the Soviet regime: a Soviet citizen who signed a condemnation of violations of law by the authorities.

began to be looked upon as evidence of the government's deep-rooted disrespect for man and his rights. In time, a basic list of problems was drawn up and became the subject of continuous attention by the human-rights movement. On the agenda were:

—the situation and treatment of political prisoners in camps, prisons, and psychiatric hospitals;

—the movement of the peoples of the USSR for a free ethnic, cultural, and religious life;

—the struggle of peoples forcibly removed from their lands during the Stalinist time to return to their homes;

—the opportunity to freely choose one's place of residence inside the country;

—the problem of those seeking to leave the country, in particular of Jews opting for emigration to Israel;

—oppression of the church and persecution of various religious minorities;

—the problem of press censorship and persecution of authors and distributors of literature in manuscript form not submitted to censorship, as well as persecution of independent culture as such;

—various socioeconomic problems of Soviet Russia.

For years persons concerned about these and many other urgent problems had knocked in vain at the doors of Soviet officialdom; now they poured out their concerns in *samizdat*. Initially, in the early 1960s, *samizdat* was devoted mainly to literary works for which a place could not be found in the censored publications. But, with time, more political material and memoirs began to appear. And toward the end of the 1960s there came a flood of letters of protest, transcripts of trials, and numerous documents testifying to the widespread violation of human rights by the Soviet regime. As the number of *samizdat* publications grew, some documents, works, and names became widely known at home and abroad; others attracted attention for a brief time and then were forgotten.

The selection of materials printed in *samizdat* did not always correspond to the significance of the problems with which *samizdat* was dealing. Rather, the selection was often determined by the level of preparedness and the ability of readers at home and abroad to comprehend the significance of problems at the time of their appearance in *samizdat*. Thus, for a long time it was not possible to attract world attention to the fate of the Crimean Tatars, barbarously exiled from the Crimea during World War II and striving for long years for the right to return home. Virtually nothing was known about the dismissal of dozens of people from their jobs for political reasons, a practice that is the most widespread and effective means of applying pressure in a country where the government remains the only employer. More information began to appear about the political camps, where people convicted for their beliefs were confined for years without the knowledge of the outside world. It was imperative to attract public attention to these and many other suppressed facts.

In response to the felt need for a publication that would reproduce the more important works in *samizdat* and document as far as possible the known violations of human rights in the USSR, *A Chronicle of Current Events* was launched in *samizdat* on April 30, 1968. The *Chronicle* quickly became an important social factor. The only information bulletin that appeared regularly in *samizdat,* it was widely read at home and, reproduced abroad, was cited as a reliable source of information. Facts distributed by the *Chronicle* in *samizdat* and over foreign radio broadcasts in the Russian language reached many people in all corners of the Soviet Union. Dissidents who were widely scattered discovered that they were not alone. Learning of each other's existence, they ceased to accept the official view of themselves as "degenerates and renegades" merely because they thought and behaved differently from their neighbors. Furthermore, when the facts of persecution in the USSR for thought and word became known abroad, people in the West who cherished these same values of freedom of thought and human rights began to show concern about the problem and to speak out in defense of the independent thinkers and the victims of persecution in the Soviet Union. The government of the USSR, despite its domestic propaganda curtain, is very sensitive to foreign opinion. This is the only plausible explanation for its painstaking preparation of information about the country for dissemination to the West. International contacts are steadily increasing, and it is becoming ever more difficult during meetings with representatives of the Western world to avoid unpleasant confrontations over political persecution and violations of human rights in the Soviet Union.

III

From this outline of the emergence and development of what we call the human-rights movement in the Soviet Union, a skeptical observer might well conclude that, although the movement comprises brave and honest people, its successes have been too few and the victims too many. Aside from its humanist slogans, the movement has no political or economic program able to attract broad-based support from the Russian people, who for the most part are probably not inclined to respond to abstract demands for respect of human rights. Skeptics may also say that the participants in the movement are too few and their progress too slow, while the regime on which they are striving to exert pressure is too powerful and too inhumane to be moved by moralizing lectures. But one should look at the movement in the context of the conditions under which it emerged.

Let us recall what Russia endured in a half-century: revolution and civil war, forced farm collectivization, invasion in World War II, and many years of terror in the epoch of Stalin. Among the tens of millions of violent deaths suffered were a disproportionate number of the most brilliant representatives of all groups of the population. We should recall, too, the demoralizing effect on the Russian people of the post-revolutionary and Stalinist terror, when informing was common behavior. Pavlik Morozov, a Pioneer of the 1930s who betrayed his own father (a "class enemy") to the authorities, was a hero for many generations of Soviet pupils. People on the street "did not recognize" the wife of an arrested friend. Newspapers printed letters from children renouncing their fathers, and from wives renouncing their husbands. A show of sympathy to relatives of an already destroyed enemy was considered a crime. It was a time when, in the words of the poet, Aleksandr Galich:

> They beat people in the mug for a show of mercy,
> And tore out one's gullet for a show of kindness.

Then it appeared that the debauch of violence, fear, and betrayal had poisoned the soul of the entire people, that the dignity of man had been trampled in the dirt, and that this damage to the soul was irreversible. But not all people were Pavlik Morozovs. Human decency and mercy did not die even in those terrible times. There were always people who, at their own risk, helped arrested friends and their relatives, and also sought to speak out in defense of the repressed. When the writer, Lev Kopelev, was arrested in 1945 and accused of anti-Soviet propaganda, thirty people came forward and signed a letter of testimony to his innocence. Subsequently, several of them were also subjected to persecution.

It was therefore natural that the first step of the human-rights movement was intuitively toward a rehabilitation of the usurped human dignity, a revival of such fundamental human values as mercy, kindness, compassion, and pity. After the arrest of Aleksandr Ginzburg, his friends went nearly every day to the apartment of his mother to give her money and to inquire about what was happening. Her home became a sort of "sympathy club," uniting persons sharing a common concern despite their fear of the KGB. A tradition arose for large groups to visit the apartments of acquaintances where searches had been carried out, and to collect money for political prisoners and their families. All of these small gestures perceptibly changed the moral climate of society and revived an almost lost tradition of the compassionate character in Russian literature. Among the Russian intelligentsia, there was an observable widening of interest in and sympathy for the oppressed and humiliated victims of the regime, and a revival of the tradition of seeing a halo around political prisoners, who for several decades had been considered political lepers. The Soviet intelligentsia suddenly understood that it was not only possible but necessary to feel shame and to protest when the Soviet Union tramples the freedom of a small country like Czechoslovakia, suppresses the national character of the Ukraine, subjects the Crimean Tatars to genocide, and extirpates the religion of the Lithuanian Catholics. A free public opinion was born in Russia, which began to look upon each new political trial as its own vital interest and to speak out in defense of every political prisoner, regardless of nationality, religious faith, or reasons for arrest. People were emboldened to write letters to an unknown prisoner behind the barbed wire, to help his family, and to take an interest in political trials in other parts of the country, in other republics of the USSR. And letters from political prisoners to their relatives were made available for all to read.

In part an extended expression of kindness and mercy, this

movement also reflected the birth of a sense of law in Soviet society. For the first time, the intelligentsia understood that the Soviet Constitution, if taken literally, defends the dignity and the rights of the citizen. The human-rights movement directed the attention of the Soviet bureaucracy, Soviet society, and the entire world to the discrepancy between the behavior of the Soviet regime and the Constitution—Soviet legality—and also to a series of international covenants and pacts for human rights, which the Soviet Union had ratified more out of concern for its international prestige than out of conviction of the need for putting their terms into effect at home. In short, the movement discovered a powerful instrument for social transformation: the law of the land.

It is here that one finds the main difference between the contemporary human-rights movement in the Soviet Union and the earlier liberation movement in czarist Russia. The human-rights movement has focused its full attention on the defense of the individual against the arbitrary behavior of the government, not on questions of state and social structure. Devoting itself to this seemingly simple and practical mission, the revitalized intelligentsia is overcoming the old intelligentsia's vice of blind faith in utopian schemes, in the creation of an absolutely just life on earth by external means. A healthy skepticism, combined with faith in durable spiritual values, has been a consequence of the decades of widespread abuse of the individual in the name of those very ideals for which the old intelligentsia had struggled. Aleksandr Galich expressed the attitude that characterizes the movement in these words:

> . . . The earth is ashes and water is tar,
> It seems there is nowhere to go.
> The roads of evil are inscrutable,
> But, people, you must not fear!
> Don't fear the ashes, don't fear abuse.
> But only fear the one
> Who proclaims, "I know the way!"
> Who says, "All who follow me
> Will have heaven on earth as reward."
>
> *   *   *
>
> Drive him off! Don't trust him!
> He lies! He does not know the way!

Czarist Russia had been unable to solve its problems and sought instead to prevent their being freely discussed. Soviet Russia has been the heir of many of the problems of czarist Russia and has since accumulated many new ones of its own. Any future Russian regime will come face to face with those inherited problems and with exacerbated new ones, and once again will not be capable of solving them in the absence of respect for human rights. While the present regime of the Soviet Union is milder than that of yesterday, tomorrow it can become more cruel and destroy all of the admittedly small recent achievements in human rights. We believe, however, that Russia will emerge from this totalitarian trap. The way to transform this belief into reality is to continue and expand the creation of democratic traditions. As I have shown, the human-rights movement has succeeded in initiating several new traditions of humanist political and social behavior in the Soviet Union. Creating this tradition forms the basis for progress in human rights in the challenging environment of the Soviet Union.

Translated from the Russian by Raymond Anderson

YORAM DINSTEIN

->>>->>>->>>->>>->>>->>>->>>->>>->>>->>> **9** <<-<<<-<<<-<<<-<<<-<<<-<<<-<<<-<<<-<<<-<<<-<<<-

Soviet Jewry and
International Human Rights

I

Not too long ago, the problem of Soviet Jewry was characterized by an uphill struggle against indifference in world public opinion. More recently, it has become highly popularized in the national and the international consciousness. The danger now is that the sloganeering required for public and political campaigns will create the impression that the issue is unidimensional and will conceal its depth. The very growing relevance of the problem, its tangibility and urgency, require careful and up-to-date analyses of the social, demographic, and psychological aspects of three and a half million Jews, who do not form one monolithic mass and whose actual plight no stereotyped description can accurately portray.[1] At the same time, there is an obvious need for a systematic and scientific discussion of the legal position of the Jews of the Soviet Union, from the viewpoint of both internal and international law, especially insofar as their human rights are concerned. It is fashionable these days to come out strongly and sweepingly for the implementation of these rights, but no serious endeavor has yet been made to define what specific rights of Soviet Jews are violated in fact; to distinguish between individual and collective rights; to examine the key role played by the element of discrimination in the treatment of those Jews by the Soviet authorities; and to establish to what extent it is permissible to introduce, on behalf of those Jews, demands for privileges denied the rest of the population of the Soviet Union.

This paper is devoted to a study of these questions through the lens of international human rights, that is to say, of human rights existing under international law. It is undoubtedly desirable to conduct a similar study from the vantage point of national human rights, viz., of human rights existing under Soviet constitutional law. But this writer lacks the necessary training for a serious examination of the internal legal system of the Soviet Union.

It is to be understood that international human rights are now in a stage of consolidation and crystallization. Many of them are controversial—in terms of their definitive formulation, if not of the very concept underlying them—and they are riddled with over-abstraction and lack of concretization.[2] These are the rights that gradually develop in customary international law. Yet there are also international human rights that are spelled out clearly and bindingly in treaties to which the USSR is a contracting party, and it cannot deny or gainsay its conventional obligations.

Obligations in what way? International human rights are rights, i.e., interests protected by law (in this case, international law). There is another side to the coin of a right—any right—namely, the corresponding duty to respect it. In the case of international human rights, the interest protected is that of the individual human being, and the protection is accorded to him vis-à-vis a state—any state—including the one of which he is a national. Consequently, when a state engages in an international convention to observe human rights, it undertakes an obligation to conduct itself in a certain way (by commission or omission) towards each and every person subject to its jurisdiction.

II

It is common knowledge that, because of its special form of government, many international human rights that are recognized in the West as a matter of course are flagrantly violated in the USSR. It is enough to refer to political human rights—such as freedom of

political opinion and the right to form political parties—for us
to realize that, in this respect, there is justification for sharp
criticism of the Soviet way of life. The internal opposition is currently identified with the movement that calls itself "democratic,"
and, in particular, with the names of several renowned scientists
and writers.[3] Not a few among the protagonists of the democratic
movement are Jews, and not infrequently its platform and aims
are confused with the struggle of Soviet Jewry. That, however, is
based on a misconception. Every Soviet citizen whose political
rights are infringed, and every person in the USSR who is denied
his civil rights—be he Jew, Russian, Uzbek, or Armenian—is
equally wronged. The Jews who endure perversions of the regime
as such, and the Jews who take a lead in an attempt to change it,
suffer and strive not as Jews but as citizens and human beings.
Their brandishing of the banner of democracy today does not
spring from their Jewishness. When one speaks of violations of
the human rights of Jews in the Soviet Union, one has in mind, of
course, those violations that take place in respect of Jews on
account of their being Jews.

The Jewish struggle in the USSR is not merely a struggle for
Jews: it is a struggle for Jews who suffer because they are Jews.
The democratic movement, by its very nature, seeks to achieve a
change of the Soviet social fabric and a discontinuance of violations
of the human rights of every and any person in the country. The
primary Jewish demand is entirely different. It may be phrased, in
paradoxical terms, as a demand for equality in deprivation. In
other words, whatever the deprivation of human rights in the USSR,
it should at least apply in parity to every person in every place. It
is only because it does not fall upon all alike—because Jews are
selected for further deprivation, over and above what happens to
their fellow-men—that there is a special problem of violations of
the human rights of Soviet Jews. Hence, whereas the democrats
regard the (equal) deprivation of human rights in the USSR as the
cardinal sin, the Jews see equality (in deprivation) of human rights
a goal well worth fighting for. Of course, the goal of equality in
deprivation is not the ultimate ideal of the Jews of the Soviet Union.
But it is a goal separate from and independent of that of the democratic movement. We must not forget that attaining one goal does
not necessarily entail accomplishing the other. Theoretically, it is
possible that the USSR will grant full civil and political rights to

Russians, but not to Jews; and it is possible that that country will deny many fundamental freedoms to all its people without distinction between Jews and others. Nothing, of course, prevents a Jew, as an individual, from fighting for the two goals together, but it is important to recognize that the two fronts do not necessarily overlap.

III

A proper analysis of international human rights must proceed along the line of distinction between ordinary rights, conferred on every individual as such, and collective rights, bestowed on whole groups (be they peoples or minorities). When ordinary rights are involved, the individual is the measure of all things. The fact that a state meticulously observes human rights in ninety-nine out of a hundred cases is not a valid response to the complaint of John Doe whose hard luck it is to be the hundredth instance. From his angle, and from that of his aggregate of human rights, statistics hardly count and it is pointless to prove that his case is the exception rather than the rule. On the other hand, when we deal with collective rights, the crux of the matter is the overall picture. The fact that John Doe or Richard Roe was denied his rights is not, in and of itself, conclusive evidence regarding the deprivation of the rights of the whole group. From the outlook of the collective, sorrow shared, far from being sorrow halved, is the very basis of claim.

What about sorrow shared pertaining to individual rights? What is the rule when a state infringes a given individual human right in ninety-nine out of a hundred cases? Does the wholesale violation turn the right from individual into collective in essence? The answer is negative. The violated right is still accorded separately to every single individual. It does not change its character as a result of the circumstances of the violation. But contravention of human rights of individuals across the board occasionally brings about a collective response. The fact that there is a popular protest movement against a massive denial of human rights by a certain regime does not signify that the rights denied belong to the group. More often than not, those whose individual human rights were affected severally gather together for a joint battle.

IV

The main collective right, granted to minority groups, was defined as follows in Article 27 of the 1966 International Covenant on Civil and Political Rights:

> In those states in which ethnic, religious or linguistic minorities exist, persons belonging to such minorities shall not be denied the right, in community with the other members of their group, to enjoy their own culture, to profess and practice their own religion, or to use their own language.

This Article may be considered as reflective of a minimal right that has evolved in customary international law.

Jews constitute the classical minority in the Soviet Union, meeting, as they do, all three alternative requirements of the Article put together: they form at once an ethnic minority, a religious minority, and a linguistic minority. There is no need to elaborate upon the religious nature of the group: no one challenges Judaism's classification as a religion. The ethnic complexion of Jews is substantiated not only by the Jewish claim to it (and actually the self-determination of the Jews is sufficient), but also by the official policy of the Soviet authorities. Jews in the USSR are regarded as a nationality—one of 108 recognized nationalities (and, in fact, the eleventh or twelfth in size)—despite their geographical distribution in all fifteen Soviet Republics.[4] Furthermore, every Jew is designated by his nationality in the registration of inhabitants and in the internal Soviet passport that he carries, and this identity tag is not a matter of free choice. The linguistic characteristic of Soviet Jews is attested by the declaration of hundreds of thousands of them in the census of 1959 and again in that of 1970—as we are informed by the data processed and published by the Soviet government itself—that their mother-tongue is Jewish (meaning, either Yiddish or one of four local dialects: Judeo-Georgian, Judeo-Tadzhik, Judeo-Crimean Tatar, and Tat).[5] For many others, a Jewish language (including Hebrew) is undoubtedly used in everyday life in conjunction with the non-Jewish mother-tongue.

Under international law, as expressed in Article 27, the USSR is in duty bound to enable the Jewish minority, as a group, to enjoy, profess, and practice its culture, religion, and language. That is a collective right of the Jewish minority. Being a collective right, we have to gauge its implementation (as explained above) by viewing the overall picture of three and a half million Jews, in contradistinction to this or that individual. Being a collective right, it is also immaterial whether or not this or that individual is interested in Jewish culture, religion, or language. The right is vested in the group, and the test of its observance is collective.

In Soviet reality, Jews are not enabled to enjoy, profess, and practice either their culture or their religion or their language. The facts have been so widely publicized that they hardly bear repetition. We can limit ourselves to listing some salient points. Culturally, there is no Jewish education in the USSR; there are no Jewish communal centers; scarcely any Jewish literature (and, in any event, no history books or publications about the Jewish heritage) or Jewish newspapers; there is no permanent Jewish theater, no Jewish museum.[6] Religiously, the number of synagogues (a few dozen that have definitely been located, and less than one hundred by Soviet admission) is entirely disproportionate to the number of Jews; the number of practicing rabbis (three throughout the European portion of the country) is dwindling toward zero; there is no religious seminary; Jewish cemeteries are being closed down; there is a shortage of religious books (including the Bible), of prayer shawls, and of ritual appurtenances; there are obstacles in the way of baking and selling unleavened bread for Passover; and grave problems arise when it comes to circumcision and kosher food.[7] Linguistically, there are no schools or other educational institutions, no teachers, and no books. Thus, the USSR in the most systematic and radical way violates the collective right of the Jewish minority to self-preservation as an ethnic, religious, and linguistic group. And it does so as the expression of a policy which is not anti-minorities as such but anti-Jewish. There is no parallel between the plight of the Jews and that of any other ethnic, religious, or linguistic group in the Soviet Union.

V

Here we get to the nub of the issue of Soviet Jewry, namely, discrimination. The principle of non-discrimination is a basic tenet in the international law of human rights. It is a procedural principle that runs through all substantive human rights, collective as well as individual, and forms an integral part of customary international law. It is embodied in a series of international instruments, beginning with Article 2 of the 1948 Universal Declaration of Human Rights (which admittedly is not legally binding per se). That Article proclaims:

> Everyone is entitled to all the rights and freedoms set forth in this Declaration, without distinction of any kind, such as race, color, sex, language, religion, political or other opinion, national or social origin, property, birth or other status.

The discrimination against Soviet Jewry is prohibited on a number of grounds, particularly on grounds of national origin, religion, and language.

It is important to clarify that, in the final analysis, the question whether, in a given state, there is forbidden discrimination—in contravention of international human rights—is one of fact and not of internal law. As the Permanent Court of International Justice stated, in 1923, in its Advisory Opinion relating to German settlers in Poland: "There must be equality in fact as well as in ostensible legal equality in the sense of the absence of discrimination in the words of the law."[8] The existence of international human rights is determined not by words but by deeds. Hence, the routine Soviet argument referring to the legislation (and even the Constitution) in force in the USSR is beside the point.

We have mentioned the discrimination against the collective right of Jews as an ethnic, religious, and linguistic minority in the Soviet Union. Had the USSR denied the rights of all minorities, without any exception, the Jewish complaint would have been drowned in the general outcry. The USSR, however, is a multinational country that takes pride in promoting the culture and language of minorities other than the Jewish, and it does not hamstring other great religions in the way that it hamstrings Judaism. Not a general policy (unlawful in itself) of a melting pot by coercion, not an involuntary removal of barriers between all communities, underlies the Soviet treatment of the Jews. The Jews are a unique people in the USSR: they have been singled out for cultural and religious suppression.

The discrimination against Soviet Jewry exists in respect not only of the collective right of the minority but also of the rights of individuals. The deprivation of individual human rights covers, in many instances, all those who are Jews and only those who are Jews.

We have pointed out that the Universal Declaration of Human Rights is not legally binding. The time has now come to mention three international treaties, outlawing discrimination, to which the Soviet Union is a contracting party: the Convention Concerning Discrimination in Respect of Employment and Occupation, adopted within the purview of the International Labor Organization in 1958; the Convention Against Discrimination in Education, adopted within the sphere of UNESCO in 1960; and the International Convention on the Elimination of All Forms of Racial Discrimination, adopted within the framework of the United Nations in 1965. We shall take a look at these three Conventions, and see to what extent each is germane to the individual and collective human rights of Soviet Jews.

VI

The Convention Concerning Discrimination in Respect of Employment and Occupation is designed to eliminate discrimination in working conditions. The term *discrimination* is defined in its first Article as a distinction, exclusion, or preference made on the basis of any of the following grounds: race, color, sex, religion, political opinion, national extraction, or social origin. The list is not as comprehensive as the comparable one in Article 2 of the Universal Declaration (thus, there is no reference here to language), but discrimination is still disallowed for reasons of national extraction and religion that are crucial to Soviet Jewry. As for the nature of the discrimination prohibited in the Convention, Article 1 lays stress on the fact that it covers not merely access to employment in general but also access to particular occupations. Therefore, not only may an unemployed man contend that he suffers from illegal discrimination, but also a person who, though employed, is denied the opportunity to gain a particular position for which he has the right qualifications. The discrimination in this Convention relates to the substantive human right to work (including the subright to free choice of employment)—which is recognized in a number of international instruments—and it is an individual right accorded to every man.

Soviet Jews do not suffer from discrimination in respect of every occupation. The proportion of Jews in some professions far transcends their ratio in the population. Yet there are several echelons where Jews are excluded. In the most essential services of the government, in positions of importance and prestige—such as the diplomatic and consular service or the foreign commercial service—there is practically a *numerus nullus* for Jews.[9] This selectiveness in the upper strata of the administration and the party runs counter to the letter and the spirit of a Convention which the USSR has undertaken to apply.

VII

The Convention Against Discrimination in Education is of paramount importance to Soviet Jewry. In its first Article, this Convention defines discrimination as any distinction, exclusion, limitation, or preference on grounds that mostly reiterate those listed in Article 2 of the Universal Declaration, including national origin, religion, and language. Apart from the general prohibition of discrimination in education, the Convention provides explicitly—that it is essential to respect the liberty of parents to choose appropriate educational institutions for their children, other than those maintained by the public authorities, and to ensure the religious and moral education of their children in conformity with their own convictions. Moreover, the Convention states: "It is essential to recognize the right of members of national minorities to carry on their own educational activities, including the maintenance of schools."

We encounter here a three-pronged approach to the problem. First, the Convention articulates the substantive human right to education (including the subright of parents to choose parochial education for their children)—acknowledged in a number of international documents—and this is an individual right conferred on every person. Secondly, the Convention gives its imprimatur to the collective right of a national minority to preserve its culture. This collective right is separate from the individual right of parents to choose parochial education for their children. The purport of the collective right is to enable the group, as a group, to establish and maintain its own schools (something that the individual parent clearly is not entitled, and is unable, to do). Finally, the Convention confirms the procedural principle of non-discrimination insofar as the discharge of both individual and collective rights is concerned.

The Convention Against Discrimination in Education is violated, in all its three aspects, in the Soviet treatment of Jews. The predominant right in the Convention—i.e., the collective right of the minority to preserve its culture—is infringed in the most blatant way. Throughout the Soviet Union, from border to border, there is not a single school offering Jewish education—Jewish culture, Jewish history, Jewish religion—in any language. Ordinarily, the problem is presented in terms of the language of teaching. And, indeed, one article of the Convention refers specifically to the right to use the language of the national minority in its own schools (although this is made contingent on the educational policy of each state). But, without underrating the teaching of the language as such, the emphasis, in the context of the Convention, must be placed not on the language of teaching but on the teaching itself. In other words, it is of less import that Jews cannot educate their children in Hebrew, Yiddish, or a local Jewish dialect. It is of greater moment that Jews cannot give their children Jewish education in any language, not even in Russian. Let it be recalled that, until 1940, there were schools in the USSR, conducted in Yiddish, where the Bible, Jewish religion, and Jewish history were not part of the curriculum. "In effect, special educational efforts were made in these schools to criticize, and uproot, the Jewish cultural heritage."[10] Plainly, even while these schools were still in existence, the Soviet Union violated the collective right of the Jewish minority to preserve Jewish culture.

The absence of Jewish schools in the USSR is not only a violation of the substantive collective right of the minority, but also grave discrimination. As a matter of fact, the discrimination committed is twofold. At the outset, there is the discrimination against Jews, as members of a minority group, in comparison with the members of the majority among whom they live. The young members of the majority in every Soviet Republic, when attending public schools, study their own heritage and culture (obviously, in their own language), and, as a group, do not necessarily require additional schools. The young members of the minority, conversely, are exposed in the public schools to an alien and assimilationist heritage and culture. As the Permanent Court of International Justice pronounced, in 1935, in the case concerning *Minority Schools in Albania*:

> [Minority schools] are indispensable to enable the minority to enjoy the same treatment as the majority, not only in law but also in fact. The abolition of these institutions, which alone can satisfy the special requirements of the minority groups, and their replacement by government institutions, would destroy this equality of treatment, for its effect would be to deprive the minority of the institutions appropriate to its needs, whereas the majority would continue to have them supplied in the institutions created by the State.[11]

The Convention Against Discrimination in Education is designed to prevent such inequality, and to shield members of minorities from the compulsion to send their children to a foreign school.

In addition to the differentiation between the Jewish minority and the majority in the USSR, there is also discrimination between the Jewish minority and other minorities. Whereas three and a half million Jews are denied the opportunity to maintain their own educational system, other national minority groups enjoy the availability of an education consistent, at least, with some of their convictions. That is the case not only of national groups concentrated in given geographical areas (*a fortiori* autonomous regions), but even of a widely dispersed national minority like the Germans.[12] Thus, the Jews suffer from double discrimination, in comparison both with the Russians and with the Germans.

Beyond the deprivation of the collective right of the Jewish minority in the Soviet Union, there is also the denial, to every Jew as a person, of the individual right to education, and once more that happens in a discriminatory fashion. First of all, in the absence of Jewish schools of the national group—even Communist Jewish schools—no parent is able to exercise his individual right to choose Jewish education for his children in accordance with the Convention. Secondly, but by no means secondarily, the Soviet Union violates the individual right of Jews to education in subjecting them to more and more discrimination in the regular institutions of higher learning. In many Soviet universities there are quotas for the admission of Jews, and some faculties have no Jewish students.[13] Consequently, the Jew is doubly hurt: not only is he deprived in the USSR of the right to gain Jewish education, but, even if he wishes to acquire a secular public education, many doors are locked to him. Thus the USSR continually violates the Convention Against Discrimination in Education, to which it is a contracting party.

VIII

The International Convention on the Elimination of All Forms of Racial Discrimination is based on a concept different from that underlying the Convention Against Discrimination in Education. The latter selects one substantive human right—the right to education—and proclaims that discrimination as regards that right, on any of the grounds listed, is forbidden. The former picks out two or three grounds of discrimination from the list and prescribes that the violation of any substantive human right on their account is forbidden.

Ostensibly, the Convention on the Elimination of All Forms of Racial Discrimination deals—as its title suggests—with discrimination on the ground of race alone. That, however, is not the case. Article 1 defines the term racial discrimination as "any distinction, exclusion, restriction or preference based on race, color, descent, or national or ethnic origin." Soviet Jews are entitled, therefore, under the Convention, to protection from discrimination based on their national or ethnic origin.

Discrimination in what sense? Article 5 of the Convention enumerates selectively (that is to say, not exhaustively) some substantive human rights—all of them individual in nature—in whose exercise discrimination is particularly prohibited. From the list of the rights spelled out here, it is worthwhile indicating those whose infringement, on a discriminatory basis, is especially significant for Soviet Jews:

1. Within the scope of the right to security of person, the right to protection by the state against violence or bodily harm. Since the Six-Day War, outbreaks of hooliganism against Jews in the USSR have been mounting in number. While there is no basis for accusing the authorities of organizing the incidents, it is a fact that

the miscreants are not caught and never punished. Moreover, since mid-1967, the mass media (which, needless to say, are all under government control) have been conducting a constant anti-Semitic campaign. The campaign expresses itself, inter alia, in a barrage of vituperative articles, *Stuermer*-like cartoons and pseudo-scientific literature (exemplified by the writings of the notorious Ukrainian anti-Semite, Trofim Kichko).[14] One must put in relief the historical-sociological background of Russia and the Ukraine, with their tradition of a popular anti-Semitism that was only too often fomented to the horror of pogroms. In view of these special circumstances, even official abstention from preventive action is tantamount to criminal negligence, all the more so as the government itself is cynically manipulating the anti-Semitic campaign.

2. The right to take part in the government at any level and to have equal access to public service. Soviet Jews do not take a meaningful part in the Soviet government today. They do not have reasonable representation in the elective bodies (the various Soviets), and, as we have seen, carry no weight in essential public services.[15] In general, there is no room at the top (of the state and of the party) for Jews.

3. Freedom of religion. This freedom, in its commonly accepted meaning, incorporates (among other subrights) freedom of religious practice, freedom of religious instruction of the faithful, and freedom to proselytize non-believers. While members of other religious groups in the USSR—not excluding religious minorities (e.g., the Baptists)—enjoy minimal rights for religious organization, churches, clergy, seminaries, religious books, and so on, comparable rights are denied the Jews.[16]

4. Freedom of opinion and expression. This freedom is, in general, circumscribed in the Soviet Union, but it should be accentuated that the restrictions on Jews are particularly stringent in all that concerns Zionist opinion. Possession of Zionist material—and the term is, at times, stretched to cover a Hebrew dictionary—arouses suspicion against the holder of engaging in subversive activities. Expression of Zionist views in public has already led to arrests and to criminal proceedings.[17]

5. Freedom of association. Unlike other national (or religious) minority groups, Soviet Jews have no communal organization, countrywide or local.[18]

6. The right to free choice of employment, which has already been discussed.

7. The right to education, which has also been discussed.

8. The right to emigrate, which is discussed in greater detail in the section following.

It follows that the Racial Discrimination Convention, no less, is grossly violated by the Soviet Union in its treatment of Jews. The violations occur while the USSR is a proud party to the Convention, and a Soviet expert is a member of the Committee on the Elimination of Racial Discrimination that was especially set up to supervise its implementation.

IX

The right to emigrate—that is, the right of every person to leave any country including his own—is enshrined in the Convention on the Elimination of All Forms of Racial Discrimination. It is also guaranteed in Article 13 of the Universal Declaration of Human Rights and in Article 12 of the International Covenant on Civil and Political Rights. This is a substantive individual human right, conferred on everyone in the USSR without distinction. At first sight, Jews are not entitled to rely on the right to emigrate qua Jews, that is, to any greater degree than non-Jews. Seemingly, the right to emigrate is subsumed under the same heading as the political rights which the USSR violates in regard to all: when the barriers of the state hem its population in, a member of the Jewish national group suffers precisely as much as a member of the Russian or the Lithuanian national group. And conversely, if a Jew gains an exit permit while the non-Jew must stay behind, there appears to be an unjustifiable preference, which is a form of discrimination, and, as such, incompatible with respect for human rights. This is how the position appears at first blush. But, in point of fact, an exact analysis of the situation is entirely different.

First, it must be observed that not every preference of a minority group is unjustifiable. Frequently, the preference is essential for ensuring the rights of the minority. Thus, under Article 1 of the Convention on the Elimination of All Form of Racial Discrimination, special measures, taken for the sole purpose of securing adequate advancement of certain racial or ethnic groups requiring protection, are permitted. The Permanent Court of International Justice ruled in the case of *Minority Schools in Albania* that "equality in fact may involve the necessity of different treatment in order to attain a result which establishes an equilibrium between different situations."[19]

Secondly, and preeminently, in studies on human rights undertaken under the auspices of the United Nations Sub-Commission on Prevention of Discrimination and Protection of Minorities, it was pointed out—in various contexts, such as the right to education and religious rights—that, in case of discrimination by a state against a particular minority group, there is a greater need for members of that group to leave the country than for the rest of the population. The Philippine judge and statesman J. Inglés—Special Rapporteur of the Sub-Commission, who prepared a study on the subject of the right to leave—emphasized that, even where a general prohibition of emigration exists, the status of members of a certain (racial, religious, or other) group which is being singled out for unfair treatment is different, inasmuch as their reasons for departure are more compelling.[20]

The denial to Soviet Jews—as Jews—of the substantive human rights (individual as well as collective) is so systematic and comprehensive, the discrimination against them so flagrant and all-consuming, the violation of the international undertakings of the USSR where Jews are concerned so unique, deep, and ramified, that the question almost presents itself whether a Jew can remain as a Jew within the boundaries of the Soviet Union. The right of every person to leave the Soviet Union—a right which is individual by nature—takes on a special meaning for those persons who belong to the Jewish minority group. One can regard the right of Jews to emigrate as a collective response to a deliberate policy of forbidden discrimination. One may say that the quantity (of discrimination) changes the quality (of the individual right to emigrate).

Nevertheless, it is important to underscore that the special right under discussion is anchored in the discriminatory policy and flows from it. If a member of the Jewish nationality is entitled to preference over all other nationalities in the matter of emigration, this is so because for him (and not for them) the alternative of national life in the USSR is barred. In popular terms, we may phrase the special Jewish right in the words of a slogan used a few years ago on behalf of Soviet Jews: "Let them live as Jews or let them leave." The formulation of the slogan as a choice is legally correct: it is the discrimination against Soviet Jews that creates the foundation for their special standing in respect of the right to emigrate. Were the Soviet authorities to desist from their anti-Jewish policy, there would be no place for a demand for preferential treatment of Jews in the matter of emigration.

Nowadays a different slogan is heard among those mobilizing public opinion on the side of Soviet Jewry: "Let my people go!" Patently, this slogan, whose biblical source is known to one and all, does not have to be taken literally. Possibly, it is merely a more sententious, more appropriate, and more familiar turn of phrase. Slogans, however, have a life of their own—irrespective of their historical genesis—and perhaps it is not unnecessary to examine the essential modern significance of this epigrammatic expression. It is noteworthy that the words "Let my people go!" relate to Jews not as individuals but as a people. They reflect not a right of individuals—reinforced on a collective basis—but a right of the collective.

The slogan has some support in the domain of international human rights. One of the collective human rights recognized at present is the right of self-determination of peoples. Self-determination means, in particular, the right of each people freely to determine its political status, and under this aegis it can, of course, secede (à la Bangladesh) from an existing state. The right is accorded to each people regardless of the good or bad life that it endures in an existing state, irrespective of elements of discrimination and independently of prior violations of the collective or individual human rights of its members. Even a people that enjoys the benefits of the land is still entitled to self-government. It is certainly arguable that Soviet Jews, as an ethnic group constituting a separate people (or, to be more exact, a part of a separate people), have a right to self-determination. But self-determination in what way? If Soviet Jews were located in a well-defined territorial region, they could have exercised their right to self-determination by seceding from the USSR. But as they are dispersed all over that country, such a possibility does not in fact exist.[21] Can Soviet Jews assert their right to self-determination by emigration? Such a conclusion has no basis in positive international law. But even if it were legally possible to speak about self-determination through emigration, we would have to tackle a question to which there is no clear-cut answer at this juncture: is it really true that most members of the Jewish people who live in the Soviet Union want this kind of self-determination? If only a segment, even a large segment, (say, half a million or a whole million out of the three and a half million Jews) wants to emigrate to Israel, it is improper to talk about self-determination of a people. Self-determination is a collective right of a people, not an individual right of its members.

Inasmuch as founding the collective right of Soviet Jews to emigrate on the ground of the self-determination of a people bristles (legally and factually) with problems, it appears that, at the present stage at all events, it is preferable to avoid this road. It is better, in my opinion, to return to the straight path of insisting on the individual right to emigrate within the collective framework. Certainly, those international conventions on human rights to which the Soviet Union is already legally committed provide sufficient basis for the assertion of the crucial and fundamental rights—including the right of emigration—that are still denied to Soviet Jews.

NOTES

1. On the precise number of Soviet Jews, see M. Decter, "Jewish National Consciousness in the Soviet Union," *Soviet Jewry* 9 (1969), 17–20.

2. For a detailed list of international human rights, discussed in terms of their concretization, see Y. Dinstein, "Human Rights: The Quest for Concretization," *Israel Yearbook on Human Rights* 1 (1971), 13–28. [Note also the reference to the origins of the term *democratic* or *human-rights movement* in Pavel Litvinov's essay in this volume.—Ed.]

3. On the democratic movement in the USSR, see A. Amalrik, *Will the Soviet Union Survive Until 1984?* (New York, 1970), p. 12.

4. On the importance of the national element in Soviet society and its pervasive impact on the analysis of the Jewish question, see B. Eliav, "The Jewish Problem and the Soviet Union," *Israel Yearbook on Human Rights* 1 (1971), 116–20.

5. For a comparison in this respect between the results of the census on the two occasions, see I.I. Millman, "Major Centres of Jewish Population in the USSR and a Note on the 1970 Census," *Soviet Jewish Affairs* 1 (1971), 13, 18.

6. See W. Korey, "The Legal Position of Soviet Jewry: A Historical Enquiry," in *The Jews in Soviet Russia Since 1917,* edited by L. Kochan (New York, 1970), pp. 76, 85–86.

7. See R. Cohen, ed., *Let My People Go!* (New York, 1971), pp. 145–47.

8. *German Settlers in Poland* 24 (1923) (B/6).

9. See J.A. Gilboa, *The Black Years of Soviet Jewry, 1939–1953* (Boston, 1971), pp. 247–51.

10. Z. Lipset, "Jewish Schools in the Soviet Union—Development and Decline," 1 *Behinot* 59, 69 (Hebrew, 1970).

11. *Minority Schools in Albania,* 19–20 (1935) (AB/64).

12. On the educational system for the members of the German national group in the USSR, see C.C. Aronsfeld, "National Cultural Facilities for Germans in the USSR," *Soviet and East European Jewish Affairs* 6 (1970), 46–47.

13. See B.Z. Goldberg, *The Jewish Problem in the Soviet Union* (New York, 1961), pp. 327–31.

14. See *Israel and the Jews in the Soviet Mirror: Soviet Cartoons on the Middle East Crisis,* edited by M. Decter (New York, 1967).

15. See Korey, note 6, at pp. 93–94.

16. For a comparison between the Jews and the Baptists in the USSR, see Z. Gitelman, "The Jews," *Problems of Communism* 16 (1967), 92–93.

17. On the first Leningrad trial, see "Exodus" no. 4, supplement to *Soviet Jewish Affairs* 1 (1971). On the subsequent trials (held in Leningrad, Riga, Kishinev, and other places), which are of major importance to the subject at hand, see "The 'Anti-Zionist' Trials," E. Litvinoff, ed., *Jews in Eastern Europe,* vol. 4, no. 7 (Nov. 1971); for a description of the Zionist material used in evidence in these trials, see particularly 209 ff.

18. See A. Yodfat, "Jewish Religious Communities in the USSR," *Soviet Jewish Affairs* 2 (1971), 61, 66.

19. *Minority Schools in Albania,* note 12, at p. 19.

20. See J. Inglés, *Study of Discrimination in Respect of the Right of Everyone to Leave Any Country, Including His Own, and to Return to His Country* (UN Doc. E/Cn.4/Sub.2/229/Rev. 1, 1963), pp. 15 and 17.

21. See, on this point, the important and interesting comments made by Rita Hauser, then United States Representative to the UN Commission on Human Rights, at the International Symposium on Human Rights at Tel Aviv University in July 1971, in *Israel Yearbook on Human Rights* 1 (1971), 361, 399–400.

MICHAEL MEERSON-AKSENOV

10

The Influence of the Jewish Exodus on the Democratization of Soviet Society

The struggle of the Jews in the USSR for freedom of emigration to Israel that began a decade ago has attracted worldwide attention. The impact of the Jewish exodus on Soviet society is an important and neglected aspect of this problem which merits examination.

The Uniqueness of the Jewish Situation in the USSR

Almost all the non-Russian peoples of the USSR—whether in the Baltic republics or in the Ukraine, in the Transcaucasus or in Central Asia—have a territorial as well as a national identity. The language, culture, and history of each group are taught (if inadequately) in the state schools. Soviet Jewry, however, has been deprived of recognition both as a national and as a religious community.[1]

Before the Bolshevik Revolution, the Jews were concentrated in the so-called Pale of Settlement. In those settlements large numbers availed themselves of the opportunity to practice Judaism, to speak Yiddish, and to learn Hebrew. After the revolution, the position of the Jews changed drastically.[2] During the 1920s and 1930s the Soviet government introduced regulations that restricted opportunities for Jews to practice their religion and keep alive their cultural heritage. At the same time, unprecedented opportunities opened up to Jews for participating in Soviet (i.e., Communist) culture. Jews moved in large numbers into many areas of Soviet economic, political, scientific, and military life.[3] However, the price paid for this broad participation was often rejection of the Jewish religious and cultural heritage in favor of Communist ideology and thus, inevitably, assimilation. For many who had been attracted by the universality of the Marxist vision and the promise of Soviet society, this rejection was voluntary.[4] But from the very beginning of Communist rule irreconcilable antagonism appeared between the regime and any national-autonomous trends such as Zionism exemplified. It is significant, indeed, that the purging of Jewish cultural and religious life in the Soviet Union in the early period was carried out in significant measure by Jewish members of the Communist party.[5]

In the last years of Stalin's reign, from 1948 to 1953, a resurgence of official anti-Semitism culminated in the destruction of Jewish national culture and the elimination of Jews from all important positions in the USSR. This Stalinist wave of anti-Semitism was the initial indicator that Soviet Jewry had no future prospects as a national entity. Assimilation was the only way for the Jews to survive—although even that was not assured.

The mood of hopelessness was eased somewhat during the liberalization of the Khrushchev era. Optimism was reinforced by the return of millions of "rehabilitated" people from the labor camps, and by the survival not only of the Jewish Communist intelligentsia but also of tens of thousands of actual or accused Zionists and Jewish cultural activists. All too soon, however, this liberalization was curtailed under Khrushchev's successors, and the growing anti-Semitism that became a part of the state ideology brought Soviet Jewry to an impasse. The promised road to assimilation began to close, yet a return to some sort of official form of national Jewish identity was impossible under the conditions of Soviet totalitarianism which doomed all nonconforming religious and cultural life.[6]

Origin of the Exodus Movement

Even when confronted with such doubtful prospects in the Soviet Union, only a few Jews chose Zionism as a possible solution prior to 1968. The memory of the cruel terror which the Russian Zionist movement had suffered was still very much alive in the Jewish population. The early Zionists had been practically annihilated in the 1920s and 1930s. The postwar wave of Stalinist terror had an even wider sweep in which Jews were often falsely charged with Zionist sympathies. The continuing persecution of Zionists during the Khrushchev era was aimed at intimidating a new generation of Jewish youth that had been cut off from the old Russian Zionist tradition and was ignorant of contemporary Zionism.[7] In Lithuania and other more recent and peripheral Soviet territories, Zionist tenets did remain alive.

Isolated instances of Lithuanian Jews leaving for Israel after August 1968, however, were not perceived as significant. In previous decades only a few hundred Soviet Jews had succeeded in leaving the USSR after many years of applying to join relatives in Israel. The vast majority of the Jewish population was so used to the idea that it was impossible to leave the Soviet Union that those early departures by daring individuals were considered to be improbable accidents. Moreover, some Jews still believed the official propaganda that explained Soviet restrictions as a response to "hostile capitalistic encirclement." For many, too, Israel was not a political reality before 1967. (Only after the Six-Day War did the image of Israel become prominent in Soviet eyes.) Still others no longer thought of themselves as Jews but regarded their existence solely in terms of Soviet culture. Nobody could foresee that the departure of members of separated families would soon lead to an exodus movement that would be transformed into a permanent revolutionary factor in Soviet life. Nor could this have been foreseen by the Soviet leadership which had started to release individual émigrés, perhaps in order to make a favorable impression on international public opinion.[8]

But the departure for Israel of isolated individuals and families which began in the fall of 1968 coincided with other relevantly significant events. That was also the year of the "Czech spring," of student agitation in Poland, and of the emergence of the human-rights movement in the Soviet Union. The slogans of internationalism, free Communism or, as it was later called, "socialism with a human face," were revived for a short time under Khrushchev, and served to rally the intelligentsia and the youth at the end of the 1950s and the beginning of the 1960s. But the gradual re-Stalinization after Khrushchev's removal showed that the Soviet regime was not, after all, in favor of liberalization. This post-Khrushchev period can be characterized as a deideologization of the intelligentsia, their abandonment of Communist values, and the formation of an independent dissident milieu.[9]

In the spring of 1968 accumulated dissatisfaction with the re-Stalinization policy of the Soviet regime found expression in written protests against the sentencing of four people at a political trial.[10] Seven hundred members of the Moscow intelligentsia participated in this unprecedented protest movement. Such open opposition alarmed the government but also inspired sympathy in dissident circles that had not taken part. The defense of the four activists marked the opening of the campaign demanding observance of Soviet law by the Soviet government. This movement for human rights, also known as the "democratic" movement, continues to formulate its demands for rights based on the Soviet Constitution or on the Universal Declaration of Human Rights, documents which had been widely cited in Soviet propaganda directed at the West. A regularly published *samizdat* bulletin, *The Chronicle of Current Events,* began to document all the official violations of the law in the authorities' relations with the dissidents.

The historical coincidence joining the success of the Zionist movement in the USSR with the emergence of the Russian democratic movement was not accidental. In the first place, the democratic movement included many Jews in its ranks inasmuch as Jews were prominent among the Moscow intelligentsia that had given birth to the human-rights movement.[11] A number of Jewish nationals were participants in both movements, and the future organizers of the exodus movement were closely acquainted with the central figures of the rights movement. Moreover, because of their vulnerable position, the Jewish intelligentsia was particularly interested in strengthening awareness in the Soviet Union of human rights and the observance of legality. Emigrating from the USSR to Israel was urged both as the inalienable right to select one's place of residence and as the right to live in the land of one's people. The

same human-rights slogans and strategies—collective and individual letters addressed to the Soviet government or to Western
public opinion—were adopted by the exodus movement. Beginning
at the end of 1968 and continuing throughout 1969, dozens of
collective petitions were prepared, many of which opened the
door to departure.[12] Now the movement began to take on a nation-
wide character.

Without constant and consistent support from abroad, however,
probably no domestic pressures would have been effective. Had
the Jewish campaign been like that of any other people claiming
national autonomy on the basis of territory, language, leadership,
and remnants of national culture, it would have been easily stifled
by the Soviet regime. Witness the case of the Crimean Tatars
whose struggle for repatriation had begun much earlier but had
yielded no positive results. By contrast, the Soviet Jewish exodus
benefitted from an unflagging source of support in the international
Jewish community and inspiration from the State of Israel. Its
very success, of course, prompted continuing efforts by the regime
to suppress the movement in every possible way: arrest of the
initiators, dispersal of meetings and demonstrations, the innumerable bureaucratic delays and humiliating procedures to which every
person desiring to emigrate must submit. Imposition on the emigrants of exorbitant taxes, and finally, in the summer of 1972, the
introduction of the so-called education tax, might have brought the
exodus to an end, had this measure not been suspended after international protest. Confronted by countervailing pressure from international public opinion, the Soviet political system revealed, for
the first time, its inability to quell an opposition movement.

It is my belief that if the Soviet Jewish attempt to emigrate
had not taken the form of a struggle for rights, foreign support
would have been lacking and the movement could not have succeeded. The wisdom of the emphasis on "rights" by the exodus
movement is confirmed by recognition on the part of the Soviet
leadership of the "legality" involved. They observe the proper
decorum of a sovereign state by granting permission to leave only
to those presenting a formal *vyzov* from relatives in Israel—although the authorities understand that many of the tens of thousands of Jews (and Soviet citizens of other nationalities) are impelled to leave the USSR for many reasons other than the desire to
be reunited with families. Both sides—those desiring to emigrate

and the ruling regime—tacitly agreed to this formula of keeping a humanitarian promise to release members of separated families.

This leads me to conclude that the idea of human rights is indeed the Achilles heel of the Soviet system, and that sooner or later they will have no choice but to accede to a movement which rests its claims on the basis of recognized legal or moral rights. It is obvious that they do so unwillingly. Despite official anti-Semitism and strong national prejudices at the summit of the party hierarchy, the regime is reluctant to let the Jews leave for a variety of reasons. Naturally, the Soviet leadership does not want to lose the specialists in various fields who are necessary to the Soviet economy and without whom a permanent crisis might result. More importantly, the exodus is an unwanted precedent, destroying the basic principle of secrecy in a totalitarian society and inevitably leading to emulation by other (non-Jewish) groups.[13] Every mass manifestation of independence weakens the totalitarian foundations of the regime. Although the authorities are unable to curtail the exodus completely, they are searching relentlessly for ways to control the movement. Within the USSR, they move to isolate it from all other forms of domestic opposition; in the international arena, they treat the exodus for the Jews as a bargaining chip in Soviet foreign policy.

All of this activity serves to point up that the Soviet leadership is beginning to understand that Jewish emigration has become a permanent factor in Soviet life. Resigning themselves to the necessity of letting the Jews go, the authorities are now attempting through their emigration policy to capitalize on this literal "fallout" from the system. In some cases, the better known and more active Jews are expelled, while others, less well known or more indispensable to the regime, are intimidated. The exit procedure is prolonged in order to cultivate "national personnel" to replace those who are leaving. One can therefore speak of the influence of the exodus as a constant domestic factor to which Soviet society must attempt to adapt.

The Influence of the Exodus

The scope of this influence is a reflection of the widespread dispersal of the Jews in Soviet society. As a result of successful assimi-

H U M A N   R I G H T S | 150

lation and the suppression of national tendencies, Jews have mingled with and become indistinguishable from the rest of the urban population. Although every Soviet citizen has his nationality (i.e., his ethnic affiliation) indicated on his identity card ("internal passport"), for some Soviet Jews this is the only remnant of their historic identity. Today, the Jew is an ordinary Soviet person, steeped in the cauldron of Soviet ideology—brought up on Russian-Soviet literature, inhaling the air of mass propaganda, completely sharing the values of his milieu—whether he is a factory worker or a merchant, a doctor in a hospital or a scientific worker in an institute, a teacher or a student. Rare is the Jew, especially if he is under forty, who knows anything about the Jewish religion, history, or language. Literally deprived of all Jewish cultural traits, he is wholly a facsimile of his society. More often than not, he attempts to stress his loyalty and ideological trustworthiness in order to maintain his position in life—which could more easily have been attained by a non-Jew with no need to stress his Communist zeal. So the Jew is not just a Soviet subject but, to some extent, a positive supporter of the system.

In the eyes of his Soviet neighbor or colleague, the status of the Jew under Soviet social laws is not different from his own. Therefore, the very fact of the Jew's sudden departure—in a country from which until now nobody could leave—must have a psychological impact that affects his outlook on his own life. One can imagine the feelings of an ordinary Soviet man when his fellow Soviet—a Jew—with whom he has been arguing in their communal apartment, sitting together at the same party or union meeting, taking a drink together on holidays, going together to vote—suddenly begins to get letters and packages from abroad, then some sort of *vyzov,* after which he announces that he "wants to return to his historic homeland." With much intensive activity, he sells his furniture, gathers money, and does indeed go abroad. Finally, he himself starts to send letters and packages to former friends and acquaintances.

For decades the entire society has lived in almost panicky fear of anything foreign, in ideologically induced fear of "capitalist encirclement" which is threatening the security of the country of "triumphant socialism." Moreover, the regime is known to punish people for foreign contacts. Consider, then, how revolutionary is his former neighbor's "exodus" to the consciousness of the ordinary

Soviet citizen. To be abroad is a mythical state for the Soviet mentality. But the departure of a neighbor and the arrival of news from him familiarizes one with that experience. "Abroad" is now populated with "my own kind of people" and thus loses its characteristic strangeness and hostility.

Preparation for departure brings with it a whole complex of events which is quite new to the structure of Soviet life. The departing person summons up his courage: his entire life is at stake once he submits his documents. As soon as a request to go to Israel has been made, this man is no longer considered reliable. From that moment on, all roads in Soviet society are closed to him—as he knows better than anyone else. There is only one way to proceed: "to fight to the finish" until he is seated on the plane at the international airport. Somehow, as if by the stroke of a magic wand, the quiet, modest, unnoticed Soviet Jew has been turned into a warrior. He goes to the local offices and threatens, demands, insists on his rights.[14] He writes letters to the government or to arouse public opinion. (The Soviet man never knew there was such a thing as "public opinion" except for the usual unanimous show of hands at a meeting!) He gets letters from abroad, and— something which really transcends the limits of understanding—he is permitted to make phone calls abroad. His friend's departure appeals directly to his consciousness: here is a man who has hurled himself into freedom.

Unconsciously aware of his own non-freedom but without ever having had the experience of political freedom, the Soviet man now has the opportunity, from the example of the emigrants, to formulate for himself what is this freedom of which he is deprived. Seeing the example of the Jews who have struggled for their right to leave and who have been faced with the necessity for buying themselves out of their Soviet citizenship, the Soviet people recognize that they, too, are the property of the state, and that their knowledge, their work, their very beings belong to the state. That bare fact, hitherto clothed in ideology, now unfolds before them. And so, a Jew fighting for his right to emigrate has been turned into a fighter for liberation; and Israel has become the invisible secret island of freedom, the symbol of liberation in the ordinary Soviet conscience.

The impact of the exodus, as several circles among the dissidents have suggested, is more than merely the possibility of flight. That in itself is a tremendous achievement in a society where people have been consigned to long terms in prisons, slave-labor camps, and insane asylums as punishment for attempting to escape. But that is not all. Taking up the struggle for the right of Jews to emigrate to Israel, the exodus has caused the entire rights movement to expand into the hearts of the Soviet people. Never before had they realized that, according to their own Constitution, these are rights to which they are entitled de jure. These are rights for which they ought to fight. Since the exodus has attracted Jews from all layers of Soviet society, its potential influence is widespread, reaching into even remote places where previously no one was aware that in Moscow or Leningrad or Kiev there were dissidents fighting for human rights. Thus, the exodus has become the movement that serves as the primary source of ferment in the society. The radical innovation and revolutionary import of this phenomenon is apparent: it has become the theme of constant conversations, discussions, arguments, among people who have no relationship whatsoever to Israel. The very success of the Jews who have been able to leave inspires others.

As the Jewish liberation movement has become a social force for spreading awarenesss of rights, the Soviet administration is at long last being forced to take into consideration the demands of the ordinary Soviet citizen. Non-observance of the law is not, after all, characteristic for Soviet society. And non-recognition of rights by the ruling hierarchy may be seen as arbitrary undermining of legality. The Jews are thus the first group of Soviet citizens to force the administration to regard them as individuals not totally subservient to the totalitarian structure, possessed of individual rights which cannot be disregarded in the impersonal atmosphere of state expediency. It is here that the influence of the exodus is most apparent—not only on the ordinary Soviet citizen but on the government and the leadership. Everyone in Soviet society is born under and raised in the same political-ideological system; all are subject to the official propaganda which, like the air they breathe, permeates all educational institutions and the mass media. The psychology of a closed society and the lack of personal rights in the face of the impersonal party regime is inherent for all social strata, from the worker and the peasant to the ministers and party organization secretaries who themselves have come up from the ranks. The exodus of the Jews has served to break down the dogmatic partitions in the consciousness of the Soviet leadership. As the pragmatism of the leadership becomes more flexible, those psychological conditions which predetermined the closed nature of Soviet society are being undermined.

One must not therefore automatically assume that the Soviet regime will become more liberal and begin to respect human rights. But it is adopting a new stance: let the people who do not want to live in this system depart. This leads to an unexpected result, which neither the initiators of the exodus movement nor the party leadership were able to foresee, namely, a resurgence of emigration by ethnic Russians. In this context it is appropriate to consider the significance of the Jewish exodus for the larger dissident movement in the USSR.

The Exodus and the Human-Rights Movement

The right to emigrate, which was formulated by the exodus movement as the right of Jews to return to the land of their ancestors, has now been adopted by the Russian human-rights movement as one of their basic demands. The centrality of this issue to the human-rights movement comes from the realization that as long as the individual has been denied the right to emigrate, and so long as he is treated as the chattel of the government, not only the expansion of his rights but even his struggle for those rights is precluded. Without the basic underlying right of free elections and without freedom of the individual from the unconditional authority of the state, all other human rights are fictional. This recognition brought the human-rights movement first to support the right of the Jews to emigrate unconditionally and then to demand the extension of that right to every Soviet citizen to emigrate as well as to return.[15]

Although this demand is still far from being fully realized, its partial acceptance by the regime (in recognizing the right of Jews to leave so as to join their relatives abroad) has opened unusual prospects for the dissident movement as a whole. Initially, the possibility of emigration was opened up by daring individuals who ventured to place themselves in opposition to the government. The result of any kind of opposition—whether Marxist, nationalistic, or religious—had always been predictable: state repression. Because the opposition did not have any positive prospects, it was necessarily limited to a small number of people who were prepared to make a conscious sacrifice. A person who protested even once found himself with no alternatives, caught in a relationship to the government which made further opposition impossible and, indeed, rendered his situation completely hopeless. Now, however, the exodus of the Jews has opened up an alternative both to the regime and to the dissidents. Recent incidents in which activists in cultural or social opposition were either exiled or forced to emigrate demonstrate that these alternatives are not merely theoretical but can be used by both sides.

It has been suggested by some critics that the very possibility of emigration has reacted unfavorably on the condition of independent Russian culture and on the dissident movement, inasmuch as the real activists were leaving the Soviet Union. Such critics, however, forget that those in the opposition movement were not born activists but developed in the process of making a personal stand for emancipation from state monism. Looking back, one can find the moment when some of these people were absolutely no different from the rest of their compatriots. Solzhenitsyn before *One Day in the Life of Ivan Denisovich,* Maksimov before *The Seven Days of Creation,* Sakharov before his famous *Reflections,* and General Grigorenko before his speech against Khrushchev's arbitrariness—none were any better known than thousands of their compatriots who shared their sentiments against the regime. Only their personal courage—and the hope that they would be heard so that there might be some future prospects for their opposition—made them into activists. Courage and independence cannot be cultivated when a person sees no hope of realizing these prospects and not even some small guarantee of personal security. During the Stalinist regime, with its camps and millions of political prisoners, there was no organized opposition; it could grow only in the period of relative liberalization of the post-Stalin years. Thus, the very possibility of emigration is itself the basis for future dissidents to regard the regime more independently. In this way the exodus has introduced a basic dynamism into the opposition movement and has become the ferment for its constant growth. As a phenomenon which by its nature contradicts the very foundation of the Soviet closed society, the exodus is an oppositional factor and, consequently, a factor provoking, nurturing, and engendering further opposition.

The possibility of emigration for the dissidents is a recent development and the ensuing results for the whole of Soviet society are not yet fully apparent. Under the most favorable conditions, a maximum of 30,000 Jews leave the USSR annually—out of a population of approximately three million Jews. So far only a small portion of the Jewish population has come to realize the desirability and necessity of emigration. But considering how slowly time flows in a country like the Soviet Union which is cut off from the rest of the world, a decade is a very short time. In 1967, only hundreds thought of the hypothetical possibility of leaving; in two years, the number who were thinking about it had grown to thousands; and since 1970, to tens of thousands.

The processes of national consciousness[16] and the internal processes in Soviet society move slowly, but in the context of the Jewish situation inside the country—where the prospects either of a national existence or of individual assimilation are diminishing—one can predict an extended exodus for many years to come. It is evident that as new recruits are attracted to this movement, new strata of Soviet society will come under its influence. Moreover, the emigrants themselves are a growing factor in Soviet life. Having grown up in the Soviet Union, they cannot help but perceive it as their homeland. Maintaining ties with their remaining relatives and friends, they can be expected to accomplish that which has been lacking for decades in the closed society of the USSR. The Jewish exodus, in breaking open a window to the world which can no longer be closed completely, could be the impetus for a gradual liberalization and revitalization of Soviet society.

Translated from the Russian by Gloria Donen Sosin

NOTES

1. L. Schapiro, "The Jews in Soviet Russia after Stalin," in *A Book About Russian Jewry, 1917–1967* (New York, 1968) cites the USSR 1959 census as numbering Jews at 2,267,814. Because of the considerable number of Jews in the USSR who conceal their Jewish origin, however, it is impossible to estimate the actual total.

2. The scope of this essay does not permit even a brief history of the Jews of the USSR, but there is a large literature on the subject in Russian.

3. For comments on the influence of the revolution on Jewry, see Y. Larin, "Territorial Regrouping of the Jewish Population," in *Revolution*

and Culture, 15 (1928), 27–40; L. Daitch, *The Role of the Jews in the Russian Revolutionary Movement* (Moscow, 1925); and V. Aleksandrov, "The Jews in Soviet Literature" and "Jewish Scholars in Soviet Russia," in *Russian Jewry*.

4. During the 1920s and 1930s the national administrations in republics with a large Jewish population (the Ukraine and Byelorussia) regarded the Jews as a Russifying element, and in order to diminish this influence Yiddish schools were made obligatory for all Jews. See Y. Mark, "The Jewish School in the Soviet Union," in *Russian Jewry*.

5. For a discussion of the role of the *Yevsektsiya* (the Jewish section of the Communist party) in the campaign against Zionism, see J.B. Schechtman, "Soviet Russia, Zionism and Israel" in *Russian Jewry*.

6. "The Jewish Question in the USSR," published in *Jewish Samizdat*, 1970, brilliantly formulates this sense of hopelessness.

7. Schechtman (in *Russian Jewry*) tells the story of the defeat of Zionism. Eyewitness accounts of prison-camp Zionists are reported in A.I. Kaufman, *Camp Doctor for Sixteen Years in the Soviet Union: Reminiscences of a Zionist* (Tel Aviv, 1973).

8. The hypothetical possibility of individual emigration was first mentioned in a speech by Premier Aleksei Kosygin in Paris, December 3, 1966. The reuniting of families subsequently became the formula on which diplomatic relations between the exodus movement and the Soviet regime were based.

9. I have traced the development of the dissident intelligentsia in several articles. See "The Birth of the New Intelligentsia," in *Self-Awareness*, edited by P. Litvinov, M. Meerson-Aksenov, and B. Shragin (New York, 1976); and "The Dissident Movement in *Samizdat*," in *The Political, Social and Religious Thought of Russian* Samizdat, edited by M. Meerson-Aksenov and B. Shragin (New York, 1978).

10. The individuals on trial—Yuri Galanskov, Aleksandr Ginzburg, Aleksei Dobrovolsky, and Vera Lashkova—had protested the sentences of the condemned writers, Andrei Sinyavsky and Yuli Daniel. Their trial was essentially the second act of a unified offensive by the regime against the dissidents.

11. The best explanation to date of the rationale for this movement and the milieu which produced it is A. Amalrik's *Will the USSR Survive Until 1984?* (New York, 1970).

12. See "The Jews and the Jewish People (Petitions, Letters and Appeals of the Jews of the USSR), 1968–1970," edited by S. Redlich, vol. 1 (Jerusalem, 1973).

13. E.g., the Volga Germans, Western Ukrainians, Armenians, Lithuanians, Pentecostalists, etc.

14. The Russian expression, "to pump for one's rights," is an excellent illustration of how deeply the lack of rights is embedded in the psychology of Soviet society. This ironic and pejorative expression depicts the uphill struggle when an individual confronted with administrative arbitrariness has to appeal to the law which is in his favor.

15. Sakharov has formulated this right with particular insistence. See his statement, "On the Right to Emigrate," in *The Struggle for Peace*, edited by A. Sakharov (Possev, 1973), p. 177; and his chapter, "On Freedom of Choice of One's Country of Residence," in the brochure, "On the Nation and the World" (New York, 1975).

16. On the process of the rebirth of Jewish national consciousness, which is essential for understanding the character of the exodus movement and its prospects but which is beyond the scope of this essay, see the *samizdat* collection by A. Voronel, "Jewishness Rediscovered," *Jews in the USSR*, no. 2 (New York, 1974).

MITCHELL KNISBACHER

The Jews of Iraq and the International Protection of the Rights of Minorities (1856–1976)

The Jewish community in Iraq dates back to the Babylonian exile, over two thousand years ago. For centuries Iraq was the center of Jewish life and scholarship. During the period of the Arab caliphs, prohibitions on usury in Islamic law and Muslim distrust of Christians led to the granting of financial autonomy to Jews, and by the ninth century Jewish bankers had succeeded in turning Baghdad into the monetary capital of the Orient. But subsequent phases of economic prosperity were intermingled with ones in which the ruling authorities used taxation and other powers oppressively against Jews, and conditions fluctuated throughout the Mongolian, Persian, and Turkish regimes which succeeded the caliphs. While the eighteenth century was marred by a series of exactions leveled against Jews to pay for public works and the lavish court of Hassan Pasha, by the middle of the nineteenth there had been a general improvement in the conditions of Jewish life.

The history of the Iraqi Jewish community over the past century provides unique evidence on the effectiveness of systems developed over the last century to provide international protection for minorities. Significantly, Iraq is the only country in the world to which more than one of the major systems has been applied or is currently applicable. They include bilateral treaties, the League of Nations Mandate and Minorities Systems, population transfers, and the United Nations human-rights efforts. Since the Jewish community in Iraq has now dwindled to less than four thousand persons, and just because its history of over two thousand years is drawing to a close, it is easier to look at it in perspective than at other Iraqi minorities such as the Kurds, whose fate is still unresolved. Further, the Jews have been the world's archetypal minority for the past two millennia, and accordingly, an examination of the operating of those systems in providing protection for the Jewish minority of Iraq may furnish insights into the adequacy or even comparative effectiveness of different general approaches to the international protection of minorities.

The need for the protection of religious minorities has been recognized in international law in Europe since the peace treaties that had brought religious warfare to an end in the seventeenth century. The principle of international protection was reaffirmed by the Congress of Vienna in 1815 when it sought to design a framework for European peace.

Throughout the nineteenth century, minorities increasingly became the subject of international guarantee. Popular sympathy for oppressed minorities spread widely and at times exerted a decisive influence on governments; the most notable example was the intervention by European states on behalf of Christians in the Turkish Empire. In the Treaty of Paris in 1856 the European nations forced the sultan to assure free exercise of religion, and provide a guarantee against discrimination on racial or religious grounds. This guarantee was reaffirmed in the Treaty of Berlin, 1878 which stated:

In no part of the Ottoman Empire shall difference of religion be alleged against any person as a ground for exclusion or incapacity as regards the discharge of civil and political rights, admission to the public employments, functions and honors, or the exercise of the various professions and industries.

The freedom and outward exercise of all forms of worship are assured to all. . . .

These treaty provisions were of major significance in the development of the modern Iraqi Jewish community.

In 1856, pursuant to the Treaty of Paris, the Turks granted the Jewish community full autonomy in internal and religious matters. Jews were also guaranteed full political rights, and, although occasional instances of discrimination at the hands of petty bureaucrats may have occurred, there were strong pointers that progress was being made. With the opening of the Suez Canal in 1869, the Iraqi economy began to flourish, and Jews came to occupy an important position in the country's commerce and foreign trade.

By the turn of the century, the Jewish community constituted one of the principal minorities in Iraq. It had been granted communal autonomy as well as representation on the local administrative councils which had been established by the Turks. The school founded by the Alliance Israélite Universelle in 1864 had taken the lead in introducing Western education. For many Jews, who moved into mixed neighborhoods and relocated outside the principal urban areas, social integration had begun.

With the revolution of 1908, the final step in the integration of Iraq's Jews was taken with the institution of compulsory military service. The practice of buying exemptions was widespread, but many Jews did enter the armed forces, and served with determination.

The political, economic, and social conditions of Jewish life in Iraq at the outset of World War I were, thus, better than they had been for centuries previously. Even the publication of the first Iraqi Zionist pamphlet demanding Palestine as a Jewish homeland had caused no alarm. But while Jews may have been tolerated, they were by no means considered socially equal to their Arab neighbors, and anti-Semitism was still latent, ready to surface at any moment. Nevertheless, the guarantees given by the Turks under the Treaties of Paris and Berlin had been respected insofar as they affected the Jewish community and, to that extent, the system was working satisfactorily.[1] It is noteworthy that these two treaties were the precedents for the guarantee of minority rights as a prerequisite to the establishment of new states in Eastern Europe after the First World War. In the aftermath of that war, the League of Nations was to espouse and expand the principle of international protection into a comprehensive minority system. Through the fact that Iraq was at first a territorial Mandate in which the League exercised special jurisdiction, and after 1932 a participant in the minorities system as a member of the League of Nations, the effectiveness of the League's minority system was of particular relevance to the development of the Jewish community in Iraq.

Protection of Minorities by the League of Nations

The plight of minorities scattered across Europe had attracted worldwide attention in 1919. Prior to the First World War, oppression of politically conscious minorities had helped to generate international tensions. It was, therefore, only natural that at the Peace Conference every effort was made to draw frontiers along ethnic and national lines. Yet there were still between twenty and twenty-five million members of minorities in Eastern Europe when the process was completed.

At the Paris Peace Conference, the minorities question was considered at the urging of Woodrow Wilson, who himself had been under pressure from Jewish organizations represented there. Although Wilson eventually lost his fight to have the provisions for minorities protection included in the Covenant of the League of Nations, he did succeed in obtaining agreement for the establishment of a separate League minorities system.

The basic premise underlying the minorities system was that "the two aims of peace and justice were correlative and interdependent." On this view, peace depended upon the internal stability of states, and that could be achieved only by guaranteeing the well-being of minorities.

It was held that the unilateral case-by-case intervention of the nineteenth century had been inequitable, and had done more to threaten than to preserve international peace. The new climate dictated that protection be undertaken on a permanent basis by an impartial international authority. Yet the creation of such an authority was still viewed as a Great Power responsibility.

In addition, national minorities demanded "affirmative protection," that is, measures which directly serve to perpetuate the culture, religion, language, or other distinguishing characteristics of the minority. While the Great Powers were hesitant to agree to such measures, they finally consented, but would not admit that minority groups possessed international legal personality.

In the end, the League system reflected a compromise between the desire of the international community, as constituted in 1919, to safeguard the rights of minorities, and its predilection for preserving the doctrine of absolute sovereignty.

The fate of the minorities system was tied up with the success of the League because of its dependence on the League's enforcement measures. When the threat of sanction was taken seriously, states trod cautiously in their dealings with League organs, but, once the threat had lost its credibility, there was little left to induce them to meet obligations forced upon them. Quiet diplomacy on behalf of protected minorities was successful only as long as there existed a threat, no matter how subtle, that other enforcement measures would be employed if the efforts at peaceful reconciliation failed.

The Period of the British Mandate

The British conquest of Iraq during the First World War marked the end of Turkish rule over the territory and the start of British. Because of a sharp increase in anti-Jewish discrimination during the war, and the hardship which the Turkish draft had worked on Jewish families, the community met the change in governing authorities with welcome relief.

During the war, the British and the French had concluded the Sykes-Picot agreement, which provided for the postwar division of the Mideast between the two powers, with the eventual intention of setting up national governments in the areas concerned. On September 27, 1924, endorsing that agreement, the Council of the League of Nations voted to grant Great Britain a Mandate over Iraq; under the terms of Article 22 of the League Covenant, the Mandatory was obligated to render administrative advice and assistance until development had progressed to the point where the territory would be ready for self-government.[2] Upon accepting the Mandate, Great Britain guaranteed fulfillment of Iraq's international responsibilities, and agreed to the submission of disputes to the Permanent Court of International Justice.

Although the League's Mandate system bore the markings of European colonialism, it was founded upon humanitarian motives as well. One of the primary reasons expressed for placing Iraq under a Mandate was the fear that it had not developed a spirit of tolerance sufficient to guarantee the rights of minorities. While protection for national and racial minorities was narrower under the Mandate system than under the minorities system, the stipulation that the obligations of the minorities system be accepted as a condition precedent to independence indicated the close relationship which existed between the two.

The British administration relied heavily on Jews, who were appointed to fill a disproportionately large percentage of posts in the administration. This occurred for two reasons: first, the Jews comprised the most highly educated group in the country; and second, many were fluent in one or more European languages. Outside of government, Jews continued to hold key places in education, transportation, banking, and finance. Although a scant 3 percent of the population, they had a major part in Iraqi foreign trade.

The decade of the 1920s was a highpoint of Jewish life in modern Iraq. Not only was there no official and little unofficial discrimination against Jews, but affirmative steps were taken by the Iraqi authorities to guarantee their rights as individuals and collectively as a community. Of primary importance were the provisions of the Constitution of 1924, particularly freedom of religion (Article 13); the right of minorities to employ their own language for instruction in the schools (Article 16); and the establishment of "Spiritual Councils of the Communities," including one which would govern the affairs of the Jewish community (Article 78). In the political sphere, the Electoral Law of 1924 stipulated that there would be four Jewish deputies—two from Baghdad, one each from Mosul and Basra.

Autonomy in domestic affairs was assured by the continuing validity of Turkish legislation granting Jewish ecclesiastical courts exclusive jurisdiction in suits relating to "marriage, divorce, dowry and maintenance payable to husband and wife." In the realm of education, the government ran several Jewish primary schools in which religious instruction was provided, while at the same time making substantial contributions to exclusively Jewish private schools.[3]

The only significant friction between the government and the community occurred over the issue of Zionism. The first official Iraqi Zionist group was established in March 1921, but it soon encountered difficulties. The Law of Associations, 1922, required governmental consent and registration for every organization, and the Ministry of the Interior had refused to process applications of Zionist groups. Eventually a gentleman's agreement was arrived at whereby the government turned its back on Zionist activity, provided it was carried on discreetly. The collection of funds, the printing of literature, and the organization of youth groups could thus go on, but the scope of these activities was reduced, particularly in the second half of the decade. Surprisingly, the anti-Zionist demonstrations, which were increasing in frequency and vehemence, still had little effect upon the community.

The relative tolerance of the Iraqi authorities during this phase is explained by the presence of the Mandatory behind the scenes at all times. Ready and willing to intrude upon Iraqi sovereignty if the need arose, the British filled the role of an impartial guarantor of the constitutional and statutory provisions which protected minority rights.

When, in its opinion, Iraq had reached the stage at which the Mandate could be terminated by its admission to the League, the British government recommended that a prerequisite to admission be a declaration which would place the country under the minorities system.[4] The condition was accepted and the text, as finally worded, was one of the most stringent drafted. Substantive rights included equality before the law, and in the exercise of civil and political rights; free use of language; freedom of religious conscience; the right to maintain religious institutions; the rights of non-Muslim minorities to use their own law in personal and family matters, to create new communal institutions, and to be equitably represented in the electoral system. Iraq recognized the obligations as a matter of international concern under the guarantee of the League of Nations, subject to modification only by consent of the League of Nations. Every Council member was entitled to bring any question of infraction before the Council, which would then take "appropriate measures." Differences of opinion on legal questions would go to the International Court.[5]

There can be no question that the Arab government of Iraq resented the fact that it had been forced to accept the minorities obligations.[6] Arab writers have claimed that before the Mandatory period there had never been any problems with minorities in Iraq. They argued that it was the League itself which had exacerbated the situation by practically creating sovereign entities within states. Moreover, it was urged that the inclusion of clauses guaranteeing minimum standards of treatment for foreign nationals and regulating Iraq's international commercial relations, carry-overs from the colonial era which were clear infringements of the newly independent state's sovereignty, tainted the image of the entire declaration.[7]

Unique in that they were the only Iraqi minority which was both ethnic and religious, the situation of Iraq's Jews differed from that of other minorities, in that they constituted an upper class in Iraqi society, and were relatively satisfied with their position during the Mandatory period. But after independence the situation was soon to change as repressive measures were gradually instituted. A statute passed in 1935 provided for the discharge of "any official who is proved to be incapable of carrying out his duties insofar as his personal efficiency or physical fitness is concerned, or to be unfit for service on moral grounds." Although the law was purported to be aimed at a reorganization of the civil service, its authority was abused in order to dismiss Jews arbitrarily from positions they had occupied since the Mandate period. Similarly, other laws were enforced selectively to discriminate against Jews. At the same time, Jewish newspapers, both Arabic and Hebrew, were shut down. And while the anti-Jewish violence which broke out in Baghdad in 1936 was brought under swift control, bomb-throwing in the Jewish quarter of the city was still being reported two years later.

Zionist work was the target of the most restrictive policies. As already mentioned, Zionists had been carrying on a broad range of activities during the Mandatory period, but after independence, the movement was compelled to go underground. In 1935, study of Hebrew in a non-religious context was banned in all schools. Jewish teachers brought from Palestine to serve in the Jewish schools were expelled. As of 1936, organized Zionist activity had ground to a complete halt, and was not to be renewed for five years. By the late 1930s, following the Peel Commission Report, the possibility of the partition of Palestine had become a key concern of government leaders and the townspeople of Iraq, and the wide support given to the program of the Palestine Defense League indicated the extent of anti-Zionist sentiment.

It should be noted that the Iraqi government, like other Arab governments then and now, professed to make a distinction between Zionists and Jews.[8] Government spokesmen often referred to the Jews as "cousins," and Jewish communal leaders were urged to issue anti-Zionist statements. But owing to the near impossibility of making an objective distinction between Zionist and Jew, even the staunch anti-Zionist stance maintained by Iraqi Jewish leadership could not prevent the brunt of anti-Zionist policies from being borne by the community as a whole.[9]

Despite the increasingly discriminatory nature of Iraq's policies during the 1930s, Iraqi Jews chose not to utilize the protective measures available through the minorities system. Several explanations can be offered. First, they probably shared the attitude which prevailed in Europe, that, in the final analysis, their well-being depended on the goodwill of their own government. Petitions to an international body, whose authority was sharply resented by Iraqi officials, were unlikely to produce positive results. Second, the Iraqi government was alleged to have interfered with the sending of petitions to the League following the slaughter of Assyrians in the early 1930s. This may have exercised a chilling effect on the Jewish community. Finally, the League's prestige fell steeply during the decade, and the notion of relying on it to protect minority rights had lost attractiveness. The withdrawal of Germany from the League and subsequent events in Europe may have embedded in the minds of many Iraqi Jews (as well as of Jews the world over) a skepticism as to the ability or willingness of the international community to deal with the problem of anti-Semitism.

The argument could be made that, even though the petition procedure was not utilized by Jews, the system may have had a prophylactic effect—that without it the situation of minorities would have been worse. But that argument is hard to sustain in light of the steadily deteriorating conditions of Jewish life, and the Iraqi persecutions of Assyrians during the period when the system was in operation. The more plausible conclusion is that the Iraqi government felt no need to abide by its obligations under the minorities declaration, probably out of a realization that the likelihood of League sanctions, or even censure, was relatively small.

It can be seen that absence of international protection during this period led to a steady deterioration in the conditions of Jewish life in Iraq. It is important to note the rather substantial German influence which had been built up in the late 1930s: Iraqi respect for Germany went back to the days of the Turkish empire, when German officers trained their Turkish counterparts. Later, the rapid growth in German military and economic power under Hitler led to a corresponding growth in that respect. Germans penetrated

Iraqi society by offering long-term credit on commercial propositions, and unqualified support for an Arab Palestine. Among
politicians, the intelligentsia, and particularly army officers, German influence spread rapidly.

The resultant shift away from democracy and toward a Fascist
militarism was accompanied by an increase in pan-Arabic, anti-
Zionist influences. Teachers from other Arab countries, Palestine,
in particular, had been brought in to fill shortages. Even more
important was the entrance, in October 1937, of the Mufti of
Jerusalem, Haj Amin el Hussein. In the name of an organization
which was formed in Iraq, he was later to conduct negotiations
with Nazi Germany over the future of Palestine, and to become
the primary public figure to make the nexus, implicitly if not
explicitly, between anti-Semitism and anti-Zionism.

The culmination of Iraqi militarism came in April 1941 when
Rashid Ali al-Gailani, a former prime minister with strong pro-
German sympathies and the backing of ultranationalists and the
army, seized power in a coup d'état. One of his first acts was an
attempt to modify the Anglo-Iraqi Treaty of 1930 and thereby
interfere with the wartime transit of British forces through Iraq.
The British reacted swiftly, landing troops at Basra, and the
Iraqis, having received only token aid from Germany, were defeated by the end of May.

But on June 1, after Rashid Ali's government had fled, leaving
a power vacuum, a full-scale pogrom broke out, creating chaos
for two days. Soldiers and police took part in rioting which led
to the indiscriminate slaughter of Jewish men, women, and children. Only with the establishment of a new government and the
imposition of a general curfew was order restored. Final estimates
ranged from 100 to 180 dead; 900–1,000 houses destroyed; and
600–2,400 stores ransacked; there were no figures for the many
rapes.

An official committee of investigation placed the blame for
inciting the riots on the propaganda of the German consulate, and
in particular on a radio station which it controlled, as well as on
the Mufti, who had been carrying on activity in the government
schools. Responsibility for the rioting itself was placed on military
elements, the youth movement, and the "avarice and greed of the
lowest mob elements."

This riot marked the start of a new era for the Iraqi Jewish
community. The succeeding years were relatively calm, as Iraqi

governments were pro-British, but thousands of members of the community, seeing little prospect of improvement, seized the opportunity to emigrate. Emigration has continued as the major mechanism of protection for Iraqi Jews in the postwar period. The development of alternative systems of human-rights protection by the United Nations, after the Second World War, even when they comprised specific commitments by the government of Iraq, did not restore the shattered sense of security of the Iraqi Jewish community.

Minorities Protection Following the Second World War

The events of the Second World War had undermined the international legal order, and the League of Nations was left totally discredited. In the course of reorganizing the international community there was a strong tendency to dissociate the new from the old. The League had failed and for that reason few people wanted the United Nations to be associated with it. The immediate postwar goal was to create a new order conducive on all levels to the promotion and maintenance of international peace.

It was to be expected that the League system for the protection of minorities would be left by the wayside. The focus in the postwar years, however, was not placed exclusively on the remnants of those minorities which had suffered at the hands of Nazi persecution. Of at least equal concern were the German minorities which were scattered throughout Europe. By the end of the war states which had hosted German minorities previously were anxious to expel them. International guarantees for the protection of minorities were to be a thing of the past. The new solution, which wasn't really new, would be the elimination of national minorities. Where feasible, borders were modified, but where border changes were politically unacceptable, the transfer of entire populations was undertaken. For those few members of minorities who chose and were permitted to remain in their host states, the policy behind population exchanges dictated against the granting of special rights or privileges. Their basic human rights and fundamental freedoms would be recognized on an equal basis with those of the members of the majority population, but the age of affirmative protection of minority rights had ended.

The transfer of populations was carried out on a wide scale

across the continent of Europe, and led to a drastic reduction in the size of minorities. These population transfers were the only action taken on behalf of European minorities immediately following the war. The peace treaties generally made no mention of minorities, nor did the United Nations Charter. Guarantees were embodied in the constitutions of several states, but there was no specifically international protection for minorities. Safeguards for minorities were to be subsumed under a new approach to the protection of human rights.

The United Nations, in abandoning the League's minorities system, shifted its focus from the protection of the minority as a group to that of the individual as a person. The guarantee of affirmative rights by an international authority was replaced by an international attempt to obtain national acceptance of standards of non-discrimination. These efforts were a reflection of a general return by the United Nations to a more absolute concept of sovereignty. Such an approach was incompatible with the broad scope of the principle of the intervention which was fundamentally characteristic of the League's minorities system.

Furthermore, as the colonial era drew to a close, the ascendancy of the principle of the sovereign equality of states foreclosed the establishment of a minorities system which would be imposed on states upon a basis of inequality, as indeed the League's was. Within the consensual framework of international law, arrangements for the protection of human rights would have to be made universally applicable. The cost of widespread acceptance would be provisions subject to flexible interpretations so that states which felt compelled to do so could avoid their obligations under any arrangements which would be created.

The Post-World War II Exodus

These trends of the immediate postwar period in the international community, with their stress on national sovereignty and their utilization of population transfer as the major mechanisms of minority protection, naturally did not allay the fears of Iraqi Jews. Their fears were shown to have been well-founded, as persecution broke out again with the passage of the United Nations partition plan for Palestine in 1947. After the Iraqi participation in the Arab invasion of Israel, the government instituted mass arrests of Jews, charging them with subversion or Communist affiliations. Zionism and Communism were condemned in popular outcries, Jews being identified with Zionists. Reports from Iraqi refugees in Israel described mass detentions in concentration camps, confiscations of property, show trials, and torture on a wide scale. By 1950, all the Jewish deputies and senators in the parliament had resigned.

Because these events coincided with the flight of tens of thousands of Arab refugees from Palestine, the question of the feasibility of a population exchange arose. Iraq, being under-populated, would have had little difficulty in absorbing the Palestinians, and a mandatory population exchange would have enabled the state to rid itself of its unwanted Jewish minority. Despite initial denials of rumors that such a project would be entertained, the Iraqi government did decide early in 1950 to permit Jews to emigrate.[10]

But even prior to the lifting of the ban on emigration, the flight of Iraqi Jews had swelled to a volume that was disquieting in terms of its effects on the economy. The exodus left a void in the commercial credit and transportation institutions which, prior to 1948, had been dominated by Jewish firms. While the hiring of Pakistanis filled the gap in skilled labor on the railways, the loss in banking presented greater difficulties.

In an attempt to compensate for this loss of manpower, and to prevent Jewish wealth from leaving the country, the Iraqis imposed severe restrictions on Jewish departures. The first was Act No. 1 of 1950, which permitted the Council of Ministers to deprive of his nationality "any Iraqi Jew who . . . chooses of his own volition to leave Iraq permanently." Standing alone, such a statute was of little importance since few Iraqi Jews who left during this period had any thoughts of returning, but the movement of property out of the country was also severely restricted. By a 1951 statute, the property of persons who had forfeited their nationality under Act No. 1 of 1950 was frozen and placed under the control of a special administrator. And later in the same year, both acts were extended to Jews who had left the country legally, if they did not return within two months of given notice.

But mass emigration went on all the same, and by the beginning of 1952 the community had been reduced to 6,000, a mere 5 percent of the 118,000 it numbered five years before.[11]

Throughout the period, there was no international authority to which Iraqi Jews could turn for help. The League of Nations minorities system was no longer in operation; the United Nations had taken no substantive steps to fill the vacuum. The very fact that, five years after the Second World War, a state could launch such an invidious campaign to expel a minority and confiscate the property of its members showed the ineffectiveness of the early United Nations human-rights efforts to protect minorities.

The Jewish community in Iraq has continued to decrease in size since the mass emigration of the early 1950s and today numbers less than four thousand. The persecution which followed the 1967 Mideast War was worse than any previously experienced. On January 27, 1969, a public hanging of four Jews before thousands of onlookers startled the world. Just one in a chain of events, it was followed in September 1972 by the abduction of ten prominent members of the community; not one has been heard from since. Numerous other incidents have been reported, of dozens of Jews arrested, of others murdered in their homes.

Not only has the physical security of Iraqi Jewry been threatened, but a host of oppressive legal measures has been imposed upon them. Under Law No. 161 of 1963, Iraqi Jews, both in Iraq and abroad, were required to apply to the Department of Passports and Nationality for identity cards, submitting evidence that they had retained their Iraqi nationality. Any Jew whose application was not approved was to be considered denationalized and his property blocked. Law No. 10 of 1968 placed restrictions on Jews, preventing them from disposing of immovable property, bonds, and securities, or engaging in other financial activities. Administrative regulations have prohibited Jews from having telephones, operating stores or pharmacies, and from government employment or university admission.

It is widely believed that the objective of these legal and extra-legal attacks has been to force out the last members of the community, so as to expropriate the extensive communal property holdings—schools, hospitals, apartment and office buildings, movie theaters, clinics, athletic fields, and parks—which were valued at nearly $200 million in 1973.

The United Nations Standards in Human Rights

When we examine these discriminatory policies against the standards laid down by international law, their violation of the minority-rights provisions catalogued above is so obvious that there is no need for reiteration. But what should be pointed out is that they also contravene the United Nations' more general human-rights standards. Those standards derive from different phases of UN activity during the past thirty years. It is true that the human-rights instruments which have been adopted by the United Nations have generally avoided the issue of minorities protection. At several stages during the drafting of the Universal Declaration of Human Rights, draft provisions for the affirmative protection of minorities were proposed. Yet no article on minorities was included in the Declaration. The Covenant on Civil and Political Rights does include the following cautious formulation of minority rights:

> In those States in which ethnic, religious or linguistic minorities exist, persons belonging to such minorities shall not be denied the right, in community with the other members of their group, to enjoy their own culture, to profess and practice their own religion, or to use their own language.

This Covenant has only recently entered into force and it will undoubtedly require a substantial period of time before the enforcement measures for which it provides can be implemented. Nevertheless, it does constitute international law, binding among state parties, which include Iraq, and is clearly, from the point of view of international protection of minorities, the most important of the United Nations human-rights conventions.

The International Convention on the Elimination of All Forms of Racial Discrimination, a binding treaty to which Iraq is a party, also touches on the question of minorities protection, but again, in a weak and indecisive manner. The Convention obligates parties to take "concrete measures to ensure the adequate development and protection of certain racial groups, or individuals belonging to them," for the purpose of securing "full and equal enjoyment of human rights and fundamental freedoms." Although the use of the phrase "development and protection" may indicate a tendency toward a recognition of positive rights, "human rights and fundamental freedoms" in the United Nations context have not generally included the right of minorities to maintain the institutions necessary for a separate communal existence.

Although the Genocide Convention deals principally with the physical destruction of groups, its definition of genocide implies the existence of a non-physical genocide as well. But the clauses referring to "cultural genocide" which had been included in some of the Convention's preparatory drafts were deleted prior to its passage.

The United Nations Educational, Scientific, and Cultural Organization's Convention Against Discrimination in Education recognizes what have been referred to as affirmative minority rights, such as the rights of members of national minorities to carry on their own educational activities, including the maintenance of schools and, depending on the educational policy of each state, the use or the teaching of their own language. The scope of the provision is extremely limited, however, as compared to the corresponding provisions in the League of Nations minorities treaties.

The international community, through the United Nations, has embraced the principle of non-discrimination as its primary means of protecting minorities, relegating the right of minorities to be provided with the means necessary to maintain their national culture and identity to weak and isolated provisions.

Accordingly, in those instances where the anti-discrimination approach has failed to provide effective protection for minority rights, it is appropriate to explore other avenues by which such protection may be obtainable. There is one alternative which has been shown to be acceptable to the international community in the past, namely, population transfers. While they involve a collective view of a given situation, the issue can be approached on the individual level by considering the right of emigration.

Article 13 of the Universal Declaration of Human Rights, passed by the United Nations General Assembly in 1948, includes the statement: "Every one has the right to leave any country including his own, and return to his country." Eighteen years later, it was followed by the International Covenant on Civil and Political Rights, of which Article 12 states: "Everyone shall be free to leave any country including his own." Protection against discrimination in respect of the right is contained in the International Convention on the Elimination of All Forms of Racial Discrimination. These provisions enjoy a strong legal standing. The International Covenant on Civil and Political Rights and the International Convention on the Elimination of All Forms of Racial Discrimination are fully binding treaties, both currently in force, and both ratified by Iraq.

Limited as they may be, the United Nations' efforts in human rights have produced a substantial base for the support of the rights of the Iraqi Jewish community if there were the political will to improve the repressive measures of the government of Iraq. First, many of the repressive measures would fall within the scope of the Genocide Convention. Second, as Iraqi Jews are recognized to constitute an "ethnic" or "national" as well as a religious minority, they are protected by the Convention on the Elimination of All Forms of Racial Discrimination. Third, the rights recognized in the International Covenant on Civil and Political Rights, by which Iraq is bound, include liberty and security of person, and freedom from arbitrary arrest and detention; freedom of movement within a state and the right of emigration; certain rights of an accused; rights of judicial due process; and freedom of religion. The Covenant is now in force, and, assuming that the Iraqi policies described are still being carried out, they violate it. Finally, one can look to the United Nations Charter itself, by which member states pledge themselves "to take joint and separate action for the promotion of 'universal respect for, and observance of, human rights and fundamental freedoms for all without distinction as to race, sex, language or religion.' " Iraqi policies have been so far contrary to the spirit and principles which they set forth as to be indefensible under the Charter.

The Current Situation

Leaving aside this consistent pattern of gross infractions of human rights, there appears to be another aspect of Iraqi policy which has surfaced over the recent years. In 1969, in a seemingly anomalous move, the government rescinded some of the most repressive measures previously enacted. By Law No. 86 of that year many of the restrictions on the disposal of property were repealed. Then, in 1970, it was announced that most of the internal restrictions had also been lifted. Not only were persons given emigration permits, but the Interim Constitution of July 16, 1970, recognized the right of free movement. The culmination of this series of moves took the form of an official publicity campaign in the fall of 1975 in which the government invited former Iraqi Jews to return. It was based on a resolution of the Iraqi Revolutionary Council (November 26, 1975) which permits Jews who have previously emigrated to return and enjoy equal rights.

While these legal maneuverings could be interpreted as a sign of a reversal in Iraq's policy towards its Jews, the actual state of affairs gives no such indication. First, despite the 1969 statute repealing the laws permitting confiscation of property, action has still been taken under the old statute. Second, although the constitutional provision does recognize the right of emigration, the qualifier "except in cases laid down by law" limits its effect to extra-legal denials of the freedom, permitting legal restrictions or even absolute denial, as has frequently been the case. Third, while ostensibly directed at Jewish émigrés, the timing and wording of the recent advertisements employed in the campaign, and the fact that many were placed in newspapers in countries such as Kenya and Finland, where there are no Iraqi Jews to speak of, suggest that its real purpose was to serve as a platform for anti-Zionist propaganda.[12] Finally, information obtained after the Yom Kippur War indicated that Iraqi Jews were still living in a state of constant fear.

Although it is impossible to know for certain whether the recent pronouncements are a ploy, there is no concrete evidence of any de-facto improvement in the situation of the country's Jews.[13] Were the problem one of securing or retaining affirmative minority rights, there might be justification for adopting a "wait-and-see" attitude. But since the question is one of physical survival, the risks involved are too high to permit such an approach.

Moreover, the international Conventions which ostensibly provide protection for the Iraqi Jewish community have proved to be of little use, for two reasons. First, the enforcement measures which they contain are inadequate in that they provide no procedures by which the parties most interested in the situation of Iraq's Jews can initiate action with respect to possible violations. For example, the International Covenant on Civil and Political Rights places the authority to bring complaints with the state parties, but, with respect to Israel, the state most likely to show a concern for the treatment of Iraqi Jewry were it to ratify the Conventions, Iraq has made the following declaration:

The entry of the Republic of Iraq as a party to the International Covenant on Economic, Social and Cultural Rights and the International Covenant on Civil and Political Rights shall in no way signify recognition of Israel *nor shall it entail any obligations towards Israel under the said two Covenants* [emphasis added].

While the Covenant has an Optional Protocol which authorizes petitions from individuals residing in the state concerned, Iraq has neither ratified nor signed it and, in the declaration accompanying its ratification of the two Covenants, has stated its intention not to be bound by it. It has similarly precluded Israel from taking any action under the International Convention on the Elimination of All Forms of Racial Discrimination by making a declaration comparable to the one just cited. Under that Convention, as well, communications cannot be accepted from individuals claiming to be victims of a violation unless the state concerned has consented.

The second explanation for the failure of the United Nations to provide viable protection for Iraqi Jews relates to the politicization of its activities. The political manipulation of human-rights issues, both in the political organs and in the bodies which undertake the preparatory work (which were generally intended to be non-political), has restricted the UN's efforts almost exclusively to consideration of situations which are of interest to certain Third World blocs, e.g., in South Africa. It is for this reason that the Commission on Human Rights, although empowered to initiate action, has ignored the violation of human rights in Iraq, as well as in many other countries in the world, and cannot be expected to do otherwise in the near future.

While the United Nations has helped to define the obligations of states in the field of human rights, it has done little to bring about enforcement. In fact, the right to petition, which was available to certain classes of individuals under the League of Nations system (persons protected by Mandates or minorities treaties) has been significantly cut back by the United Nations practice which, until recently, had subjected that right wholly to the consent of the state.[14]

Current minorities-protection arrangements being inadequate, it is necessary to consider the feasibility of emigration as a solution to the problems of Iraq's Jewish minority. As noted, Iraq has recognized the right of emigration under several different human-rights instruments. But, not surprisingly, its stance on Jewish emigration in recent years also violated international legal standards. Enforcement of property forfeitures and other restrictions on emigration which apply only to Jews are violations of the International Convention on the Elimination of All Forms of Racial Discrimination. Second, judging the periodic bans on Jewish emigration against the standards of the International Covenant on Civil and Political Rights, one can find little justification for the Iraqi policy. It would be difficult to see how one could rationalize the denial to Iraqi Jews of the right to emigrate on grounds of national security when no Jew has occupied a sensitive position in the government or armed forces in several years. Besides, if one reckons the size of the community and its position in Iraqi society, one would be equally hard pressed to argue that restrictions on emigration can be justified by the need to safeguard "public order, public health or morals or the rights and freedoms of others."

As for the feasibility of full-scale emigration of the community, there would appear to be few obstacles in the way. The overwhelming majority of the community has already emigrated, most of them resettled in Israel, where permission to enter is given as a matter of right under the Law of Return. Moreover, because of the large number of Iraqi Jews in Israel, the social and cultural absorption of any future group of immigrants is likely to proceed more smoothly than would otherwise be expected.

It should be recognized that grave losses are likely to be incurred in the economic sector, since Iraq may very well set forfeiture of the Jewish communal holdings as the price of emigration. That would impose a heavy burden on the emigrants and mean a windfall for Iraq, which would be taking many times the amount necessary to compensate it for any adverse effect that the emigration may have on its economy. But monetary losses must be considered along with all the other relevant factors, and large-scale emigration appears to present the only practical approach to the current predicament of the community. If current conditions were minimally acceptable, one could propose a policy of waiting until the United Nations' human-rights system has had an opportunity to develop fully. But Iraqi Jews, at present, are in such imminent danger, in my view, that only the transfer of the entire community can assure that a disaster will be averted.

NOTES

1. It should be emphasized that these comments refer only to the situation of the Jewish community. Other minorities, the Assyrians in particular, did not fare as well, despite the fact that the stipulations of the Treaties of Paris and Berlin had originally been inserted with the primary object of protecting non-Jewish minorities.

2. No formal mandate was ever issued, but the Council approved the terms of a British communication as "giving effect to the provisions of Article 22 of the Covenant." When the British and French announced their decision to grant independence to the countries in the Mideast, in 1919, non-Muslim minorities in Iraq were sharply concerned, as they placed little faith in the Arabs. The Jews of Baghdad immediately forwarded a petition to the British government, requesting permission to become British subjects if Iraq were to be placed in the hands of an Arab government.

3. Such aid was granted under the authority of the "Law for the Grant of Financial Aid to Schools and Public Institutions No. 18 of 1926," *Compilation of Laws and Regulations 6.* It should be noted that comparable grants were being made to Christian and Muslim schools as well.

4. The minorities system was designed to be applied to those European states which had either been defeated during the war or were newly created after it. Its legal authority derived from a treaty or declaration made by a state to the League's Council, or among two more states and placed under the guarantee of the Council; eighteen such agreements were concluded during the course of its operation. The treaties and declarations were all similar, and to a great extent the rights protected and the conditions of supervisions were identical. Termination required the consent of the League.

5. Final action was taken on October 3, 1932, when, acting on the recommendation of the Sixth Committee, the Assembly voted unanimously to admit the Kingdom of Iraq to full membership.

6. It should be noted that when the obligations were imposed on Iraq the principal concern was for the Assyrians and Kurds. Nevertheless, the arrangement did not prevent the eruption of serious disturbances by members of the Assyrian community shortly after independence. The massacres of Assyrians which were alleged to have ensued led to serious questioning of the effectiveness of the system and widespread disillusionment with it. Nolde, *L'Irak, Origines Historiques et Situation Internationale* 228, 237 (1933). See generally Malek, *The British Betrayal of the Assyrians* (1935). The Kurds have fared little better, having been involved in continuous controversy up to the present day, with still no resolution in sight.

7. The arguments glanced over the fact that the only right guaranteed foreigners was that of a judicial system to protect their rights, and that the standard of protection appeared to be the "minimum standards" of international law, and not a "national treatment" standard. Similarly, the principal commercial privilege was the obligation upon Iraq to grant members of the League most-favored nation status, but such arrangements were to be reciprocal, and special provisions were included to protect Iraq in the event of a balance of payments disequilibrium.

8. See *18 League of Nations Off. J., Spec. Supp.* 175, *37–38* (1937); LN PMC, 20th Session, at 123 (1931). LN Doc. C422M176 (1931), 6.

Arab writers have frequently claimed that there has never been a "Jewish problem" in the Mideast, but that it has been an exclusively European phenomenon. They take the position that, if a solution had to be found for the "Jewish problem" in Europe, then it should have been found at the expense of Europeans, and not Arabs.

9. As late as the early 1940s Zionism was reported to have been viewed as "distasteful and potentially ruinous" to a large segment of the Iraqi Jewish community.

10. Possible reasons for the Iraqi decision to permit emigration were to confiscate the property holdings of Jews, and to appease Western public opinion. See A. Cohen, *The Jews in the Middle Eastern Countries (1860–1971)* (Hebrew, 1972), 39. Cohen gives the desire to turn over positions held by Jews to Muslims as a third reason, but, given the fact that the vacancies created a strain on the economy, the argument is less persuasive, unless the assumption is made that the Iraqi government underestimated the effect such emigration would have.

11. This was the 1947 census figure. Unofficial and probably more accurate estimates placed the number at 150,000.

12. See "Iraq's Phony Invitation," *Toronto Star,* February 3, 1976. One clear indication of this was the fact that the advertisements, aside from announcing the resolution, denounced Zionism by attempting to distinguish it from Judaism: "The latter [Zionism], however, is a racist movement particularly directed against Palestinian Arabs and consequently vehemently opposed by all justice-minded peoples the world over and the United Nations."

13. The text of the advertisement in the *New York Times,* December 15, 1975, also claimed that "Iraqi Jews enjoyed a prosperous life in Iraq before they unilaterally decided—under Zionist instigation and terror—to leave the country." See also *New York Times,* January 11, 1976. Because of restrictions on the press it is extremely difficult to obtain current information on Iraq's Jewish community.

14. It is not likely that Iraqi Jews will petition the Commission on Human Rights, owing both to the severe restrictions under which they are currently living and the high risks which such a communication would entail for its signatories.

SHIMON SHETREET

›››-›››-›››-›››-›››-›››-›››-›››-›››-››› **12** ‹‹‹-‹‹‹-‹‹‹-‹‹‹-‹‹‹-‹‹‹-‹‹‹-‹‹‹-‹‹‹-‹‹‹-‹‹‹-‹‹‹

Freedom of Conscience
and Religion in Israel

The question as to whether freedom of religion in all its varieties
is adequately protected in any society can be answered by a careful examination of the relevant doctrines and practices of its legal
system. There are significant sources for the protection of religious
liberty in Israeli law. There have also been various efforts to incorporate religious norms or restrictions that reflect religious
sources into the law of the land and an evaluation of these is part
of any investigation of Israel's adherence to principles of freedom of
conscience and religion.

Legal Protection for Religious Liberty

The Palestine Mandate of 1922 contained a number of provisions
ensuring freedom of religion and conscience and protection of
holy places, as well as prohibiting discrimination on religious
grounds. Further, the Palestine Order in Council of that same year
provided that "all persons . . . shall enjoy full liberty of conscience and the free exercise of their forms of worship, subject

only to the maintenance of public order and morals." It also laid down that "no ordinance shall be promulgated which shall restrict complete freedom of conscience and the free exercise of all forms of worship."[1] These provisions of the Mandate and of the Palestine Orders in Councils have been recognized in the Israeli legal system and are instructive of Israeli policy in safeguarding freedom of conscience and religion.

Israel's Declaration of Independence, promulgated at the termination of the British Mandate in 1948, is another legal source that guarantees freedom of religion and conscience, and equality of social and political rights irrespective of religion. Although the Declaration itself does not confer any legally enforceable rights, the Israeli High Court has held that "it provides a pattern of life for citizens of the State and requires every State authority to be guided by its principles."[2]

To support the fundamental existence of the right of freedom of conscience and religion, the courts have also relied on the fact that Israel is a democratic and enlightened state. In one significant court decision, Justice Moshe Landau stated: "The freedom of conscience and worship is one of the individual's liberties assured in every enlightened democratic regime."[3] In dealing with questions of religious freedom, as well as other human rights, the Israeli courts have also resorted to the Universal Declaration of Human Rights and the International Covenant on Political and Civil Rights, that reflect "the basic principles of equality, freedom and justice which are the heritage of all modern enlightened states."[4] In doing so, the courts have required that two conditions be met: that the principle in question is common to all enlightened countries and that no contrary domestic law exists. In this regard, Justice Haim Cohn has said:

> It is decided law that rules of international law constitute part of the law prevailing in Israel insofar as they have been accepted by the majority of the nations of the world and are not inconsistent with any enactment of the Knesset (Parliament). The principles of freedom of religion are similar to the other rights of man, as these have been laid down in the Universal Declaration of Human Rights, 1948, and in the Covenant on Political and Civil Rights, 1965. These are now the heritage of all enlightened peoples, whether or not they are members of the United Nations Organization and whether or not they have as yet ratified them. . . . For they have

been drawn up by legal experts from all countries of the world and been prescribed by the [General] Assembly of the United Nations, in which by far the larger part of the nations of the world participates.[5]

An interesting situation follows from this ruling: The State of Israel need not sign, ratify, or otherwise adhere to a given international treaty and will, therefore, not be bound by it in international law, yet the private Israeli citizen may rely on the treaty in court proceedings if it meets the conditions necessary for judicial recourse.

On the other hand, Justice Yitzhak Kister has expressed the view that, because of the special nature of the Jewish religion, "it is not possible, or at least very difficult, to employ with regard to the Jewish people and the Jewish religion the forms and definitions common among the peoples of the world in respect of freedom of religion."[6] With that view, the author cannot agree. There is nothing to prevent resort to principles common to foreign legal systems and accepted by civilized peoples, so long as the special considerations stemming from the peculiar character of the Jewish religion and a Jewish state are not ignored, where they have their proper place. It is noteworthy that the Israeli Supreme Court customarily avails itself of leading principles in foreign law in matters of religious freedom, and this course is followed even by those of its judges who explicitly recognize the singularity of the Jewish religion.[7]

Many provisions of Israeli statutory law are devoted to the protection of holy places and sites which serve for prayers and other religious purposes.[8] It is an offense under penal law to cause damage to any place of worship or to any object sacred to any religion with the intention of affronting the religion of any class of persons. There are, for example, penal sanctions for trespass on places of worship and burial, for indignity to corpses, and for disturbances at funeral ceremonies. The Supreme Court has dealt very stringently with acts which offend religious sentiment.

Religion-State Relationship and Freedom of Religion

The prevailing view in comparative international law is that the establishment of religion and its recognition by the state, or the separation of religion from the state, do not, as such, violate religious freedom or constitute unlawful discrimination for religious reasons or religious intolerance. The nature of the regulation matters and the measure of statutory protection of religious freedom does not vary with states where separation exists or where there is a state-recognized religion.

Many countries which separate church and state nevertheless grant exemptions from certain legal duties such as military service on grounds of religious beliefs, while other countries which have a state-established religion do not. The relationship between church and state has no significant effect on the free exercise of religion and, thus, the International Draft Convention on the Elimination of All Forms of Religious Intolerance provides that neither the establishment of a religion, nor the separation of church from state, in and of itself, is an interference with the freedom of religion, unlawful discrimination on religious grounds or religious intolerance.

Of course, if in consequence of the state's recognition a particular religion or its adherents are given preferential treatment over other religions or over persons who are not members of it, this involves an infringement of the principle of religious freedom which requires the equal treatment of all religions. The same applies where the separation of religion and the state leads to preferential treatment of people with no religion, or disbelievers, as against others.

It should be noted that, irrespective of state recognition of a particular religion, the religious beliefs of the majority of the population inevitably affect the life of the state. In the United States, for instance, this phenomenon is reflected in the prescription of Sunday as the weekly day of rest. By contrast, in Israel it is Saturday, and the Jewish festivals are also rest days. (The right is reserved to non-Jews to choose the rest day customary among them.) In Israel, the phenomenon is also manifested in the status enjoyed by the Chief Rabbis.

Issues of Integration of Religion and State

There is no separation of religion and state in Israel. At the same time, there is no recognized religion in the accepted sense. Some have argued that the peculiar nature of Judaism, which embodies a pattern of daily life and not merely a set of religious dogmas, and which intermingles religious and national elements, is not conducive to separation of religion and state. As David Ben-Gurion put it, "The convenient solution of separation of church and state, adopted in America not for reasons which are anti-religious but on the contrary because of deep attachment to religion and the desire to assure every citizen full religious freedom, this solution, even if it were adopted in Israel, would not answer the problem."[9]

Apart from the peculiar nature of Judaism, there is the difficulty attending separation which flows from the approach of the law in Israel to matters of personal status. This approach, predating establishment of the state, rests on religious affiliation, religious law, and religious jurisdiction. Other difficulties in the relations between religion and state in Israel have their origin in the absence of clearly defined rules in Jewish law as to its relationship with an independent Jewish state.[10]

The integration of religion and state in Israel is visible in many fields, some expressly regulated by statutory law, some relying on a legal regulation. Among them are the application of a religious test to the Law of Return (which provides for automatic Israeli citizenship to Jews wishing to reside permanently in Israel), the exclusive application of religious jurisdiction and religious law in matters of marriage and divorce, the conduct of religious education financed out of state funds, and the establishment of a special Ministry of Religious Affairs.

Those who are opposed to regulation in the religious sphere do not, in fact, desire absolute separation, but they contest those provisions which force religious norms upon the individual and compel recourse to religious authorities. What is asked for is not, for instance, the abolition of marriage by religious ceremony, but the alternative of civil marriage. Jewish religious law, it is our position, has discourse not with the state but with the individual.[11] And since the individual is entitled to religious freedom, it is incumbent upon the state to enable the individual to observe his religious prescripts without interference.[12]

Imposition of Religious Norms

The most difficult problem relating to religious liberty in Israel is posed by the imposition of religious norms and restrictions of a religious nature on all Jews, whether or not they are religiously observant.

To determine whether the enforcement of a norm of religious origin infringes freedom of conscience and religion, a distinction must be drawn between a norm of religious origin which is not generally recognized and adopted by the society and one which is. The enforcement of a norm of the first type—such as the application of religious law in marriage and divorce—involves a violation of religious liberty; the enforcement of a norm of the second type—such as the prescription of a day of rest—does not, for in that case the enforced norm is treated like any norm, regardless of source, which has been accepted by society, and which the state may enforce through legislation. As Justice Simon Agranat, the President of the Supreme Court, has observed:

> The function of the State, so democratic theory teaches, is to fulfill the will of the people and give effect to those norms and standards which it prizes. It follows from this that the common conviction must first form among enlightened members of society that these norms and standards are true and just, before we can say that a general will has been created to give them binding force, to stamp them as positive law and attach its sanctions.[13]

This opinion involves the much-debated issue of whether the state may legislate morality or compel a moral norm.

With regard to Jewish law, Justice Landau has proposed to distinguish between "rules which prescribe man's behavior to his fellow man and those which affect the relationship between man and Divinity."[14] On this view, coercion of the former upon non-believers does not derogate from freedom of conscience and religion. The difficulty I find with this distinction is that it implies that there would be nothing wrong with the enforcement of conduct, religious in origin and in substance, provided only that it concerns human relations. A law, for instance, which compels the sending of Purim gifts, or the opening of one's doors to the poor on Passover (following the injunction of the Haggadah, "Let all in need come and eat"), or the consolation of those in mourning, would be entirely valid because it relates to man's conduct toward his fellow men, although its source and substance are religious. Furthermore, the distinction is not clear-cut. By what criteria could one determine whether a norm is of one or the other kind? By a religious yardstick or a secular one? And where a rule is measurable by both yardsticks, which prevails?[15]

Admittedly, the compulsion of rules affecting man's relations with his Maker is a more serious invasion of freedom of conscience, still in the realm of man's conduct toward his fellow men, enforcement of norms which have not secured the societal approval that is generally considered a prerequisite for their enforcement offends against freedom of conscience. It should be added that the enforcement of the provisions of private law drawn from Jewish sources, such as those relating to bailees, guarantee, sale, and the like, does not violate religious freedom provided that the inherent religious elements have been filtered off.

Justice Moshe Silberg has distinguished between the "rational" and the "credal" commandments of Judaism.[16] While the former may, in his opinion, rightly be enforced on the public without prejudicing religious freedom, the coercion of the latter does not offend against that freedom. Again, I cannot agree with this distinction. That a religious norm is rational does not justify its compulsion until it has won the social approval required to render it a norm binding upon society. It is possible also for such societal approval to be gained by credal norms. Moreover, does this mean that, before deciding to enforce any norm, one must inquire and ascertain whether it is "rational" or "credal"? Justice Agranat has held alternatively, that one must find out whether the general public will exert itself to turn the religious norm in question into a norm of socially binding effect.[17] I agree with that view. The point is that the test of whether a norm having its source in religion deserves to become a binding one in society cannot be a religious test—namely, its classification as "rational" or "credal" within the Jewish religion—but solely the test of whether it has won contemporary social consensus.[18] Ultimately, the test for justifying coercion of norms is not their content but the measure of social consent which they have received.

Further, when the question arises whether to impose an obligation regarding an act which may affect religious freedom, it is not enough to inquire generally into the nature of the proposed norm. A religious norm may, in its totality, be a positive social norm, but the specific acts involved may not have gained the necessary consensus that would justify coercion. Thus, no one disputes that the introduction of the Saturday day of rest, for all its religious origin, is a positive social norm, but one should not infer that every restriction regarding the kind of things that may be done on the Sabbath is thereby justified and involves no invasion of religious freedom. Army regulations relating to the Sabbath and the festivals provide that entertainment in army units should be so arranged as to avoid "profanation" of the holiness of the day. Soldiers have thus been prohibited from listening on those days to the radio and recordings in messes and clubrooms. Manifestly, these regulations have nothing to do with the positive norm of a rest day that has social value but are connected with the religious prescript in Jewish law against "profanation" of the Sabbath day. From the fact that observance of a weekly rest day is, in general, a positive norm, no inference can be drawn that these particular regulations are, or are not, repugnant to religious freedom.

Israeli law, at present, provides examples of coercion of religious law that are not accepted norms within Israeli society. The application of Jewish law to marriage and divorce, and the subjection of citizens and residents to the exclusive jurisdiction of the religious courts in such matters, are an improper coercive enforcement of a religious norm. And the very necessity to marry before a religious authority results in a number of restrictions of wider ambit. A woman who has left the faith loses property rights. The marriage of a *kohen,* a man whose descent is traditionally traced to the ancient priesthood, and a divorcee is forbidden. None of these matters are to be found in any statute.

Justice Landau has observed that "the enforcement of religious law in marriage and divorce . . . is not actually the same as the full operation of all the halachic rules affecting marriage and divorce. . . . [The Marriage and Divorce Law of 1953] is not to be read as imposing any prohibition which is really religious in origin and substance on the Jewish population of Israel, including those for whom the observance of religious prohibition is not a matter of religious belief."[19] The law, he argues, "is not intended to offend against freedom of religion guaranteed to all citizens of our State or to impose the observance of religious precepts on the non-religious public." Justice Landau urged that the law of 1953 that had granted jurisdiction over marriage and divorce to the Rabbinical Courts be interpreted in ways which would avoid inconsistency with the basic principles of freedom of religion that are part of the law of the land.

Because the army controls the lives of soldiers in service more closely than the state controls the lives of its citizens, religious norms are enforced to a larger extent on soldiers than on civilians. Army regulations regarding the High Holy Days, for example, provide for obligatory participation in educational activities conducted by the army chaplaincy. The Minister of Defense has explained in the Knesset that this does not involve any assault upon freedom of conscience and religion, for two reasons. First, the regulations do not oblige any soldier to do anything apart from listening to talks on the moral values of the Jewish festivals. Second, the talks correspond to those on other subjects given by education officers of the army, where attendance is also mandatory. It seems to me, however, that the information work of the education officers has nothing in common with the educational activities of the chaplaincy. The army regulations are also invalid in my view because, at least in theory, they make it a duty for all soldiers to attend, including Druzes, Circassians, and other non-Jewish soldiers.

A similar problem arises in connection with the study of the Bible in state schools. While the State Education Law does assert that elementary education is to be based on "the values of Jewish culture," the use of the Bible and other religious literature as "religious instruments" within the compass of prayer or religious preaching is appropriately forbidden as repugnant to freedom of conscience and religion. Such a use is totally different from the use of this literature as an "educational instrument" for teaching Jewish cultural values or even for inculcating moral values.[20]

The Secular Primary-Purpose Test

In legal terms, the difference between religious norms which are not part of the societal consensus and norms with religious roots which have been adopted by the society assumes the form of the secular primary-purpose test. If the primary purpose meant to be served by the law is secular—that is to say, is acceptable to enlightened members of society—no improper coercion is involved, even if a religious purpose is incidentally served. For instance, the designation of Sunday as the general day of rest in the United States would prima facie constitute the coercive enforcement of a Christian religious norm on the entire population, but since the primary purpose is a secular one, the incidental result of enforcing a religious norm does not invalidate such a law.

The secular primary-purpose test is acceptable to the courts in Israel, whether or not they apply it explicitly. Justice Silberg has held that where a religious purpose is not primary to a law but the provisions of that law can be justified by the secular purpose achieved, no infringement of religious freedom occurs, even if the statutory provision also serves some religious purpose.[21] And Justice Zvi Berinson has held that the fact that a municipal by-law, dealing with the opening and closing of businesses, accords with religious demands will not invalidate all or any part of it "if the primary purpose sought to be achieved by means of it is not a religious purpose."[22]

A legislative or administrative act serving a religious purpose, if effected by an administrative authority, possesses force only on the condition that the religious purpose is incidental or marginal to the secular primary purpose. Thus, the Israeli Supreme Court has decided that the introduction into an import license of a condition whereby the importer of food must produce a certificate of *kashrut* from the Rabbinate to obtain clearance of the goods from customs does not serve the economic purposes of the law restricting imports. Therefore, the court found that the authority, in imposing such a condition, had improperly exercised its powers in order to attain a religious purpose.[23] Similarly, the Supreme Court has denied validity to an order of the Food Controller that prohibited the breeding of pigs in certain areas by virtue of his general power to regulate the inspection of food. In its ruling, the court noted that "the sole firm grounds, or at least the primary and decisive grounds, for the Food Controller's administrative and legal acts in this matter were national-religious and not economic grounds inherent in the purposes of food control."[24]

National-Religious Norms

A special problem arises with what are termed in Israel national-religious norms. Certainly, religious freedom is consistent with the imposition of national norms that bind a society to its historic values and cultural heritage. The intermingling of national and religious elements in Judaism requires, however, that a distinction be drawn between purely religious norms and norms which display national features.

National-religious norms are enforceable upon individuals only when they have secured societal consensus. However, their introduction into official state institutions may be warranted, even when their enforcement upon the individual citizen is not justified. Thus, the State of Israel may properly require that Jewish symbols and values should be preserved by governmental authorities and the official representatives of the state in the course of their duty even though these may lack the consensus which would transform them into norms binding on all citizens. Analogously, it is my view that the observance of the dietary laws in the army is justified, not because military standardization and national unity make it undesirable to set up two kitchens in every army unit or because there is no hardship involved in non-observant soldiers eating *kosher* food while the alternative policy creates severe hardship for many soldiers. The observance of the dietary laws in the army can be justified on the ground that it forges a bond with the past of the Jewish people by means of one of the most conspicuous of Jewish symbols.

Governmental Response to Religious Needs

In Israeli law, religious matters are regulated only by the national legislature. In the absence of specific legislation, there is no warrant for the enforcement of any religious norm by the executive branch of government. But, in contradistinction to the enforcement of religious norms, governmental administration may, within the scope of its general authority, include religious considerations along with others in the regulation of public life. Such is the case, for example, in ordering the closure, during the hours of prayer, of a section of road adjoining a synagogue. The court held that "in attaching some value to the consideration that motor traffic along the roads concerned on a Jewish festival and the Sabbath disturbs worshippers during their prayers in the Yeshurun Synagogue and prevents them from praying in tranquility, [the Traffic Controller] gave thought to an interest of a religious character.

However, this does not invalidate his decision, just as it would not be invalid had he had in mind some cultural, commercial, health or other like interest."[25] Consideration of interests having a religious character is justified "provided they affect an appreciable part of the public" and do not impose a "burden which cannot be borne."[26] The justification for taking account of religious considerations and interests derives, as has been suggested, from the fact that they fall into a wide category of matters which may properly be given consideration for the purpose of exercising authority.[27]

Concluding Note

It is proposed to embody individual rights ("Rights of the Man and the Citizen") into what will eventually become the written Constitution of Israel.[28] Section 14 of the Draft Basic Law reads: "Every man is entitled to freedom of worship of God."[29] This proposed wording is seriously deficient in that it is limited to just one aspect of freedom of religion, freedom of worship, and fails to extend its protection to numerous other aspects of religious liberty, such as the freedom from imposition of religious norms. Further, it does not deal with the right to convert and its corollary, the right to proselytize. No doubt, the narrow scope of the proposed wording stems from well calculated, mainly political, considerations (apparently to satisfy the demands of religious political parties). It is to be hoped, however, that this section will be amended before it is enacted into law and becomes part of the Constitution of Israel.

NOTES

1. See Articles 2, 13–18 of the Mandate for Palestine, and Articles 83 and 17 (1) (a) of the Palestine Order in Council of 1922.
2. H.C. 262/62, *Perez* v. *Kfar Shmaryahu Local Council,* 16 *Piskei Din* 2101, 2116 (per Justice Sussman).
3. Cr. A. 112/50, *Yosifof* v. *Attorney General,* 2 *Piskei Din* 486, 598, 612 (per Justice Landau).

4. H.C. 301/63, *Streit* v. *Chief Rabbi,* 18(1) *Piskei Din* 598, 612.

5. H.C. 103/67, *American Orphan Beth El Mission* v. *Minister of Social Welfare,* 21(2) *Piskei Din* 325.

6. H.C. 132/66, *Segev* v. *Safad Rabbinical Court,* 21(2) *Piskei Din,* 560.

7. See, e.g., Cr. A. 217/68, *Izramax* v. *State of Israel,* 22(2) *Piskei Din* 343, where Justice Silberg resorted to American case law regarding the Sabbath to justify the prohibition of the opening of a petrol station under a by-law.

8. E.g., Section 3 of the Local Authorities (Vesting of Public Property) Law, 1958, excludes property used for religious purposes and services from that which a local authority is empowered to acquire compulsorily for public purposes.

9. *Nezah Yisrael,* 154–55.

10. See B. England in 22 *Molad* 702–03 and the authorities that he cites. Cf. Y. Leibowitz, "Jewish Law as the Law of the State," 3 *Sura* 495.

11. In a Jewish state, however, there is the further requirement that the ancestral past of Judaism should not be forgotten.

12. See England, "The Relationship between Religion and State in Israel," 16 *Scripta Hierosolymitana* 274 (1969).

13. H.C. 58/66, *Shalit* v. *Minister of the Interior,* 23(2) *Piskei Din* 477, 602.

14. H.C. 51/69, *Rodnitzki* v. *Rabbinical Court of Appeal,* 24(1) *Piskei Din* 704, 712.

15. This critique of the distinction set up by Justice Landau also applies to the one suggested by Justice Silberg.

16. Cr. A. 217/68, *Izramax* v. *State of Israel,* 22(2) *Piskei Din* 343, 354 et seq.

17. H.C. 58/66, *Shalit.*

18. Even were the distinction adopted, it is not practical nor can it always help to justify the coercion of norms. Justice Silberg himself faced difficulties in explaining the nature of the Sabbath commandment and found in it both "rational" and "credal" elements intermingled. He also found it difficult to justify the closing of businesses on Jewish festivals and had to appeal to the fact of those festivals being national values. See Cr. A. 217/68, *Izramax,* 356–58.

19. H.C. 51/69, *Rodnitzki,* 712. There are further grounds for this view, but they lie outside the scope of the present study.

20. State Education Law, 1953, Section 2: "The object of State education is to base elementary education in the State on the values of Jewish culture and the achievements of science, on love of the homeland and loyalty to the State and the Jewish people."

21. In Cr. A. 217/68, *Izramax,* 353, Justice Silberg sums up the secular primary-purpose test adopted in the United States.

22. Cr. A. 217/68, *Izramax,* 362.

23. H.C. 231/63, *Retef Ltd.* v. *Minister of Commerce and Industry,* 17 *Piskei Din* 2730.

24. H.C. 105/54, *Lazarovitz* v. *Food Controller,* 10 *Piskei Din* 44, 55, per Justice Berinson. It may be contended, however, that prohibition of pig-breeding in respect of Jews is warranted, because the entire matter is rooted in Jewish national tradition.

25. H.C. 174/62, *League for Prevention of Religious Coercion* v. *Jerusalem City Council,* 16 *Piskei Din* 2665, 2668.

26. Cr. A. 217/18, *Izramax,* 362. Justice Berinson states: "As between one way of doing things in disregard of religious considerations and another way having regard for religious considerations but without placing upon the public too heavy a burden, the second is certainly to be preferred."

27. A similar reason serves in the United States to justify government acts supportive of religion. See P. Kurland in *Law and Religion* 18, 122 (1962).

28. *Hatza'ot Hok (Legislative Bills of the State of Israel)* (No. 1085) 448 [1972/73].

29. As no capital letters are used in Hebrew, it is not clear whether the section should be read as "worship of God," or "worship of god," any god. Also, *Elohim,* which is the Hebrew word for both God and gods, raises doubts and gives rise to construing the section as protecting freedom of worship of monotheistic religions only.

JEROME J. SHESTACK

>>>->>>->>>->>>->>>->>>->>>->>>->>> **13** <<-<<<-<<<-<<<-<<<-<<<-<<<-<<<-<<<-<<<

Human-Rights Issues in Israel's Rule of the West Bank and Gaza

Throughout modern history and for the greater part of ancient history Jews have been ruled by others, treated as strangers in alien lands. They won political and civil rights slowly and only after deprivation and suffering. And when enlightenment had seemingly arrived their world was torn asunder by the Holocaust. Jews know both how precious freedom is and how fragile.

In 1967, for the first time in modern history, Jews found themselves ruling over others, a large population not part of their own state. Because of the Six-Day War, Israel occupied the West Bank and the Gaza Strip and found it necessary to administer lands inhabited by over a million Arabs who, for the most part, were hostile to Israeli rule.

This was a strange and unwanted role for Jews. Had the Arab states been willing to make peace after 1948 it would not have happened. But events decreed otherwise and there has been no peace treaty or political solution since. For over ten years now Israel has ruled over the West Bank and Gaza.

What kind of rule has it been? How has the Jewish commitment to human rights stood up to the test? Has Israel met the standards one would expect of a Jewish state? These are not easy questions to answer. For even as Israel continues to occupy the West Bank and Gaza, it is surrounded by hostile neighbors and, indeed, a hostile world. In a state of siege one is likely to be defensive, not introspective.

I

As an objective matter, it would seem relatively simple to ascertain the condition of human rights in the West Bank and Gaza.* However, such is not the case. Emotions override objectivity on both sides of the ledger. A major complicating factor is that part of the Arab strategy is to make Israel appear a violator of human rights, with the result that the issue of human rights has become a political pawn in the Arab-Israeli controversy. Hence we are presented with the spectacle of Arab states whose own human-rights records are abysmal constantly complaining about human-rights violations in the occupied territories. One need have no particular astuteness to recognize that these complaints stem not from solicitude for human rights but from a design to arouse world opinion against Israel. This does not mean that those with partisan motives may not sometimes raise valid points, but it does signify that the charges must be looked at carefully since they are often fabricated for political ends. Moreover, in this situation, minor transgressions are magnified out of proportion and an overview is seldom taken.

In making human-rights evaluations one must know at the outset the standards to be applied. Even this is not a simple matter. In peace time, the Universal Declaration of Human Rights sets the standards for human-rights observance. While few nations can be said to comply fully with the Universal Declaration, the Declaration sets out the obligations against which performance can be measured. But the Universal Declaration of Human Rights was not intended for times of war or belligerency. The standards applicable during states of belligerency are far more limited. These are embodied in the law of belligerent occupation codified at the Hague Peace Conference in 1899 and 1907, often referred to as the Hague Regulations. In addition to the Hague Regulations, the

* For detailed sources, see Notes at end of essay.

duty of an occupying power is governed by the Geneva Convention of 1949, which contains various humanitarian provisions designed to protect the inhabitants of the occupied territory.

The international community assumes that Israel's presence in the West Bank and Gaza is that of a belligerent occupier and that, therefore, it is subject to the Hague Regulations and the Geneva Convention. Israel claims that an occupying power is a nation which displaces a legitimate sovereign; it contends that Jordan and Egypt, the previous ruling powers, respectively, did not enjoy that status in the West Bank and Gaza. Therefore, Israel regards itself more as a trustee than as an occupying power. From this, Israel argues that the Geneva and Hague rules do not technically apply. However, Israel maintains that it voluntarily abides by the Hague Regulations and the Geneva Convention. Thus, as a practical matter, the Regulations and Convention set forth standards by which the international community evaluates the Israeli administration.

The guiding principle of the Hague Regulations is found in Article 43, which requires an occupant to "take all steps in its power to re-establish and insure, as far as possible, public order and safety while respecting, unless absolutely prevented, the laws in force of the country." This provision requires Israel generally to keep in force the Jordanian and British Mandate laws in effect in 1967 in the West Bank and the Mandate laws then in effect in Gaza. For the most part, Israel has followed a policy of "non-interference" as required by international law. Thus, in the West Bank the local courts continue to administer local laws unchanged from those of the period prior to the occupation. In Gaza, how-ever, an administrative change was necessitated because the judicial functions there had been carried out by Egyptian personnel. In 1967 Israel reinstalled local Palestinian judges.

Although the local laws have largely remained in effect, Israel has taken the position that changes in local laws enacted for the *benefit* of the local population are not a violation of the laws of belligerent occupation. While one might dispute this position as a matter of technical international law, one could hardly quarrel with it in humanitarian terms. For example, in 1968 Israel changed the existing penal laws of the West Bank by abolishing the death penalty, certainly a humane change. The Arab courts have not questioned that amendment to the local laws. Another example was Israel's amendment of the Jordanian electoral law to extend suffrage to non-property holders and to some 33,000 female residents of the West Bank. Although Jordan denounced the amendment as illegal, it was a change which could reasonably be considered to benefit the local population. Because of that change the number of electors in the local elections of 1976 was considerably expanded.

Of course, whether or not a particular change is beneficial may become a point of controversy. Concepts which Israel may deem to be beneficial under its standards of democratic pluralism may appear foreign to the residents of the West Bank and Gaza. Similarly, improvement of conditions in the occupied territory may be beneficial to the local population but may also serve to make the territory dependent upon the occupier. For this reason, even so-called beneficial changes must be approached cautiously under international law. By and large, Israel has done so.

Israel's policy of non-interference encompasses not only the courts and administration of justice but also the range of government services in the territories. There is a minimal number of Israelis employed in government services in the West Bank and Gaza. The latest figures are not available, but as of June 1975 only about 3 percent of the personnel in the civil administration of the occupied territories was Israeli.

Non-interference is the standard of international law generally applicable to occupying states. A better test of Israel's humaneness is the extent to which Israel applies more liberal provisions of human rights than international law requires—derived from standards it applies to its own society. This is a difficult test for any occupier because an occupier inevitably faces security conditions which require restraints which would not be imposed under peace-time conditions. Considering the security problems, Israel appears to have displayed a remarkable sensitivity to the civil liberties of the inhabitants of the West Bank and Gaza.

An important human-rights standard, to which Jews are particularly attuned, is freedom of movement. Early in the occupation Israel set up a policy of "open bridges" between Jordan and the West Bank. Under this policy there has been considerable movement of people and trade between east and west. (However, many Arab travelers complain of harassing and undignified searches.) As of the middle of 1975 nearly 750,000 persons had crossed the bridges from east to west and over 600,000 from west to east. Travel between Israel proper and the West Bank was limited at first, but since July 1971 has been liberally allowed, as is permission for local inhabitants to visit other Arab states.

Another act of the Israel government, in June 1967, was to establish unqualified freedom of worship and access to holy places and full protection for the religious shrines of all religions. This did not exist under Jordanian rule. There has also been no impediment to the conduct of religious schools for Muslims in the occupied territories nor to the opportunity for religious teachers to train in Arab states. Israel has helped young residents of the territories to take examinations leading to Egyptian qualifications and there are over 7,000 persons who hold such qualifications. There have been complaints that Israel excised anti-Israel propaganda from Arab textbooks, but there is no privilege to inflammatory propaganda under international law or even under peace-time human-rights conventions.

Israel has also permitted considerable freedom to the media. Although subject to censorship, Arab newspapers are published in the territories and are often outspoken in criticizing Israel. There is no limitation on radio or television broadcasts from Arab states. Foreign correspondents have ready access to Arab inhabitants.

The holding of municipal elections is another liberal measure. Considering the risk of electing officials hostile to Israel, under international law Israel might have suspended local elections on security grounds. Major municipal elections took place in 1976 with a voter turnout of 68 percent. The result was the election of a list of radical and nationalistic Palestinians. Many of these officials have been quite vocal in expressing their hostility to Israel.

Still, implicit in any military occupation are restrictions on civil liberties because of security requirements. Political organizational activity is curtailed. Demonstrations have been forcibly dispersed. Curfews are imposed from time to time, sometimes of a fairly prolonged nature. Identity cards are required. Vehicles are frequently stopped for inspections, particularly in Israel proper. Homes are searched without warning. Such restrictions vary in severity with perceptions of security needs. There is always the danger of overreaction by nervous security forces and there have been instances of this in the West Bank and Gaza. Israel claims that its security restrictions are authorized under international law. Whether that is so depends, of course, on the value judgment one makes regarding security needs. A "sympathetic" judgment, however, does not lessen the indignity of the restrictions from the Arab viewpoint.

Considering the Israeli administration as a whole, Israel would seem to have more than met the requirements that international law imposes with respect to civil liberties of residents of occupied territory. Israelis note that in many ways the residents of the West Bank and Gaza enjoy more civil liberties than they did under Egyptian and Jordanian occupation and, indeed, more than the nationals of many Arab states. It is a fair point but not one likely to assuage local inhabitants opposed altogether to the Israeli presence. No matter how humane and decent Israel may be as an occupier it cannot make its presence welcome. This dilemma lies at the heart of the Israeli occupation, and it is not likely to be resolved in the absence of an overall peace settlement.

Another aspect of human rights relates to economic and social development which generally include such matters as employment, health care, sanitation, educational opportunity, and standard of living. International law provides few guidelines here other than to prohibit the occupying power from exploiting the occupied territory for its own purpose. The available statistics indicate that the economy of the West Bank and Gaza has advanced significantly since 1967. The gross national product has substantially risen each year and real per capita income since the Israeli occupation has increased by 80 percent in the West Bank and 120 percent in Gaza. Unemployment since 1967 has decreased, dropping from about 13 percent in the West Bank and 30 percent in Gaza to around 1 percent or less. Part of this, however, is due not to economic development in the West Bank and Gaza but because a significant number of residents of these territories are employed in Israel. Consumer goods, too, have increased: for example, there were six times as many family-owned refrigerators in the West Bank in 1976 than in 1967, and nine times as many in the Gaza Strip.

Under Israeli administration, housing conditions have also improved considerably. In Gaza, for example, the Egyptian administration had kept most of the Arab refugees in camps, where the housing conditions were deplorable. Although a great deal of substandard housing still exists, a substantial amount of new housing has been provided. The Commissioner General of the UN Relief and Works Agency for Palestinian Refugees (UNRWA) recently reported that 65 percent of the refugees in camps now live outside.

Health care has also improved substantially: for example, infant mortality in the West Bank has been reduced from 120 per 1,000 to 50 per 1,000. The ratio of physicians and nurses to population has increased sharply and the per capita expenditure for health services has more than tripled. Recently, a team of World Health Organization experts reported favorably on such developments but, since the report was favorable to Israel, it was not officially received at the United Nations. There are many other impressive statistics of this kind.

Israel frequently cites such statistics to show that the general standard of living in the West Bank and Gaza is better under the Israeli administration than it was under Jordanian and Egyptian rule. This is undoubtedly so, yet critics of Israel are more likely to make comparisons with the standard of living in Israel proper. Israel is a full-fledged parliamentary democracy with a progressive economy and the economic level in the territories does not match that of Israel. Such a comparison is not entirely irrelevant so long as Israel chooses to exercise jurisdiction over the West Bank and Gaza. Relevant or not, the dichotomy between Israel proper and the territories poses a continuing vulnerability for Israel.

II

The most controversial aspect of Israel's administration has arisen with respect to the question of whether Israel has violated international law by its treatment of security offenders. Although security offenses of persons in the territories are under Israeli military jurisdiction, defendants have available various due-process safeguards. All persons arrested are allowed counsel of their choice; some of the prominent defense lawyers of alleged terrorists have included outspoken critics of Israel. A person cannot be convicted by his confessions alone; corroborative evidence is needed. Application for relief to the Supreme Court of Israel can be made by any inhabitant of the occupied territories. There are also other safeguards for defendants. Israeli judges are independent and generally sensitive to the requirements of a fair trial.

A general test of the fairness of trials is the number of acquittals. In 1976, of the persons tried before a military tribunal, 408 were acquitted, which was a substantial percentage of those apprehended. Only twenty-six persons received more than ten years' imprisonment, and these included persons convicted of regular crimes as well as acts of terror.

However, Israel has come under attack principally with regard to the specific measures of administrative detention, treatment of detainees, deportation, and demolition of homes. It is claimed that these measures are contrary to the provisions of the Hague Regulations and the Geneva Convention. There is no doubt that Israel has engaged in deportations, detentions, and demolitions, although the extent of such measures is a matter of dispute. Israel claims that as a legal matter such measures are authorized for security reasons under the British Mandate regulations and in some cases under the Geneva Convention as well. A United Nations Special Committee that has addressed itself to this area is of the view that the Geneva Convention is the applicable law and that the threat to Israel's security has never been such as to warrant such controversial measures.

There is a fundamental difference in philosophy underlying these two positions. The United Nations Special Committee began with the premise that the Israeli occupation is unjustified and that there is a legitimacy to the Palestine Liberation Organization (PLO), *including* its terrorist activities. Israel, on the other hand, regards its occupation as a legitimate exercise of its right to self-defense and it views the PLO and other terrorist organizations as wanton, random murderers. It is not within the scope of this discussion to analyze terrorism or to draw distinctions between various types of terrorism. It bears emphasis, however, that the Palestinian brand of terrorism has been largely aimed at innocent civilians. Moreover, the terrorist activities are directed not only against Israelis but often against civilian Arabs who show cooperation with the Israeli administration. Such terrorism, of course, is a gross violation of human rights and severe security measures are warranted to restrain it, within the bounds of international law. Put another way, the Israeli experience with the

Palestinian terrorists in Maalot, Kiryat Shimona, the Tel Aviv highway, and other places would appear to evidence a sufficient threat to Israel's security to warrant strict measures to combat terrorism. Still, the issue cannot be satisfactorily dealt with in generalizations and particular security measures must be examined.

One of the controversial measures relates to the administrative detention of persons without trial. The essential justification for detaining a suspected terrorist without trial is for reasons of security. The information on the detainee may come from local inhabitants or intelligence agents whose lives might be jeopardized if they testified at an open trial. Under the Fourth Geneva Convention, such detention is permitted for imperative security reasons provided certain procedures are met, such as the availability of appeal and periodic review. Israel has provided procedures which more than meet the requirements of the convention. For example, every detention is reviewed every six months regardless of whether the detainee has appealed. If a detention is to exceed nine months, it must receive cabinet approval. Additionally, an Area Advisory Committee appointed by the Israel High Court reviews detention procedures at least three times a year.

Notwithstanding the sanction of administrative detention by the Geneva Convention, from a human-rights viewpoint there is a fundamental lack of due process in holding a person in prolonged detention without trial. The right to a prompt, fair trial in which one faces one's accuser should be considered a fundamental right for everyone, including terrorists.

Administrative detention is now less of a problem than it was in the period after the 1967 war, when the number of detainees probably reached over 2,000. This number has steadily decreased either by conviction or release, so that the number of such detainees is now less than 50. Recently, the attorney general of Israel indicated his opposition to administrative detention and some detainees have been released. It is to be hoped that all remaining detainees will be brought to trial promptly or released if the government chooses not to try them.

A controversial, related question is how detainees are treated. It has been alleged that when prisoners are first captured and interrogated they have been tortured and mistreated. Here there is no issue as to an interpretation of international law. Israeli officials agree that torture is wrong and without justification. The dispute arises as to whether it occurs in practice and, particularly, whether such abuse is government-sanctioned.

The principal official charges of torture have come from reports of a United Nations Special Committee, composed of nations having no diplomatic relations with Israel and openly hostile to the Jewish state. Unfortunately, the committee has often ignored accepted rules of evidence and received the loosest type of un-evaluated hearsay from highly partisan sources.

Israel has cited various examples designed to expose the un-reliability of the committee's reports. One such case on which the Special Committee reported is that of Mohamed Kader Derbas, who testified that he had been arrested by the Israelis in Gaza and castrated by them in an Israeli hospital. Committee experts supposedly verified this by visiting Derbas in Gaza. However, the records of the Gaza health department revealed that Derbas' tes-ticles were removed because of a tubercular infection at a hospital in Gaza prior to the Israeli occupation. Another example concerns the testimony of a former mayor of Ramallah, who stated that two Israeli soldiers had wrongfully shot and killed two Arabs and had not been punished. The committee reported that the testimony deserved "credence." A rudimentary investigation would have un-covered that an Israeli court had sentenced both soldiers to life imprisonment. There are many such examples which weaken or negate the committee's credibility. The reliability of the commit-tee's sources does not seem to have improved appreciably with sub-sequent reports.

Torture, of course, is a particularly emotive concept and various private groups that can be described as PLO sympathizers or Marxist-inspired have echoed the Special Committee's charges. Jewish groups generally react angrily to such charges, exposing the motives of the accusers and asking why they express solicitude for terrorists but not outrage at the acts of terror.

However, there have also been charges of mistreatment by re-sponsible groups. For example, in 1970, on the basis of inter-views, Amnesty International stated that a prima facie case has been made of abuse of prisoners in interrogation centers, warrant-ing an independent inquiry. And in 1977, a team of reporters from the *London Sunday Times* also claimed to have found ev-idence of torture and mistreatment of a number of detainees in interrogation centers. The *Sunday Times* report was widely quoted. Later, some of these charges, but not all, were shown to be inaccurate, casting doubt on the objectivity of the report. When the *New York Times* tried to verify the *Sunday Times* story, it found that the evidence did not meet its standards, and it did not treat the story in depth for that reason.

Israel has consistently tried to provide specific refutation of the alleged cases of mistreatment, but not always conclusively. It is usually difficult both to verify charges of torture and to refute them. The physical evidence looked at long after the fact is generally inconclusive. There are motives to make spurious charges. A prisoner who confesses voluntarily may claim he was tortured to protect himself against retribution from his fellows. Moreover, some of those who claim to have been tortured are highly politically motivated persons who are part of the terrorist organization. A terrorist who has no scruples against killing children is not likely to have scruples against lying about torture.

There are also motives to make spurious denials. Interrogators do not have the sensitivities of high-court judges, particularly in dealing with terrorists. Interrogators invariably deny any wrongdoing and can be skillful in protecting each other. It is not easy to resolve who is telling the truth.

Israel has vehemently denied any government-sanctioned torture. It has issued strict orders against such brutality. While it acknowledges that "rogue policemen" sometimes violate these orders, it claims to punish violators. Israel also cites its adherence to the rule of law and points to various procedures in its court system designed to discourage mistreatment. These include full hearings in court on charges of torture or coerced confession and refusal to accept a confession without corroborative evidence.

After the *Sunday Times* report, Israel adopted a policy that allows International Red Cross observers to visit detainees after the first fourteen days of their detention in an interrogation center and sooner in special circumstances. Under the Geneva Convention, saboteurs or persons suspected of activities hostile to the security of the occupying power may be regarded as having forfeited rights of communication. The present move, therefore, is a forward step and has been welcomed by international human-rights organizations. However, an even shorter access period would be desirable.

Various human-rights organizations have urged Israeli officials to allow a non-governmental commission to conduct a formal inquiry into the charges. So far, Israel has not invited such an inquiry although Israel does allow reporters and other investigators to interview prisoners and former prisoners. This in itself has prophylactic value, since nations which engage in systematic torture do not generally afford access to prisoners. However, informal access is not a substitute for a formal inquiry. One can understand a refusal to allow an inquiry by hostile and partisan United Nations committees, but there is no sound reason for rejecting an objective investigation by an independent, non-governmental human-rights commission. On the contrary, by encouraging such an inquiry, Israel would have the opportunity to put to rest conclusively the charges of mistreatment.

In Israel, convicted terrorists are not executed but imprisoned. Most of the complaints about the prisons revolve around crowded conditions, visitation privileges, recreation facilities, and the like, but rarely mistreatment of prisoners. The International Red Cross has access to these prisons, as do other human-rights organizations. There is a severe problem of overcrowding and lack of recreational and work facilities in the prisons, about which the International Red Cross has complained. Crowding is a condition found in most prisons around the world; and Israeli authorities have indicated their concern over that problem. However, to date they have not taken sufficient remedial action to cure the problem. Generally, however, it would appear that Israeli prison officials administer humanely the prisons in which security offenders are jailed. Of course, prison conditions vary from prison to prison and the battle for decent treatment of prisoners is a never-ending one, even in progressive societies.

III

Another area of controversy concerns the deportation of civilians from the occupied territories. Article 49 of the Geneva Convention prohibits deportations to the territory of the occupying power or to that of any other country. Israel claims that this provision was inspired by Nazi practices of deporting prisoners to work in slave and labor camps and Israeli officials assert that it does not apply to persons guilty of severe security violations, such as terrorists and saboteurs, who would otherwise be tried and imprisoned. From a human-rights viewpoint, deportation to the East Bank is certainly less severe than detention or imprisonment in the West Bank. Nevertheless, such deportations are punishments; they have sometimes been carried out without affording adequate notice and the opportunity to face one's accusers at a trial, essential elements of due process. Human-rights organizations, therefore, correctly oppose such practices. Israel claims that in recent years, deportation has been used infrequently. However, even for a small number it is an undesirable practice.

The question of demolition of houses allegedly used to shelter and aid terrorists also has been the subject of much controversy. Israel claims that such measures are authorized both under the British Mandate Defense Regulations and Jordanian laws in effect in 1967. Under the Geneva Convention, however, such action is prohibited unless rendered absolutely necessary by military operations. Israel contends that such necessity has existed, while Jordan and many international agencies claim the opposite. Such demolition would also seem to contravene the provisions of the Geneva Convention against collective punishment, although Israel maintains that only those guilty were punished.

There have been varying reports of the numbers of houses demolished. The largest number of demolitions took place during the period immediately following the 1967 war, when they may have reached the thousands. Thereafter, the number decreased sharply. A United Nations Special Committee reported 109 demolitions between May 1970 and April 1971. The number has been much lower since.

Israel has defended such demolitions as necessary to counter and deter terrorist activity from the occupied territories. It may well be a deterrent; most harsh measures are. Nonetheless, from a human-rights viewpoint, demolition is not a desirable practice, since the owners of the houses are not afforded an opportunity to defend against the charges of harboring terrorists. The practice now appears to have virtually stopped in the territories.

One other controversial issue sometimes raised in a human-rights context is that of Israeli settlements in the West Bank. The number of Israeli settlers in the West Bank is in dispute, but as of the latter part of 1978, they probably did not number more than seven or eight thousand. There are arguments pro and con regarding the legality of the settlements, but the weight of legal opinion is that they violate the Geneva Convention. Apart from the legal issue, emotions run high on the issue of settlements. Israelis recall that in many cases they lived in these areas for decades before being driven out by the Arabs in the 1929 riots or in the 1948 war. Arabs tend to view the settlements as a prelude to annexation. For now, the issues involving the settlements are largely political ones. However, a human-rights issue arises if the settlements displace inhabitants or misappropriate their resources. To the extent that this has happened it is wrong and should be redressed by the Israeli government.

It is also argued that the settlements jeopardize self-determination in the territories, and that self-determination is a human right. One of the most complex issues in international law is that of self-determination—for whom is it appropriate and when? It is pertinent that during the nineteen years of the Egyptian occupation of Gaza and the Jordanian occupation of the West Bank there was no talk of self-determination for those areas. From a human-rights viewpoint self-determination may be counter-productive, for instance, where it results in rule by a dictatorial, irredentist regime—which would certainly be most likely if the PLO came to power. In any event, some 8,000 settlers among a population of over a million will hardly affect the issue of self-determination one way or another. The settlements issue undoubtedly will not be resolved except in the context of a comprehensive peace treaty.

IV

What, then, is a fair overall conclusion? Compared to the human-rights performance of other occupying nations in modern history, Israel's record in the West Bank and Gaza ranks high. Using the standard of applicable international norms, Israel's record is still commendable. Judged by the standards one would expect of a Jewish state with a religious and historic tradition of humanistic values, there are deficiencies but also many credits. On balance, despite some strains, Israeli rule has been decidedly humane.

Of course, Israel will not be judged fairly by most of the international community. This fact is a source of distress to Israel. Israelis are outraged that their every act is scrutinized with no similar scrutiny for actions of neighboring states. Israelis consider it unfair that minor transgressions in the territories are censured while serious abuse of human rights by other nations goes unaddressed. Israelis deplore the lack of recognition of their humaneness. All this is certainly unfair, but such, unfortunately, are the political realities.

What of the future? Israel can cope with unfairness—but can a Jewish state cope with what the occupation does to its own values? So long as Israel remains in the West Bank and Gaza, security considerations will keep it from giving the inhabitants there the full measure of liberties Israel permits its own citizens. This double standard must perforce be repugnant to Jewish values. Even worse, if agitation in the territories increases, Israel may have to engage in repressive counter-measures or reprisals. The pity of this would be not only for the inhabitants of the territories but for the Israelis as well. Decent, humane societies cannot be built under the tensions of confrontation.

Leaving the West Bank and the Gaza Strip may, indeed, pose a threat to Israel's physical security; staying there may pose a threat to its moral values. Other options create their own acute dilemmas. Jews have never had easy choices.

This essay was written before the Camp David accords of October 1978 and the subsequent developments. The various observations that I have made here remain pertinent. Negotiations over the West Bank and Gaza will undoubtedly continue for some time to come; indeed, security problems there may become aggravated during any future negotiations, testing further the Israeli commitment to a humane administration. It is to be hoped that full peace in the areas under consideration will become before too long a reality. In any event, the Israeli role in the West Bank and Gaza during the crucial decade of 1967–78 will continue to be examined critically and evaluated. That should surprise no one. Throughout the ages Jews have been held accountable for actions which departed from Jewish values—and that, perhaps, is the key to Jewish survival.

NOTES

The literature on the subjects dealt with in this essay is voluminous. However, most of it is quite subjective or openly propagandistic and of little value in attempting to reach an evaluation. The observations here are based on a study of the available literature, numerous interviews, and first-hand inspections, including investigations of a number of Israeli prisons detaining security offenders. Some of the sources that the author found useful on the principal topics discussed are the following:

The Applicability of the Geneva Convention to the West Bank and Gaza and the Question of Sovereignty

Thomas S. Kuttner, "Israel and the West Bank: Aspects of the Law of Belligerent Occupation," *Israel Yearbook on Human Rights* 7 (1977), 166 (hereafter, *IYHR*); statement of Ambassador Chaim Herzog to the General Assembly of the United Nations, October 26, 1977; Allan Gerson, "Trustee-Occupant: The Legal Status of Israel's Presence in the West Bank," 14 *Harvard International Law Journal* 1 (1973) (presentation of Israeli position); Morris Greenspan, "Human Rights in the Territories Occupied by Israel," 12 *Santa Clara Lawyer* 377 (1972).

Reports of the United Nations Special Committee to Investigate Israeli Practices Affecting the Human Rights of the Population of the Occupied Territories

Dov Shefl, "The Protection of Human Rights in Areas Administered by Israel: United Nations Findings and Reality," *IYHR* 3 (1973), 337; Nigel S. Rodley, "The United Nations and Human Rights in the Middle East," 38 *Social Research* 17 (1971); John C. Bender, "Ad Hoc Committee and Human Rights Investigations: A Comparative Case Study in the Middle East," 38 *Social Research* 241 (1971); Kuttner, *supra;* Greenspan, *supra.* Reports of the United Nations Special Committee: Report A/8389 (Oct. 5, 1970, Sept. 17, 1971); Report A/8389/Add. 1 and Add. 2 (Dec. 10, 1972); Report A/9148 (Oct. 15, 1973); Report A/9148/Add. 2 (Nov. 20, 1973); Report A/9817 (Oct. 25, 1974); Report A/10272 (Oct. 13, 1975); Report A/31/218 (Oct. 1, 1976); Report A/32/284 (Oct. 24, 1977); Amiel Najari, statement of November 14, 1977, analyzing the Report of the UN Special Committee, UN Doc. A/SAC/32/Sr. 23.

Military and Judicial Administration of the West Bank and Gaza

Meir Shamgar, "The Observance of International Law in the Administered Territories," *IYHR* 1 (1971), 262; Nitza Shapiro-Libai, "Territories Administered by Israel, Military Proclamations, Orders and Judicial Revision: Extracts" in *IYHR* 1 (1971), 419; "Law and Courts in the Israel-held Areas," Institute for Legislative Research and Comparative Law, Hebrew University (1970); "Three Years of Military Government, 1967–1970," by the Coordinator of Government Operations in the Administered Territories, Ministry of Defense (Israel) (see also supplements updating this report).

Economic Development in the West Bank and Gaza

Brian Van Arkadie, *Benefits and Burdens: A Report on the West Bank and Gaza Strip Economies Since 1967* (Carnegie Endowment for International

Peace, 1971); see also Israel Kimbi and Benjamin Hyman, *A Socio-economic Survey of Jerusalem, 1967–1975* (1978); Kuttner, *supra;* Herzog, *supra;* Anne Sinai and Allen Pollock, eds., *The Hashemite Kingdom of Jordan and the West Bank* (American Academic Association for Peace in the Middle East, 1977). For a highly critical view of Israel, see Abdeen Jabara, *Israel's Violation of Human Rights in Arab Territories Occupied in June 1967* (Association of Arab-American University Graduates, September 1976).

Human-Rights Issues in the West Bank and Gaza (Detention, Deportation, Torture, Etc.)

Stephen M. Boyd, "The Applicability of International Law to the Occupied Territories," *IYHR* 1 (1971), 258; Morris Greenspan, "Human Rights in the Territories Occupied by Israel," 12 *Santa Clara Lawyer* 377 (1972); Kuttner, *supra;* Jabara, *supra;* Arie Pach, "Human Rights in West Bank Military Courts," *IYHR* 7 (1977), 222; Annual Reports of the International Committee of the Red Cross; David Libai and Nitza Shapiro-Libai, "Freedom from Arbitrary Detention, Israel Law in the Light of International Instruments," *IYHR* 4 (1974), 335. The *London Sunday Times*, story referred to in the text, appeared on June 9, 1977; response in the *Times,* September 18, 1978; transcript of press conference with Israel State Attorney Gabriel Bach, July 29, 1977 (Israel Office of Information). Israeli replies to the charges were transmitted by the Permanent Representative of Israel to the Secretary General of the United Nations on November 15, 1977, UN Doc. A/SPC/32/Sr. 23; critical comments on the *Times* report by David Krivine appear in the *Jerusalem Post,* August 5, 1977, October 28, 1977, and October 17, 1978 (international edition).

TWO

THE HISTORICAL DEVELOPMENT IN
JEWISH THOUGHT AND EXPERIENCE

Classical Sources

HERBERT CHANAN BRICHTO

14
The Hebrew Bible on Human Rights

The concept of human rights is commonly believed to be a product of Western thought in the last few centuries. It was in the eighteenth century that the idea found full expression, when the French rationalists and the American colonial Deists promulgated universal, natural, or human rights as a revolutionary doctrine. In this campaign they were confronted by several groups, including royalty, nobility, or clergy who resorted to scriptural authority to justify their claims to special status. Such proclamations of biblical sanction for human inequality did not go unchallenged, of course, and Scripture was often cited to confound claims made in its name. The rationalists' response in this debate, however, was to ground the absolute rights of all men in the absolute status of man—a status derived from the primary ultimacy which man enjoyed by nature rather than by grant of a divine monarch. Note as confirmation of this, which term holds pride of place in the phrase, "the Laws of Nature and Nature's God." In the rationalist view, once man's absolute value was freed of dependence on a divine king, the justification of human

equality was no longer vulnerable to the citations or interpretations of a sacred text.

The Vocabulary of Human Rights

The absence of an explicit vocabulary of human rights in the
Bible would also appear to support the conclusion that the
search for this concept in biblical literature is a futile, anachro-
nistic exercise. Thus, a concordance of the Bible in English has no
entry for *human,* and the listings under *right* do not contain the
abstraction expressed today by the plural *rights.* This linguistic
argument, however, is misleading. Literal translations often distort
meaning, and a mechanical lexical approach veils rather than re-
veals the concepts which a civilization will express in a given
language. Biblical Hebrew, for example, has an overwhelming
preference for concrete and particular formulations over the
general and the abstract.

The subtle ambiguities of biblical Hebrew that are relevant to
any search for a concept of human rights in the Bible may be
illustrated by the fact that there is no single word to express the
idea of justice. There is a word, *mishpat,* which has a host of
meanings: custom, tradition, wont, norm, mores, judgment. And
in addition to standing for the entire judicial process, *mishpat* may
represent any component of that process; that is, arraignment,
indictment, trial, verdict, sentence, execution of sentence. Another
term *tsedek,* or *tsedakah,* has the sense of right or rightness. The
abstract term *justice* is best expressed in Hebrew by a hendiadys,
that is, by two terms joined by the conjunction *and* which together
express a single idea, as, for example, "good and mad," "very
angry." Thus, the Biblical phrase *tsedek umishpat,* literally "rightness and judgment," means "right judgment," and hence it is the
term which is appropriately translatable as "justice."

If we pursue this illustration further, it will become clear why
the interpretation of biblical thought requires the translation of
concepts rather than of words. The moral ideas cannot be read
literally, out of context, as is often done from a handful of
passages. The root of *tsedek,* for example, may express in addition
to "rightness" the following: merit, justification, victory, vindication. Accordingly, the *tsadik,* the person to whom the property of
tsedek is ascribed, in one context is a righteous individual, and in

another, a litigant who is in the right in a particular suit. The contrary person, called a *rasha,* may be a wicked person or a litigant whose case has no merit. It follows that a righteous person can be the *rasha* in a particular suit while a scoundrel can in such circumstances be the *tsadik.*

Contextual Interpretation of Biblical Categories

The expression *human rights* involves a double assumption. First, that there is a universal, humanity. (The term *human* implies that considerations of differences in such subcategories as race, creed, nationality, sex, and social rank are not relevant.) Second, that entitlements accrue to anyone by virtue of his belonging to that common humanity. Where membership in any of the subcategories listed entails lesser rights, we would have to conclude either that such membership makes the person in some sense less than human, or that the full rights spoken of may not be characterized as rights qua human.

The Bible presents us with a perplexity. On the one hand, it contains the most sweeping definition of man and ascribes to him supreme dignity and sanctity, endowing him with a charter of rights which are considered virtually absolute. On the other hand, it discriminates among humans in terms of kinship, polity, sex, ideology, and social status—and this to such an extent that one might conclude that there are no human rights as such, or that only a tiny proportion of what passes for mankind is to be classified as human with human entitlements. Thus, if life, liberty, and the pursuit of happiness comprise a charter of human rights, then the entire charter in principle and in detail may be seen as nullified by biblical prescription of capital punishment, war, conquest, execution for transgression of taboos, bride sale and purchase, slavery, and so on.

The key to the resolution of this perplexity lies in the recognition that the Bible, even while setting forth an ideal of man, attempts to cope with the existential facts of human divisions and of human failure to exercise freedom in obedience to the divine will.

The supreme dignity of man, in contradistinction to all other living species, is expressed in man as a special act of Creation, in his characterization as "the very image of God" and in the mandate of sovereignty given to him (Gen. 1:26,28; 2:7). The biblical language of Gen. 9:6 explicitly interprets this divine image as symbolic of the sanctity of human life.[1] That all the races of man are included in this category is made clear by the tracing —first from Adam, then from Noah—of the descent of all from a common ancestor.

The failure of universal man to live up to this standard of dignity is mythopoeically expressed in several crises, each of which eventuates in a new beginning. The Fall of Adam is followed by human propagation outside Eden; the Deluge, by the subsequent division of the earth by settlement by Noah's sons; the Tower of Babel, by a new dispersion of mankind. These failures prepare the stage in the biblical story for the emergence of Israel as the instrument of God's plan for mankind. Universal man, though failed, is not abandoned. A particular segment, the stock of Abraham, is now charged with showing the way to all mankind: ". . . Abraham is to become a great and populous nation and all the nations of the earth are to bless themselves by him. For I have singled him out, that he may instruct his children and his posterity to keep the way of the Lord by doing what is just and right . . ." (Gen. 18:18,19). In the biblical drama, the rest of mankind waits in the wings as Israel holds center stage. It is Israel's career now which will determine whether mankind can have a model for success, or whether man will fail in this particular prototype as he previously had in the universal history.

The covenantal relationship between God and Israel[2] is to be understood, then, as the same kind of relationship which the Deity would have between himself and mankind. The latter He holds in abeyance while testing Israel in that relationship. Covenantal morality and law, which applies to all members of the covenant community, is therefore prototypical of the law and morality which would apply to all mankind—were all mankind to constitute itself, as God had first willed, a covenant community. Every right enjoyed by an Israelite is thus, in ideal terms, a human right; just as every disability suffered is a limitation of a human right. Scripture, however, focuses on the existential, not the ideal, with the consequence that while universal moral standards must govern the relationship between the covenant community and other communities, the overwhelming proportion of biblical law and precept applies to the closed world of the covenant community. To put it differently, biblical law and morality is primarily tribal. Since this characterization is almost always associated with the negative and pejorative connotations of clannish loyalty and xenophobic license, let us call it tribe-contextual rather than tribal.

This transposition of context is the crucial interpretive perspective required in order to understand the issues of biblical law and society. A contextual approach excludes any effort to mechanically apply such categories as inequality and discrimination to specifics of covenantal (tribe-contextual) law and precept. For a relevant analogy, consider how misleading it would be to censure as discriminatory a life-insurance company on the grounds that it does not extend death benefits to non-policyholders, or denies them to those in default of premium payments. It will, nevertheless, be instructive to examine the stance of the covenant community in regard to the rights of others, both individuals and communities.

Two caveats before we proceed. First, the scriptural world-view cannot be appreciated except by reference to neighboring societies and cultures in the ancient Near East. While many biblical values emerged in response or reaction to those of the pagan ambience, many biblical values represented the achievement of pre-Israelite civilizations and were integrated as axiomatic in the scriptural value system.[3] Our exposition of biblical values, therefore, implies neither a claim that these are necessarily original in Israel nor an implication of invidious comparison with other ancient value systems. Second, while it is both convenient and meaningful to speak of rights as absolute, even such absolute values as the right to life and liberty may clash with each other. In any such conflict, there is a hierarchy of values which compels one to yield to another. But this is not a negation of the defeated or defeasible value. Thus, for example, the prescription of capital punishment for murder or for any other serious crime is not a negation of the absolute value of human life but rather a forfeiture deemed necessary for the preservation of that absolute value.

On Race, Racialism, and Racism; War and Genocide

In its purely descriptive sense, the term *race* is essentially a kinship concept designating a group descended from a common ancestor or ancestral stock. *Racism* is the assignment of different degrees of value—dignity, capacity, entitlement—to kinship groups on the assumption that they represent different species, that is, groups that are derived from no single stock or far removed from a common stock. The racist view asserts that these qualitative distinctions determine disabilities and justify discrimination in assignment of rights. The term *racialism,* however, we shall use to designate the sense of consciousness of racial differences without prejudice as to value.

The striking conclusion from an analysis of the Bible is that neither in ancient Israel nor in the world around it is there a shred of evidence attesting to racism. As for racialism, the consciousness of genetic families seems to have entailed little significance for biblical man. Accordingly, membership in one or another of the three great divisions of humanity—as descendants of Shem, Ham, or Japhet—does not determine Israel's relationship of amity or enmity, tolerance or discrimination, vis-à-vis foreign groups.[4] The category of consequence for human relations was the *family as a religious entity,*[5] constituted of the ancestral dead, the living generations, and future descendants. Human existence outside the context of the religion-family was virtually inconceivable. Individual needs and rights derived from any yielded precedence to the needs and rights of this family. Thus, the right of an individual to life itself or to any of its benefits might be forfeited when in conflict with the survival needs of the family.

An important documentation of this thesis is found in the biblical attitude toward capital punishment. Capital punishment is not viewed as a negation of the human right to life. Even when applied in connection with the transgression of a taboo, it represents the forfeiture of that right as the consequence of an action which jeopardized the life of the family. In like manner the existential human condition of war[6] poses the ultimate threat to the family's existence. It therefore warrants the taking of life in self-defense, just as it justifies the hazarding of the lives of the individual defenders for the sake of preserving the religion-family.

Perhaps no aspect of biblical morality is so shocking to modern sensibilities as the ancient convention of the war of extirpation, referred to by the biblical phrase, *herem*-war. This aspect of Israel's pagan heritage must be viewed in the light of the religion-family concept. Real property was for the ancients a religious, rather than simply an economic or political, concept. The sundering of a kinship group from its ancestral soil represented a death sentence not only for the generation in exile but for the entire religion-family—for generations yet unborn and for the ancestral shades in the afterlife. Imperialist wars had as their object the exaction of tribute from neighboring nations—and many a prophet counseled Israel to pay such tribute rather than resort to rebellion against a foreign suzerain. However, the pressure of national and tribal migrations in the ancient world inevitably created a situation in which incompatible populations struggled for territorial survival.[7]

What is noteworthy in Scripture as concerns the program of war against the populations which Israel is to supplant in the Promised Land is that the victims are not regarded as less than human or as inferior racial stock. Self-serving as the justification may be, Israel's predecessors on the land are seen as having defaulted on their right to territory and survival by reason of a long history of inveterate immorality.[8] By contrast, the divine Landlord who brings Israel to populate the territory to be vacated warns his new tenants against encroaching upon neighboring peoples who had in earlier times, by God's fiat, also supplanted elements of the original sinful stock.[9]

The clue to a people's essential incompatibility with Israel is the injunction against intermarriage. The noteworthy point is that, except for the Amorites, who are "sinful," this injunction is extended to only two peoples, the Ammonites and the Moabites, *both of whom are Israel's kindred.* The injunction against intermarriage is grounded on an historic trespass of kinship obligations. The Edomites and the Egyptians are explicitly excluded from this prohibition, which applied to no other of the many peoples with whom Israel had contact.[10]

Accordingly, concepts of racism derived from modern experience fail to explain the relationships prevalent in the culture of the biblical Middle East. The patterns of group and ethnic conflict are real, but they are complexly woven and do not fit by any means into a modern framework of racist interpretation.

On Freedom and Slavery, Social Equality and Inequality

As peace and freedom are the ideal condition of man, while war and enmity are his existential and sinful condition, so freedom and autonomy are the biblical ideal, while subjugation, servitude, and slavery are all too often the existential rule. The ideal of freedom for all men is implicit in the equality of all men as a consequence of their descent from a common ancestor. This ideal is often expressed explicitly in regard to a number of institutions prescribed for Israel, characteristically associated with the number seven: the weekly Sabbath; the seventh year of release from debt; the six-year limitation on servitude, marking the seventh year as that in which freedom is to be regained.

Freedom is essentially the capacity to dispose of time. The Sabbath is recognized as a symbol of such freedom by its association with the liberation of Israel from Egyptian bondage.[11] What has not generally been perceived is that same symbolism in the association of the Sabbath with the divine act of Creation.[12] God's lordship over the substance of the world and over its denizens is clear in His being their Creator.[13] God's lordship over time is expressed in the symbolism of His performing the acts of Creation in six days, abstaining from work on the seventh day and hallowing it. Israel's observance of the Sabbath expresses recognition of His lordship over time by the act (as it were) of returning time to its lord every seventh day: "Six days *may* you labor, the seventh is the Lord's."[14] Despite the fact that the theology of freedom is for the most part expressed in the Bible in symbolic and mythopoeic fashion rather than in categorical proposition, there can be little question that God does represent the principle of freedom and is the Author of man's freedom. As a consequence, service to God is considered to be the highest celebration of human freedom.

The limitations of freedom are generally expressed in biblical Hebrew by a form of the term *eved*. This term has a broad range of connotations and is incorrectly rendered by the word "slave." The *eved* of an emperor may be a vassal king, just as a vizier may be the *eved* of a king, or a foreman of a landowner. Slavery in the sense of *humans as property* is very rarely the denotation of forms of the root *eved* in Scripture. A case in point is the status of the Israelites who were liberated from Egypt. As distinguished from the normal denotation of a slave class, that is, chattel, the Israelites in Egypt owned property in the form of vast flocks, had unimpaired rights to the grazing lands of Goshen, maintained their family and tribal integrity, and constituted an autonomous community within the Egyptian homeland. The servitude they endured, as described, was a (possibly) discriminatory form of corvée labor. Work quotas assigned by the Pharaoh were enforced by *Israelite* headmen. Egypt as "the house of bondage" is an expression emblematic of a society ruled by a god-king. Hence Egypt is the "iron furnace" in which all men are reduced under the monolithic tyranny of a mortal monarch held to be divine. Egyptian society may be contrasted to Mesopotamian societies where the rule of law was asserted as subjecting the monarch himself to its standards.[15]

Within Israel itself, slave status as such was for the most part restricted to non-Israelites, usually captives taken in war or purchased. As in Bedouin societies until today, even these slaves were considered members of the religion-family. Upon manumission they took their places as free mmbers of the family, entitled to all perquisites and subject to no disabilities, regardless of racial or national origin.[16] To see a discriminatory idea in this restriction of slave status to non-Israelites is to overlook the existential position of the covenant community in a non-covenantal world. For Israel to have yielded the universal prerogative of warring peoples to enslave captives in the name of the ideal value of human freedom would have been analogous to unilateral disarmament in a world of bellicose states. God's covenant with Israel does not require Israel to commit ethnic or national suicide.

The basic pentateuchal legislation in regard to the *eved* deals not with slavery but with *indentured service,* which but for the setting of a time limit would eventuate in slavery for all practical purposes. While the phrase *eved ivri*[17]—usually translated as "Hebrew slave"—is normally assumed by both the rabbinic tradition and contemporary scientific scholars to refer to Israelites alone, the available evidence is that the term refers to indenture and is applicable to native or foreigner.[18] Nevertheless, the basic legislation in regard to the *eved ivri* appears in intercovenantal (tribe-contextual) context and must be seen, almost certainly, as having reference to fellow Israelites.[19]

We revert now to our definition of freedom as the capacity to dispose of time. That it is this capacity which the *eved* surrenders to his master emerges from the relevant biblical passages. A master who strikes an *eved* dead is subject to the normal penalty of retribution for murder. The right of the master to discipline his *eved* by means of physical punishment is explicit, on the grounds that "he is his money"; that is to say, the *eved* represents an investment of the master's capital (his labor has been paid for in advance and he receives his subsistence) and the master is entitled to the labor due him. Hence it is that death of an *eved* occurring some time subsequent to a beating is viewed as a happenstance and does not subject the master to retribution. On the other hand, should a blow by a master destroy the eye or tooth of an *eved,* he immediately gains his freedom—without any recompense to the master for any labor yet due him in terms of his capital investment. The logic behind this is clear. Since the *eved* is a bound servant, his time (temporarily) is not his own, but his life and person is. Any impairment of his person, or his faculties, which extends beyond the period of his service results in default by his master, a default which may represent a loss considerably greater than the normal payment for comparable mayhem committed upon a free man.

On Economic and Political Status

The collection of writings which constitutes the Hebrew Bible derives from a time span of almost two thousand years. Accordingly it reflects problems and remedies of a society in historical flux. During this span, a semi-nomadic pastoral family evolves, both genetically and by accession, into a complex of clans and tribes. These tribes infiltrate a territory which is the land bridge between Asia and Africa and which, therefore, has been the scene of many waves of mass migrations and successive settlements. Tribal autonomy yields to everchanging degrees of central administration—federation, monarchy, theocracy—all the while that family and tribal mores continue in force wherever they are not usurped or supplanted by central authority. Pastoralism is succeeded by an agricultural economy in which the family holds inalienable title to its sacred real estate, a claim which becomes increasingly difficult to maintain as cities proliferate, feudal or oligarchical lords expropriate the peasantry, and new classes of artisans, merchants, professional soldiers, and royal officials emerge.

It has been argued that the biblical ethos has provided the sole ideological base for democracy, asserting as an ideal the fatherhood of God and the brotherhood of man, yet recognizing the existential sinfulness of man. Man is delivered from anarchy and its evils only by the various institutions of social and political authority. Scripture condones these emergent political institutions although it does not prescribe them. Whatever its political form or organization, society is required by Scripture to uphold the standards of minimum human dignity. These standards include, for example, the right of any Israelite to satisfy his hunger at his fellow's expense but not to harvest his fellow's labors. Among the provisions for the administration of justice are many examples of social legislation such as those permitting the poor and the alien access to harvest gleanings, unreaped borders, and the forgotten sheaf. Another illustration of these egalitarian standards is the protest against the creation of landed estates.

What must be emphasized is that these precepts inculcating care and concern for underprivileged individuals and classes are attempts to palliate the existential consequences of a society which is less than ideal. They are by no means to be taken as condonation of the inequable condition. The prophetic demands that society's stewards take up the suit of the widow and the orphan[20] is a consequence of the vulnerability of those who have no protection, not a reflection of intrinsically inferior status on entitlement. Similarly, the alien was normally propertyless and underprivileged, but not intrinsically or necessarily so. So, too, membership in the Levites, a hieratic caste, entailing high privilege in one set of circumstances, might at another time result in straitened condition. Reduction to penury was not yet the worst of fates; indebtedness was. Failure to repay a loan or the accumulating interest was the chief cause of distraints on property or persons, culminating in a termless form of indenture comparable to peonage. Hence the precept against charging of interest. That such a precept applied only to a fellow Israelite and not to an outsider in no way constitutes a double standard. The "foreigner" (the Hebrew term used is *nokhri*—as distinct from *ger,* the resident alien) was not subject to the moral obligation to lend without interest. Hence, by principle of reciprocity, he was not privy to the privilege of borrowing without interest.

Perhaps the single greatest obstacle to our appreciation of the essentially non-discriminatory and non-xenophobic nature of biblical law and precept is the argument that there is in the Bible a refusal to tolerate any religion beside its own. Israel's monolatrous or monotheistic passion is commonly understood as spilling over from ideological intolerance to discrimination against adherents of incompatible religions.

We would argue, to the contrary, that the fanatical biblical zeal for monolatrous or monotheistic worship of the Lord must be recognized in its restricted reference to the covenant community and its sacred territory. While the one true religion of Israel is seen as the model and exemplar for all peoples and nations, nowhere in the biblical record is there even the thought of exporting it in coercive fashion beyond Israel's territories or of subjecting non-Israelites to its canons of faith and praxis. In Deuteronomy the proscription of human sacrifice and nature-worship for the covenant community explicitly states that the Deity Himself has allotted such false worship to all the other peoples on earth (Deut. 18:9–14). While Israel's covenant with the One God is seen as a boon and privilege entailing the obligations of grateful loyalty, Scripture's attitude to pagan religion is one of condescension and contempt: the pagans are more to be pitied than loathed. Crucially, paganism is not in itself grounds for the discriminatory oppression of its practitioners—even within the borders of Israel's sacred territory.[21] Hence it is that while an Israelite may not worship other gods even outside Israel, the sacrifices brought by pagans to Israel's God in Israelite shrines are not predicated on their abandoning their own deities. Participation in the sacrifical Passover rite is the only occasion for which circumcision is a prerequisite for the resident alien or *ger*.[22]

On the Status of Women

Every age indulges in the luxury of invidiously comparing its values with those of the past. As accumulation of scientific knowledge and technological innovation expands the reach of humankind increasing the range of its moral options and eliminating some of the exigencies of survival, our vision of human potential continues to expand. Perhaps, then, it is only to be expected that from our own age of egalitarianism—which has been rendered possible and feasible by changes in the patterns of specialization and division of labor—the Bible would be viewed as a textbook of male chauvinism. In the light of our vast knowledge of the civilizations of the ancient Near East, however, this criticism cannot be sustained. Only in the most recent decades, and only in several Western societies, has the female sex succeeded to higher standards of dignity and entitlements than those available to women in ancient Mesopotamia. Scripture gives evidence that Israelite society resembled Mesopotamian society in this respect.

The ideal of woman's status and dignity is expressed in one compact sentence, "God created man *(ha'adam)* in His image, in the image of God He created him; male and female He created them" (Gen. 1:27). The mythopoeic narrative in Genesis 2, after telling of the man's (correct) failure to recognize his counterpart in any of the animal species, and of his mate's creation out of his own flesh and bone (the Hebrew idiom for "essence"), reaches a climax in the perplexing gloss (verse 24): "Hence a man leaves his father and mother and clings to his wife, so that they become one flesh." The perplexity lies in the male's leaving his parents, whereas in biblical patriarchal society it is the woman who cuts her ties with her parents to join her husband's family. Attempts to solve the problem by the adducing of evidence for a matriarchal social organization in the geographical or temporal ambience of the Bible have proved fruitless.[23] The resolution of the perplexity lies in the consideration that the Hebrew language has no neuter gender, only masculine and feminine. When the Hebrew speaker wishes to say "one another" in regard to people or things he must have recourse to "the man his brother" or "the woman her sister," depending on the gender of the noun in question.[24] When two nouns of differing genders are in question, Hebrew begins with or opts for the masculine. The intent of Genesis 2:24 is not to confuse us with a statement contrary to fact (that the male leaves to join the female); it has reference mutually to man and woman, both of whom separate from their parents to create a new unit. The closest of human bonds is the genetic one between parent and child, yet it yields to and is superseded by the marital bond between a man and a woman who, in keeping with the incest taboo, are at least minimally removed in terms of consanguinity. This anomaly of the human condition is resolved here in terms of the mythos: the marital bond represents a recreation of primal man, a fusion with his own essence, the reunion of the sundered twain which is the human whole. Here, in short, we have the Hebrew version of the Greek *androgyne* myth, preserved for us by Plato.

While it would be irresponsible to overlook the essentially subordinate status of the woman in a patriarchal society, it is erroneous to assume that woman enjoys higher status in a matriarchal or matrilineal society. But it is wrong to infer that a woman was deprived of human rights qua woman in biblical society. Nor, for that matter, is it acceptable to overlook the gradations in social rank among women, or among men and women. As in the folk song where it is the farmer who takes a wife and not vice versa, so in the ancient Near East it was always the man who took the woman in marriage. Yet there is little question that the free woman (who, in the Code of Hammurabi, for example, in order to marry a slave had to "cause him to take her,") retained her edge in rank, even as Queen Elizabeth II remains the sovereign of Prince Philip. Similarly, we must distinguish between the free woman of high rank who entered wedlock with all her entitlements contractually guaranteed and the *amah*. The *amah*, usually translated as bondswoman, was no more a female slave in the sense of being a commodity than the *eved* was a male slave. With monetary recompense for the loss of her services to the family that had nurtured her, she was acquired for the basic purpose of being married within and adding to the strength of the adopting family. If the paterfamilias of the latter decided against taking her for himself he might designate her for his son, but failing this he could not transfer her to another family, even in Israel. Space again forbids our expatiating on the rights guaranteed to the woman in the relevant biblical passages, but these express the concern of Scripture to protect the woman in her vulnerability to her husband.[25]

Further, it is important to realize that polygamy, as biblically sanctioned, does not of itself necessarily represent deprivation of rights or dignity for the sex which shares a consort. Thus, the polygamy practiced by the patriarch Jacob did not demean his wives, Rachel and Leah. Despite the fact that the definition of marriage in a polygamous system leaves the husband free to cohabit with unmarried women while denying extramarital relations to his wives, there is no double standard in regard to the crime of adultery: the penalty for the offense is the same for both adulterer and adulteress.

The Modern Context

The seemingly increasing irrelevance of the Bible in modern times has not weakened the inference that a book whose specificities derive from the contexts of a remote culture and civilization runs counter to the "new" concepts of "natural" or "human" rights. The contemporary humanism that has asserted the murderer's right to life and parole, the homosexual's claim to indulge in his or her natural tastes, or a woman's right to abort an unwanted fetus does not readily find the source of its concept of human rights in a literature which, on particular occasions, has prescribed capital punishment, female subjugation, and death for both the sodomite and the desecrator of the Sabbath.

The secular criticism of biblical roots of human rights has an interesting irony. While many religious persons cannot conceive of a ground for human dignity and moral values except in a transcendent Creator who is the Author of physical and moral law, many secular persons view such a ground as itself demeaning to man and diminishing his dignity. They would rather root man's value in man's collective ultimacy, which somehow transcends the impersonal Nature of which he is a part. On the secularist view, human transcendence of unthinking Nature and of Nature's unthinking components derives from the uniqueness of Man's intellectual and moral capacities.

There is a further irony, therefore, that some of the secular promulgators of human rights have most recently sought to extend the category of human rights to include the rights of the nonhuman. I refer to recent movements to assert the legitimacy of the rights of animal life, of vanishing species, and of ecological habitats. Yet this extension of morality to the environment rests in the capacity of the human imagination to personify that which is not now human.

In this personification, the modern imagination resembles biblical expression. Scripture expresses horror over murder, for example, by personifying matrix earth being forced to drink the blood of her offspring. In the biblical imagery, crimes *pollute* the soil and the land will *vomit* its polluting population into exile. The modern concern with preventing the extinction of various species of animal life is in resonance with the biblical prescription not to collect the dam with her chicks but to release her to hatch another generation. Cruelty to animals is proscribed in such prescriptions as not to yoke animals of different strengths (ox and ass) to the plough or not to muzzle the ox which treads the grain. Ecological considerations are exemplified in the prohibition of sowing the vineyard's aisles with a second crop or the destruction of defenseless fruit trees while waging war in enemy territory. Such concerns must be perceived for what they are—a sensitivity to the human capacities for greed, rapaciousness, wanton cruelty, and ingratitude, capacities which cross over from the human realm into the non-human.

In Scripture, as in the modern context of most human-rights theorizing, the environment—animate and inanimate—is the stage for man's activities. Damages to the environment, accordingly, are crimes only to the extent that they impair the rights of other human beings, analogous to a passenger's not having the right to bore a hole in the floor of his part of the lifeboat. But the integrity of the material of the lifeboat, in itself, has no place in a discussion of human rights.

Conclusion

For some readers, the foregoing presentation will have the ring of an apologetic for Scripture. It is nothing of the sort. The argument stands or falls on its philological merit. What requires emphasis is that in dealing with a literature deriving from an ancient society it is the structure of values of that society, and not the particulars accidental to time and place, which must be discerned when the focus of the investigation is itself an abstraction—such as "human rights." What emerges from our contextual interpretation of biblical values is their relevance, appositeness, and congeniality with the conceptual frame of human rights. This should occasion no surprise. Biblical values did not become sacred because of their appearance in the Bible; rather, the Bible itself became sacred because its values speak to our sense of the sacred.

NOTES

1. The scheme of the early chapters of Genesis actually allows for the sanctity of all animal life; cf. Gen 1:29–30, which envisages all animal species as herbivores. Gen. 9:6, which associates the sanctity of human life with the imagery of "the human form divine," is in the context of permission to man to become a carnivore, thus pointing to illicit carnivorousness as the specific content of the term *hamas,* the lawlessness of all creatures which led the Deity to bring on the Flood. See my discussion "On Slaughter and Sacrifice, Blood and Atonement," *Hebrew Union College Annual* 47 (1976), 19–56 (hereafter cited as *HUCA*).

2. The covenantal relationship has both vertical and horizontal vectors. It is the vertical vectors between the various tribes of Israel, on the one hand, and God, on the other, which enjoin the horizontal ties of mutual obligation among the tribes, thus creating the covenant people.

3. See my discussion of the Decalogue in "On Faith and Revelation in the Bible," *HUCA* 39 (1968), 35–53.

4. Racialism was based not on genetics but rather on practices such as circumcision which, common to Israel and the Amalekites (a clan of Edom-Esau), rendered them kin regardless of enmity; and separated Israelites from Philistines and Shechemites, even though ties of amity and alliance might prevail. Cf. Gen. 34 and Judg. 9:1–29. As for the Cushite wife of Moses in the conflate account of Numbers 12, it is an error to read a racial significance into what is basically a geographical rather than a gentilic appellation. Cush apparently embraces not only Ethiopia and parts of the Sinai peninsula but also the Sudan, which had a varicolored population.

5. For the far-reaching consequences of the concept of the religion-family, discerned for the ancient Indo-European by Coulanges and for the Semites by this author, cf. "Kin, Cult, Land and Afterlife," *HUCA* 44 (1973), particularly §2.

6. That history begins with war is expressed in the fratricide mythos of Cain and Abel, the two men representing at that moment the future of the entire human race. The religion-family as the quintessential condition for human life is expressed in the penalty of banishment as the equivalent of, and alternative to, a death sentence. See Gen. 4:11–14 and my discussion of the banishment term *arur* in "The Problem of 'Curse' in the Hebrew Bible," Society of Biblical Literature Monograph 12 (1963), particularly pp. 84, 87–92; also "Cain and Abel" in Supplemental Volume of *Interpreter's Dictionary of the Bible.*

7. In the light of real property as a religious rather than an economic concept in the frame of the religion-family, the adjective "territorial" modifying "survival" is a redundancy. See note 5 above. Comparison of the biblical ethos in this matter with similar problems in our own age cannot but yield absurd conclusions unless we keep in mind that autochthony is a claim precluded for all but a tiny fraction of the human race.

8. Cf. Gen. 15:7, the promise of the land; 15:14, "I will pass judgment on the nation they shall serve" (i.e., the Egyptians); and 15:16, "the iniquity

of the Amorites has not yet reached the full measure"—i.e., of wrong to warrant immediate expulsion. Cf. also such passages as Deut. 9:4 ff.

9. Deut. 2:4–5, 9–12, 19–23; Amos 9:7.

10. The chronological ordering of biblical books according to critical canons would indicate that most of the insistence on the obligation to extirpate the original inhabitants of the land are written from a retrospective point of view, i.e., what should have been done to insulate Israel from the pagan practices of these inhabitants. Similarly, all the evidence is for free intermarriage with kindred peoples in the pre-monarchical as well as in most of the monarchical period. What the Deuteronomist had in mind by the tenth, or the third, generation in Deut. 23:4–9 is not at all clear.

11. Deut. 5:15 (the Decalogue).

12. Exod. 20:11 (the Decalogue).

13. See "Kin, Cult, Land and Afterlife," §12b.

14. The rubric, "evening and morning" for the days preceding the creation of the sun point to the culmination of the Creation narrative in the Sabbath, all seven days together symbolizing God's creation of time as well as matter. The rendering of the imperfect tense of the verb "to perform (labor)" as an imperative rather than a permissive is without any support in the text or the ethos of Scripture, which regards labor as both necessity (a sad one when it is arduous) and privilege (from point of view of its yield in benefits).

15. See E.A. Speiser, *Genesis,* The Anchor Bible, p. xlvi; and H.A. Frankfort, *Kingship and the Gods* (Chicago, 1948).

16. Cf. "On Slaughter and Sacrifice, Blood and Atonement," paragraphs two and three, and "Kin, Cult, Land and Afterlife."

17. Exod. 21:2–6 and its parallel in Deut. 15:12–18, where "your brother the *ivri"* points to the possibility that the latter term may also refer to non-Israelites; cf. Jer. 34:8–16. Different terminology covering the same or similar situation appears in Lev. 25:39–46.

18. See note 17 above; for other instances of "Hebrews" referring to non-Israelites, see 1 Sam. 13:3, 7, 19.

19. Note that Deut. 23:16–17, forbidding the return of an *eved* to his master and prescribing for him generous treatment and asylum, almost certainly refers to a non-Israelite slave, fugitive from a non-Israelite master.

20. See, e.g., Isa. 1:17, 23. The injustice to be remedied is more akin to our contemporary need for Legal Aid Societies. The impoverished widow and orphan fail to get a judicial hearing because the pillars of society who should sit in judgment as a civic duty refuse to do so without payment (*shohad,* mistranslated as "bribe").

21. The intolerance of worship of other gods by non-Israelites in the land of Israel is explicit in such historical accounts as that of Elijah's struggle with Jezebel's Baal-priests. The prohibition of the consumption of animal blood to *ger* as well as Israelite (Lev. 17:10–14) is due to the symbolism of returning the blood (=life essence) to the Lord of all life; within the sacred precincts of the Promised Land, even a non-Israelite had to acknowledge the sovereignty of the God of Israel.

22. Exod. 12:43–49; cf.. preceding note and Lev. 22:18, 25—verses which reveal that sacrifices to Israel's God might be offered on behalf of both (an uncircumcised) *ger* and non-resident foreigner *(ben nekhar).*

23. Aside from the fact that biblical society is consistently patriarchal (despite some evidence of fratriarchy in the [Hurrian] ambience of Aram in patriarchal times), the determining consideration is the following: even in a matriarchal society the groom/husband does not leave his own maternal family to take up residence with his bride's family. The husband has visiting rights with his wife; the children of the union relate to their mother's

brothers for "paternal" protection, just as the husband plays the role of "father" to the children of his own sisters.

24. The entire account, to be sure, is written from the masculine point of view. The force of the mythos, however, is to express the sense that "human" is not "man" but "man-woman."

25. In my paper on Num. 5:11–31, "The Case of the *Sota* and a Reconstruction of the Biblical 'Law,' " *HUCA* 46 (1975), 55–70, I propose a new interpretation of the supposed ordeal undergone by a woman suspected of adultery. It turns out that the real import is not to discriminate against the woman but rather to protect her from the jealousy of her husband.

DAVID DAUBE

⟫⟫⟫⟫⟫⟫⟫⟫⟫⟫⟫⟫⟫ 15 ⟪⟪⟪⟪⟪⟪⟪⟪⟪⟪⟪⟪⟪⟪
The Rabbis and Philo
on Human Rights

Terms

There is no rubric *human rights* in rabbinic literature or in Philo, yet the documentation bearing on the topic constitutes a veritable *embarras de richesses*. A systematic exploration, not here attempted, might begin by investigating a number of terms such as *kevod haberiyyoth*, "the honor of human creatures." It occurs, for instance, in the maxim that a substantial portion of the religious law is suspended where it clashes with a person's dignity. Suppose somebody points out to you, what you did not know, that your jacket is made of forbidden material. You need not discard it at once in public and thereby be open to ridicule and shame.[1]

Creature is normally employed where the condition of man as such, irrespective of nation, rank, or the like, is in question. (In the traditional grace after a meal, God is thanked for sustaining "the whole world . . . He giveth bread to all flesh . . . and provideth food for all his creatures whom He hath created."[2]) The word is not met in this sense in the Hebrew Bible; it is no doubt among the achievements of the last two or three pre-Christian centuries. The earliest extant mention of *the honor of creatures* demonstrates the expansive, generous thrust of the concept. Rabbi

Johanan ben Zakkai, of the first century C.E., is puzzled[3]—as are scholars to this day—why, according to a biblical statute (Exod. 21:37), the thief of an ox is liable to fivefold restitution, but that of a sheep to fourfold only. His explanation is that, while an ox can be pushed along, a sheep must be carried—a humiliating job. God, sensitive to *the honor of creatures,* makes up for it by imposing a lighter penalty.

Another phrase worth looking into is *mippene darke shalom,* "for the sake of the ways of peace." It is prominent in regulations extending to Gentiles a privilege, strictly speaking, reserved for Jews. For example, a congregation's welfare chest is to be used equally for both, "for the sake of peace."[4] The notion has found its way into a fair number of New Testament teachings. Paul argues that if only one spouse converts to Christianity but the other, though not converting, is willing to stay on, that should be accepted since "God has called us to peace" (I Cor. 7:12–15).[5] Jewish apologists are not in general very happy with this motive. The aim of smooth coexistence with the outer world—and an outer world which has all the power—seems much less noble than, say, pure love. Perhaps, however, this is to take too much *au pied de la lettre* those who profess to be guided by the latter alone.

God and Fair Judgment

Actions ascribed to God frequently mirror activities and aspirations on earth. Take the struggle against discrimination, antedating by far the epoch on which I am concentrating. Not surprisingly, the Rabbis and Philo, in their theodicies, are eager to prove God free of this taint: there must be no favoritism. The Jews were vouchsafed the Sinaitic revelation, the Rabbis affirm,[6] because they alone were willing, all others having declined. Noah and Abraham, Philo contends,[7] were singled out because of their saintly natures.

Resentment of downgrading is even more ancient and basic. Strictly speaking, to be sure, favoritism and groundless downgrading are merely two aspects of the same action. This does not alter the fact—a far from negligible one—that Jacob is perceived as preferring Joseph (Gen. 37:3–4), or the prodigal son's father as preferring this son (Luke 15:11–32); whereas a bastard, an

Ammonite, or a Moabite, none of whom may "enter into the assembly of the Lord" (Deut. 23:3–4), are perceived as being placed at a disadvantage. Which aspect is emphasized depends on what is deemed to be the standard. If it is the inferior position— that of Joseph's brothers or the prodigal's brother—the superior one will be attacked as enjoying favoritism; if it is the superior position—that of the bulk of the nation participating in the assembly—the inferior one will be attacked as suffering groundless downgrading. In short, it is the deviation from the norm that is noticed.

Here is a typical example of how God is dissociated from unwarranted downgrading. The Bible tells us (Gen. 4:3–8) that when Abel and Cain sacrificed to Him, He responded to the former but not to the latter, with disastrous consequences. No reason is given. Historically considered, the narrative in its original setting had an etiological character: it was designed to impress the superiority of bloody sacrifices (Abel offered sheep) over vegetarian ones (Cain offered fruits).[8] The Rabbis, however, are no historians. They take it for granted that Cain deserved his treatment.[9] God is perfection and perfection implies justice. Accordingly, they press a little oddity out of the biblical wording. While Abel brought "the choicest of the firstlings of his flock," Cain brought "from the fruit of the soil"; not, the Rabbis point out, "of the first-fruits." Ungratefully, he gave God what was of least value. Philo takes over this indictment of Cain and adds that he grudgingly delayed even his mean offering.[10] In support, Philo invokes the circumstantial formulation of the text: "In the course of time, Cain brought an offering. . . ." *

In a sense, arbitrary punishment is a form of negative discrimination. Judah's firstborn son Er, we read in Gen. 38:7, "was wicked in the sight of the Lord; and the Lord slew him." Just as in the case of Cain's sacrifice, one might gain the impression that God acted from simple dislike, and this would indeed be a ground-

---

*It would lead too far afield here to set out why I assume Philo to be indebted to the Rabbis rather than the other way round. I think that, as a rule (to which there are exceptions), where the two coincide, priority belongs to the Rabbis. Often, admittedly, Philo is indebted to a version of their thought slightly different from that preserved. Again, I do not mean to deny that they, in turn, may have conceived of the idea in question under Hellenistic influence.

less killing. The sages could never tolerate such a construction.[11] Er must have been guilty of misdeeds meriting his fate; only their precise nature may be argued. Philo stresses the phrase "in the sight of the Lord."[12] Er was not killed for any cause obvious to the multitude. He stands for the body, which is a drag on the soul. Ordinary people do not understand this, but God and His friends do: the body is evil "in the sight of the Lord." Actually, it is never anything but a corpse; God "slew it" from the outset, i.e., created it dead. (In this case it is less certain that Philo draws on the Rabbis; the two may be quite independent of one another. Yet even here it is arguable that he received some stimulus from them.) Despite differences as to details, the sages are all agreed that Er sinned by giving in to lust: he practiced coitus interruptus so that his wife's beauty should not be spoiled through childbearing.[13] Philo, like the Rabbis, would not admit an arbitrary infliction of hurt by God.

God and Fair Procedure

Er (the body) is discussed by Philo in connection with another being that is evil per se: the serpent of the so-called Fall.[14] Once more, God is to be defended from any imputation of discrimination. What lends this section particular interest, however, is that we learn of a right to a hearing before being condemned. The demand for this right is not nearly as old or as universal as that for the absence of discrimination. Even nowadays, though counted as of almost equal importance, it is made light of to a greater extent than commonly realized. Every avoidable excess, for example, allowed to the police in dealing with accused persons in their custody infringes upon this right.

When the couple in Eden have tasted the forbidden fruit, God challenges Adam: "Did you eat of the tree?" Adam, not too gallantly, tries to shuffle off responsibility on Eve: "She gave me of the tree, and I ate." He even insinuates that God Himself is somewhat to blame. The full text reads: "The woman You put at my side—she gave me of the tree. . . ." So God next demands an explanation from Eve: "What is this you have done!" And she refers Him to yet another instigator: "The serpent duped me."

Whereupon He metes out dire retribution to all three—first the serpent, then Eve, lastly Adam.

The Rabbis notice that God debated (in Hebrew, "to take and give") with Adam and Eve, but not with the serpent.[15] He knew— that is how they account for it—that the serpent was wicked, a master of excuses. As an example, the Rabbis produce this argument on the part of the serpent: You told them not to eat of the tree, I told them to eat; they were perfectly aware that what You said was valid, what I said, invalid; why should I be held culpable for an utterance everybody recognized as empty? It is all their business.

Philo concentrates on Adam's denunciation of Eve and Eve's of the serpent. For him, the question is why God automatically accepted the latter but not the former. God himself (in Deut. 19:17) ordains—"properly," "reasonably," in Philo's estimate (the Greek is *eikos*)—that an accuser is not to be believed till the accused has had an opportunity of defending himself. Philo's answer is that Eve represents sense-perception, which can go right or wrong; hence she must be heard. (As must, of course, Adam, who represents the mind.) By contrast, the serpent represents pleasure, inherently bad; so a hearing would serve no purpose.

Thus the Rabbis and Philo both justify the distinction God made between the culprits. Philo, however, speaks in far more strictly legal terms than extant rabbinic tradition. The latter contains no quotation of a law requiring a hearing. Even so, most likely he is acquainted with it, or some version of it. That a hearing formed an essential part of the Jewish procedure of the time is certain—the best-known illustration being the trial of Jesus. The provision cited by Philo is also used by the Rabbis as a scriptural basis in this matter: "The two men who have the controversy shall stand forth before the Lord, before the priests and the judges."[16] Actually, the Rabbis deduce from this verse the need not only for a hearing but for a hearing in the presence of the accuser. *Audiatur et altera pars* is not enough; the accused is entitled to a confrontation. The result is reached by attaching weight to the fact that the text reads "the two men shall stand forth," instead of merely "the men"; i.e., they must appear together. The observance of this principle is indeed the duty of the parties no less than of the court.

The Universality of Justice

In importing these canons into the stories of Cain, Er, and the serpent, the Rabbis and Philo are endowing them with a wide validity. All three stories refer to the period before the Sinaitic covenant; two of them antedate Abraham and, indeed, the Flood; and one refers to the very beginning of life and struggle on earth, the expulsion from paradise. In principle, evidently, these are rights not restricted to any sector of mankind.

This liberal application of elementary notions of fairness can be traced far back into the Hebrew Bible. Abraham wrests from God the promise that Sodom will not be destroyed if some decent people can be found there (Gen. 18:20–32). Sodom is a heathen town; the first attack on communal responsibility is mounted for the sake of heathens. Significantly, Abraham reminds God of His position as "the Judge (or Ruler) of all the earth." Similarly, it is in answer to a heathen's protest that God admits that a man taking another man's wife without knowing of her status should be spared (Gen. 20:1–7). This is the problem of "essential error" in crime: if things were as believed, the deed would constitute no wrong. The external criteria for culpability are all there, yet the doer is innocent at heart. The Greek prototype, of course, is the saga of Oedipus. The earliest scriptural recognition of the demands of this situation occurs in the narrative of the king of Gerar who, misled by Abraham into thinking that Sarah is only his sister, includes her in his harem. At a later stage, we come across the general plea of man's creatureliness and lack of insight as mitigating his accountability. It is advanced in the Book of Jonah in defense of another heathen city, Nineveh (Jon. 4:11). Job's anxiety about theodicy could be voiced by any sufferer anywhere. These fundamental claims have a knack of disregarding fortuitous barriers of race or culture. Or it might be put this way: pioneering minds break through to the deepest concerns shared by all.

Escape by a Slave

Let us leave the doings of God and pass on to a specific injunction in the Fifth Book of Moses: "You shall not turn over to his master a slave who seeks refuge with you from his master. He shall live with you in any place he may choose among the settlements in your midst, wherever he pleases; you must not ill-treat him" (Deut. 24:16–17). From "the settlements in your midst" it is clear that a fugitive from abroad is contemplated. The provision displays a somewhat unrealistic bounteousness. For the most defenseless, wretched figure of the outside world, entry into Israelite territory is to spell not only safety but also freedom, and freedom not only as opposed to slavery but also in the sense of unrestricted selection of domicile and absence of ill-treatment. It is in line with other deuteronomic precepts designed for a community able to afford the ideal, for example, "Three times a year . . . all your males shall appear before the Lord your God in the place that He will choose" (Deut. 16:16); and, in particular, able and concerned to look after the underprivileged: "the Levite, . . . the fatherless, and the widow in your settlements shall come and eat their fill" (Deut. 14:29).

It is noteworthy that, whereas the version of the Ten Commandments offered in Exodus (20:11) gives the Creator's rest on the seventh day as the reason for the Sabbath, that in Deuteronomy (5:13–15) gives the nation's past in Egyptian slavery. Moreover, Deuteronomy adds a special clause, " so that your male and female slave may rest as you do." It even expands the reference to beasts. In Exodus, the Sabbath embraces "your cattle"; in Deuteronomy, "your ox or your ass, or any of your cattle." That these are purposeful insertions is beyond doubt. A remarkable injunction in Exodus (23:12), outside the Ten Commandments, represents the Sabbath as entirely in the interest of slaves, beasts, and strangers: "On the seventh day you shall cease from labor, in order that your ox and your ass may rest, and that your bondman and the stranger may be refreshed."

How does the lawgiver reconcile this welcome for a foreign runaway with slavery within the state? Part of the answer may be that a slave living in this community is supposed to be normally well treated and to enjoy adequate protection if abused. As for a Hebrew slave in particular, Deuteronomy (15:12–18), in contradistinction to Exodus (21:2–6), takes it for granted that any family he may have shares in his release in the seventh year. Furthermore, Deuteronomy considers it possible—as Exodus does not—that a slave may waive this release from no other motive than love for a good master. Manifestly, the theory at least is rosy.

A usual reply, when our modern conventions for the safeguarding of the personality are decried as ineffectual, is that at least they are there ready to take over if a favorable constellation arises; and that occasionally happens. Those who hold this view may derive comfort from the fate of the direction under discussion: though never fully enforced, it functioned as a permanent stimulus. The actual regulations as to escapees derived from it would be more or less liberal in different periods and regions, but at least the matter received continuous attention.

A notable divergence of Philo[17] from the Bible is his view that the slave may not be handed back even if his owner belongs to the same state as the person to whom he flees. Indeed, Philo seems primarily to think of just this case. It is no doubt connected with this change that the slave does not become free. There are two alternatives. Preferably, negotiations between him and his master will lead to his return on acceptable terms. Failing such agreement, he is to be sold to a third party, the master getting the proceeds. The way the apostle Paul sends back Onesimus to Philemon, with a letter outlining the happy relationship to be established, comes near the former course (Philem. 1:8–19). With regard to the latter, Philo reflects that, while there is no saying how the new owner will turn out, an uncertain evil is lighter than a certain one—the opposite of the familiar warning, "Better the devil you know than the devil you don't know," or Shakespeare's "and makes us rather bear those ills we have than fly to others that we know not of" (Hamlet 3.1.81).

From Philo's use of the statute in his allegorical system,[18] it looks as if a friendly arrangement with the original owner appeared to him practically unattainable. (The situation in the Epistle to Philemon is obviously very exceptional.) Even sale to a third party is not really incorporated in his symbolism. Instead, it is as if the slave were to become the property of the person with whom he takes refuge. He is likened to one casting off the severe yoke of foolish passions and seeking out a wise and kind master, who will not let him be subjugated again by his inner tyrants and who may eventually even grant him freedom.

It is widely held that Philo is borrowing from Attic law. Quite possible; but it is also possible that he is following certain among the Rabbis (who, to be sure, may themselves owe something to non-Jewish institutions). At any rate, by about 300 C.E. there were those who paid heed to the owner's financial stake, even if he lived abroad and his slave reached the land of Israel. The latter indeed gains his liberty, but he owes the former his own value.[19]

The Bible says nothing about the particular circumstances in which the slave ran away. They are plainly of no account. Neither, up to a point, are they in the post-biblical era, and Philo expressly declares the provision applicable even if the flight was motivated by consciousness of misdeeds. (Onesimus, one has the impression, was not the most honest of servants.) Where a crime proper is in question, however, the general laws take precedence. This comes out in a legend about King Jehoiakim[20] who—as the Rabbis see it—wickedly rebelled against his overlord Nebuchadnezzar. The latter approached Jerusalem but told the Sanhedrin that he would depart if Jehoiakim was given up. When the Sanhedrin informed Jehoiakim, he pleaded the prohibition of surrendering a runaway slave to his master. (In Hebrew, it must be remembered, *slave* may denote *vassal*.) The Sanhedrin, however, was not moved. The story, incidentally, with its fanciful extension of the ordinance to a domain for which it was never designed, testifies to a lively interest in the basic idea.

The rabbinic material[21] preserves traces of a tendency to promote, or demote, the precept to a more theological import, that is to say, to construe it as for the benefit not of a fugitive slave proper but of a proselyte: he had been a slave to his evil idols and is now to enjoy the security of right belief and companionship. Philo, as we saw above, assumes the law to enshrine a comparable philosophical tenor having to do with an individual's spiritual development. Maybe he is inspired by these rabbinic circles. But he does not substitute the philosophical teaching for the justiciable content: an escapee is entitled to assistance. And there is the deeper lesson: a man abandoning passion will find a haven with wisdom. By contrast, the doctrine here in question is not concerned with allegorization, the detection of a second meaning beneath the apparent.[22] It is concerned only with the latter, the justiciable content, to which it gives a radical twist, asserting that it has regard to a proselyte. How far religious fervor accounts for this reinterpretation, how far the immense difficulties in applying the statute to actual slaves, it is hard to decide. We must not forget that even to shelter a proselyte was not always a simple affair. Anyhow, it is interesting that the theologizing tendency did not prevail.

Josephus presents a problem. In the famous anti-suicide speech[23] he argues that, as the punishment of runaway slaves is approved even if they have fled from bad masters, to flee from the best of masters, God, is all the more objectionable. Perhaps he has in mind fugitives recaptured and not falling under the deuteronomic injunction. Or perhaps the protection even of slaves not re-captured was more or less suspended at the time. We must not forget that a rebel like Simon son of Gioras enticed many slaves to join his band by promising them liberty.[24] In his selection of Jewish customs,[25] Josephus does not advert to the provision here discussed—unless it lurks behind his statement that Jews may not kill whatever takes refuge in their homes; from the context, the reference appears to be to animals.[26]

Escape by a Captive

A remarkable ruling goes back at least to the first half of the third century c.e.: a slave who escapes from prison becomes free.[27] Whatever the legal reasoning, a major consideration must have been that to force back into servitude one who has taken this risk to shake off his chains would be barbarous. Doubtless the prison envisaged is a non-Jewish one and, no matter what his offense, conditions are presumed to be of a sort no one should have to suffer. A benediction forming part of the daily morning prayers runs: "Blessed are thou, O Lord our God, King of the universe, who loosest them that are bound."[28]

It may be appropriate here to cite a dispute respecting Jews, whether initially free or slaves, who are captives in heathen hands.[29] The sages hold that, though it is a duty to ransom them, one should not further their escape, "for the sake of the main-tenance of the world." The implication—easily overlooked—is that, ideally, piety does require us to aid them to flee; only the reprisals certain to be taken against Jewry at large are too fearful, so we must forgo this good work. Perhaps there is in this decision a slight inclination to law and order in general. It is challenged by Rabbi Simeon ben Gamaliel, or rather, he substitutes a slightly different *ratio legis*. One should refrain from furthering escapes, he holds, not "for the sake of the maintenance of the world," but "for the sake of the treatment of captives." In other words, it is not the danger to the community that militates against such assistance but the likelihood that, if escapes are assisted, captives will be kept in even severer confinement—not to mention the fury that will be vented on any who remain behind after one has got away.[30]

The Rabbis do not fail to note a practical consequence: on the basis of Simeon's view, if the heathens hold one captive only, it is indeed right to help him escape.[31] Simeon, it may be observed, had narrowly missed imprisonment and death in the Hadrianic persecution and had been in hiding for years. His standpoint came to predominate.[32] So much so, indeed, that post-talmudic commentators have consistently assimilated the dissenting view to his as much as possible.[33] The sages, too, it is claimed, are guided solely by sympathy with the captives. The difference between them and Simeon—an extremely subtle one—is that whereas the latter takes account of present captives only—so that, if there is only one, his flight can cause none to suffer—the former take account also of future captives; that is why no flight is ever to be supported. The sages are thus cleared of harboring any expedient thought for the safety of the community. Yet the expression "for the sake of the maintenance of the world" points to precisely this thought; and it cannot have the meaning imposed on it by the commentators, definitely not when opposed to "for the sake of the treatment of the captives."

Suicide

Freedom to die is about to graduate as a human right. Neither in the Hebrew Scriptures nor in the New Testament is suicide reproved. In the Book of Tobit (3:10), Sarah, in extreme distress, refrains from suicide not because it is intrinsically reprehensible but because it would reflect on her father: people would say that he could not look after her.

By the first century C.E. at the latest, however, there is a strong current against the deed. Josephus[34] knows of a practice—presumably supported by an extensive interpretation of a pentateuchic law (Deut. 21:22–23) concerning an executed criminal—to leave a suicide unburied until sunset. In rabbinic writings, not only is a prohibition of suicide read into God's warning to Noah, "For your life-blood, too, I will require a reckoning" (Gen. 9:5),[35] but also a comprehensive duty to preserve oneself intact is established, with appeal to such texts as "take utmost care and watch yourselves scrupulously" (Deut. 4:9).[36] When Rabbi Hanina ben Teradyon, in a Hadrianic persecution, was slowly burnt at the stake and his disciples wanted him to open his mouth in order that he might die faster, he replied that "one must not injure oneself"—a very general phrase: *haval* or *hibbel*.[37] (He did accept the executioner's offer to raise the flame.) Philo does not take up the topic of suicide *ex professo*. There is, however, a memorable chapter[38] on a plan by the Jews of Jerusalem, should Caligula persist in his resolve to erect a statue in the Temple, to be faithful both to him and to God by total self-immolation.

In the final analysis, it will never be easy to settle the limits of the right to die. And no easier to settle those of the fetus's right to be born.

NOTES

1. Babylonian Talmud, Menahot 37b.
2. Simeon Singer, *Authorised Daily Prayer Book* (1890), p. 280.
3. Mekhilta on Exod. 21:37.
4. Palestinian Talmud, Demai 24a.
5. See David Daube, *Pauline Contributions to a Pluralistic Culture*, pp. 233 ff. pp. 233 ff.
6. Mekhilta on Exod. 20:2.
7. *Allegorical Interpretation* 3.24.77, *On the Giants* 14.62 f.
8. See Daube, "A Note on a Jewish Dietary Law," *Journal of Theological Studies* 37 (1936), 289–91.
9. Genesis Rabbah ad loc.
10. *The Sacrifices of Abel and Cain* 13:52 ff.
11. Genesis Rabbah ad loc.; Babylonian Talmud, Yevamot 34b; cf. Book of Jubilees 41:2 f., Testament of Judah 10:2 f.
12. *Allegorical Interpretation* 3.22.69 ff.
13. On some aspects of his conduct, see J.T. Noonan, *Contraception* (Cambridge, 1965), pp. 34, 50 ff.
14. *Allegorical Interpretation* 3.21.65 ff.
15. Genesis Rabbah ad loc.

16. Siphre Deuteronomy ad loc. Deut. 1:16 and Exod. 23:1 figure in Babylonian Talmud, Sanhedrin 7b.

17. *On the Virtues* 24.124.

18. *Allegorical Interpretation* 3.69.194.

19. Babylonian Talmud, Gittin 45a.

20. Genesis Rabbah 94 on 46:26 f., Leviticus Rabbah 19 on 15:24.

21. Jerusalemite Targum ad loc.; Siphre Deuteronomy ad loc.; Babylonian Talmud, Gittin 45a.

22. For the difference between allegorization and ordinary reinterpretation, see my essay, "Allegorizing," in D. Daube and R. Yaron, *Ancient Law* (forthcoming).

23. *Jewish War* 3.8.5.373.

24. Ibid., 4.9.4.508.

25. *Jewish Antiquities* 4.8.4.196 ff.

26. *Against Apion* 2.29.213.

27. Babylonian Talmud, Gittin 38a.

28. Singer, *Authorised Daily Prayer Book* (1890), p. 6. The source is Babylonian Talmud, Berakhot 60b.

29. Mishnah, Gittin 4.6.

30. An example may be found in Ecclesiastes Rabbah on 7:15.

31. Babylonian Talmud, Gittin 45a.

32. Tosephta, Gittin 4.4; Babylonian Talmud, Gittin 38a.

33. Their understanding of the dispute seems to go absolutely unquestioned; see, e.g., H. Danby, *The Mishnah* (London, 1933), p. 311.

34. *Jewish War* 3.8.5.377.

35. Genesis Rabbah on 9:5; see Daube, "The Linguistics of Suicide," in *Philosophy and Public Affairs* 1 (1972), 398.

36. Babylonian Talmud, Berakhot 32b. See Daube, "Limitations on Self-Sacrifice in Jewish Law and Tradition," in *Theology* 72 (1969), 299.

37. Babylonian Talmud, Avodah Zarah 18a.

38. Embassy to Gaius 32.229 ff. See also Daube, *Civil Disobedience in Antiquity* (Edinburgh, 1972), pp. 92 ff.

S. D. GOITEIN

Human Rights in Jewish Thought and Life in the Middle Ages

Medieval Jewish philosophers and thinkers were concerned with God, not with man. The nature of God—His actions in the visible world, in particular His manifestations in the Hebrew Scriptures; as well as the capacity of the human soul to perceive and serve Him properly—these were the topics which occupied Jewish thought in the Middle Ages.* A mere glance at the table of contents of Moses Maimonides' *Guide of the Perplexed,* or Saadya Gaon's *Book of Opinions and Beliefs,* brings home this fact. They studied human society as a vehicle for strengthening, or at least not impeding, the individual soul in its endeavor to reach perfection and, ultimately, salvation. The relations between man and his fellow creatures as such and, consequently, human rights, were not their concern.

To be sure, even if they had not been trained in Greek philosophy, the medieval Jewish thinkers would have recognized that only an orderly human society could vouchsafe the spiritual pursuits which alone, they believed, made life worthwhile. Maimon-

*This essay is concerned mainly with developments within the orbit of Islam.

ides explains this in some detail in his Guide (III, 27). But they did not consider in any depth the structure of such an orderly and just society. What Muslims and Jews alike had to say about this matter mainly centered around the image of the ideal ruler, and particularly the question of whether and to what extent he was to be a man of special spiritual gifts that would enable him to guide his subjects to the service of God. Other than that, their interest focused on the individual, not on the body politic; on the duties of men, not on their rights. Each section of Maimonides' Code of Law is superscribed: "This section contains the following obligations." Actually, his book, like the corresponding Muslim works, was a manual of duties, not a code of law.

The tenth and last chapter of Saadya Gaon's *Opinions and Beliefs,* the only one dedicated to man's behavior in and for this world, contains eminently reasonable guidelines for proper human conduct. But these guidelines clearly were not motivated by consideration for the needs and rights of fellowmen; their aim was self-perfection, the attainment of the ideal of the accomplished sage, who was the secular counterpart of the true servant of God.

"The duties of the heart," discussed by Bahya Ibn Pakuda in the book bearing that title, were exclusively duties toward God. Naturally, some of these religious virtues also presupposed decent behavior toward God's creatures.

Judah Ha-Levi's theological chef d'oeuvre, generally known as the *Kuzari,* but actually named *In Defense of the Despised Nation,* displays a bias in its very title. It stressed the natural inequality of men with regard to their choicest spiritual gift, their faculty for religious experience—an inequality that will disappear only in messianic times, when the nations will be integrated into Israel's religion and endowed with true prophetic vision comparable to that of the ancient prophets of Israel.

I hasten to add that the belief in the exclusive truth of Israel's religion—with all the limitations on general rights this concept implies—was shared by practically all Jewish thinkers, especially Maimonides. It need not be emphasized that the spiritual leaders of the two other monotheistic religions held the same views concerning their own dogmas. The difference, of course, was that Islam and Christianity, as ruling religions, did great harm to the minorities living within their orbit, while the Jewish community was saved from such misdeeds by its lack of power.

A noteworthy exception to this general trend in medieval thought is found in a place and time where we would not have expected it: in Yemen in the time of Maimonides. Nethanel ben Fayyumi, in his book poetically titled *The Orchard of the Intelligence,* states that nothing prevents God from sending unto His world whomsoever He wishes whenever He wishes, since the world of holiness unceasingly sends forth from the sphere of light to the world of matter emanations to liberate the souls from the dark and coarse sea of matter. Consequently, Islam is to be regarded as a true religion. Using many quotations from the Koran, Nethanel attempts to prove that Muhammad thought that this was true also of Judaism; that therefore the advent of Islam had not annulled the Torah. As Solomon Pines of the Hebrew University has shown, Nethanel's views, as much as they appeal to us, were not rooted in a more broad-minded approach to man's relations to man, but in his philosophical theory of God's relation to the world: the sphere of holiness is in a constant state of emanation; therefore, on its receiving end, human prophecy and religion must be possible wherever and whenever needed, and not confined to a certain place, such as the Holy Land, or any period, like that of biblical Israel or the days of the Messiah.[1]

This preoccupation with theology and seeming lack of attention to human rights had both a negative and a positive reason. Systematic thinking about the nature of God and His guidance of the world had been almost completely absent in the pre-Islamic Jewish world where Greek was not spoken. But human rights, and relations among men in general, had been fully established in the Bible and the Talmud, and these formed the very substance of medieval Jewish beliefs and practices. The Jewish thinkers of those days did not consider it their task to lay down new principles or to formulate laws for safeguarding human rights, for they never regarded themselves as lawmakers: "The Law is God's," as the Bible says (Deut. 1:17), and has been promulgated by Him in the Scriptures. It was incumbent on man to study God's law to understand it, as expounded in the disquisitions of the Talmud. Thus, the first answer to the question of medieval Jewish attitude toward human rights must be that it was basically and mainly identical with the teaching of the Bible as interpreted in the Talmud.

However, it would be a grave error to assume that the medieval

Jewish thinkers' use of their spiritual heritage was merely codifica-
tion and transmission. In the centuries of transition from late
antiquity to the Middle Ages, the Jewish people underwent a
revolutionary transformation that had a profound impact on the
practice, and to some extent also on the theory, of its law. In
late antiquity the Jewish population of Palestine had been pre-
ponderantly agricultural and parochial, and that of Babylonia
largely so. Through a long process already discernible during the
Persian rule over Babylonia and the Byzantine rule over Palestine,
and accelerated by the rise of the Middle Eastern bourgeoisie in
early Islamic times, the Jewish farmer was replaced by the urban
craftsman, merchant, and professional. The predominantly peasant
and parochial Jewish society had become urban, mobile, and
cosmopolitan.[2]

This socioeconomic transformation was matched by an equally
profound cultural change. For one thousand years, from Alexander
the Great to Muhammad, the Jews of Palestine had lived within
the orbit of Hellenic civilization. But the struggle for the preservation of their unique religion and ethics forced them to reject Greek
philosophy and science. Judaism retained its spiritual identity, but
at a price: it did not participate in the world culture of its day,
which was Hellenic. Hence, also, the unfortunate dichotomy between Aramaic- (and Hebrew-) speaking Jews and those whose
mother tongue was Greek. The estrangement was so deep that the
writings of Philo, the greatest Jewish thinker of the time, never
reached the bulk of the Jewish people; and the majority of the
Greek-speaking Jews assimilated to their environment and were
lost to Judaism.

With the advent of Islam there was a complete change. The
world, so to speak, had become Jewish. That is, the countries inhabited by Jews were now under the rule of the two religions
whose basic doctrines were identical with Judaism. The Muslims,
in particular, were described by Abraham, the son of Maimonides,
as "those who have adopted our system of religion." There no
longer was any danger from polytheism, materialism, and hedonism
of pagans. On the other hand, the new class of merchants and professionals had the means, the leisure, and the desire to partake
in the new world culture, which was a product of the Judeo-
Christian-Islamic tradition and the Hellenic heritage. This widening of cultural horizon, together with the exigencies of the new

socioeconomic situation, affected both the concepts and the substance of law and brought about many changes in the attitude toward human rights.

It appears that these changes were effected in four different ways: first, by bold interpretation, which shaped moral principles enounced in the Bible or in the Talmud into positive legal injunctions; second, by statutes, *takkanot,* promulgated by the Gaons, or heads of the *yeshivot,* the Jewish high councils, or by local authorities or communities; third, by official recognition of the international law of the merchants as law applicable in the Jewish courts; finally, by the acceptance of local usage, especially in family law. Let us illustrate these methods by example.

Slavery in Medieval Judaism

The first concerns slavery, a topic particularly sensitive to the question of human rights. To be sure, when we speak about slavery within the orbit of Islamic civilization, and particularly Judaic civilization within Islam, we must free ourselves entirely from the notions formed through our knowledge about the fate of slaves in the workshops of Athens, the *latifundia* of Rome, and the plantations of the American South. Male slaves were very rare in Jewish bourgeois society and were mainly employed as business agents; as such they had a respected position, derived from the power and riches of the lord whom they served. Female slaves were common; they provided domestic help and nurses in the middle- and upper-class households.

Both male and female slaves belonged to the family. They were greeted in letters, and they themselves extended greetings to relatives of the family. A traveler was reminded to bring home a present for the maidservant, as for his children and his wife. Reports about slaves running away from Jewish households were virtually nonexistent.

The sages of the Talmud seemingly had little regard for slaves and even objected to their manumission. The biblical "You may keep them as slaves forever" was explained by them as an injunction: "You shall keep them forever." But this is a theoretical clarification rather than a practical recommendation. A certain Jewish sect had adopted the idea—adhered to also in Christianity and Islam—which sees in the freeing of slaves a pious deed. This principle was not recognized by the talmudic scholars, because the slave of a Jew enjoyed religious privileges—for instance, the Sabbath rest—which he would lose as a free pagan. But freeing a slave and introducing him into the Jewish faith was indeed a meritorious action, and in the Middle Ages the manumission of slaves was extremely common, as is abundantly proved by the documents of the Cairo Geniza, which are discussed below. We possess documents bearing directly on the emancipation of slaves and many others that refer to freedmen and freedwomen. I might add that I am not certain that the frequency of manumissions was indeed an innovation of the Jewish Middle Ages, for the term freedmen appears quite often in talmudic discussions.

There are, however, certain aspects in the attitude toward slavery in medieval Judaism which are perhaps novel and deserving of special attention. In some deathbed declarations the maidservant was set free, but it was left to her whether to remain in the house and serve the testator's heirs, or to leave and try a life of her own. From other documents we learn, too, that the slave was not regarded as an object but as a human being with a will and personal preferences.

With manumission, a slave became a full member of the Jewish community. Unlike the situation in Roman and Islamic law, the master or his family had no claim on the freedman, and whenever doubts arose about this question, the courts were quick to dispel them. Conversely, when the freedman was in trouble, the family of his former master would volunteer to help him, since as a former member of the household he had a moral claim on such support. Numerous documents prove that freedmen and freedwomen had Jewish spouses; in other words, the stipulation, included in the deed of manumission, that the slave liberated was entitled to marry a Jewish person was not theory but daily practice. Occasionally, documents also show that the former maidservant brought into the marriage a considerable dowry, no doubt solely or mainly contributed by her former proprietors.

Another specific trait, and perhaps innovation, of the Jewish Middle Ages was the practice of buying little slave girls, bringing them up in the Jewish faith, and then liberating them, equipped with means for a livelihood (on condition that they remain within the Jewish fold). Since being a Jew was regarded as the highest form of human existence, this pious work of education, liberation, and support must have been believed particularly meritorious, for it bestowed upon the person concerned the most precious of human rights: freedom, sustenance, and the true faith—but leaving to the beneficiary the choice of accepting the offer or not.[3]

After this brief survey of the position of slaves in the Jewish High Middle Ages within the orbit of Islamic civilization, we now turn to the principles underlying that position, as pronounced by Maimonides in his code. Having dealt in 115 long paragraphs with the minutiae of the mostly obsolete ancient laws of slavery, he states in the concluding paragraph the religious and moral obligations toward slaves and expounds the ideas on which they are based. In order to understand his statement properly, we must remember that the Bible says only with regard to the Hebrew and resident alien slave that he should not be treated with harshness. Consequently, according to the exact wording of the text, it was permissible to be harsh with others, subsumed under the term Canaanite slaves. To be sure, at the time of Maimonides there were no Jewish or resident alien slaves; all slaves were legally "Canaanites." We are now prepared for reading Maimonides' Code on this question (Book 12, section "Slaves," chapter 9, paragraph 8):

> It is permissible to treat a Canaanite slave with harshness. This is the law. But piety and reason oblige a man to be merciful and just toward his slave, not to overburden him with work, not to cause him grief, but let him share all food and drink taken by himself, as was the custom of our sages of old. . . . He should not humiliate him by infliction of corporal punishment nor by words. He should not shout at him angrily, but talk to him quietly and listen to his arguments. This is clearly expressed in the beautiful words of Job in praise of himself: "Have I ever disregarded the rights of my slave or those of my bondwoman, when they had an argument with me? . . . My Creator has made me and him in one womb and has formed us in one womb."

But the general human obligation of regarding our fellowmen as brothers did not suffice Maimonides in his appeal for the proper treatment of slaves. He continues:

> Cruelty and brutality are characteristic of pagans and idolators, but the seed of our father Abraham, Israel, have mercy

with everyone, because God bestowed upon them teachings
and religious obligations in plenty, which represent just laws
and ordinances. And of God, who has ordered us to imitate
Him, it is said: "He has mercy with all his creations."

Thus it is not only the human rights of our fellowmen, but also
what may be described as the general spirit of Jewish law, which
obliges us to behave humanely toward our subordinates. Moreover, we are held to imitate God, and must strive to be merciful
like Him.

The imitation of God is pronounced as an obligation in Leviticus
19:2, where God commands: "You shall be holy, for I, the Lord
your God, am holy." But the formulation itself is found in Plato's
dialogue *Theaetetus,* and appears again and again in later Greek
thinking.[4] Thus, it is not precluded that the talmudic formulation
somehow was influenced by Greek popular philosophy. In any
case, we see here that Maimonides' specific legislation concerning
the humane treatment of slaves is based, on the one hand, on the
general idea of the unity of mankind, as poetically expressed in
the Book of Job, and, on the other hand, on the idea of the
imitation of God, as found in the Talmud. But the detailed formulation of the moral postulate is entirely his own, although it was
shared by the finest thinkers of the two other monotheistic
religions.

Innovations in Medieval Jewish Law

A similar procedure, namely, basing a specific ruling on a general
idea expressed in the classical sources of Judaism, although that
ruling evidently opposes an explicit decision made by the ancients,
is to be observed in the second type of innovation noted for the
Jewish Middle Ages, the statutes, or *takkanot.*

The most important requisite for the protection of human rights
is security, safeguards guaranteeing their proper execution. But
safeguards efficient in one socioeconomic situation may become
obsolete in another. A Jewish wife did not inherit from her husband; her economic security depended on her marriage contract,
stipulating the sums to be paid to her and the dowry to be returned to her in case of a divorce or the death of her husband. In
order to guarantee the payment of these sums, a husband had to

mortgage all his real estate. This ancient law was efficient as long as the average Jewish householder possessed landed property. But after the radical socioeconomic transformation of the Jewish people, which took place in late antiquity and early Islamic times, only limited numbers of Jews held agricultural land, and the value of their urban real estate often was below that of the *ketuba,* the sums stipulated in the marriage contract. Under these circumstances the heads of the two Babylonian *yeshivot,* together with the presidents of the high courts attached to the *yeshivot* and the *Resh Galutha* ("Head of the Diaspora" from the House of David, who at that time still wielded ecumenical authority), issued a statute decreeing that a husband, and indeed any debtor, stood surety for his debt with all his possessions, mobile property included.

This statute was accepted all over the Jewish world, but with a provision that is most instructive. Since the gaonic decree flatly contradicted talmudic law, it was followed in practice but not in theory. What actually happened was this: as the Geniza shows, any *ketuba,* and any other document involving a monetary obligation, contained the condition that the husband or debtor stood surety with all his possessions, real estate and mobile, "and even the coat from his shoulders." According to the Talmud, everyone was free to take upon himself financial obligations. By inserting this condition into every contract, both the talmudic law and the gaonic statute were heeded, and the main object of both, the protection of the rights of wives and of creditors, was achieved.[5]

The Jewish community sometimes had to protect its rights against overreaching leaders. The most notorious example was "the Head of the Jews," Abu Zikri Zutta, who, in the turbulent times of the transition from the Fatimid to the Ayyubid rule in Egypt, succeeded in obtaining that post by promising a yearly contribution to the government, which he himself tried to levy by appointing judges who would pay him part of their yearly income. This practice, known in Europe as simony, was common in Islam, but unknown in Jewish Egypt. There the *dayyanim,* the judges and spiritual leaders, were of two types: professionals, that is, scholarly persons who received a modest remuneration from the community in their capacity as scholars who devoted their time to study instead of seeking a livelihood and, in addition, took fees for the writing of legal documents (not for giving judgment, as is often erroneously stated); and men of affairs—merchants, physicians, government officials—who volunteered to serve the community. Zutta intended to streamline the entire juridical and communal system on Islamic lines, making the dispensation of justice a source of substantial revenues, especially for himself. This was incompatible with the letter and the spirit of Jewish law, and would have forced many incumbents of the office of *dayyan* to resign.

In a beautifully styled *takkana,* the Jewish community of al-Mahalla, a provincial town in Lower Egypt, describing themselves as "adherents of the law of the living God, who seek His propinquity, detest evildoers, and love Godfearing men," declared that Zutta's regime completely undermined the position of the "sons of the Torah" (meaning the local spiritual leaders); that by trying to exchange them for more docile officials, he caused endless communal strife, which in itself was a great sin (quoting Hosea 10:2). Consequently, the community would not accept any *dayyan* sent by Zutta, pay him a salary, join him in prayer, or heed any of his rulings. They would retain their own judge as long as he agreed to stay with them. (He intended to settle in the Holy Land in his old age.) Moses Maimonides was asked to confirm the legality of this *takkana,* which he did with great aplomb. The example of al-Mahalla certainly was followed (or perhaps even preceded) by other communities, and in a few years the usurper Zutta lost his position. Thus the concerted effort of the community, theoretically underpinned by the words of the prophet, upheld the rights of the individual judges and safeguarded the traditional communal organization of public life in Jewish Egypt.[6]

A certain affinity with the ordinances of the heads of the *yeshivot* is to be found in the third type of innovations of the Jewish Middle Ages: the recognition by the Jewish courts of the customary law of the merchants and its application in juridical practice. In the wake of a farflung international trade, which had developed in late antiquity and early Islamic times, new forms of mercantile contracts and financial practices had developed, and these were at variance with forms and practices recognized in the Talmud. The Jewish merchants, even when dealing with one another, mostly adopted the new ways of business; but they were still accustomed to, or held fast to, the principles of bringing their disputes before Jewish courts. The only efficient way of protecting the rights of the contestants was to judge them according to the laws under which they had made their transactions or undertaken their joint ventures.

The Jewish courts lived up to the situation and, led by the Gaons, boldly replaced talmudic law by the new practices. It is true," writes Hay Gaon in the eleventh century, "that our sages have said that one should not send bills of exchange, but we see that people actually use them; therefore, we admit them in court, since otherwise commerce would come to a standstill, and give judgment according to the law of the merchants." The very wording of Hay Gaon's responsum proves that he refers to an established practice of the Jewish courts. It should be noted that in a collection of Christian (Nestorian) statutes and judgments, compiled around 800 C.E., the "customs of the merchants" were also recognized by the courts. At the time of Hay Gaon, friendly relations prevailed between him and the Catholicos, the head of the Nestorian church.[7]

The changes brought about by the new customary law of the merchants were particularly evident in the field of partnership, especially in overseas undertakings, where it developed a specific form, which, under the name *commenda,* was also in vogue on the northern shores of the Mediterranean. In this contract, labeled by the Jewish courts "partnership of the gentiles," the investor of the capital received two-thirds of the profit, and the manager, who undertook the perilous sea voyage and did all the work, got the remaining third, but was not responsible for losses. In the corresponding ancient Jewish *'iska* contract, the opposite relationship prevailed: the manager, who did the work, received two-thirds of the profit, but was responsible for losses. There is no need here to search for the reason for the differences between the two laws: whether Jewish law was perhaps more appreciative of the value of labor, or whether capital had become scarcer; or whether it was discovered that under the new conditions of huge overseas undertakings managers were often unable to bear the losses, so that the stipulations of the Jewish law had become unrealistic. The important point for us is that the "partnership of the gentiles" was recognized as law by the Jewish courts because it was practiced by the majority of merchants.

Finally, it was local practice that furthered the practice and concepts of Jewish law and promoted the cause of human rights. Local custom was recognized as a legitimate source of law in the

Talmud, but its exact character, origin, and historical development
are not easy to define. Its beginnings are mostly shrouded in dark-
ness. A certain usage might have been introduced by a great
teacher, ordered by an ecumenical authority, or resolved upon by
public acclamation; and since that origin had been forgotten in the
course of time, it came to be regarded as customary law. But
precisely this status as a law unwritten but recognized as binding
by the community endowed it with moral force.

Polygamy was permitted by both biblical and talmudic laws.
However, the marriage contracts of the twelfth century, which are
preserved in great numbers in the Cairo Geniza,* prohibited the
husband from taking a second wife. At the same time, the letters
and documents related to family life in the eleventh century prove
that the Jewish family then was not less monogamous than in the
twelfth century. What happened here was that, for reasons unknown to us, it was found necessary at a certain time to incorporate
in explicit form a generally recognized practice in the marriage
contract. It is the same process as the one observed above with
regard to the stipulation found in every marriage contract, according to which the husband stands surety for his wife's *ketuba* with
all his possessions, mobile and real estate. There was no need to
include it, since it was a solemnly promulgated gaonic statute. But
(as Maimonides remarks), the "scholars of the West" once
ordered that it be expressly stated.[8]

The same was true of the monogamy clause. Since the local
usage at the turn of the eleventh century clearly was at variance
with the freedom granted to the husband by Bible and Talmud,
some scholars—perhaps those who had emigrated to Egypt from
Palestine in the wake of the First Crusade—found it proper for
the husband to include that prohibition in the marriage contract as
one of his obligations. As is well known, in Western Europe the

*Our main source for the actual life of the Jews under Islam during the
High Middle Ages (approximately 950–1250 C.E.) is the letters and documents of the Cairo Geniza. Geniza is a place where discarded writings on
which the name of God is, or might have been, written are kept to preserve
them from desecration. The so-called Cairo Geniza was a room attached
to a synagogue in the ancient capital of Islamic Egypt. That Geniza differed
from other genizas in its enormous size—hundreds of thousands of leaves—
and, in particular, in that it preserved, in addition to religious and other
literary writings, great masses of nonliterary, secular material, such as letters
and documents of all descriptions.

ban on polygamy was ascribed to Rabbenu Gershom of Mainz-Mayence, who lived around the year 1000; but in literature the ban makes its appearance only in the twelfth century, that is, at the time the monogamy clause is regularly included in the marriage contracts found in the Geniza. In reality, monogamy had become the established practice in both areas many years before.[9]

Human-Rights Developments in Domestic Relations

After having examined the methods by which the Jewish Middle Ages progressed in matters of human rights, we are now able to define with greater precision these achievements. Naturally, they were primarily in those areas of law and social institutions which the state (or, one should perhaps say, the ruling religion) left to the autonomous discretion of the Jewish community: family law in the broadest sense of the word, including, for example, education and care of the needy. Because of the size of the Jewish communities in Islamic countries in those days, its civil law, unlike that of Christian Europe, was also largely the domain of the Jewish courts and therefore an area for the development of human rights.

The monogamy clause in the marriage contracts of the Cairo Geniza has already been discussed. Another clause that was most often connected with it was one prohibiting the husband from keeping a maidservant whom his wife disliked. To be sure, sexual relations with a slavegirl were strictly forbidden by Jewish (as by Christian) law. The new provision aimed at further protection of the wife and the preservation of domestic peace. In view of the extensive concubinage practiced by the Muslim majority, this was a particularly difficult task; but, as proved by the rich documentation of the Geniza, it must have been carried out satisfactorily to a remarkable degree. Later, in Christian Spain, the Jewish authorities were less successful in this respect.

There was another aspect of domestic life in which the example of the Muslim environment was harmful. An Islamic saying has it that the ideal wife passes the threshold of her husband's house only twice: when she enters it after her wedding and when she leaves it for her eternal abode. Islamic law gave the husband considerable rights to limit his wife's freedom of movement. It is natural that Jewish husbands, especially of the lower classes, tried to usurp the same rights, although they were not granted by Jewish law. Here we see the Jewish courts taking a strong stand. A Jewish woman was free to visit any place where a respectable Jewish woman was supposed to go, such as the synagogue, the bath-house (in those times, a kind of club house, where one passed the better part of the day), parties of congratulation or condolence (also very long-drawn affairs), the bazaars of the clothiers, and, of course (though husbands sometimes objected), her family. Maimonides, who came from the fanatical Muslim West, took a far less liberal stance on this question than the Jewish judges who preceded him in Egypt.[10]

Maimonides' strictness has been particularly noted with regard to the grave problem of wife-beating. According to him, a wife should be forced to do the work she is obliged to do, "even with a stick." This strange pronouncement was motivated by the belief that idleness produced looseness of morals. Yet, as Abraham ben David, the Provençal critic of Maimonides remarks, there is noth-ing in the classical sources of Judaism that would authorize a hus-band to physically castigate his wife. This was permitted, and perhaps even recommended, by the Koran; but not by the Jewish Scriptures. Modern writers who have compared the advice of Maimonides and the rebuke by his Provençal critic incorrectly see in them the contrast between the Muslim and the Christian environments. Wife-beating was as common in Christian Europe as it was under Islam, and it was also theoretically justified by Christian theologians. On the other hand, many documents of the Geniza show that the Jewish judges took a very serious view of this matter, imposed fines on husbands, or threatened them with forced separation or even divorce. Muslim judges, too, protected maltreated women, and there were Christian theologians who dis-approved of wife-beating. This was not a difference between Islam and Christianity but a split of opinion about human rights which intersected the three monotheistic religions; and it was not always the most prominent thinkers who took the most progressive stance.

A medieval Jewish woman (and perhaps the woman of the early Middle Ages in general), while married, remained strongly attached to the house of her father, the family into which she was born. Her financial resources after the death of her husband, or in case of divorce, were mainly the possessions she had brought from her father's house; and, in case of disputes with her husband, she had to take refuge with her father or brothers. Therefore, one of the most precious human rights of a married woman of those days was the privilege to live in the propinquity of her paternal family. The right of choosing the domicile of the young couple often was given to the wife in her marriage contract, or established after marital strife. It was one of the most characteristic aspects of Jewish marriage as revealed by the Cairo Geniza.

Women frequently appeared in court, made transactions of the greatest possible variety, and served as executrixes of wills and as guardians of children. Essentially, I believe, all this was perfectly legal also under ancient Jewish law; but the mass of new materials on such activities found in the Geniza seems to prove that, despite the hampering influence of the seclusion of women under Islam, the socioeconomic transformation of the Jewish people, discussed above, remarkably enhanced the economic independence of the Jewish woman, and with it, her legal position.

A similar change is to be observed in the right to education. In talmudic times, the parents were obliged to provide education for their children, and in the absence of parents, or where they were destitute, it was up to the local community to provide the necessary service. In principle, the situation was the same in the Geniza period. The difference is that here we see the law generally accepted and put into force. The communities either kept special classes for orphans and the children of the poor or paid teachers for admitting them to their schools. Many marriages were concluded to safeguard the proper upbringing of the children of one widowed partner or both, and the relevant contracts also give us an idea about the time required for this (e.g., ten years for upbringing, two for paid vocational training). They also show another side of the child's human rights: the stepfather must never castigate his stepson physically, nor humiliate him verbally—a formulation reminiscent of Maimonides' words regarding the treatment of slaves.[11]

The rights of the needy were an area in which particularly conspicuous progress was made during the Middle Ages. The goal was not to liquidate poverty. This was neither possible—for the numbers of paupers compared to the householders sustaining

them was far too large, nor was it intended—for poverty was a
state decreed by God and it was up to Him, not man, to make
the poor rich.[12] The greatest attainment of the age was the strictness with which the idea of the rights of the needy was put to
work, that is, the care taken that all funds destined for the poor
would really reach them. Revenue was created by collections made
throughout the year, special drives, and, to an ever rising degree,
by income from properties donated to the community for the
purpose. Bread was distributed to the poor regularly, twice a
week. There was also distribution of wheat, clothing, and money,
and special allocations for such other needs as education, health
care, and burial.

All this was done by adhering to strict legal procedures. No one
could receive handouts from the community without being a
certified needy, a status which was checked at short intervals. The
lists of contributors, beneficiaries, and revenues from, and ex-
penditures on, public property were posted in the synagogue
where anyone could scrutinize them. Sometimes the *parnassim,*
social-service officers, who had compiled these lists, and the three
communal judges, who had examined them, would affix their
signatures. Often even small matters of public charity were brought
before the *Nagid,* Head of the Jews, for any misuse of money
intended for the poor would be an impingement on their rights.
Although the means of the Jewish community were limited, its
insistence on strict legal procedure in this matter must have been
a great relief to all concerned. It may have been necessitated by
the practices rampant in the far richer Muslim environment, where
the misuse of funds destined for the poor was proverbial.[13]

Finally, it was the courts of justice which were the upholders
and promoters of human rights within the Jewish community. The
Muslim *qadi,* like the late Roman provincial magistrate, dispensed
law in splendid isolation, which opened the door to partiality,
venality, and miscarriage of justice. The Jewish court consisted of
at least three men. The bench was normally shared by a professional scholar and men of affairs, so that legal tradition and
practical experience worked side by side. The procedure consisted
of fact-finding and statement of the legal situation. Once this was
done, the parties usually settled and the judges signed the agreement as witnesses. From Spain to India the same law and procedures were observed by the Jewish courts. This greatly enhanced

the legal security of merchants engaged in international trade, or rather of most people, for even persons with limited means had shares in one or another venture of the international trade. There was no force compelling the litigants to apply to a Jewish court. Those who went to a Jewish court did so because they believed this to be a more expedient and safer way to obtain their rights than to go to the *qadi.*

The Jewish courts of the High Middle Ages were not mere committees of arbitration. The cases were decided according to the law of the Torah, traditional Jewish law, as it had developed by that time. This is clearly evident from the countless responsa, or legal opinions, on actual litigations still preserved and from many direct references. Once the legal situation was established, the courts preferred settlement to outright judgment (which, of course, was also given when absolutely necessary), for any faulty dispensation of the law of the Torah was a grave sin. The law of the Torah was heeded, but it was, one might say, taken out of the hands of God and placed into the hands of men.

Summary

The Jewish craftsmen and merchants of the Middle Ages were involved on a daily basis with their fellows, customers, and competitiors, and therefore they evolved sensitivity to human relations. This was one source of the progress made in that period toward the safeguarding of human rights. Yet that concern for human rights did not develop from an idea of equality. Maimonides took pains to explain in detail that even in the days of the Messiah there would be poor and rich, powerful and wretched people.[14] On the other hand, we remember his warm words advocating humane treatment of slaves, because they are sons of Eve like ourselves. In a similar appeal, Solomon ben Judah, the eleventh-century head of the Jerusalem *yeshivah,* quoting Malachi (2:10), exclaims: "Do we not all have one father, has not one God created us all?" The father alluded to here is not Abraham, the father of the faith, but Adam, the father of mankind.[15] Thus the basis of human rights was not *egalité,* for there prevailed a profound sense of the God-ordained natural inequality of men, but *fraternité,* the idea of human brotherhood.

NOTES

1. See Solomon Pines, "Nathanel Ben al-Fayyumi et la théologie ismaélienne," *Bulletin des études historiques juives,* I (Cairo, 1946), pp. 5–22.

2. S.D. Goitein, "The Rise of the Middle Eastern Bourgeosie in Early Islamic Times," in *Studies in Islamic History and Institutions,* Leiden, 1966, 217–41. What I have said there with regard to the Jewish community, p. 241, was later qualified by me in my paper, "Some Major Problems of Jewish History," *Proceedings of the Fifth World Congress of Jewish Studies,* Jerusalem, 1972, pp. 100–106.

3. See Goitein, "Slaves and Slavegirls," in *A Mediterranean Society: The Jewish Communities of the Arab World as Portrayed in the Documents of the Cairo Geniza,* vol. 1, University of California Press, Berkeley, 1967, pp. 130–47, 431–37.

4. Lawrence V. Berman, "The Political Interpretation of the Maxim: The Purpose of Philosophy Is the Imitation of God," *Studia Islamica* 15 (1961), pp. 53–54.

5. H. Tykocinski, *Die gaonaeischen Verordnungen,* Berlin, 1929, pp. 37 ff. where the relevant material is carefully collected. See Salo W. Baron, *Social and Religious History of the Jews,* vol. 6, p. 132, and 392, n. 152.

6. This *takkana* is preserved in two parts. The lower was edited by S. Assaf in *Melilah,* Manchester, 1950, vol. 3–4, 224–29, and reprinted in J. Blau. *R. Moses b. Maimon Responsa,* Jerusalem, 1960, vol. 2, pp. 516–19. The upper part was discovered by me later and published in *Tarbiz* 32 (1963), pp. 191–94.

7. Hay Gaon in Harkavy, *Responsen der Geonim,* Berlin, 1887, p. 216, no. 423. Goitein, *A Mediterranean Society,* vol. 2, pp. 328 and 599. N.V. Pigulevskaja, Die Sammlung der syrischen *Rechtsurkunden des Ischobocht und der Matikan,* in xxiv. Internationaler Orientalistenkongress, Akad. Nauk, USSR, Moscow, 1957. Goitein, *A Mediterranean Society,* vol. 1, 1967; vol. 2, 1971.

8. Maimonides, Code, *malveh ve-loveh,* chap. 11, para. 11. S.W. Baron, *Social and Religious History,* vol. 6, p. 132.

9. Z.W. Falk, *Jewish Matrimonial Law in the Middle Ages,* Oxford, 1966, pp. 13 ff. Mordechai A. Friedman, in *Perspectives of Jewish Learning,* Chicago, 1972, pp. 26 and 36, n. 26.

10. See article "Woman" in *Encyclopaedia Judaica,* XVI, p. 627. About wife-beating in Europe see G.G. Coulton, *Medieval Panorama,* 1938, reprint Meridian Books 1958, pp. 614–28 (with illustration).

11. See numerous examples for such stipulations in marriage contracts in my *Jewish Education in Muslim Countries, Sidre Hinnukh* (Jerusalem, 1962, 29–31 [Heb.]). A number of others have been found by me in the interim.

12. *A Mediterranean Society,* vol. 2, pp. 139–42, and 443.

13. Ibid., pp. 91–143, 411–510, 542–50.

14. Maimonides, *Commentary on Mishna,* Sanhedrin, 10, Introduction (edition Qafeh, Jerusalem, 1965), pp. 197, 207.

15. Unpublished manuscript, still in private possession, Mosseri L 210.

Modern Movements

SALO W. BARON

17
The Evolution of Equal Rights:
Civil and Political

The very term *emancipation* has been deeply tinged with emotion. Emerging in the press and the literature after the 1828 Catholic emancipation in England, this term denoted, as did its ancient Roman prototype, liberation from bondage. The tendency for the protagonists of Jewish emancipation was to overstress the existing or past "bondage" of the Jews and their discriminatory treatment by law and society, as against the forthcoming era of freedom in which Jews would be participants in the historic careers of the surrounding nations as citizens equal to all others in their rights and duties.

Out of this overemphasis upon the pre-emancipation status of discrimination and segregation grew not only the misconception of the meaning of medieval Jewish "serfdom," but also the long-prevailing lachrymose conception of Jewish history in the Diaspora as being essentially a *Leidens- und Gelehrtengeschichte*. Ultimately, many people started talking of a pariah status of the pre-emancipation Jew. This term was supported by the great authority of Max Weber, who, in the introduction to his penetrating essay on the social ethics of ancient Judaism, had bluntly declared:

"Sociologically speaking, what were the Jews? A pariah people. This meaning, as we know it from India, a guest people which is ritualistically segregated from its social environment either formally or actually." Forgetting the qualifications suggested by Weber himself, the Indian parallel has haunted many Jewish minds ever since. In fact, however, it is without justification.[1]

I

This somewhat simplistic contrast between the modern Jew and his ghetto ancestor tended to overlook some basic lines of evolution which preceded and followed the American and French revolutions. In many of the works on Jewish emancipation, the main emphasis has been on the legal and political aspects of equality of rights for Jews. These developments were usually best dated according to the legal enactments guaranteeing such equality under the constitutions of the respective countries. The process of Jewish entry into general society, however, depended much more on basic demographic, economic, and intellectual developments than on legal pronunciamentos. Very frequently legal enactments were merely a form of ratification of socioeconomic and cultural developments which had already taken place, sometimes over a period of generations. True, the law, once enacted, added new vigor and acceleration to those underlying trends. In some cases, however, when it was precipitately promulgated out of consideration for general principles, it proved quite ineffective in practice, because society was not prepared to follow its lead. We need but refer to the obvious dichotomy between the generally egalitarian constitutions of the Soviet Union and of many Arab lands and the actual treatment of Jews by the existing regimes.

Nonetheless, with the general penchant of the revolutionary and post-revolutionary generations before World War I to attribute supreme importance to formal enactments and the belief in the sanctity of constitutional provisions as well as of international treaties, the struggle in the late eighteenth and most of the nineteenth centuries took the shape of political battles for the securing of such egalitarian pronouncements. Characteristically, this struggle was led not by the Jews but rather by progressive forces in the various states, whose spokesmen, often subconsciously, felt that

Jewish emancipation was an even greater historic necessity for the modern state than it was for the Jews themselves.[2]

Most prolonged and widely debated was the struggle for Jewish equality in the German-speaking countries. The problems were aired in endless discussions, from the days of Mendelssohn, Lessing, and Dohm to the Congress of Vienna, the basic constitution of the Germanic Confederation, the upheavals of 1848, and the numerous legal enactments in the various German states culminating in the Austro-Hungarian constitution of 1867 and that of the German Empire of 1871. These debates continued with great passion thereafter because of the unceasing anti-Semitic attacks on Jewish equality and the Jewish, as well as general, apologias for it. One major item under dispute was whether Jewish emancipation was so intimately interwoven with Jewish assimilation that it entailed a sort of contractual obligation on the part of Jews to become assimilated to German culture. Some Jew-baiters argued that, because Jews had not surrendered their ethnic identity, they had not kept their part of the contractual bargain and that, hence, emancipation ought to be revoked.[3]

At the same time, Jews—and particularly spokesmen of the rising Jewish nationalist movement—argued not only that legal inequality of any segment of the population was incompatible with democracy but also that all ethnic minorities as such were entitled to enjoy both equality of rights as citizens and specific safeguards for the cultivation of their cultural heritage. They demanded, therefore, both equality and so-called minority rights. These debates led up to international guarantees, in the Peace Treaties of 1919, of both full emancipation and minority rights for the Jews living in the countries between the Baltic and the Aegean Sea. Before long, however, these attainments were completely cancelled out by the Nazi revolution, which not only denied Jews legal equality but gainsaid their very right to existence.

During the two centuries of debate, the Germans emerged with a clearer conception of the distinction between what they called the *bürgerliche Gleichberechtigung* and the *privatbürgerliche Gleichberechtigung*. The former implied complete equality in both political and civil rights and duties. The latter was intended to grant Jews socioeconomic equality, particularly in the occupational sphere, while denying them the political rights of public office, political franchise, and the like. This distinction underlay, for instance, the famous Prussian emancipatory decree of March 11, 1812. In Articles 7–9 it provided for full equality of Jewish *Einländer* with the Christians and even opened up to Jews all academic, teaching, and municipal posts. But it added: "We reserve for ourselves the right to provide in the future as to the extent to which Jews shall also be admitted to other state functions and offices."[4]

At times, such limited equality also implied certain differentials in the duties of citizenship; for example, in military service. On the other hand, Jewish participation in the military forces was demanded in Austria and in Russia even before the enactment of general legal equality. Remarkably, the Russia of Catherine the Great was ready to concede to the Jews electoral rights in municipal governments—rights formally granted in that period only to the Jews of Tuscany, where the Jewry of Leghorn had long played a noteworthy role in the grand duchy's affairs. Simultaneously, however, the Russian government imposed upon the Jews significant new residential and occupational disabilities to meet certain demands by powerful segments of society at large.[5]

II

In assessing the aftermath of emancipation, one must not overlook the fundamental fact that equality of rights for Jews was unthinkable in the general European corporate structure prevailing before the great eighteenth-century revolutions. There existed no equality of rights for other groups of the population. Each corporate body, such as the nobility and the clergy, the bourgeoisie and the peasantry, whether free or living in a state of villeinage, lived according to its own system of rights and duties. Very frequently, the privileges granted to one city greatly differed from those granted to another in its immediate vicinity. In Poland some so-called *jurydiki* formed enclaves within the cities, the jurisdiction over which was in the hands of their private owners, especially nobles or churches, who independently regulated the rights of the respective groups in their domains. Even within individual cities the legal status of patricians often differed from that of the plebeians in both theory and practice. And among various artisan guilds regulations differed in accordance with their respective statutes. Under such a system Jews formed a corporate body apart, whose rights and duties were regulated by special privileges granted by monarchs or other masters, privileges which often varied from locality to locality and from period to period. It was the great historic accomplishment of the modern state to have swept away these multifarious regulations which often came into direct conflict with one another and led to endless controversies and even court litigations sometimes lasting for decades.

For Jews the distinction between political and civil rights was of great importance. Civil rights, which primarily involved the removal of certain occupational disabilities, were of paramount concern to a people which was at that time rapidly increasing in numbers and badly needed an enlargement of its economic base. If my population estimates are at all correct, it appears that in the mid-seventeenth century the total world Jewish population had declined to less than one million, but subsequently rose to well over two million at the beginning of the nineteenth century, and reached some sixteen million in 1939.[6]

With such a population explosion, Jews could not possibly live on the few limited occupations open to them under the restrictive legislation of the pre-emancipation period. Hence, there was practical unanimity among their leaders about the desirability of the removal of the civil disabilities, although the admission of Jewish pupils to general schools (the public-school system, started in Prussia in 1802, was rapidly gaining ground throughout the Western world in the course of the nineteenth century) was not necessarily considered a blessing by the staunchly Orthodox, who viewed their children's attendance at such schools as a threat to the survival of some of the most cherished elements in their intellectual heritage. But the threat to such survival from political emancipation was infinitely greater. Among the new duties imposed upon the Jews loomed full participation in military service, which increasingly meant compulsory drafts of masses of young men in each country. Quite apart from such excesses as came to the fore in the Russian *recrutchina* of 1827–55, such service often demanded from Jewish soldiers violation of the Sabbath and neglect of the dietary laws.[7]

More generally, the integration of the Jews into the political structure of their respective countries usually presupposed curtailment of Jewish self-government in communal affairs. The judicial

authority of the Jewish courts of justice, especially, now necessarily had to give way to that of the general courts. Nor did the
Jewish community function any longer in behalf of the state as the
main tax-collecting agency among Jews; it was happy to receive
governmental guarantees for its right to impose limited taxation on
its members in order to provide the now greatly reduced communal
needs. Otherwise, Jews as individuals were to be taxed, on a par
with the other citizens, directly by the government's fiscal organs.
On the other hand, the major political right, namely that of the
franchise, was rather meaningless to the masses of Jews living in
countries such as Russia, and even Austria or Prussia, before the
proclamation of their more liberal constitutions. In absolutist
states, the diets possessed very limited legislative powers, and the
right to vote in their elections meant very little in practice. Even
after, the aforementioned right of the Russian or Tuscan Jews of
the eighteenth century to elect or be elected aldermen in their
municipalities carried very little weight, since the municipal organs
largely continued to be controlled by often hostile burghers.

For these reasons, many traditional Jews were more afraid of
political emancipation than of a continuation of the existing discriminatory laws. Even in such Western communities as those of
Amsterdam in 1796 and the Grand Duchy of Baden in 1846, the
conservative groups often strenuously objected to the sweeping
declarations of complete equality of rights. Understandably, the
opposition was more intense in the East European mass settlements where most Jews were able to live a full Jewish life and
undisturbedly cultivate their ancestral mores. In the Duchy of
Warsaw, created by Napoleon I after the Battle of Austerlitz out
of the eastern provinces of Prussia, the rumors spreading among
the population about an impending enactment of a broad-gauged
egalitarian constitution created consternation in the Orthodox communities. Not surprisingly, some leading rabbis called upon the
Jews of the entire duchy to observe fast days and convoked special
worshipful assemblies to recite Hebrew prayers imploring the Deity
to forestall the feared catastrophe. More practical elders instituted
a large fund-raising campaign in order to dispatch a delegation to
Warsaw to lobby there against the forthcoming legislation. As it
turned out, however, the constitution proved to be far less egalitarian than expected. From a slightly different angle, half a century
later, Galician Orthodox communities feared that the weakening

of the traditional internal controls resulting from the political egalitarianism proclaimed by the Austrian Constitution of 1867 would result in replacement of their own chosen leaders by outside authorities whom they had been accustomed to mistrust and fear. The popular Yiddish humor equated *Konstitutsie* with *konst du, tist du* (if you can, you do)—meaning that the new individual liberties would replace the existing moral order by uncontrolled license and anarchical behavior. Nevertheless, in the long run, political and civil rights became so intertwined, and the needs of both the Jewish people and the modern democratic states to establish a general system of equality of rights so imperative, that all such negativistic attitudes on the part of the Jewish minority proved utterly futile.[8]

III

The leaders of governments and of public opinion were not unaware of the Jews' reluctance to give up their accustomed way of life in return for some dubious benefits of political equality. Opponents of Jewish emancipation, such as Abbé Maury of the French National Assembly, harped on the theme of the Jews being a "state within the state." The abbot, and many of his successors in various lands, insisted that the Jews would always remain such a self-segregating entity within the body politic despite equality of rights. On the other hand, the proponents of an egalitarian system often outspokenly or tacitly presupposed that Jewish emancipation would automatically entail Jewish assimilation to the majority culture. In his famous dictum at that assembly, the Girondist Count Clermont-Tonnèrre emphasized that the new constitution ought to give "to Jewish individuals all rights, to the Jewish nation none," which was a clear call to the Jews to give up their separatism. To reinforce that nexus, this protagonist in the struggle for Jewish equality added a most significant clause: If the Jews would accept this arrangement, well and good; but if not, "let them say so, and then let them be banished!" In other words, even Clermont-Tonnèrre thus reverted to the old medieval intolerance of Jewish ethnic distinctiveness. In the Middle Ages total assimilation could be achieved only by the Jews' accepting conversion to the dominant faith of their compatriots, whereas since the Treaties of Westphalia of 1648 European nations had learned to live peacefully together with a variety of Christian sects, and assimilation to their secular cultures was deemed sufficient.[9]

Even more remarkably, when after considerable struggle the Congress of Vienna passed the basic Constitutional Act of the newly formed Germanic Confederation under the guarantee of the Great Powers, it inserted the well-known Article 16 referring to Jews, which read in part:

> The Confederate Diet will take under advisement . . . as to how the enjoyment of citizens' rights could be granted to the adherents of the Jewish faith in the Confederate States in return for their assumption of all the duties of citizens.

Evidently, the sponsors of that resolution, including the chief defenders of Jewish rights at the Congress—the Prussian representatives, Chancellor Carl von Hardenberg and Wilhelm von Humboldt—wished to make sure that the Jews would accept that condition.[10]

Yet, as it turned out, granting the Jews political rights encountered considerable resistance among the conservative groups in Prussia and the other Confederate States, and the promise of Article 16 was not to be implemented for several decades. For ideological even more than for practical reasons, many members of the ruling classes resented Jews holding public office and thus exerting political "domination" over Christians. As a small but irksome residuum of the medieval discrimination, German Jews, though obliged to serve in the army and navy along with their Christian compatriots, were kept out of the officers' corps and higher administrative posts from 1871 to 1914. At the same time, civil equality encountered even greater practical obstacles. Many Christians, entrenched in certain occupations, fiercely resisted the Jews' entry out of fear that their own sources of livelihood would thereby be subject to much stiffer competition. That is why the progress of civil equality usually was quite protracted and particular disabilities were removed only step by step, until society and government were ready to decree total equality by a sweeping declaration.

When, in the era of resettlement, Holland pioneered with the readmission of Jews and the extension to them of many civil rights, the eminent jurist Hugo Grotius realized that there were insurmountable obstacles to granting the Jews full equality in civil occupations. Although advocating in 1616 that Amsterdam admit Jews on the basis of fundamental equality, subject only to specific disabilities, his famous *Remonstrantië* consisted of some forty articles primarily devoted to spelling out such disabilities. Foremost among the proposed discriminatory provisions was a continued prohibition on Jews engaging in any retail trade because increased competition in this field might undermine the livelihood of many Christian burghers. On the other hand, Jews were welcome to engage in banking, stock-exchange transactions, membership in the East and West India companies, the establishment of sugar mills and other factories, and in international trade—all desirable occupations from the standpoint of the Christian majority because they thus helped to enlarge the occupational arena not only for themselves but also for the Dutch people as a whole.[11] Similar considerations governed the readmission of Jews by the city of Hamburg, as well as by Glückstadt, then under Danish suzereinty.

Most noteworthy was the law passed in England in 1697 with respect to the London Stock Exchange. So desirable appeared the presence of Jewish brokers with their extensive international contacts and a clientele in control of considerable capital that the law provided for a total Stock Exchange membership of 124, of whom 100 were to be men enjoying the freedom of the city, 12 foreigners, and 12 Jews. Ironically, Jews were thus granted the privileged position of permanently holding nearly 10 percent of the total membership, at a time when they constituted an insignificant fraction of the inhabitants of the English capital and when the prevailing legal fiction still assumed that no Jews were allowed to live in the country.[12]

Another major obstacle to Jewish entry into various occupations stemmed from the existing guild monopolies. In many areas Jews were not only refused admission to the guilds which, incidentally, often were as much religious brotherhoods and social fraternities as occupational leagues, but were frequently prevented from competing with guild members in the production of their respective goods. At times, only crafts connected in some form with Jewish religious requirements, such as meat processing and tailoring (because of the biblical prohibition of mixing wool and linen), were exempted. In Central and Eastern Europe the perennial Jewish conflicts with existing artisan (and merchant) guilds formed a highly significant, often tragic, chapter in the history of the Jewish people. On many occasions the guilds appeared in the forefront of the struggle to eliminate Jews entirely from a city or country. Only slowly, and largely under the pressure of other groups, did decisive economic factors prevail over such narrow class interests. Jews were allowed to form guilds of their own in Poland and Lithuania. To cite the English experience again, such admission was gradual; for instance, Jews were allowed to become solicitors in 1770 and were admitted as barristers in 1833, long before the change of the oath of office of newly admitted members of Parliament in 1857 enabled Jews to be elected to office and subsequently to take their seats in the House of Commons.[13]

In Britain's North American colonies, however, Jews, like other white immigrants, were often welcomed as much-needed manpower to populate and exploit the vast open spaces in the New World. Thus, they could more readily overcome any economic disabilities. The saga of Asser Levy and his successful struggle in 1654–64 for permission to open a butcher shop, acquire real estate, and to stand guard instead of paying a special tax, was a noteworthy example of how quickly such obstacles could be overcome. It was not surprising, therefore, that in the following century Myer Myers was not only admitted to membership in the Gold and Silversmith Guild in New York but was even elected its president twice, once seemingly before the American Revolution.[14]

Most remarkably, the exercise by Jews of certain political rights, such as voting in elections for colonial legislatures—which were far more meaningful than municipal elections in most European countries of the period—caused hardly a ripple among the North American colonial public. Only once, when in 1737 a defeated candidate to the New York Assembly raised an objection to Jews having been allowed to vote in the election, did the New York Assembly declare that, as in the mother country, Jews ought not to enjoy political franchise. This declaration seems to have been subsequently disregarded, especially after the enactment, by the British Parliament, of the Naturalization Act for the North American colonies, in which special allowance was made for Jews' religious scruples, in order to facilitate their becoming naturalized citizens. Not long thereafter, in 1774, Francis Salvador, a young English Jew but recently settled in South Carolina, was readily elected to the First and Second Provincial Congress of that colony which, in 1776, became the first general legislature of the state of South Carolina. Nor do we hear of any objections against the admission of Jewish volunteers to the revolutionary forces, or to their serving as officers in command of Christian detachments.[15]

IV

Partly because of its legal disabilities and partly for other historic reasons, pre-emancipation Jewry in most countries had an economic stratification at variance with that of the majority of the population. This imbalance often served as a target for anti-Jewish attacks, Jews being called by their enemies usurers, unsavory merchants *(Schacherer)*, and exploiters of the populace. The Jewish minority of reformers and protagonists of equality were prepared to admit some of these charges and merely argued that not the Jews but the existing laws were responsible for this awkward disparity.[16]

To remedy that disequilibrium, progressive Jews from the Mendelssohnian age on, were ready to cooperate with the governments in teaching Jewish youth to engage in "useful" and "productive" occupations, and thus to make them better citizens for the countries concerned. In most Western countries Jewish communities organized regular societies for retraining young Jews and for channeling their energies into productive work. Some governments, beginning with Joseph II of Austria and Alexander I of Russia, adopted large-scale programs for colonizing Jews on land so as to convert a people of petty traders and craftsmen into farmers and agricultural laborers.[17]

This ideal of restratification, of course, ran counter to the prevailing economic trends which during the last several generations were driving untold millions of peasants into cities and constantly diminishing the ratio of the farming population in all Western lands. But such a reversal could appear, to quote a well-known Hegelian simile, as "placing history, where it belongs, on its head." This ideal dominated Jewish thinking throughout the nineteenth and early twentieth centuries: it was the hallowed watchword of the *Am Olam* movement for the Dispersion and of the Zionist pioneer movement for Palestine.

Yet such a defiance of prevailing economic trends is never easy or completely successful. We do not have adequate Jewish occupational statistics, not even for the contemporary United States. Historically, even in countries where demographic data were more readily available because the recurrent governmental censuses have identified Jews as members of either a religious or an ethnic group, their occupational distribution often is inadequately known. However, on the basis of whatever information is now available we may have to come to an amazing conclusion: if one compares the Jewish economic stratification along broad occupational lines as it existed in the year 1800, as against that of a hundred years later, one finds rather little statistical change. Despite the considerable efforts at rebuilding the Jewish economic structure and the opening to Jews of untold new economic opportunities in the rapidly expanding economies of the Western world, the major occupational categories do not seem to have changed very greatly. According to the best available estimates, in 1800, about 2 percent of Jewish households engaged in farming, some 30 percent derived their living from various crafts, while almost 50 percent lived from commerce, including moneylending, and allied occupations; only a small percentage were in the ranks of professionals and public servants, many of the latter holding offices within the Jewish community as such. There was also a considerable residuum of so-called *Luftmenschen* who derived a meager income from occasional odd jobs, or lived on private or communal charities.

In 1900, notwithstanding the great colonizing schemes for Jewish immigrants in the United States, the efforts of the Jewish Colonization Association to settle East European Jews on land in Argentina and other countries, and the early Zionist plan to develop the Palestinian Yishuv with an emphasis on agricultural colonies, the percentage of farmers in the Jewish world population seems not to have exceeded the 2 percent of a century before. Similarly, the industrial segment did not go beyond one-third of the gainfully employed Jews in the world. Perhaps the largest change consisted in the diminution of the ratio of *Luftmenschen* and the growth of the number of Jews in the liberal professions and other service industries.

Needless to say, there is a qualitative difference between the large number of Jewish petty artisans and their apprentices who formed the majority of those engaged in industrial endeavors in the early 1800s and the legions of Jewish factory workers in Eastern Europe or the United States a century later. Similarly, there is a qualitative difference between a mass of Jews owning small retail shops and the multitude of employees in, or agents for, large business corporations; not to speak of the mercantile elite which controls large retail chains or department stores. The important role played by Jews in arts, sciences, journalism, and other forms of communication may not be accurately reflected in the occupational statistics, but from the point of view of economic well-being and sociopolitical influence, such differences are of basic importance.

Nevertheless, these transformations are not quite so radical as they appear on the surface. In short, what happened in the course of the nineteenth century was not so much that, by securing wider civil rights, the Jewish economic structure had begun resembling that of the general population, but rather that, because of the prevailing economic trends in recent generations—as I had paradoxically contended back in 1937—"the world has become, so to speak, increasingly 'Jewish' in its economic stratification. Once more Jews may merely have anticipated the general developments."[18]

NOTES

1. See Max Weber's *Gesammelte Aufsätze zur Religionssoziologie.* 3 vols., Tübingen, 1920–21, vol. 3: Das antike Judentum, pp. 2 f.; and my remarks thereon in *A Social and Religious History of the Jews,* 2d ed. revised, vols. 1–16, New York, 1952–76, esp. vol. 1, 297 n. 7, and on the meaning of medieval Jewish serfdom, ibid., vol. 11, 4 ff., 289 ff. and the literature listed there. My rejection of Weber's thesis has by no means been weakened by its defense on the part of the English translators of Weber's *Ancient Judaism,* Glencoe, Ill., 1952, pp. xxiv f.

2. This aspect has been more fully developed in my essay, "Newer Approaches to Jewish Emancipation," *Diogenes,* 29 (Spring, 1960), 56–81 (also in its French and Spanish editions).

3. See Harry Sacher's succinct reply to these contentions in his *Jewish Emancipation—The Contract Myth,* London, 1917.

4. See the text and the discussions preceding its enactment in Ismar Freund's *Die Emanzipation der Juden in Preussen unter besonderer Berücksichtigung des Gesetzes vom 11. März 1812.* 2 vols., Berlin, 1912.

5. On the manifold vagaries in Catherine's Jewish legislation, see the

brief summary in my *The Russian Jew under Tsars and Soviets,* 2d ed. rev. and enlarged, New York, 1976, pp. 15 ff.; and W. Bruce Lincoln, "The Russian State and Its Cities: a Search for Effective Municipal Government, 1786–1842," *Jahrbücher für Geschichte Osteuropas,* 17 (1969), 531–41.

6. See my *A Social and Religious History of the Jews,* first ed., 3 vols., New York, 1937, vol. 2, 165 ff.; and my article "Population" in the new *Encyclopaedia Judaica,* vol. 13 (1971), 866–903.

7. On the excesses of the Russian cantonist system, which left a permanent imprint on the Russian Jewish community, see esp. the graphic description by Saul Ginsburg in his *Historishe Verk,* 3 vols., New York, 1937–38, vol. 2, 3–20; vol. 3, 3–135, 357–69.

8. E.N. Frenk, *Yehude Polin bi-yeme milhamot Napoleon* (Poland's Jews during the Napoleonic Wars), Warsaw, 1912, p. 23; Philip Friedman, *Die galizischen Juden im Kampfe um ihre Gleichberechtigung (1848–1868),* Frankfurt, 1929.

9. See the text of Count Clermont-Tonnèrre's oft-quoted address of December 23, 1789 (including the final threat of banishment), reproduced in the *Revue des grandes journées parlementaires,* ed. by Gaston Lebre and G. Labouchère, vol. 1 (1897), p. 10. On " 'A State within a State'—The History of an Antisemitic Slogan," see Jacob Katz's essay under this title in *Proceedings* of the Israel Academy of Sciences and Humanities, vol. 4, (1969), 3. However, Katz himself admits that the same slogan was also used against such other disliked "separatist" groups as the Jesuits and the Freemasons.

10. Johann L. Klüber, ed., *Akten des Wiener Kongresses 1814 und 15,* 8 vols., Erlangen, 1815–19, esp. vol. 2, 456 ff., 590 ff.; and other data analyzed in my *Die Judenfrage auf dem Wiener Kongress auf Grund von zum Teil ungedruckten Quellen dargstellt,* Vienna, 1920.

11. See Hugo Grotius, *Remonstrantië nopende de ordre dije in de landen van Hollandt ende Westvrieslandt dijent gestelt op de Joden,* reed. by Jacob Meijer, Amsterdam, 1949; Meijer's analysis of "Hugo Grotius' Remonstrantie," *Jewish Social Studies,* 17 (1955), 91–104; Herbert I. Bloom, *The Economic Activities of the Jews of Amsterdam in the Seventeenth and Eighteenth Centuries,* Williamsport, Pa., 1937; and the additional sources quoted in my *Social and Religious History of the Jews,* 2d ed., vol. 15, 390, n. 30.

12. Lucien Wolf, "The First Stage of Anglo-Jewish Emancipation," in his *Essays in Jewish History,* ed. by Cecil Roth, London, 1934, pp. 115–36.

13. H.S.Q. Henriques, *The Jews and the English Law,* Oxford, 1908, pp. 203 ff.

14. The sources cited in my "The Emancipation Movement and American Jewry," first published in Hebrew in *Eretz-Israel,* vol. 4 (1956), 204–214 and subsequently reproduced in a revised English trans. in my *Steeled by Adversity: Essays and Addresses on American Jewish Life,* ed. by Jeannette M. Baron, Philadelphia, 1971, pp. 80–105, 592–98.

15. Ibid., pp. 92 ff., 595 ff.

16. Characteristic of that approach was Christian Wilhelm Dohm's *Über die bürgerliche Verbesserung der Juden,* rev. ed., 2 vols., Berlin, 1783, partly written under Mendelssohn's inspiration, and enthusiastically greeted by some Jewish contemporaries. On the "Dessau philosopher" role in this enterprise and his own divergent views on some details, see now Alexander Altmann's comprehensive work, *Moses Mendelssohn: A Biographical Study,* Tuscaloosa, Ala., 1973; and his "Letters from Dohm to Mendelssohn," *Salo W. Baron Jubilee Volume,* ed. by Saul Lieberman, 3 vols., Jerusalem, 1974 [1975], vol. 1, 39–62.

17. See, for instance, J.M. Isler, *Rückkehr der Juden zur Landwirtschaft. Beitrag zur Geschichte der landwirtschaftlichen Kolonisation der Juden in verschiedenen Ländern,* Frankfurt, 1929.

18. See my *A Social and Religious History of the Jews,* first, 1937 ed., vol. 2, 409. Certainly the American farmers who, though consisting of but some 4 percent of the gainfully employed persons in the United States, are able not only to meet the needs of their own society but also help to feed untold millions in other lands, statistically resemble much more closely the small minority of Jews living on agriculture in Eastern Europe in 1800 or in the United States in 1900 than did the Christian farmers in those countries in either period.

JACOB KATZ

18

Post-Emancipation Development of Rights: Liberalism and Universalism

I

The emancipation of Jews, that is, their acceptance as permanent residents of a country and equal citizens of the state, was the result of a historical process that transformed Western thought as well as social reality. In the realm of thought, it meant the transition from a theologically conditioned orientation to one wedded to nationalism. In the realm of reality, it meant relinquishing religious commitments by the state in favor of purely secular objectives and a shift from the feudal structure of society toward the free mobility of individuals. All these mutations were of a universalistic nature insofar as they pertained to society at large. The results concerning the Jews represented a kind of by-product. European thought, once liberated from Christian dogma, could envisage the Jew as a human being unencumbered by the deficiencies attached to him by Christian tradition. The state, conceiving itself as a political organization whose main function was the mundane welfare of its citizens, could ignore their religious affiliation. Similarly, once society accepted an individual's capacity as the only criterion for assigning available functions, access of Jews to places formerly barred to them could not be denied.

Thus, Jewish emancipation could be viewed as accidental, lacking a dynamic and driving force of its own. Yet such a concept of the historical process is no more than a sham, far from doing justice to the concrete events which were of a much more involved and complicated nature. This oversimplified concept must be corrected on two counts.

First, it is not true that once the universalistic trends on the intellectual, political, and social levels became evident Jews were automatically drawn into their orbit. Jews having represented, in social reality as well as in the realm of thought, a case sui generis, a special effort was needed to include them in any universalistic category. Strong social and psychological inhibitions had to be overcome in order to realize what on the plane of pure logic may well suggest itself as a matter of course. Many instances in the history of political and social emancipation will bear this out. The French National Assembly abolished estates and declared all Frenchmen to be equal. But the Jews did not become citizens of the state by virtue of this declaration. A special legal act—or, rather, two, one for the Sephardim of the south and another for the Ashkenazim in Alsace—became necessary in order to include them under the general rule. The reason for this is simple. Jews lived on French territory, but their being a part of the body politic was not at all a settled issue—as was the case with the most destitute peasant or the proscribed Protestants. The peasant and the Protestant, albeit suppressed and persecuted, counted as Frenchmen, and the abolition of the estates and declaration of religious freedom put them on an equal footing with their compatriots. Jews, on the other hand, even if rich and influential, were still regarded as a nation apart to whom the laws and declarations of the French institution were not automatically to be applied.

An even more telling example can be adduced from the realm of social acceptance: the history of freemasonry. The first paragraph of the freemasons' constitution, promulgated in 1723 by the united Grand Lodge of London, the fountainhead of the whole movement, made eligibility to the lodges dependent on belief in God and life after death, besides possession of a high standard of morality. Affiliation to the church or commitment to a set of dogmas was explicitly discarded, since—in accordance with the prevailing trends of deism—the three specified tenets were deemed sufficient to bind together those who aspired to a common brotherhood. Logically, this definition embraced not only Christians of all denominations but also Jews. Nevertheless, when some ten years later the first Jews appeared on the scene, asking for admission to the London lodges, it was not taken for granted that their being Jewish was not an impediment to complying with their request. In England, it is true, the issue was resolved in the affirmative after some discussion. But not so on the Continent. In France, the exclusion of Jews, in spite of the adoption of the English constitution, remained almost universal until the Revolution; in Germany, the controversy over the admissibility of Jews dragged on throughout the nineteenth century and beyond. I have described this sideline of the Jewish struggle for social emancipation in my book, *Jews and Freemasons in Europe* (Cambridge, Mass., 1971). Here I should like only to stress the difficulties with which the Jews were confronted even where the principles of universality had been accepted.

The promoters of the masonic constitution, in defining their aim in universalistic terms, meant only to obviate the requirement of confessing to the dogmas of any of the Christian churches or sects. That their definition would automatically include Jews may not even have occurred to them. Jews, having lived on the margin of Christian society, were absent from people's thoughts—unless brought to mind by a special reason. Thus, even though the actual wording of the constitution contained no reservation with regard to Jews, their inclusion could only be secured by a special decision, and the effort of overcoming traditionally conditioned mental inhibition.

These impediments and inhibitions deriving from the particular status of the Jews necessitated an active campaign in favor of civil rights for Jews in European polity and society by both the Jews and their supporters. The intellectual combat in support of the Jewish cause was conducted on two fronts, at times clearly distinct, at times converging. The prejudices and misconceptions concerning Jews and Judaism—that Jews were by their very nature irredeemably corrupted, or that Judaism was an antiquated and immoral religion—had to be dispelled. Then the universalistic character of the institutions—the state, the societies such as the masonic lodges—had to be stressed and conceptually substantiated. This line of argument, although initiated by a concern for the Jews, reinforced and broadened the foundations on which the principle of universalism rested. The cause of universalism in general greatly benefited by drawing into its orbit the case of the Jews.

II

This conjunction of Jewish interest with the stress on, and even evolution of, general principles is evident already in the thoughts and activities of Moses Mendelssohn—the first Jew who combined partnership in European intellectual creativity with an active role in paving the way for his brethren to become members of society and citizens of the state. Mendelssohn advanced the theory of a modern state liberated from its attachment to the church or to any form of organized religion. He delineated the boundaries of authority as well as the obligations of both the state and the church, attributing to the first the juridical control of people's conduct and to the latter the cultivation of their moral sentiments. Implicit in this theory was a denial of the exclusive claim of any one church to being the sole partner of the state. Any religious association could assume the task traditionally allotted to the Christian churches. The immediate object of this theory was, of course, that the equal standing of Judaism with Christianity would be accepted as a sufficient guarantee of its adherents' loyalty and morality.

One of the main prerequisites for citizenship in the modern state was secured for Jews by virtue of this theory—as was access to society through the enlightened sentiment that valued general human qualities over attachment to any particular (Christian or other) doctrines. Mendelssohn figured in his lifetime as one of the most eloquent proponents of this humanistic trend, as well as a principal exponent of the idea of the secular state. He, indeed, came to be looked upon as the embodiment of the human ideal of enlightenment, and it was not without reason that, with the appearance of Lessing's *Nathan the Wise,* people believed that in this literary creation could be discovered the actual characterization of the author's friend, Moses Mendelssohn. While upholding this generally valid human ideal, Mendelssohn was deeply committed to the community of his origin and felt this ideal to be in complete harmony with its tradition; indeed, he believed he was doing no more than exposing the genuine Jewish teaching of religious tolerance and humanism. Whether historically this was a correct assessment—and we shall return to this question later—is less important than the fact that by upholding both the ideal of universal tolerance and freedom and the Jewish aspiration to acceptance and civic equality, he substantially contributed to the advancement of both.

Joining the peculiar Jewish endeavor to the mainstream of social and political liberalization of European society became, in the course of time, a major tactical weapon in the fight for both. This combination also had its linguistic expression. The first catchword under which the Jewish cause had been propagated—"civic betterment of the Jews"—had an outspokenly particularistic ring. This phrase first appeared in the title of Christian Wilhelm Dohm's famous book, the publication of which (Berlin, 1781) initiated the public discussion on the future of the Jewish community in the modern world. Dohm's suggestion for gradual integration of the Jews into state and society was based upon belief in the intrinsic equality of all human beings, the capacity of all men to adapt themselves to changing conditions, and the independence of human rights from racial origin or religious affiliation. Still, the implementation of these principles with regard to Jews required, according to Dohm, a process of accommodation. The state must gradually relinquish its traditional restrictions and reservations against Jews—gravitating in the course of this process toward the model of a secular, rationalistically conceived, and rationally conducted state.

Indeed, Dohm hoped that the absorption of the Jews into state and society would incidentally provide an incentive for implementing reforms warranted for their own sake. The recommendation of Jewish acceptance was therefore linked also in his conception with a general reform in state and society. Nevertheless, as an official of the state, conservative as it was in spite of the enlightened rule of Frederick II, Dohm had to be careful not to publicize his reformative views in too obvious a fashion. The title of his book, *Über die bürgerliche Verbesserung der Juden,* suggested that it was concerned exclusively with the Jewish issue.

III

The term *civic betterment* held sway for the better part of two generations, having served as the key term in the discussion of the

Jewish problem from the 1780s until the end of the 1820s. Then, in 1828, the expression *emancipation* made its appearance, supplanting almost with one stroke the older expression. I have traced the course of this remarkable linguistic evolution elsewhere,* and shall recall here only what seems to be relevant to the problem under consideration. The term *emancipation*—of juridical provenance, meaning to release a slave from his bondage, or a child from parental control—had been in vogue in England since the last decade of the eighteenth century, when the Irish began their political struggle for freedom. When, in the 1820s, the Catholics in England took up their fight for political equality, this went under the popular expression, "the Catholic Emancipation." Achievement of their objectives with the abolition of the Test Act in 1828 had a direct effect on the Jewish community, since it left them as the only politically underprivileged group. Immediately, some well-wishers in Parliament raised the issue of the Jews' claim to political equality, and thus the Jewish struggle under the password *Jewish emancipation* began. The term was quickly caught up in Germany where, with the emergence of the liberal movement, the second phase of the Jewish fight for acceptance and equality started. The term *Jewish emancipation* became a mighty weapon, for, in contradistinction to *civic betterment,* it carried with it an emotional quality, an appeal for justice for the victimized and oppressed.

Nor did the expression remain on this second level of application. Once it had been extracted from its original setting, the Catholic struggle, it was set free, so to speak, to be used whenever a similar invocation seemed appropriate. This transcendence by the term of its primary context is clearly manifested in a striking manner by Heinrich Heine, who was one of the first to resort to the newly discovered weapon of political propaganda. Speaking about the obvious disintegration of the old estates and the hoped-for changes in the whole structure of European society, Heine declared: "What is the great assignment of our times? It is the emancipation, not only of the people of Ireland, of the Greeks, the Jews of Frankfurt, the blacks of West India, and similar deprived peoples, but the whole world, especially Europe, which came of age and is now tearing itself away from the iron bonds of the

* "The Term 'Jewish Emancipation': Its Origin and Historical Impact," in *Studies in Nineteenth-Century Intellectual History,* edited by A. Altmann (Cambridge, Mass., 1964), pp. 1–25.

privileged, the aristocracy." The emancipation of the Jews thus became a single point in a grandiose scheme of liberation on a worldwide scale and, more concretely, in the process of the democratization of Europe.

Fifteen years later, in the famous controversy between Bruno Bauer and Karl Marx on the "Jewish Question," the transplanting of the term from the Jewish to the general human scene became an overt argument. Both Bauer and Marx contested the Jewish claim to a special act of emancipation. They made the Jewish advancement dependent on a wider scheme of liberation, Bauer on the liberation of the state and society from religion and Marx on the liberation of society from the oppressive power of the state itself. No doubt echoing the words of Heine, Bauer declared: "The question of emancipation is a universal question, the question of our time in general. Not only the Jews but we, too, wish to be emancipated." Bauer maintained that the Jews, while clamoring for their own emancipation, failed to contribute to the emancipation of the state and society at large. Marx gave his contention an even more anti-Jewish slant: "The emancipation of the Jews is in its final significance the emancipation of mankind from Judaism"— Judaism identified here with the whole system of capitalism. The two controversialists were in agreement in their negative attitude toward Jews and Judaism. The solution of the Jewish question was, in the conception of both, identical with the dissolution of Judaism that would come about in a new phase of society projected into a utopian future. For both these thinkers, the Jewish question became the occasion for evolving a conception of a universal human freedom—albeit at the cost of the individual Jewish existence.

The transposition of the term *emancipation* from the special Jewish domain into the universal human realm foreshadows its penetration into the sphere of philosophy and theology. Following the trend of thought revealed by the two disputants, the term assumed the meaning of liberation, the removal of artificial fetters from individuals and groups. The emotion-laden connotation that clung to the word from its sociopolitical application was carried over into its philosophical and theological meaning, containing as it did not only the cognitive statement of the possible liberation but also the normative demand and obligation to do so. Thus the expression became an ideological tool also in the theoretical sphere, postulating the progressive delivery of man for external as well as internal impediments and inhibitions. In the social and political sphere, the term found varied and widespread application, once again owing to its evocative quality. The liberation of the Russian peasants in the years 1862–63 went (at least in the West) under the name of emancipation, while the same act in Prussia fifty years earlier was unconnected with this slogan. Then the abolition of slavery in the United States, although executed by the state and not by the owners—thus approaching the term's original meaning but not covering it—was called and propagated by means of this ideological expression. Toward the end of the century came the emancipation of women, then the emancipation of children, and— once again returning to a more philosophical import—erotic and sexual emancipation. In short, the term ran the gamut from the original juridical meaning to all possible ideological applications, the term *Jewish emancipation* serving an important, almost seminal, role.

IV

The role of Jews in furthering the trend of social and political liberalization was not limited to this linguistic contribution. With the entry of Jews into European politics and society, the liberal camp received a substantial contingent of members who were unreservedly and unconditionally committed to their adopted cause. Theoretically, Jews, once emancipated, were free to choose among the different parties and factions competing for the conduct of the country's affairs. In fact, however, Jews were drawn in the direction of the left wing of society, joining the parties and assisting the associations which strove for change and liberalization in politics as well as other walks of life. This was the case even in France, where Jews had already acquired citizenship in the course of the Revolution but, unless absorbed into their environment through baptism, felt themselves moving on the fringes of French society far from having free access to its inner circles. Whether these French Jews were at the same time committed to some particular Jewish objectives, like Adolph Crémieux and his associates in the Alliance Israélite Universelle, or rather regarded themselves as free of any special obligations, their hope of being ultimately integrated into French society depended upon the implementation of the ideals of the Great Revolution: liberty, equality, and secularization.

The validity of these ideals was contested by the conservative and clerical wing of French society, and the Jews naturally felt called upon to support the other half of France that made itself the trustee of the revolutionary heritage. Such support did not necessarily lead to complete self-effacement on the part of Jews. On the ideological level, Joseph Salvador succeeded in a lifelong effort to assign Judaism a central role in leading modern society to its destination, an integral part of which was to be the absolute equality between man and man. The Alliance believed its function in establishing a worldwide organization in support of backward Jewish communities—preparing them by modern education for ultimate emancipation—to be nothing else but paving the way for the universal implementation of the French revolutionary ideas. Whether on the plane of thought or on that of action, Jews involved in public affairs in France in the nineteenth century allied themselves with the proponents of liberalism. In no other country was the identification of the Jews with a well-defined sector of society as obvious and outspoken as it was in France.

In Middle Europe, especially in Germany where Jewish emancipation was achieved only in the course of a long drawn-out process, the link of the Jewish cause with that of liberalism was revealed during the fight for political emancipation proper. True, the affinity between liberalism and Jewish emancipation was a one-sided affair: all Jews who fought for emancipation leaned toward liberalism, but not all the liberals embraced the idea of Jewish emancipation. Some of the most violent opponents of Jewish emancipation—for instance, the theologian Heinrich E. Paulus of Heidelberg—came from the liberal camp. The Jewish combatants had a double front. They fought the conservatives who were reluctant to concede to the Jews any rights or privileges traditionally preserved solely for gentiles. At the same time, they had their quarrel with the liberals, who twisted their own principles in order to avoid the consequences with regard to Jewish equality.

But it was just this confrontation with the hesitant and half-hearted adherents of liberalism that offered the best opportunity for demonstrating the absurdity of the position that would uphold the principles of liberty and equality but limit them to gentiles. Jewish intellectuals, headed by Gabriel Riesser, used all the tools of polemics—logic, eloquence, irony, and derision of the opponent—in order to persuade and convince. And, of course, by elaborating the principles of liberalism with regard to Jews these principles themselves gained in clarity, cogency, and conclusiveness. Indeed, the Jewish advocates of their own cause found it more and more possible as well as appropriate to participate in the political struggle for liberalization of society at large. They not only influenced the course of events through the press but also joined parties and associations active in the service of the liberal trend. This was one of the obvious signs of change in the general climate. In the aftermath of the Napoleonic era, Loeb Baruch, dismissed from the office he had occupied with the Frankfurt municipality, decided to employ his talents by launching a literary and political periodical, but saw not the slightest chance of success in doing so as a Jew. He converted and set out on his career as one of the staunchest crusaders for liberalism and democracy under the name of Ludwig Börne. Similar motivation prompted Heinrich Heine and many others less well known to resort to baptism. By converting, Börne and Heine did not abandon the cause of the Jews, to which they were committed. Börne defended the Frankfurt Jews' claim to citizenship in a pamphlet in 1816, and Heine belonged to the famous *Kulturverein* of Zunz in Berlin. Yet they believed they could be more effective by dissociating their own lot from that of the community, enhancing, as it were, their credibility by promoting a general principle rather than a particular interest.

Gabriel Riesser, on the other hand, preferred a frontal attack against the adversaries of Jewish emancipation, using discrimination against the Jews as an example of the distortion of a universally valid truth. Time proved Riesser right, at least on the personal level: admitted to the bar in Hamburg in 1840 and elected a member of the revolutionary Parliament of 1848 in Frankfurt, ascending to the office of vice president. On the public level, too, things changed for the better; the idea of Jewish emancipation gained more and more ground in an obvious interaction with the process of liberalization in society at large. By the beginning of the 1870s, the Jews of Germany, Austria-Hungary, Switzerland, Italy, and Great Britain attained, in the wake of a hard struggle, the status of full citizens that had fallen to their brethren in France in the sudden windfall of the revolution. The impact of the Jewish presence in European society began to be felt from the moment the first step toward emancipation was initiated. Let us now attempt to define the nature of this impact.

There is no doubt that by the influx of Jews into European society the cause of liberalism, in the widest sense of this word, acquired an immense source of energy. Jews provided a heavy contingent of critics of everything obsolete and antiquated; they became the heralds, the producers as well as the consumers of innovations in economics, the promoters of newly founded associations, patrons and clientele of the latest form of literature and art. On the plane of political principles, the support for universally valid laws and human rights became almost a self-understood Jewish concern.

This avant-garde role of the Jewish minority was, as might be expected, not universally acclaimed. The conservative elements in society, whether religious or social, resented deviations from inherited ways of life. They therefore transferred their resentment to any group that conspicuously participated in the promotion of the new, with its inevitable entanglement in the disintegration of the old. Modern anti-Semitism drew much of its emotional vigor from this more or less consciously experienced resentment. Of course, what was deemed blameworthy by the conservatives elicited the admiration, often tempered in time by overtones of envy, of the more advanced. Then, there were the Jews themselves who, conceiving the sector of society with which they were involved as representatives of the future, saw in their achievement only a reason for self-congratulation.

In historical retrospect, we ought perhaps to refrain from passing judgment on the social process under consideration and even more so on those who were evaluating it from their naturally limited contemporary vista. We should rather make an attempt to penetrate to the deeper reasons for the peculiar role that fell to the Jews in modern society in the post-emancipation era. Such an analysis may also be a better guide to an understanding of our present situation— in spite of the qualification due to all historical analogy—than the application of hindsight when sitting in judgment on the naiveté of past generations. Some of the reasons for the Jews being staunch supporters of innovations in the political, social, and cultural fields are readily apparent. Newcomers to the social, cultural, and, in many respects, also to the economic scene, they found many of the avenues to the established ranks of society, to the sources of wealth and livelihood, and especially to positions of political power barred to them. In the field of cultural creativity, Jews lacked the bonds and commitments to the often religiously permeated symbols—with Christian connotations, of course—by which the imagination of the artist was nurtured.

Jews had hardly any chance to share the benefits of social or cultural life, or even to participate in their development, unless a thorough change took place in their structure and content. Such change was at any rate imminent, given the forces at work which were about to transform Western society from its pre-modern shape into its modern metamorphosis. Jews, having sensed the direction of the change—their formal access to membership in state and society itself being an indication of it—joined with the elements that promoted the desired transformation. Jewish participation in the promotion of change is observable in almost every field of social and cultural activity, but it is perhaps most obvious in the sphere of political and social advancement that concerns us here. The support by Jews of the political parties that stood for enfranchisement of more and more enlarged circles and layers of society is statistically substantiated, and there is sufficient evidence for their active assistance to all the movements that aimed at what they conceived of as the realization of basic human rights. In striving for their own interests, they at the same time sustained the interest of many others.

V

The question that poses itself now is whether this Jewish self-interest was the only motivating force of Jewish behavior, or whether there were other less obvious and less egoistic stimuli by which their conduct might have been spurred. Jewish contemporaries would have, no doubt, protested any attempt to attribute their joining the forces of what had been regarded as the cause of progress to egoistic motivation. Even if the linking of the Jewish concern to this cause had been consciously experienced—and this need not always have been the case—it did not necessarily blunt belief in the justice and appropriateness of the cause. Most of the Jews who adopted the liberal cause felt, no doubt, that they were engaging in a struggle for the best interests of their class, their country, and humanity itself. Those who still maintained their ties with the Jewish community and its religion were prompted to harmonize their political and social goals with the teachings of Judaism. The social and political philosophy of men like Adolph Crémieux and Gabriel Riesser was interspersed with more or less overt hints and references to Jewish sources and concepts. Moses Mendelssohn, committed as he was to the full extent of Jewish tradition, was at pains to present his theory of Judaism and his enlightened political philosophy as of one piece.

Others, perhaps not so well versed in Jewish tradition but still attached to some of its teachings—men like Joseph Salvador, Elijah Benamozegh, Ludwig and Martin Philippsohn, and Moritz Lazarus —sought to underpin their political views and social ambitions by Jewish props. In fact, all the exponents of Judaism—theologians and philosophers as well as historians—strengthened the trend toward liberalism by portraying Judaism at the fountainhead of humanitarianism and of the idea of equality of men. The dissemination of these teachings and working for their implementation they conceived to be the Jewish nation's mission. For all the differences of creed and religious practice between the Orthodox Samson Raphael Hirsch and Abraham Geiger, in the identification of Jewish teachings with such modern ideas they were in complete agreement. Whatever the merits or demerits of these theories as a historically valid interpretation of Judaism, at the time of their appearance they went a long way in assisting Jews to combine some commitment to Judaism with political and social activity in state and society at large.

It is easy for us to disavow these claims of nineteenth-century ideologies and even to smile at their naiveté. We have meanwhile learned the craft of exposing high-sounding ideals and theorems as mere ideologies, the function of which is simply to secure individual or collective interests. Still, we should be careful not to dismiss the possibility of an intrinsic connection between Judaism and the liberal trends just because joining with the liberal camp also served Jewish interests. Although it is true that Jews were prompted to join the liberals because of such motivations, it is still a remarkable fact that they could do so without finding insurmountable impediments in their tradition or inhibitions in their mentality.

Contrary to the popular version of the theory of ideology, it is not true that every human group can adapt itself to any situation by evolving or absorbing the most fitting set of ideas that would protect and foster its vital interests. Historical experience as well as sociological analysis show that this is not the case. There are marked differences in the capacity of nations in this respect, and even of groups within nations; for instance, Catholics and Protestants were found to differ in their responsiveness, owing no doubt to their respective religious conceptions. The outspoken readiness of the Jews to adopt the ideal of liberalism must also have originated in the system of Jewish thoughts and beliefs.

I am not suggesting a similarity of content in the way of nineteenth-century theologians. We would certainly reject and even laugh off attempts at recovering the symbolic meaning of modern connotations in ancient Jewish ritual in the manner of Samson Raphael Hirsch, or the interpretation of talmudic morality as the prototype of Kantian ethics as Moritz Lazarus wished to have it. In seeking the reasons for the historically established affinity between Judaism and liberal ideas, one has to disregard the details of Jewish symbolism and ethical teachings. Rather, one must have recourse to the basic assumptions of the belief system, the far-reaching accountability of man for his deeds and his destiny—minimizing the role of divine grace and blind chance—the emphasis on this world as the main scene of individual human endeavor as well as the scene of history's course and consummation, the concomitant absolute evaluation of human life, and the high premium set upon securing the means to sustain it.

These more or less explicit trends of religious sentiments may have had a bearing on Jewish adaptability to the newly created conditions with the emergence of the modern era. Some of the explicit teachings of Judaism, manifested especially in the prescriptions of religious practice that kept the community apart and infused it with a sense of singularity and aloofness, were certainly not conducive to liberalism. But these practices and the assumptions on which they rested were now assailed and undermined by both the Jewish enlightenment from within and the critics of Judaism from without. These overt manifestations of Jewish life, traditionally conceived of as the very essence of Judaism, yielded with surprising ease. As a result of the external and internal pressures, religious practice was largely abandoned, leaving large circles of Jewish descendants without overt bonds that might have

impeded their accommodation. Others reduced religious observance to a minimum and did so under the sanctioning wings of the
Reform movement in Germany or the United States, or in the
shadow of traditional but extremely tolerant and compromising
communal institutions, as in France and Great Britain. Even modern Orthodoxy of the Frankfurt school, in spite of its adherence to
the rules of Halakhah, succeeded in creating a modus vivendi that
would permit its adherents to participate in the economic and
cultural life of the environment with a clear conscience. At any
rate, the consistently observant Jews became a small minority, and
even they were not prevented from throwing their weight in favor
of liberalism in its political, economic, and cultural aspects in
society at large. The more latent components of the Jewish mentality, on the other hand, operated among all Jews as long as they
did not transfer their allegiance to Christianity by genuine
conversion.

Conversion did occur and, due to the transmuting force of
religious experience, it seems at times to have changed the whole
mental identity of the convert. That is why we find among the
Jewish converts zealous defenders of the Catholic church—the
brothers Ratisonne, for instance, in France—and ideologues of
political and social conservatism—such as Julius Stahl in Prussia.
And the second or third generation of converts might not have
evolved any Jewish traits at all, for the mentality we are talking
about is not a genetic or a racial propensity but rather a culturally
transmitted and socially conditioned set of attitudes and behavior.

How and to what degree the social stimuli and the cultural
tradition coalesced in the life of individual Jews as well as in that
of certain groups is dependent on circumstances. What seems certain is that hardly any escaped their impact and very few with-
stood their determining influence. Yet the concurrence of Jewish
responses to the challenge of modernization—the positive attitude
toward social change, the adoption of universalistic ideals, and
especially the opting for human rights—all that characterized the
reaction of the Jewish minority in far-away places and at distant
times cannot be fortuitous. While a sociological analysis is unable
to accept purely altruistic motivation, it does allow for an appreciation of the objective gains won for the Jews' own benefit and,
not entirely accidentally, also for the benefit of others.

LESLIE C. GREEN

19
Jewish Issues on the Human-Rights Agenda in the First Half of the Twentieth Century

I

It is a commonplace that Jewish communities have suffered from the denial of human rights since the Dispersion. It is, therefore, natural that both Jewish groups and individuals have figured frequently in the struggle to secure respect for such rights. At the beginning of the modern period, with the enactment of religious emancipation in Europe, many believed that Jews would attain full civic equality. It is true that the civil rights of Jewish communities improved markedly during the eighteenth and nineteenth centuries in almost every European country. The record of continuing domestic and international protests both by individuals and by governments,[1] however, provides dramatic evidence that the Jews of Europe were still far from enjoying equality in the exercise of many basic human rights even after the period of emancipation.

A general characterization of the Jewish situation in Europe at the beginning of the twentieth century would have to include the systematic denial of fundamental human rights in several states and the pervasive threat of anti-Semitic sentiment in many regions. Frustrated at the failure of their earlier expectations for civic and social equality, many Jewish groups and individuals began to

search for other routes to security and freedom from oppression.
Thus, the shock of a series of pogroms in 1881 in Russia led Leon
Pinsker to formulate a philosophy of Zionism, while the Dreyfus
trial in France similarly served as the impetus for Theodor Herzl
to organize a political Zionist movement. Zionism advanced a new
direction for the achievement of Jewish emancipation and human
rights: national self-determination through the founding of a
Jewish state. For Herzl, as for many early Zionists, the establishment of a Jewish state represented a continuing expression of the
effort to guarantee universal human rights for Jews. Herzl therefore stressed the continuity of the laws of his proposed Jewish state
with the liberal ideology of his time: the rule of law, the separation
of church and state, and the protection of individual rights. A reading of Herzl's *The Jewish State* provides illuminating evidence of
the laws and institutions that he projected for the human rights of
all residents of the envisioned state.

   Though Zionist ideology derived from several sources and from
plural traditions, Herzl's Zionism placed special emphasis on the
belief that the Jewish state would mark the decisive end of anti-
Semitism. Herzl's views were given force by continuing anti-
Semitic outbreaks in his last years, such as the Kishinev pogrom in
1903. This particular pogrom provoked public indignation in the
British press, official protests by the United States, and a Memorial
by leading American Jews to the Russian government. This
Memorial has a significance that transcends its immediate context,
for it provides an illuminating introduction to several issues that
have been part of the continuing discussion of international protection of minority rights throughout this century. The Memorial
presents an interesting formulation of the claim that other members of the international community have a legitimate interest in
the violations of human rights committed by sovereign states upon
their own citizens. It rebuts the view that such violations represent
only an "internal" matter[2] in the following terms:

   . . . We believe ourselves to be justified in insisting that the
   claim of the Russian Government that the question of the
   condition of the Jews in Russia is a purely domestic one with
   which the people and governments of other countries have no
   concern, can no longer be maintained. When a government,
   either through the application of exceptional laws or by other
   means, forces great masses of its subjects to seek to improve

their condition through emigration to other countries, the people of these countries which gave an asylum to such refugees from persecution and oppression may, with entire propriety, criticize the conditions which have caused an influx into their country, and may properly insist that these conditions shall be improved in such manner and to such extent that the causes of the forced emigration shall cease to exist, and this without justifying the charge that they are meddling with affairs that should not concern them.

In the light of the recurrence of these issues in the past decade, there is a special irony in the Memorial's rejection of proposed Russian solutions, whether mass emigration or the gradual granting of civic rights, and its insistence instead upon full and immediate civil rights for the Jews in Russia.

The Kishinev pogrom that motivated this document was not a unique event. The years before the outbreak of the First World War witnessed a series of such occurrences. In Russia, between 1903 and 1906, there were more than 300 pogroms; in Romania, the position of the Jews was equally precarious. It is against this background that sentiment grew among the Allied Powers during World War I for postwar treaties and postwar organizations that would protect minority groups, whether racial or religious. The envisaged dissolution of the Austro-Hungarian Empire and its replacement by multinational states precipitated expressions of concern for the situation of linguistic and cultural minorities in the successor states, prompting the promulgation of Wilson's Fourteen Points. The minorities themselves, however, were not in a position to make any significant contribution toward solution of their own predicament. The view of Allied leadership at the time is well summed up in the comment by Lloyd George concerning the situation in Central Europe, "where there existed an inextricable mixture of races and a confusion of tongues that rivalled Babel":

> Sometimes the various races were apt to form groups or little communities of their own. But not infrequently in the same town or village there were huddled together Czechs, Magyars, Germans, Poles, Slovaks, Ruthenians—and everywhere Jews. . . . It was recognised very early in the course of the Peace Conference, that the question of the protection of the minority population in the Succession States was one of paramount importance. There was common agreement amongst all the parties concerned that assurances for the protection of these

minorities must be given as one of the essential conditions of a peace settlement. Apart from the inherent justice of such a position, we foresaw trouble in the future if any of these minorities were ill-treated.[3]

The staff of President Woodrow Wilson were equally concerned. It was their concern about the security of religious groups in Europe that led to the express recognition of a need to provide for international underwriting of religious toleration. Thus, the supplementary agreement attached to Wilson's third draft of the League Covenant stated:

> Recognizing religious persecution and intolerance as fertile sources of war, the Powers signatory hereto agree, and the League of Nations shall exact from all new States and all States seeking admission to it the promise, that they will make no law prohibiting or interfering with the free exercise of religion, and that they will in no way discriminate, either in law or in fact, against those who practice any particular creed, religion, or belief whose practices are not inconsistent with public order or public morals.[4]

This proposed obligation was amended in a later draft, and the link between war and intolerance was removed. In its place an injunction was suggested against the enactment of discriminatory legislation. In the end, the Covenant of the League of Nations made no reference to either racial or religious persecution. The minority groups were left with such protection as they could derive from the Peace Treaty, the Minorities Treaties, and the Minorities Committes of the League of Nations.

II

Perhaps foreseeing that the nations of the world would not take adequate steps to protect the Jewish minority, several Jewish groups, particularly the Zionists, sought political support for their efforts at self-determination and recognition of their national identity. Their goal was Jewish statehood in Palestine rather than protection of minority status in Europe. A group led by Chaim Weizmann, which included Lionel Rothschild and Alfred Mond from Britain, as well as Louis Marshall, Felix Frankfurter, and

Eliahu Lewin-Epstein from the United States, was able to secure the support of a number of British political leaders. In November 1917 Lord Balfour promulgated the Declaration which carries his name, and which proclaimed:

> His Majesty's Government views with favour the establishment in Palestine of a national home for the Jewish people, and will use its best endeavours to facilitate the achievement of this object, it being clearly understood that nothing shall be done which may prejudice the civil and religious rights of existing non-Jewish communities in Palestine, or the rights and political status enjoyed by Jews in any other country.

Despite the reservation in respect of "the civil and political rights of the existing non-Jewish communities in Palestine," there can be no doubt that the intent of the Declaration was the same as that of the Jewish leaders: complete national independence. Thus, Balfour clarified the phrase "a national home" by adding that this "did not necessarily involve the early establishment of an independent Jewish State, which was *a matter of gradual development in accordance with the ordinary laws of political evolution*"[5] [emphasis added]. Insofar as the British Cabinet was concerned, Lloyd George reported that:

> It was not their idea that a Jewish State should be set up immediately by the Peace Treaty without reference to the wishes of the majority of the inhabitants. On the other hand, it was contemplated that when the time arrived for according representative institutions to Palestine, if the Jews had meanwhile responded to the opportunity afforded them by the idea of a National Home and had become a definite majority of the inhabitants, Palestine would thus become a Jewish Commonwealth.[6]

Wilson's view was similar, as he explained to the American people: "I am persuaded that the Allied nations, with the fullest concurrence of our Government and our people, are agreed that in Palestine shall be laid the foundation of a Jewish Commonwealth."[7]

The Jewish leaders, too, recognized that the establishment of an independent state was a matter of progressive development, and certainly accepted the proviso that all the rights of the present inhabitants of the region were to be protected. Thus, in February 1919, Nahum Sokolow, as spokesman for the international Jewish community, advised the Supreme Council concerned with drafting the Peace Treaty that, in its mandate,

> Palestine shall be placed under such political administrative and economic conditions as will secure the establishment there of the Jewish National Home, and ultimately render possible the creation of an autonomous Commonwealth, it being clearly understood that nothing shall be done which may prejudice the civil and religious rights of existing non-Jewish communities in Palestine, or the rights and political status enjoyed by Jews in any other country.[8]

There was one other aspect of the struggle for the National Home that is particularly relevant to the theme of universal human rights. The Zionist movement was concerned to secure international recognition of what is now generally considered to be a fundamental human right: the right of national self-determination.

Weizmann had proposed to the Supreme Council that the Mandatory power should "accept the co-operation in such measures of a Council representative of the Jews of Palestine, and of the world that may be established for the development of the Jewish National Home in Palestine and entrust the organisation of Jewish education to such Council."[9] In due course, the Jewish Agency came into existence. Eventually, the Mandate for Palestine was drawn up with Britain as the Mandatory power formally committed to securing the purposes set out in the Balfour Declaration and affirmed in the preamble to the Mandate, with the further obligation that:

> An appropriate Jewish agency shall be recognised as a public body for the purpose of advising and co-operating with the Administration of Palestine in such economic, social and other matters as may affect the establishment of the Jewish national home and the interests of the Jewish population in Palestine, and, subject to the control of the Administration, to assist and take part in the development of the country. . . .
>
> The Zionist organisation, so long as its organisation and constitution are in the opinion of the Mandatory appropriate, shall be recognised as such agency. It shall take steps in consultation with His Britannic Majesty's Government to secure the co-operation of all Jews who are willing to assist in the establishment of the Jewish national home.

It may be contended that in this organized effort at national self-determination the Jews as a people were not contributing directly and in a positive fashion to the establishment and protection of human rights. Yet in this instance, as in respect of religious toleration and self-determination, they were the medium for achieving international recognition of such rights. This is true, in my view, even if the "right" of self-determination is to be interpreted as more a political than a legal right. There is a striking element of legal innovativeness in the Mandate's recognition of the principle of self-determination. It provides an example of a government submitting to the requirement of international law to cooperate with private individuals who do not enjoy diplomatic status, where these individuals are drawn not from the territory affected by the treaty, nor from among the nationals of the sovereign state which was assuming the obligation. The Mandatory power was required to recognize the interest of a minority group scattered throughout the world, and to acknowledge that this group, organized as it thought fit, had a legal right to participate in fulfilling a treaty to which it was not—and could not be—a party. The fact that the Mandatory was given discretionary control in deciding how far the agency concerned could help it to achieve the treaty's purpose does not detract from the significance of what had been achieved in terms of the rights of minority groups.

This is so even if difficult questions remain as to the extent to which the Mandatory carried out its obligations under the Mandate, and even if some of the terms of the Mandate may have been self-contradictory. Let it suffice to note that the Jewish organizations in Palestine during the Mandate period were responsible for promoting the economy of the country, as well as the health and labor conditions of all its inhabitants—and this to an extent that is perhaps only now being recognized on an international level through the medium of such instruments as the International Covenant on Economic, Social, and Cultural Rights.

III

Insofar as the Jewish question was concerned, the main issue of the Peace Treaties was the status of Palestine. Yet it was recognized that there were also legitimate concerns about the protection of the rights of Jewish minorities outside of Palestine. In some of the countries with which Minorities Treaties were being drawn up—as in Poland, Romania, Greece, and Lithuania—this concern was expressly stated. In fact, the protection provided by these treaties was to some extent observed. Thus, the former Director of the Minorities Question Section of the League of Nations was able to state:

> During the fourteen years of my service in the League of Nations, I do not remember the Jewish minority in Poland ever raising any question or making any complaint concerning its treatment by the Polish authorities. And in my constant visits to Poland, and in my very numerous discussions with Poles, both officials and others, and with the representatives of the minorities, on questions concerning the situation of the latter, I gained the increasingly vivid impression that the process of uniting the Jewish elements to the new Polish State was progressing so rapidly that it could have been cited as a model of governmental policy towards minorities.[10]

However, the Director's sanguine view of Poland's treatment of her Jewish population was not universally shared. Thus, it has been observed[11] that international protection proved inadequate to ameliorate the condition of Polish Jewry in the interwar period. In fact, as a result of a combination of economic factors and anti-Semitic policies, the condition of the Jews in Poland was actually deteriorating. Thousands of Jewish families subsisted on charity supplied by Jews in the West, while many other thousands sought relief in emigration. Finally, Poland announced in 1934 that she no longer regarded herself as bound by the Minorities Treaty, on the ground that the obligation of minority protection should be universal rather than selective. The Western powers in the League acquiesced, partly to avoid Polish opposition to the admission of the Soviet Union to League membership. But it was not long before the League itself abandoned any major concern with regard to the treatment of minorities in Europe—in 1934—only one year after the accession to power of the Nazis in Germany.

As awareness grew of the manner in which the Third Reich was treating its minorities, and particularly its Jewish population, pressure increased for some commitment by the rest of the world to the idea of promoting, protecting, and guaranteeing human rights for all, regardless of racial, religious, or national origin. This movement, however, did not gain any real official government backing until after the outbreak of the Second World War. Even then it is difficult to be sure how far this was sincere and not just a wartime propaganda ploy. After all, between 1933 and 1939, the British government had maintained that it was ignorant of what was occurring in Germany; or that the reports were exaggerated; or that, even if true, international law and comity precluded any intervention (even verbal) in the internal affairs of another state. Nevertheless, once at war with Germany, Britain published a White Paper concerning the treatment of German nationals in Germany,[12] which made it perfectly clear that the British government had been aware all along of developments under the Nazis. The United States had consistently taken a stronger stand, but with only equivocal results.

As increasing numbers of Jewish refugees from Germany became clients of the Jewish organizations in Britain and the United States, these groups threw themselves into the campaign to secure international recognition of human rights. Of the many efforts, two are of particular relevance.

One was launched by Hersch Lauterpacht, the architect of proposals for an international bill of the rights of man, who wrote:

> The idea of an International Bill of the Rights of Man is more than a vital part of the structure of peace [for it] is expressive of an abiding problem of all law and government [and so] long as that problem remains unsolved, it will continue to be both topical and urgent long after declarations of war and peace aims have become a matter of mere historical interest and after the effective elimination of war has become a reality.[13]

Lauterpacht's proposed Bill of Rights was not adopted by any state or embodied in any international instrument. It did, however, play a major part in the discussions and preparatory work which ultimately led to the references to human rights in the Charter of the United Nations, and, still later, to the detailed exposition of such rights in the Universal Declaration.

The other effort was inaugurated by Raphael Lemkin, who invented the word *genocide* that has since become part of the vocabulary of international law. He defined it as follows:

> Generally speaking, genocide does not necessarily mean the immediate destruction of a nation, except when accomplished by mass killings of all members of a nation. It is intended

rather to signify a coordinated plan of different actions aiming at the destruction of essential foundations of the life of national groups, with the aim of annihilating the groups themselves. The objectives of such a plan would be disintegration of the political and social institutions, of culture, language, national feelings, religion, and the economic existence of the national groups, and the destruction of personal security, liberty, health, dignity, and even the lives of the individuals belonging to such groups. Genocide is directed against the national group as an entity, and the actions involved are directed against individuals not in their individual capacity, but as members of the national group.[14]

As early as 1933, Lemkin proposed to the Madrid International Conference for Unification of Criminal Law that it declare the destruction of racial, religious, or social collectivities a crime under the law of nations. Subsequent events in occupied Europe made him all the more determined to secure recognition of this new crime. In 1948, on the same day as it adopted the Universal Declaration of Human Rights, the General Assembly adopted the Genocide Convention which came into force in 1951.

Perhaps the basic flaw of the Genocide Convention is the absence of any international criminal tribunal—although its ultimate establishment is envisaged. Pending the creation of such a court, the crime is punishable by the courts of the country in which it was committed. Yet, broadly speaking, it may be doubted whether genocide can ever be committed as a matter of private enterprise. It is far more likely that, as in Nazi Germany, it will be committed either at the instigation, or with the condonation, of state authorities. Thus, it is highly unlikely that a national trial will ever take place.

With the establishment of the State of Israel, it has become possible for a Jewish community to make a positive contribution, on the level of sovereign responsibility, to the establishment of respect for human rights. Perhaps the first such contribution was the enactment of the 1950 Law of Return. Although ostensibly concerned with nationality and immigration, it is in fact statutory recognition of the right of asylum. This right is proclaimed in the Universal Declaration as belonging to all persecutees, although no obligation to grant asylum is imposed on any state and the right has in fact disappeared from the international covenants. The Law of Return enabled the large numbers of Jews among the stateless refugees in the aftermath of World War II in Europe to settle in

Israel. But this humanitarian legislation has also created problems, particularly with respect to the definition of a Jew—since it is only the Jew who has the statutory right of return. Disputes between the religious and the secular authorities over the definition of who is a Jew have been resolved essentially with the views of the religious community prevailing.

The problems created in Israel by this type of religious issue call for a special sensitivity in respect to human rights. Israeli courts have ensured that there is no religious discrimination, and that tolerance and equality shall be maintained among all religious groups. Thus, they have held that "if the state allocates money from its budget to assist in upholding a certain religion and its rituals, and education for the children of its members, another sect may expect similar assistance to the extent required and within the limits of the state's means."[15] Similarly, a judicial decision asserted that the authorities have an obligation to protect the spirit and culture of a minority "who are members of a religion and a community with a way of life, customs, and traditions of their own."[16]

Contemporary Jewish interest in the promotion and protection of human rights has not become exclusively centered on the State of Israel. Jewish organizations have maintained continuous interest in human rights in the various countries of the Diaspora, an interest not limited to the rights of Jews alone. In my view, this is as it should be. Since Jews constitute only one segment of humanity, if human rights were guaranteed for all, in any practical and meaningful sense, then Jews as such would benefit. Moreover, I believe that if each minority group were to become introverted, concerned only with its own self-interest, then an attack on any one would render comparatively easy the destruction of human rights for all.

NOTES

1. See, e.g., C. Adler and A.M. Margalith, *With Firmness in the Right: American Diplomatic Action Affecting Jews, 1840–1945* (New York, 1946).

2. This is a forerunner of the type of argument later put forward by those who favored bills of rights, including the right of suffrage, but who

made such rights subject to local law, because of, e.g., the question of franchise of the Negro population in the United States or in South Africa.

3. D. Lloyd George, *Memoirs of the Peace Conference,* 2 vols. (New Haven, 1939), vol. 2, p. 881.

4. D. H. Miller, *The Drafting of the Covenant* (New York, 1928), vol. 2, p. 105.

5. Lloyd George, vol. 2, p. 735.

6. Ibid., p. 736.

7. Ibid., p. 737.

8. Ibid., p. 747.

9. Ibid., p. 748.

10. P. de Azcárate, *League of Nations and National Minorities* (Washington, 1945), p. 34.

11. Adler and Margalith, p. 167.

12. H.M.S.O., Cmd. 6120 (1939).

13. H. Lauterpacht, *An International Bill of the Rights of Man* (New York, 1945).

14. R. Lemkin, "Genocide" in *Axis Rule in Occupied Europe* (Washington, 1944), p. 79.

15. *Abu Ghosh-Kiryat Ye'arim Music Festival Society* v. *Minister of Education and Culture,* 25 *Piskei Din* 821 (1971).

16. *Halon* v. *Chairman of the Local Council,* 25 *Piskei Din* 591 (1971).

BEN HALPERN

Jewish Nationalism:
Self-Determination as
a Human Right

I

It is a common belief that nationalism was the primary cause of war in the nineteenth century. Liberal internationalists still view with dismay the unexpected, but continuing, eruption of national conflicts in our own time. Certainly the perennial debates about the definition of *nation, nationality,* and *national rights* that fill many shelves in any university's law and political-science library were never merely academic. By appropriate definition of these terms one could either legitimize or disqualify the claims of a people to territory, statehood, or corporate existence—even, as Hitler demonstrated, the very survival of its individual members.

These terminological disputes, which set nation against nation and people against people in violent opposition, are often assumed to have an opposite effect upon the internal cohesion of a people involved in national conflict. It is generally believed that in the face of a common national danger the unity and solidarity of an embattled people is strengthened. This may well be generally true in the case of independent nation-states, but it is far from being the invariable experience of ethnic and religious minorities and colonial dependencies. Among self-conscious racial, religious, and national communities whose freedom is restricted by outside rule, ideological quarrels over issues of self-determination, and over the alternative categories of rights to be sought under the alternative definitions, have regularly produced internal political division. In the case of the Jews, the rise of Zionism (or, for that matter, of religious reform) was a fertile source of communal rivalries and disputes for the past hundred years.

Only in retrospect, and anachronistically, could it be said that Jews in the 1940s "saw no inconsistency between belief in international human rights and a Jewish homeland," even with the qualification that some Jews became Zionists because of their "skepticism as to whether Jews could find security elsewhere, even in liberal Western societies."* At the time in question, Jewish nationalists and anti-nationalists were sharply divided over proposals for a Jewish commonwealth, on the one hand, and an international bill of rights on the other. There were certainly those, who even at the time, saw nothing inconsistent in favoring both propositions at once, but the general community unquestionably construed the two proposals as rival programs of politically opposed factions.

Integration or self-segregation, emancipation or national liberation, assimilation or nationalist revival—these opposed options are common lines of cleavage in the recent history of many "colonized" peoples and ethnic minorities. They correspond to fault lines along which the Western structure of equal citizenship tends to fail. Government based on equal individual citizenship has regularly run into roadblocks owing to deeply rooted habits of preference and discrimination on grounds of race, sex, religion, national origin, clan, family, and other emotional ties or barriers between individuals. From the liberal point of view, the remedy for these lapses and shortfalls in the realization of legal equality is a greater, more consistent, commitment to liberalism. From the point of view of ethnic and racial minorities, it may be precisely dogmatic liberalism that is the perceived threat. The Jews, at any rate, were faced with disparate options from the moment that the French Revolution made available a liberal alternative to the Jewish community. The rival programs during World War II of national self-determination and an international bill of rights reflected a long-standing ideological split in which the imperatives of continuity in

* S. Liskofsky, "International Protection of Human Rights," in *World Politics and the Jewish Condition* (New York, 1972), p. 280.

the Jewish tradition strained against the presumed requirements of integrationist liberalism.

II

It is easy to reduce to absurdity the long quarrel between individual and collective rights. The one approach rests on an atomistic liberalism which posits man as an indeterminate entity who contracts all his relations to others in total freedom: a procedure that guarantees legal equality, even if it has no other appeal to human sentiment. The fatal flaw in this idea is that before any man can act freely (and not merely under coercion of biological drives) in seeking to create contractual relations with others, he must have his own secure identity; and that is something created out of organic personal relations, which are not chosen but given. Collective rights, then, are conceived and justified as natural extensions of man's organic, given relations to others. But this, too, is a conclusion which logically reduces to absurdity; for to construct institutional relations that simply ratify and reinforce organically established relations, without any leeway for freedom of contract, is to make everyone a slave. In actuality, of course, no pure or ideal society, built entirely on one or the other principle, has ever existed or could ever survive. The concrete differences that divide advocates of the individualist and the collectivist approach to an international system of human rights occur over intermediate issues; they concern proposals that lean to one or the other side but are not rigorous applications of either rationale.

The force that initiated, and to this day sustains, a principled drive toward international government in a united world is the survival into the twentieth century of nineteenth-century liberalism. The contemporary expression of this force is the movement for an international human-rights regime. But most of the concrete problems encountered today, in the difficult birth of a new international order, are caused by the counterpressures of recently awakened collective interests against the perceived injustices of a dogmatic international liberalism. Included among these problems, to every liberal's dismay, are issues of national self-determination raised by groups based on religious and racial criteria, as well as demands for economic and social equality between collective entities—demands, in both cases, sharply clashing with the assumptions of a new order based on the legal equality of freely contracting individuals. The result has been that our emerging international order, such as it is, is the product of conflicting forces and represents a loose and shifting structure of compromise built to contain them.

Liberalism, upon whose sustaining force the drive for a broadening sphere of international government essentially depends, has made its ideological adjustments to successive new issues as they arose; but it has often done so by conceding points to the opposition in a kind of rearguard action, and in the hope of a more liberal world in the future. Economically disadvantaged groups, religious communities oppressed by the dominant forces in their homeland, and similar collective interests that demand institutional recognition in the world order can be accommodated by liberal internationalists on the tacit assumption that special arrangements for their benefit are needed as a provisional measure until they wither away in the more perfect future.

An early case in point was the liberal construction of the idea of nationalism itself in the nineteenth century. Rationalist liberalism was opposed on principle to this particularist aberration. Romantic liberalism, however, adopted it, at least in part, in the doctrine of national self-determination, combining ethnic, local loyalties with the concepts of citizenship and popular sovereignty. But this doctrine obviously complicates the simple liberal idea of individual human rights by adding a clashing category of collective rights; and it also, of course, acknowledges a wide range of discriminations between nationals and non-nationals inherent in national systems of law. On the basis of such discrimination, nationalist Romania could consistently persecute its Jews by considering them aliens.

Such restrictions on complete legal equality of individuals are easiest for liberals to justify in terms of their fundamental beliefs when they are based on the impersonal, objective criterion of territory. The nation-state, covering a substantial territory and including a considerable population, represented, according to a widespread liberal assumption, the effective limit of government, given nineteenth-century techniques of production and communication. With further progress in the twentieth century, the sphere of government, having already spread from clan, tribe, and village to the nation-state, was expected to be extended by soon-to-be-available technological methods to a united world. The disappointing revival of nationalism precisely in our time can only be condoned by the liberal mind as a temporary expedient needed to help disadvantaged new nations catch up with the rest. Herein lie some of the psychological difficulties in accepting *Jewish* nationalism among Jewish liberals, who hold themselves to be part of the avant-garde, both as Jews and as internationalists, and not part of a disadvantaged group entitled to special consideration.

Quite clearly, the criterion for making national distinctions that was hardest for Western nineteenth-century liberals to accept was, and in some ways still remains, the criterion of religion. Western nationalism, almost as much as Western liberalism, could only arise out of the collapse of a religiously-ordered, or religiously-divided, continental, political, and social system. Occidental Christendom had to be displaced, or gradually made to yield its hegemonic sway, in order for the essentially secular, technical, and, eventually, democratic order of Western civilization to emerge. Together with the rise of national territories, national languages, literatures, and histories superseded the culture and hierarchy of religion as the formative principles of the European political system. Religion was accommodated as a subordinate aspect of the national cultures of Western liberal countries under their guarantee of the individual freedoms of conscience and association. Wherever religious boundaries still served to define political units, these were regarded as an obstacle to the complete realization of the liberal nationalist vision.

Religion, of course, still persists as a significant force in forming political entities. Belgium and Holland, like Poland and Russia, were constituted by religious no less than by ethnic cultural distinctions. Lutheran Germany insisted on regarding itself as a Christian state, and French legitimists fostered a national consciousness inseparable from Catholicism, well into the nineteenth century. So, too, the constitutionally liberal Anglo-Saxons, who condemned such reactionary principles when explicitly propounded by rightist Continental ideologues, tacitly (and, in some respects, formally) excluded from their society ethnic, especially immigrant, religious minorities. Nevertheless, liberalism remained, in principle, firmly opposed to religion as the basis and regulating definition of national entities; and though the newly liberated Third World has compelled acceptance within the international order of precisely such combinations of religion and nation-state as Pakistan or Libya, liberal acquiescence has been grudging and conditional. The problematic church-state and sect-nation union is interpreted as a transitional development; and it is most easily accepted when a major, or at least substantially large, territorial base gives it adequate politico-economic justification.

This does not mean that religion is totally debarred from political functions in a thoroughly liberal society. In fact, de Tocqueville's observation about the paradoxical strength of religion in America after the separation of church from state need not be confined to the social, infrapolitical sphere. The liberation of the secular polity from the constraints and limits of religious affiliation affords an opportunity for new, manifest as well as latent, political functions for religious institutions. Among the outstanding functions of the clergy in America is certainly the role they are expected to play in contributing the leaven of idealism, of zeal and elevated moral standards, to our political life—and they can play this role precisely because their removal from any specific, operational responsibility in civic affairs gives them the imputed distinction of having a disinterested commitment to absolute standards and the general good. The recent social activism of Catholic worker-priests in France and elsewhere in Europe also comes after a period when the secular state thoroughly denuded the church of those manifold political and infrapolitical functions which had once vested it with such an executive authority.

Even more significant than these manifest functions is the extraordinary latent function of religion (more specifically, of Christianity) in the political world of full-fledged secular nationalism. A good part of the manifest powers of administration exercised by the clergy in earlier times had been taken over by absolutist monarchs before the era of popular sovereignty completed the work. Finally, nationalism, completing what science and secular humanism had begun, was to divest religion of its dominance in the sphere of culture: language, literature, and the consciousness of history were all detached from the church and raised to the most prized hallmarks and attributes of the nation, the essential presuppositions of its political life. Yet this expropriation of culture from the church was incomplete, leaving to religion an essential area of culture and a vital political function.

National culture, including language, literature, and historical consciousness, is heavily weighted on the side of the aesthetic. It comprises an individuality of style and taste and a distinct perspective which unite national groups and set them apart from others in matters of judgment. What it does not provide are precisely those universal norms by which individual men, the irreducible identities who are called upon to know things objectively and to act upon presumptively universal rules, are able to live under the rule of conscience. Those norms are only possible under the conception of a human universe that transcends national distinctions. The concrete ethical and metaphysical assumptions which articulate these assumptions are not random among individual members of nations and civilizations; if that were the case, the minimal basic consensus that makes civilization possible would exist only by accident, and, no doubt, be as fleeting as accidental conjunctions usually are. Instead, the assumptions of common sense and a common morality underlying civilizations derive from the broadly shared religious and philisophical culture of continental regions—in the case of Occidental civilization, from Western Christianity and humanistic science. The national cultures of the West, beyond the essentially aesthetic styles and perspectives that distinguish and divide them, are united in a common civilization based on shared ethical, metaphysical assumptions of their Christian, humanistic, and scientific traditions.

National self-determination, therefore, is a conception still imbedded in the very matrix from which it had to be torn in order to be born. The national idea asserts the right to foster individual and distinctive national value styles and perspectives, freed from the tyrannous universality of both rationalist liberalism and hegemonic religion; but the nation also lives, and can only survive, by respecting the ethical universality of standards that are still derived, in their concrete form, from religious culture and humanistic philosophy.

III

Jewish nationalism is peculiarly difficult for the liberal mind to adopt—and not merely because so many Jews feel that a rigorous liberalism should offer them an escape, by integration with others, from the misfortune of their birth into a religious community that has lost its meaning for them. More objective considerations also make this nationalism especially unpalatable for liberals. The conditions which produce Zionism combine, in a high concentration, the very features that liberals find least acceptable, if not downright obnoxious, when proposed as a basis for political nationalism: first, the Jews are constituted an ethnic group by religion; second, far from occupying a territory large enough to be administered by a nation-state, they occupied no territory at all until recently, but were dispersed, as a small minority with special economic functions, in many countries.

The ethnic implications of religion, both Jewish and Christian, complicated the question of the civic emancipation of the Jews and their acceptance as citizens with equal rights into the political society of the countries they lived in. In spite of the principle of the separation of church and state, Jewish citizens were effectively precluded by the ban of religious difference from full and equal participation in political society. In conservative states, and during conservative periods, the exclusion of Jews from a full share in public affairs was explicitly imposed on the grounds of the Christian quality of the state. Where liberalism prevailed, social convention, sometimes openly and sometimes tacitly, denied Jews free access to those social circles which control informally the flow of power and influence over public affairs in formally democratic countries. The Jews were segregated not only in the synagogues where they voluntarily assembled in exercise of their freedom of conscience; nor were only those Jews segregated who were religiously committed and affiliated. Owing to the wide and profound influence of religion in channeling social contacts, Jewishness was enough to bar citizens from broad areas of contact and activity of decisive importance in public affairs; and short of conversion to Christianity, the exclusion was no less effective against irreligious, or anti-religious, Jews than it was against believers and observers of the Mosaic faith.

The most obvious result of these conditions has been a change in the self-definition and institutions of the Jews far more radical than anything comparable in the history of the emancipation of other religious minorities. The long-standing cohesiveness of religious practice and doctrine among Jews, which was variegated but not divided by regionally developed traditional styles and customs, was now supplanted in Western countries by a kind of denominationalism closely approaching that of the Christian majority. In all countries, the rise of the secular state produced a new kind of Jew, no longer self-identified by his religious affiliation; and in the dense ethnic concentrations of Eastern and Central Europe such Jews found an adequate expression for their condition in some kind of ethnic self-assertion: Zionism, territorialism, Diaspora nationalism, or Bundist Yiddishism.

A militant Jewish liberalism, as well as a developed ideological movement of religious reform, arose among acculturated young Jews of the mid-nineteenth century in reaction to the manifest inadequacies of the initial emancipation. In one respect, that of religious reform, the response was an explicit commitment by Jewish liberals to the collective survival of Judaism in the face of new challenges posed by the secularized nation-state; and these were challenges that were expected to wax rather than wane as restrictions against Jews were lifted. Another response, that exemplified by Gabriel Risser's journal, *Der Jude,* and by the creation of the Alliance Israélite Universelle in 1860 and the Centralverein deutscher Bürger jüdischen Glaubens in 1893, had no more than a nominal relation to the survival of Judaism as such, for these circles took a non-partisan position on sectarian issues, and concerned themselves directly with removing any remaining legal or social discriminations against Jews. But this, too, served a latent function in consolidating a collective Jewish identity, especially among religiously unaffiliated Jews.

The communal consensus of Western Jewries remained explicitly committed to a liberal, integrationist view. Their de-facto segregation, produced not only by societal restrictions but by the objective effect of their own institutional creations, posed no clear, widely perceived challenge to this intellectual position. But militant liberal Jewish organizations could never confine themselves to the legal, social, and political problems of their own country alone. The international dispersion of the Jews continually posed problems of civil rights, or simple human oppression, in other countries; and these often raised questions whose ideological difficulty was hard to ignore. The involvement of French or British Jews with Jewish problems in Algeria and Persia, Romania and Russia, Switzerland, Hungary, and Syria could be explained away as simply a legitimate concern for one's coreligionists, not a matter of clannish solidarity, but it still remained problematic. It might be reasonable, under standard Western conceptions, to justify a brotherly charity, going beyond mere humanitarianism, towards one's co-religionists, but it put those conceptions under strain to make them cover the broad and markedly political program of activity which Western Jewish organizations mounted in all countries where Jews were oppressed.

The international action of Western Jews on behalf of their oppressed Jewish brethren really continued a long ethnic tradition of Jewish mutual aid, necessitated by the global dispersion both of Jews and of Jew-hatred. Two more current developments also commended such activity especially to Jewish liberals. On one hand, the expanding area within which Western countries eagerly took up the "white man's burden" called for parallel activity of bodies like the Alliance Israélite Universelle among Jews. On the other hand, the growth of an internationale of political anti-Semites made it inescapably clear that, in spite of different local conditions and forms of expression, the forces of prejudice that produced ritual libels, expulsions, involuntary infant conversions, and anti-Jewish riots in North Africa, the Ottoman Empire, the Balkans, and Eastern and Central Europe were one and the same as those that Western Jews still had to fight in their own countries. Western Jews worked on behalf of their coreligionists in foreign areas in the same spirit of liberalism as on their own behalf at home. The same objectives of equal citizenship and human rights were publicly pursued in democratic national assemblies and parliaments in the West as were discreetly pressed in the chancelleries of Eastern autocrats, and at international postwar conferences, from Vienna (1815) and Aix-la-Chapelle (1818) to Berlin (1878). But solutions in tune with ruling assumptions in London and Paris often clashed jarringly with the conditions and assumptions prevalent in backward agrarian countries like Russia or Romania. In the latter country, liberal Western Jews were forced to recognize by 1870 that the standard remedies of political emancipation and equal economic opportunity could not be applied within the foreseeable future of that generation of persecuted Romanian Jews. They were compelled reluctantly to accept as an emergency measure there—and, later, in Russia—the alternative solution of emigration (or even, as American Jews proposed, full evacuation)—which was tantamount to conceding ideological defeat.

Soon enough, the ideological issue was explicitly raised by Russian and other East European Jews. They faced directly those consequences—eviction and expulsion, boycott and expropriation—which universally befall racial and religious minorities fulfilling commercial and financial functions, when the oppressed, xenophobic native peasantry begins to rise up and rebel. They had to recognize that their troubles were not transient or accidental but permanent and basic features of an untenable position. Such an open challenge to liberalism (pointedly stressed when the earliest classic Jewish nationalist manifesto, in opposition to the principle of emancipation, was given the militant title of *Auto-Emancipation*) could not be evaded. The Alliance Israélite Universelle, which had previously been active in promoting Jewish agriculture and immigration in Palestine, now proclaimed its open opposition, and Western rabbis sharpened their anti-nationalist formulations for polemical effect.

In the end, however, the new national consciousness that arose in the East left its impact upon the perceptions and ideas of all of world Jewry. This was caused only in part by the agony of East European Jewry, the largest pre-Hitler Jewish community. The sense of Jewish ethnicity also rose as it became evident, and generally acknowledged, that national consciousness is the appropriate expression in our time of the basic structure of Jewish existence.

IV

Nationalism arose in Western Europe by detaching itself from religion; and yet, religion remains a powerful, formative element in the national consciousness of even the most secular Western states. Gallic Catholicism, British Anglicanism, German or Swedish Lutheranism, and, among the varied WASP sects of America, Congregationalism in the North and Presbyterianism in the South, stamped their peculiar characteristics upon the national consciousness and self-awareness of the several nation-states. This is even more significantly true of many newer nationalisms, beginning with the Slavic movements and continuing with the new Asian-African nations of the Far and Middle East. Sectarian differences are often the primary causes that divide them from one another, and all of them, each according to the world religion that dominates its region, are set off collectively against Occidental Christendom by a major religio-cultural division—not to say, opposition. Their national self-consciousness is not simply a special cultural differentiation out of a common Occidental ethico-religious stock, as is the case with Western nations. They are not part of Western civilization, but of competing Eastern civilizations. The original cause of their nationalism is, in most cases, resistance to the pressure of Occidental civilization as represented by the political, economic, and cultural domination of one or more of its national representatives. The subsequent liberation of secular nationalism from religion may occur among them in a parallel way to its Western development, but only against a background of the liberation of their own religious civilization from Western dominion.

The case of the Jews, while unique and uniquely complicated, resembles in certain ways the development of the newer, anti-Western nationalisms. Jewish nationalism, too, arose in rebellion against submitting to Western domination in the ways Western Jewry had done; and its slogan of "auto-emancipation" was a banner of protest against the nationally demoralizing illusions of the liberal emancipation ideology. This meant that the initial movement of Jewish nationalism, in terms of its cultural dimension, was to revive the traditional ideas of national Exile and national Restoration (or even Redemption) which Western Jews had abandoned in adjusting to a status of equal citizenship. The Zionists reclaimed those symbols, which tapped deep sources of Jewish national self-consciousness, because they powerfully expressed the national destiny of Jews in the future as well as the ethnic singularity of their millennial past. And, in so doing, Jewish nationalism began by moving toward the history-laden values of traditional Judaism, which were threatened by Western Jewish liberalism.

Of course, Jewish nationalism, no less than others, had sharp conflicts with religious conservatism throughout its history. The first Jewish nationalists rebelled against the pious quietism of the traditional cult of Exile just as sharply as against the self-abnegation of Western Jewish liberals who denied the historic concept of Exile. Anti-Zionism then arose among some Eastern religious traditionalists in as emphatic a form as among some Western religious reformers. The rise of the State of Israel projected the quarrel between Orthodoxy and the secularist wing of nationalism into continuous prominence as a political issue. The modern Jewish community of Israel is no longer made up of uniformly traditionalist believers and observers of talmudic Mosaism. Each infusion of immigrants from Western countries or from Russia brings with it new Jewish nationalists who are not Orthodox, and often not religious. The Jewish state is required by its very structure to foster a national consciousness that comprehends them all; and this demands a degree of separation between national and religious consciousness.

Zionism, however, encounters particular difficulty in accomplishing this task which it shares with other nationalisms. Unlike the others, it is tied to a religion which extends to only one ethnic group, and which dominates no major geographic region, but only, since the creation of Israel, a small notch of territory occupied by a single nation-state. If the Jewish state seeks to base its national culture on the Hebrew language and Jewish history alone, it is not then able to rely on a moral ethno-religious consensus shared with others in its region or beyond. Unless Israel roots its ultimate frame of reference in Judaism—that is, in an ethos shared historically with no other people—it risks the obscure menace of a history without deep roots. But, in any event, Israel finds itself still involved in the religiously-based antagonism between Jews and other groups—notwithstanding the predictions of Zionist ideology that anti-Semitism would disappear together with its presumed cause, Jewish national homelessness.

These complications are vaguely reflected in the conflicting positions taken toward the relations of Jews to Judaism, and of both to non-Jews, by various recent schools of more or less articulate Jewish opinion. A symptomatic, if not a more substantial, significance attaches to the ideological position of the so-called Canaanites, who enjoyed a certain notoriety shortly after Israel's emergence. These Zionist ultras, or post-Zionists, proposed a radical solution: to detach Israel entirely from Judaism and attach it instead to a conveniently antique and presently nonexistent regional civilization of Canaanism which they could imaginatively construct in the new Israeli regime. Not surprisingly, this vision evoked no enthusiasm in the surrounding region; in Israel, where it represented a reductio ad absurdum of certain logical possibilities contained in Zionism, Canaanism exercised the kind of indefinable influence common to marginal extremists.

Another approach to the problem of Jews vis-à-vis Judaism and other religions also lay largely beyond the range of any possible Israeli consensus but exerted a pervasive influence on the thinking attitudes of Western Jewish communities. An equal share for Judaism in the common ethos said to be expressed in our "Judeo-Christian" civilization was a claim often voiced by Reform and Conservative Jews, but one not shared by outspoken Orthodox leaders. This proposition assumes an indefinable essential praxis, or doctrine, which is shared; and it ignores, of course, the concrete historical fact that Judeo-Christian relations represent a symbiosis of mutual antagonism. Such a dubious abstraction may rob the concept of a Judeo-Christian ethic of any significance in real history, but it is unquestionably convenient for both Jewish and Christian liberals. For the former, it conforms with the abstract, ahistoric public presentation of Judaism that they prefer, and it legitimates them (however minimally, superficially, and delusively) in their particular nationality and regional civilization; for the latter, it allows them to be tolerant toward Jews in terms of a pro forma rather than a substantive brotherhood.

Just how limited and insubstantial is the imputed brotherhood was made clear in the inconclusive Jewish-Christian ecumenical consultations and negotiations that have marked the recent past. The current Christian drive for ecumenism was certainly motivated to an extent by revulsion from the Holocaust years; but a more enduring and effective motivation was the encounter with the emerging nations of Asia and Africa and the non-Christian, or non-Occidental, civilizations they represent. In the event, the latter motivation, by far the more powerful and dominating, proved one of the main barriers to successful conclusion of the kind of symbolic reconciliation to which liberal Jewish theologians aspired.

This entire complex, as already noted, lies largely outside the range of solutions for the relation with non-Jews that could conceivably sustain an Israeli consensus. The Judaism that could mean anything to Israeli Jews must rest solidly on an ethos whose symbolism is fully attuned to the Jewish national history of Exile and Restoration. The privileged position of Orthodoxy in Israel is maintained not merely because of complex political considerations involved in government coalitions, but on more solid ground. Israeli secularist Jews reclaimed through Zionism a sense of history for which Orthodox tradition provides the bulk of its significant symbolism. They bear the inconvenience of Orthodox privilege, in part, because this is the only ethos they know which is fully attuned to their national history. Their continued apathetic response to the discriminations suffered by liberal Western Jewish denominations rests in part on their inability to feel that such versions of Judaism are equally attuned to the historic Jewish national experience.

The full acceptance of Jewish nationhood is still blocked by gentile incomprehension or (in the case of Christianity and Islam) antagonism toward Judaism. The existence and self-assertion of Israel pose the ecumenical problem in a different form from that pressed by Western Judaic advocates. Israel represents for the Christian West (and for Islam) the challenge of a distinct civilization, based not merely on an abstract religious, but on a concrete territorial—that is, social, political, and economic—foundation. This is a challenge which most effectively moves the ecumenical spirit when backed by substantial regional strength. Given the modest magnitude of Israel, not even the memory of the Holocaust produced a true ecumenical acceptance of this new form of the Jews-Judaism phenomenon. Such acceptance and recognition is the only road to peace, justice, and international order in the Middle East; but only repeated demonstrations of sacrificial devotion by Israel and the Diaspora Jews may at last attain it.

The relations between religion and nationality, and the deeply-lying problems of ethos and politics which they involve, are central to the future of Israel and world Jewry. The concrete shape of the questions at issue only began to emerge in public debate upon the creation of the Jewish state in 1948. Other problems, arising out of another peculiarity of the Jews—their dispersion among the nations—became salient issues of international, as well as of Jewish, politics in 1914, when Turkey's entry into the war signaled the approach of the Ottoman Empire's long-expected collapse. The alternative self-definitions and new statuses then advocated by rival Jewish factions raised novel questions in international law and new issues of political ethics. Attempted solutions were closely connected with the halting development of an international order, initially under the League of Nations Covenant and, subsequently, under the United Nations Charter.

V

In Russia and Austria-Hungary, where long and sad experience proved emancipation to be an idle hope for Jews in backward, agrarian regions and under autocratic regimes, there had developed in 1914 a new range of legal and political formulas for Jewish liberation. Apart from a bourgeois faction of assimilationists and a radical internationalist proletarian movement, the bulk of East European Jewry joined in assuming a fundamentally ethnic, or national, definition of their condition. Within this consensus, different proposals concerning an appropriate status for the Jews were favored. The range ran from the purely cultural (Yiddishist) national program of the Bund in Russia, Poland, and Lithuania, the minimal expression of a considerable variety of Jewish Diaspora-nationalist doctrines, to an evacuationist version of Zionism, the maximal expression of the rejection of Diaspora existence which was shared, in greater or lesser degree, by various "territorialist" doctrines.

The consensus of Western Jewries still clung to the liberal individualistic principles of integration and equality, and tried to press upon their governments plans to establish those principles in the postwar regimes envisaged for the Russian, Austro-Hungarian, and Ottoman empires. To the extent that Jewish nationalist ideas penetrated the West, this was an effect of Eastern European immigration and of those native dissenters from the Establishment who regarded the condition of Eastern, rather than of Western, Jewries as the authentic contemporary expression of the perennial Jewish problem. At the same time, it was the problem of European and Ottoman Jews that would face Western Jewries, should the Allies win the war. Thus, if they wished their plans for postwar reorganization to be related to objective Jewish realities, they would ultimately have to consider East European views, as well as to confront specific East European situations.

Doctrines of national self-determination applied to the Jewish situation were crystallized by the end of the war in two major proposals: the demand for national minority rights, in treaties to be signed by successor states of the vanquished multinational empires, and in the provisions for a Jewish national home, incorporated in the international Mandate for Palestine entrusted to Great Britain. Both these programs were adopted by the main Western Jewries, American and British, only after an internecine struggle during the war years. They were backed, in spite of reservations, by Western Jewish delegations at the Peace Conference.

The national-minorities treaties will be dealt with here only in relation to our main topic, the right of national self-determination. Suffice it to say that such treaty guarantees of far-reaching autonomous rights for national minorities within the new nation-states seemed open to liberal criticism on at least two grounds: they appeared to be discriminatory, since minority rights were guaranteed internationally only for specified states, and not by a universal rule; and they seemed to endanger national unity in the new nation-states by encouraging minority separatism. In fact, however, the minority treaties availed very little to establish a viable form of ethnic autonomy for the national minorities in the new states. Instead, they served as an instrument for the introduction in such countries of the ordinary, individual civil rights implied in the liberal institution of equal citizenship.

The doctrine of national self-determination was most fully applied to the Jewish case. Some of its most thorny issues arose in relation to the establishment of the Jewish national home and, later, the Jewish State of Israel. The ideological, legal, and politico-ethical problems were most complex, and the considerations most sophisticated, in the early years of international relations under the Versailles Peace Treaty and the League of Nations system. In that initial period there was a general Jewish consensus combining support for both national minority rights and the project of a Jewish national home in Palestine. (It was, however, opposed by significant groups of recalcitrants and dissenters, and masked sharp latent disagreements that were only temporarily submerged.) Among non-Zionist leaders of the Jewish delegations at the Paris Peace Conference, these demands for collective rights were supported with important reservations, as already noted. Among Zionists, there was broad but rather diffuse adherence to a vaguely defined conception that united the two demands, of national minority rights and a national home, in a single, synthetic doctrine. Some aspects of this doctrine were fundamental to any possible claim for Jewish national self-determination. Other aspects proved to be rocks of division that divided radical Diaspora-nationalists from Zionists, and one stream of Zionists from another.

The immediate intellectual background of these Eastern European ideas (and, to a large extent, of Wilson's adoption of the principle of national self-determination in the Fourteen Points) may be traced to the theories of nationality, and national autonomous rights within a federal system, developed in the 1890s by Austrian Social Democratic ideologists. Their proposals not only favored a federal reorganization of the empire (as well as of the Social Democratic Party), granting national minorities autonomous rights in the regions they dominated, but also the extension of such autonomy to national minorities in regions where they were not concentrated and dominant. This principle was adopted by theoreticians of the Bund, the Socialist Zionists, and the Folkist and Sejmist Parties in Galicia, Poland, and Russia, who claimed (variously defined) rights of "national-personal" autonomy for Jews (within the federally reorganized empires and the Social Democratic Party) on the grounds that dispersed, exterritorial minorities, no less than regionally dominant minorities, were entitled to a form of self-determination.

Such a conclusion, applying the Austrian doctrine of exterritorial national autonomy to the Jews, far from being accepted, was explicitly rejected by the originators of the underlying theory. They made it clear that an ethnic entity like the Jews, which was based on the outdated principle of religion, might exist as the artificial product of obsolete conditions in the reactionary, autocratic, and underdeveloped regime of Russia but, they argued, political and economic progress would, and should, inevitably assimilate Jews into the general population, as it had already begun to do in the advancing, industrializing countries. The disqualification of the Jewish claim was also logically required if one adhered to the specific doctrine of the Austrians, instead of adopting only its broader outlines. Their proposal of exterritorial national autonomy was meant to apply throughout the Austro-Hungarian Empire to such dispersed ethnic groups as the Germans, who, while minorities elsewhere, were the majority in at least one of the Empire's proposed federal regions. The projected national minority unions would provide, autonomously, for the cultural needs of all their members, outside as well as inside the national region; but only such minorities as were qualified by their dominance in a federal region could enjoy these benefits. This distinction necessarily disqualified any possible Jewish claims in Austria-Hungary, where the issue was merely theoretical; and when the doctrine was actually applied, in Soviet Russia, it was the grounds for the many difficulties under which Jewish attempts to sustain a degree of national autonomy constantly labored.

At the war's end in 1918, however, Eastern European Zionists were passionately convinced that the opportune moment had come to achieve national liberation in Palestine, together with national autonomy in the Diaspora. This stance was in line with a synthetic doctrine of national self-determination such as the Russian Zionist Helsingfors Conference of 1906 had implicitly projected. The new circumstances, involving a postwar reconstruction of Central and Eastern Europe, the Balkans, and the Ottoman Empire, permitted—indeed, required—a further elaboration of the approach on an international scale.

The conception generally entertained was one that assumed democratically constituted Jewish national assemblies in each Diaspora country (or democratically elected community structures in Western countries that might not establish autonomous national minority institutions). Where such assemblies were authorized, they would elect executive bodies to administer Jewish (Yiddish or Hebrew) schools and welfare institutions, which would be supported by tax receipts, allocated by the several governments on a proportionate, equitable basis.* The several assemblies and communities would create a World Jewish Congress as the ultimate authority for international Jewish policy in regard to both Palestine and the Diaspora. Palestine, claimed for the Jews on the grounds of their ancestral rights, would serve as the territorial base essential to the full exercise of national self-determination; and during the period prior to the establishment of a Jewish majority there,† the World Jewish Congress, or its representatives, would

---

* There were obvious parallels to the millet system of the Ottoman Empire, with major differences: the millets were primarily ecclesiastical, administering religious laws of personal status, and were self-financed.

† The question of the status of world Jewry in the Jewish state, after it had a Jewish majority, did not arise before 1948.

share directly in the Mandate government. (In this way, self-governing institutions could be established in Palestine in accordance with democratic principles without the danger that the local Arab populations might block Jewish immigration and relative increase by virtue of their initial majority positions; for world Jewry, and not only the already settled Jewish community, would be counted, en bloc, in the democratic electorate of Palestine.)

Western Jews, as noted, were ready to support national minority rights for Jews in countries where other minorities obtained them, and to accept and assist the development of a Jewish national home in Palestine. They adopted this stand in spite of their own liberal preference for a regime of equal individual rights and their rejection of collective rights in their own country, because Eastern Jewries were those directly involved, and their views and special situation had to be considered. But they utterly rejected the notion of an international elected body authorized to conduct Jewish policy or to share in the government of Palestine as the representative of world Jewry. This, in their eyes, was a blatant example of dual loyalty, a sin of which anti-Semites had always accused the Jews. To the extent that such a conception was believed to be implied in Zionist proposals, non-Zionist collaborators turned into anti-Zionist foes. Shifts back and forth between non-Zionism and anti-Zionism continued to characterize bourgeois liberal Western Jews up to World War II, as the suspicion rose or fell that Zionist plans essentially implied a (democratically constituted) world Jewish entity with quasi-sovereign political functions.

But this very conception was rejected in regard to Palestine, with almost equal emphasis from the start, by the proposed Mandatory power, Great Britain; and anyone who, like Chaim Weizmann, relied primarily on cooperation with England had to disavow it as well. Thus, even before the Balfour Declaration was obtained, Weizmann was already compelled, in May 1917, to warn his fellow Zionists not to expect to be granted either explicit statehood or immediate government powers in Palestine. In other respects, however, the Zionists were able to introduce aspects of their general conception into the Mandate instrument. The British (partly on their own motion, partly after strenuous arguments by Zionist negotiators) formulated this document; and the League of Nations approved it, in terms which recognized the special claim to self-determination in its historic homeland of a people dispersed and no longer occupying its territory.*

The British drew a clear distinction between the Palestine Mandate and other "A" Mandates in order to conform with the intent of the Jewish national home clauses in the instrument: that is to say, they recognized by implication that Jewish self-determination applied to Palestine in respect to potential immigrants, not only settlers already established, and should be proportioned to the reserved rights of world Jewry, and not only the vested rights of the Palestine Jewish community. On these grounds, portions of Article 22 of the League Covenant which "provisionally recognized [other "A" Mandate countries] as independent states subject to the rendering of administrative advice and assistance by a Mandatory until such time as they are able to stand alone" were omitted from the Palestine Mandate; the requirement in other Mandates to prepare an Organic Statute speedily was also omitted; and instead of "rendering administrative advice," the Mandatory for Palestine was given full rights of legislation and administration, as in a Crown Colony. In other words, in order to secure the self-determination of the dispersed Jews in their homeland, the British Mandate draft did not grant world Jewry a proportionate representation in the Palestine government, but instead indefinitely suspended self-government in Palestine, pending an ultimate political settlement of claims, both Jewish and Arab.

The right of the dispersed Jews to seek their full self-determination in Palestine stage by stage, by means of continuing settlement and not on the basis of present occupation, was implied also in Article 4 of the Mandate, which provided for "a Jewish agency . . . for the purpose of advising and cooperating with the Administration of Palestine. . . ." This body was to be recognized as "a public body" and authorized to advise and cooperate with the Mandate government "in such economic, social and other matters as may affect the establishment of the Jewish national home and the interests of the Jewish population in Palestine and, subject always to the control of the Administration, to

---

* The principles involved in this case also applied to one other, the proposed Mandate for the Armenian people in their homeland, but this was never instituted owing to the victories of Turkish nationalism in Anatolia.

assist and take part in the development of the country." The Jewish Agency, then, was not part of the Palestine government, as the Eastern European (and Palestinian) Zionists had wished; but it *was* recognized as a public body and given specifically limited but broad powers—powers which were justified only if Jews were entitled to seek to become a majority and set up a government. This right, moreover, clearly referred not simply to Jews already settled, but to those who might come; and the Zionists (at their own suggestion) were required to "secure the cooperation of all Jews who are willing to assist in the establishment of the Jewish national home." The latter injunction invited the World Zionist Organization, which represented both Diaspora and Palestinian Jews, to seek still broader support in world Jewry. The aim here, too, was clearly limited: the underlying conception was not of a World Jewish Congress responsible, among its other international tasks on behalf of Jews, for everything relating to the establishment of a national territorial base in Palestine; the broadened constituency of the Agency was to recruit for the limited purpose of supporting the Agency's defined tasks. Such a defined role, and such a restricted status, were, in the event, acceptable to non-Zionists who, in 1929, joined the "extended Jewish Agency." Zionists who cherished the broader conception, especially those in Eastern Europe who were strongly committed to Diaspora nationalism, resented and resisted the non-Zionist participation; other Zionists, chiefly concerned with the steady growth of the national home in Palestine, welcomed it.

By the beginning of the 1920s, then, the limits of the possible realization of early East European concepts of Jewish national self-determination had been demonstrated, and more or less accepted. Dreams of autonomous national assemblies and cultural ministries (such as had functioned in a brief postwar interlude in the Ukraine), with governmental authority to foster Jewish culture, made little or no headway in the states subject to national-minorities treaties. As a "weak minority," the Jews found it safer to be sparing in appeals to the League of Nations when those rights they did secure, both individual civil rights and tax-supported Hebrew and Yiddish schools, were increasingly infringed upon or denied. At the same time, "strong minorities" like the Germans, with powerful conational neighboring states, aggressively exploited and abused the provisions of the treaties in a campaign to destroy the whole Western system under which national minorities were nominally protected.

In Palestine, the claim to national self-determination, based on the national need of the dispersed Jews for a territorial base in their historic homeland, was embodied in the fundamental structure of the Mandate and, roughly speaking, guided the Administration's policy through the decade of the 1920s; but only at the price of a Zionist renunciation of any share in the Palestine government for a representative world Jewish organization. The Jewish Agency as a "public body" symbolized the basic right of Jewish self-determination in Palestine; but its clearly delimited functional scope also demonstrated that this right remained one of principle only, and its full realization was contingent on the success of Jewish efforts, for which Britain undertook no guarantee. The accession of non-Zionists to the Jewish Agency left no doubt that they understood this body to be in no way the quasi-sovereign, authorized representative of world Jewry in all its political concerns; and they also made quite explicit their confidence and hope that a Jewish state need never arise in Palestine. Such non-Zionist hopes were, of course, not shared by Zionists. The Jewish Agency partnership (which enjoyed no remarkable success in the 1930s) was a compromise masking severe differences. The fatal rise of Hitler not only forced those differences into the open in the 1930s and early 1940s; it also prepared the grounds for the more solid consensus that a traumatized Jewish public forced upon its institutions in the closing years of the Holocaust and during the difficult prenatal struggle of the State of Israel.

In the closing decades of the Palestine Mandate, the shifting British policy, eventually leading to the virtual abandonment of the Mandate, caused the Jewish consensus to be repeatedly solidified in opposition. Both Zionists and non-Zionists, associated in the Jewish Agency, protested vehemently when, in the wake of Arab uprisings in 1929 and 1936, the British announced policies at variance with the accepted interpretation that the Mandate authorized, for an indefinite period, Jewish immigration limited only by (Jewish-supported) economic absorptive capacity. This unity continued into the war period in the common opposition of Zionists and non-Zionists to the 1939 White Paper and the 1940 Land Transfer Regulations. In this stand, the Jewish public was also able to rely on the adverse opinion of the Permanent

Mandates Commission on the new British policy, as well as on the outspoken opposition to the White Paper of outstanding foes of the whole prewar appeasement policy, like Winston Churchill and the British Labour Party. Although united in opposition to British policy, non-Zionists and Zionists did not share the same reasons for opposition. They could join in condemning the immigration and land-sale restrictions as being contrary to the Mandate, and as discriminatory against Jews and confining them to a ghetto in their own internationally recognized homeland. But non-Zionists, who had always been uneasy about the privileged position of Jews under the Mandate, became seriously alarmed when partition, involving the creation of a Jewish state in a portion of Palestine, was suggested as a way out of the impasse. Zionists could only welcome the prospect of a Jewish state, however much the drastic limitation of its area aroused their antagonism.

VI

The end of the Second World War precipitated the political problem of Palestine's future. It soon became utterly clear that, without a solution permitting the speedy creation of a Jewish state, no possible humane solution, but only new disasters, could be anticipated for the Jewish "displaced persons." The British Labour Party, coming into power in the postwar election, reaffirmed the White Paper policy, and under Foreign Minister Ernest Bevin, pursued it with increasing ferocity. The Palestine Jewish community initiated measures of active resistance ranging from open and, at times, armed defiance of the blockade against Jewish immigrants to guerrilla war against the British Mandate itself and its military and police forces. Under these pressures, the Zionist Executive in August 1946 initiated a renewed proposal of partition and gained the support of the American government and of the American Jewish Committee. In later years, the American government wavered in its support of the partition proposal but the American Jewish Committee did not, thus closing a nearly complete circle of communal solidarity in favor of full national self-determination through the creation of a Jewish state in part of Palestine.

The solution of the Palestine problem was ultimately approved by the United Nations in November 1947; but not because the nations accepted completely the right of a dispersed people to territorial self-determination or were prepared to accept explicitly what was implicitly understood and all too obvious: that this was the essential prerequisite to any humane solution of the postwar Jewish problem. The first recommendation of the Anglo-American Inquiry Committee, in 1946, states: "We have to report that such information as we have received about countries other than Palestine gave no hope of substantial assistance in finding homes for Jews wishing or impelled to leave Europe." Notwithstanding this finding, the Committee then propounded the following principle: "But Palestine alone cannot meet the emigration needs of the Jewish victims of Nazi and Fascist persecution; the whole world shares responsibility for them. . . ." United Nations bodies and member states have frequently stated very similar views.

The creation of Israel represented an acceptance by international consensus—in spite of continuing Arab opposition—of the fact of the Jewish national home's existence rather than a straightforward recognition of its moral basis. Nevertheless, the moral claim of a homeless people to national self-determination in its homeland (as the only possible place for such an achievement) played a role, only manifest at moments of crisis, which cannot be ignored in the political history of Israel's rise. At the very zenith of enthusiasm for national self-determination, during and after the First World War, leaders open to idealism, or preferring to appear as such, perceived that self-determination should apply not only on a property-rights basis to majority populations occupying their own land, but also on a human-rights basis to minorities not effectively occupying any land but with profound traditional ties to an historic homeland. The Armenians as well as the Jews exemplified this case, though only the Jews were able to realize the claim. That they were able to do so was the consequence of the rather fortuitous and shifting confluence of their claim with the interests of one or another power or powers—and, in the end, to the tangible force they themselves represented. But, on the other hand, decisive victories based on sufficient force have not yet sufficed to establish Israel's legitimacy in the eyes of the Arabs—precisely because they repudiate the Jews' claim to their historic homeland as a just title. Just as the diplomatic gains of Jewish nationalism rest on no more than a partial, often suppressed, recognition of the moral claims of a homeless people, so the repeated failures to gain Arab recognition rest on a partial, rather than total, repudiation of the principles involved. One somewhat paradoxical consequence of Jewish nationalism, and its specific innovations in doctrine and law, has been the extent to which these precedents have been picked up and utilized by others, including its opponents, and above all by the Arabs.

If there is any recent notable application of Diaspora nationalist notions like those of Eastern European Jewry in the early twentieth century, it is obviously the theory and practice of American black nationalism. The recognition accorded to "peoples" in Article 80 of the UN Charter, in response to Zionist urging, was extended (in a manner which not only the American Jewish Committee but also the American Jewish Congress opposed) to the International Covenants on Human Rights and on Economic, Social, and Cultural Rights, both of which somewhat incongruously recognize "self-determination" of peoples as *individual* rights.

The most notable instance of the adoption of Jewish (in this case, of specifically Zionist) doctrines of national self-determination is, of course, that of the Palestinians. They have imitated, in detail, the method and procedures as well as the theoretical justification of Zionism. They proclaim themselves a homeless people—not only exiled from Palestine but homeless in other Arab countries, such as Lebanon, Syria, or Jordan, and even on the Palestine West Bank, should they or their ancestors once have lived within Israel's borders. They cultivate this sense of homelessness by schooling, by a kind of nationalist liturgical writing, and by refusing adamantly to be resettled. They declare that only in the area usurped by Israel (now occupied by an unquestionable Jewish majority for over a quarter of a century) can their national homelessness be resolved and their just rights of self-determination be secured.

One would think that, having generalized Zionist theory to apply to their own case, Arabs should recognize it in the original, Jewish case; but this would be too simple a conclusion. Even before the Palestinians, Arabs did not base their rejection of Zionist claims to Palestine on a simple denial of the claim that a dispersed, homeless people was entitled to a territory for its self-determination. They sometimes recognized the abstract right to such a claim, but argued that the obligation to compensate the Jews was that of Europeans, who had oppressed Jews, whereas the Arabs (as they asserted) had never done so; accordingly, Jews should have a territory in Europe, not in the Arab lands. The present Palestinian theory more closely duplicates the Zionist case (and undercuts the earlier Arab argument) by stipulating that, because of an indissoluble emotional bond, *only* Palestine—and no other land, no matter how similar in culture and society—can resolve the need for Palestinian sovereignty; but this leads to no greater willingness to universalize the principle to include the original case, the Jews. Some Palestinians quite flatly state that their pseudo-Zionism is a "tactical" weapon and commits them to no "strategic" aim—in other words, once Israel disappears, there will be no further need for Palestinian nationalism. Others, more fully committed to a Palestinian entity, equally flatly insist that Israel must be "de-Zionized" (that is, disappear, since the army, economy, society, and culture as well as the state must be de-Zionized, and Jewish immigrants since 1917—or 1948—be removed) in order to make room for a Palestine that will be not only "secular, democratic" but also, plainly speaking, Arab. The extension of "Zionism" to the Palestinian case, so conceived, is a claim to nullify real Zionism; that is, it seems to be a right claimed for the specific purpose of eliminating an existing right. But the only practical possibility for the inclusion of a Palestinian nationality under an international order (should Palestinians truly wish, even after the war ends, to constitute a national entity separate and distinct from the rest of the "Arab nation") would be through the conclusion of a peace with Israel.

International recognition of a principle or a right may launch it and give it some political impetus in world affairs, but its actual weight, in this as in other cases, must rest on the recognized adjustment of power relationships. To realize rights in practice, it is always necessary to build supporting strength; and to prevent distortion and abuse of principles, once introduced, it is also necessary to exert continuing strength. This lesson has been thoroughly inculcated in contemporary Jewish consciousness by the tortuous course in recent world history of the idea of national self-determination for a dispersed people united for nearly two millennia only by the moral universe of historical Judaism.

JACOB L. TALMON

Mission and Testimony:
The Universal Significance
of Modern Anti-Semitism

The fate of the Jews during the last two hundred years is indis-
solubly connected with issues which form the very core of the
condition of modern man. Jews played so important a role in
modern history, not because they had a mission to carry out
(though this aspect should not be belittled), but because it was
their fate to serve as a testimony, as a living witness, a touchstone,
a whipping block and symbol all in one.

I

If the French Revolution may be considered as the beginning of
an era that has not yet come to an end, we can view the 1880s
as the beginning of a historical wave—with anti-Semitism as one
of its motive forces—which may, for all we know, not yet have
been brought to a halt in 1945. Jewish emancipation in the French
Revolution was an offshoot of the triumph of rationalism and the
idea of the rights of man. More than that, it sealed the complete
victory of these values, since the Jews were a marginal case. The

anti-Semitic rage that erupted in Europe eighty years ago was not a by-product, but the point of departure and focus of a vast political and ideological movement. From its Archimedean point of anti-Semitism that movement was driven on to repudiate everything affirmed by humanist rationalism, and indeed everything taught by its parent, Christianity.

The tragic paradox of the Jews in modern times has been the fact that their existence and success have been dependent upon the triumph of the idea of oneness as represented by liberal democracy and socialism, while the very phenomenon of Jewry is an unparalled demonstration of the enormous power of the element of uniqueness. The Jews did not want and could not escape the fact of their uniqueness; the general community would not and could not be made oblivious of it.

The liberal state which accorded full rights to its Jewish citizens on the same basis as to all others, including freedom of economic pursuit, a share in the running of the nation's affairs, took its stand on the theory of a social contract concluded between men of reason. Racial origin, religious affiliation, social class, and all those deep but elusive differences, rooted in and exemplified by habit and custom, reflex and prejudice, instinct and frame of mind, disposition and manner of reasoning, which separate and isolate men, were considered irrelevant, when compared with the forces of conscious deliberating reason. On the other hand, the texture of the liberal state was limited from its very inception to a legal framework. Outside it, the citizen was free to follow his own judgment. Such a regime was ideal for the Jews: but to their misfortune it never even came into being. Liberalism came to the fore partnered with nationalism. The universalist principle of common citizenship replaced the feudal structure based upon class and caste distinctions, but the new national brotherhood strove after homogeneity which would mark it off from all the other national communities.

From the very day when the nation-state appeared on the scene of history it began—as does every vital institution—to develop an ethos of its own by trying to enrich and deepen its own contents. Every nation went out of its way to stress its own uniqueness based on blood, common memories, common symbols of a remote past in which the Jews had no share and which very often only served to remind them of past persecution, and to emphasize their status as aliens. Even during the honeymoon of emancipation after the victory of the French Revolution, the slogan was coined: "Everything for the Jews as individuals, but nothing for them as a nation." And if the Jews were unfortunate enough to be irrevocably committed to the preservation of a national identity and their historic uniqueness, they would have to be expelled, for there was no place for a state within a state. Napoleon did not merely compel the Jews to forget Zion and the Messiah who, the Jews believed, would someday come to redeem Israel. He went further, planning to force the Jews to intermarry "so as to dilute their blood."

In Western Europe there were ancient nation-states with developed economies, a balanced social structure, a rich and varied cultural heritage, and small Jewish communities. The Jews soon abandoned their separate language, became assimilated to the culture of the environment, and discarded most of those religious observances which served to separate them from their neighbors.

Of course many Jews became totally assimilated. Others assumed the color of their surroundings so that they lost almost all distinctness in the eyes of their neighbors. Yet the process of assimilation was never completed. Among other factors, it was continuously disturbed by waves of Jewish migrants from the East European pale. Their arrival in the West infused new vigor into the local Jewish communities. At the same time there developed a stereotypical image of the alien Eastern Jew, an image that was transferred in the minds of many to all Jews.

II

The murderous assault did not come from the side of the conservative, feudal, and clerical forces which were opposed to equal rights for Jews because the "arrival" of the Jews was in their eyes a symbol of a libertarian repudiation of all traditional values, the overthrow of hierarchical order, and the end of the Christian state as it had existed for centuries. Nor did it come from those who in the name of national homogeneity demanded that the Jews should become totally assimilated. The attack came from men who started as devotees of the democratic ideals, but, incensed by the Jewish phenomenon, were swept from a refusal to respect human dignity in the Jew to a denial of the very idea of human rights based on the conception of human equality.

Nothing demonstrates this shift more strikingly than the brochure *The Jews and Music* which Richard Wagner published in 1850, only two years after the composer's fight on the barricades of Dresden at the side of the arch-revolutionary and anarchist Mikhail Bakunin. "There will never be true liberty for humanity so long as there are still oppressed men left anywhere in the world, however few and far between they happen to be," the young Wagner wrote. In his discourse on *The Jews and Music* so soon after, Wagner (made to feel uncomfortable by the Jewish composer Meyerbeer) dwells on the contradiction between reason that teaches men to view the Jews as human beings like all other humans—in this case like all other Germans—and the stubborn fact that the actual Jews whom he saw around him were in his eyes still German-speaking Orientals, despite the 2,000 years they had been living in Germany. This led Wagner to speculate on which was more real: The abstract idea, pure reason, postulating the unity of mankind, or the concrete fact of group peculiarity? The unity of the human species, or racial uniqueness? What should be, or what is? Humanism was teaching men to treat the Jews in a spirit of tolerance and respect for the human personality, for all men were created in the image of God, but a primeval and spontaneous instinct found expression in hatred of the Jews. When was a man truest to himself, when engaging in ratiocination or when obeying the voice of blood? Which had a higher claim to be the truth—the logical syllogism or the intuitive response?

The implication of these questions, once posed, reached out far beyond the subject of the Jews. The very nerve center of rationalism and indeed Christianity itself was attacked here. The concept of a universal natural law was also repudiated. The individual as a creature of a reason common to all men was no longer, as he had been for millennia, the primary and most important fact. The collective group of the race became primary and fundamental. Language and art were invoked by Wagner and his followers as the conclusive proof of this primacy, because they bore the unmistakable and indelible imprint of race. These were not contrived deliberating by reason, but sprang from dark forces and hidden wellsprings.

The two pamphlets by Karl Marx on the Jewish question and

its connection with capitalist liberalism, published just a few years before Wagner's pamphlet, reveal an attitude not entirely dissimilar to that represented by Wagner. To Marx, liberal-capitalist society appeared to be founded upon fraud. It had declared itself in favor of equal legal and political rights for all, irrespective of social origins and economic status. In other words, inequalities of wealth were proclaimed irrelevant, and hence beyond the limits of governmental intervention. The fraud, according to Marx, consisted in the fact that with the abolition of all other privileges—racial origin, family status, religious association—the privilege of wealth had become the most decisive social datum. In law, differences in wealth and property no longer existed, but in actual fact it was they that shaped society. In theory, the parties in a state struggled over formal principles. But in fact, hidden and "unacknowledged" interests, one may say illegitimate interests, were turning the wheels of history. That unacknowledged and illegitimate force which had become omnipotent was embodied in and symbolized for Marx by Judaism.

The liberal constitution accorded full rights to the Jews on the ground that their religious affiliation was irrelevant, and in so doing did away, as it were, with Judaism. But instead of doing away with Judaism, it enthroned it, giving it free rein, liberating it from all restraint, as it had declared status and wealth irrelevant, while in fact giving supreme power to money to dominate society. For "money" read "Jews." The liberation of mankind therefore meant the liberation of mankind from Judaism. "Following the liberation of society from Judaism will come the social liberation of the Jews themselves," Marx wrote in the concluding section of his second pamphlet. The annihilation of Judaism would bring with it the liberation of the Jews. "There is only one possible way of redeeming the Jews from the terrible curse that hangs over them—annihilation," Wagner wrote in the concluding passage of his essay on *The Jews and Music*.

Despite these passages in Marx, it would be a distortion to label him or the socialist movement of Europe as anti-Semitic. It is easy to collect many anti-Semitic quotations from the works of the early socialists such as Fourier, his pupil Toussenel, who wrote the book *The Jews, the Rulers of the Age*, and from the voluminous writings of Proudhon. Anti-Semitic opinions, which lesser socialists voiced as empirical statements, would inevitably be integrated by the great systematizer, Marx, into a cohesive weltanschauung. Yet anti-Semitism could never become an essential prop to hold up the doctrine of socialism. The primacy of the class war on a world scale runs counter to the belief in race as a factor of decisive importance. And the vision of a universal classless society is inspired by the idea of the unity of the human species. In the messianic visions of the socialist pioneers the international proletariat was destined to become humanity itself.

But if responsibility for anti-Semitism cannot be laid at the door of the socialist movement, neither should socialism be looked upon as the sworn and consistent defender of the Jews against anti-Semitism, certainly not before the end of the nineteenth century. Socialism emerged as a shield only when the modern mass movements of the nationalist Right began to steal the socialist clientèle by directing social wrath into channels of hatred of Jews and diverting it from the idea of class war. That process began about the year 1880, with the emergence of anti-parliamentary mass movements.

III

The attack on parliamentary government was launched in the years when European liberalism had reached its apex. In the 1870s constitutional regimes were celebrating their triumph in all countries of Europe except Russia. And even Russia had taken the road of reform in the 1860s. Czar Alexander II was about to grant a constitution when he was struck down by terrorists. It was also the golden age of liberal capitalism. The principle of free trade was acknowledged as the very token of the harmony of interests between nations. Every European country was overflowing with enterprise and economic activity. On the morrow of the war of 1870 Germany was swept by a frenzy of joint stock activity. New companies vied with each other in daring ventures. France changed from an agricultural country into a nation that served as a banker on a worldwide scale, financing railways in Russia and the Suez and Panama canals. In both France and Germany it was not long before wild speculation was overtaken by Nemesis. Many persons who had started with high expectations found themselves grievously disappointed and cheated.

It was the contradiction between the triumph of parliamentarism, on the one hand, and the disasters wrought by the workings of capitalism, on the other, that gave birth to the anti-parliamentarian mass movements of modern times. The masses had been led to believe in representative government and elected bodies as a panacea for all the ills and deficiencies that beset society. Representative government was seen as the omnipotent sovereign, and the people had, after all, the power to elect or dismiss its representatives at will. And so it was natural that the belief should spread that the failure of representative institutions in the fulfil-ment of their prime duty—the assurance of social-economic stability—was proof of some deep-seated illness. And when crises were accompanied by scandals involving politicians and statesmen, the cry went up that the people's representatives were the servants and the agents of the men at the stock exchange who pulled the strings in a plot against the innocent masses. As European society became more democratic, the parliamentary regime became pro-gressively more threatened.

The Jews played an active and extremely important part in the development of capitalism. Emancipation had set free forces that had been lying dormant for hundreds of years. The emancipated Jew did not feel that he had reached a haven. He had cut himself off from Jewish tradition, but he had not been accepted by the society in which he lived, and many doors remained closed to him. He wanted to escape from his deprivation by intense activity in fields to which he had free access. The social mobility of the Jews exceeded that of any other group. Jews thronged to the cities which are the most sensitive arteries of any country, illuminated by pub-licity and public attention. When Jewish names then surfaced in public scandals, they attracted disproportionate attention.

Among the principal victims of these crises and scandals that afflicted society were the lower middle classes rather than the proletariat which had little or nothing to lose, let alone invest. The petty bourgeoisie grew impoverished while lacking any real sense of identity or cohesion as a class, for they had no organi-zational equivalent of the workers' trade unions and socialist parties. At the same time they dreaded the specter of sinking into the ranks of the proletariat. Nationalism, which was capable of giv-ing them a feeling of belonging to the national brotherhood on the same footing as the upper classes, appeared as an anchor of salva-tion and a compass in a world shaken by upheavals. Lower-middle-class chauvinism found in anti-Semitism one of its main props. This anti-Semitism permitted many shopkeepers or artisans to feel superior to the Jewish intellectual or businessman, especially when menaced by the two "Jewish conspiracies"—international finance and international communism—both allegedly intent upon disrupting national unity. Nationalism was everywhere in ascendance.

The nationalist sentiments which from 1870 divided the two greatest and most advanced nations in Europe, France, and Germany, put a decisive brake upon revolutionary socialist internationalism. The patriotic sentiment of the workers and their leaders proved to be incomparably stronger than international working-class solidarity. Concomitantly anti-parliamentarism with its social and anti-Semitic flavor had emerged in several European countries and, in special form, in the Austro-Hungarian Empire.

The conditions in the Austro-Hungarian Empire during its twilight period exerted the most direct and decisive influence on the shape of modern German Nazism. In *Mein Kampf* Hitler admits that all his political and social ideas were born under the impact of the political realities he was able to observe in Vienna, especially the two pan-German anti-Semitic movements; one founded by Georg von Schoenerer, the other the Social Christian movement led by the popular mayor of Vienna, Karl Lueger.

The basic problem of the Austro-Hungarian Empire, as Hitler saw it, was the bitter struggle of the German-speaking part of the population to remain the masters of the country's destiny, despite the fact that other races—and in particular Slavonic peoples—formed the majority of the country's inhabitants. A parliamentary regime based on numerical majorities, and the principle of "one man one vote" threatened the special status of the Germans in the Empire. Two alternatives presented themselves: either to dismantle the Empire and annex the German-speaking areas to Germany to form a Greater Germany, or to reject democratic parliamentary government in favor of the principle of a governing élite—in which case the party system would have to make way for government by an inspired leader. Viewed from this angle, the Social Democrats and the Jews were the most dangerous enemies. The German-speaking socialist in Austria who contended that the Czech worker was closer to him than the German bourgeois was undermining the unity of the German race. Austrian socialists found themselves reluctantly defending the unity of the

Empire, while demanding wide autonomy for its component peoples, because the break-up of the Empire was calculated to be interpreted as a victory for isolationist nationalism at the expense of international unity.

The only racial group in the Austro-Hungarian Empire that was fully committed to the Hapsburg ideal of a multiracial kingdom was its Jewish population. The Jews were convinced that change in the multiracial, supranational empire, where groups and entities of all kinds were assured the right of self-expression, would be to their disadvantage. Moreover, the principal leaders of the Social Democratic party in Austria were Jews. So the conclusion could easily be drawn that there was a Jewish-capitalist-socialist-democratic plot to destroy the German race in Austria. The equality of all the citizens of the country, the principle of the sovereignty of the numerical majority, the parliamentary regime with its political parties, could be viewed as a screen laid by the Jews for their cunning schemes to liquidate racial élites. The destruction of the élite and the consequent weakening of the nation was an opportunity for the Jews to exercise their destructive tyranny without hindrance. In *Mein Kampf* Hitler singles out the Soviet Union and France as proof of the correctness of his doctrine.

Hitler's criticism of the two anti-Semitic movements of the Austro-Hungarian Empire deserves attention. He praised the pan-German movement for its adherence to the principle of race, but criticized it for its lack of social orientation and its remoteness from the masses. The chief virtue of the Social Christian movement, on the other hand, was its closeness to the masses and its understanding of the techniques of mobilizing the masses. But Hitler found it wanting in that it did not have a doctrine of race and had its loyalties divided between Germany and the Roman Catholic church. Without a racial doctrine, Hitler thought, anti-Semitism was bound to remain a tepid affair. It is no accident that a high proportion of Nazi leaders were from multiracial areas, where the Germans had played the part of a master race: Alfred Rosenberg came from the Baltic; Rudolf Hess was born in Cairo; Darré originated from the Argentine; quite a few, like Hitler himself, came from Austria-Hungary, and especially the Sudeten.

Hitler believed that the secret of political success was to concentrate on one enemy. Success in politics required the selection of a principal enemy who could be shown to embody the characteristics of all the other enemies and to arouse fiercer revulsion and hatred than any of them. In this way the principal enemy could be isolated, other rivals for power could be identified with him and held up to contempt and ridicule. The Jews presented an ideal target. Crudely understood Darwinist biologism, when juxtaposed with the inter-racial struggles of the peoples of the old Hapsburg Empire, created the vision of an interracial war of destruction. The words *Ausrot-tung, Vernichtung* ("destruction," "annihilation") crop up countless times in Hitler's writings, and not just as picturesque expression or vivid metaphor. Since the conflict between races was a life-and-death struggle, there could be no laws to regulate it other than the law of the stronger. Such a war demanded masses of soldiers who would fight relentlessly and, even more, a quasi-religious ideology—a weltanschauung to stir men and fire them to action by rousing their fanaticism (another word that Hitler never tired of using). That faith must be based upon a set of ideas as few and simple as possible. The creed should not be confused by complicated questions, side issues, and unresolved problems such as religion or economic policies, for the main thing was to seize power. If there was no power to act, there was no point in putting forward political programs; and once power was won, everything would come in its wake. In essence, the fight was not concerned with who was more right—we or they—but which one of us was it going to be? We personify the new faith of the master race. Our enemies are the forces of Satan.

The movement initiated in the 1880s by the German court preacher, Adolf Stöcker, offers us an insight into the transformation of anti-Semitism from traditional hatred of the Jews into the demoniacal racial mass movements of our age. German conservatives of the old school were at first attracted by the crusade that Stöcker, himself a commoner, was waging against the Progressist-Socialist heresy which denied God, the Kaiser, and the Fatherland. The campaign for the saving of souls was welcome to them, and incitement against the Jews did not particularly upset German Junkerdom: they were rather pleased by the discomfiture of the Jews. Kaiser Wilhelm I himself expressed his satisfaction with Stöcker's efforts to put the Jews in their rightful place, for he thought they had become far too impertinent. However, the Kaiser hastened to add, although it was true that the Jews had been granted too many opportunities, this was a fait accompli and these rights had been incorporated into the statute book of Germany, and he (the Kaiser) had sworn to uphold the constitution. Similar opinions were voiced in the Reichstag when a petition with a quarter of a million signatures was introduced demanding an end to Jewish emancipation in Germany.

In his youth Bismarck used to say that he would never be able to serve under a Jew or to obey a Jew, and in the debate on the German defense budget of 1879—a date of prime importance in the history of Germany and the world—the Chancellor did not shrink from attacking his Jewish rivals, Edvard Lasker and Ludwig Bamberger of the Liberal party, by dropping hints about those who "neither spin nor sow, yet reap rewards." Although Bismarck had no liking for Stöcker, he advised his son, who was a candidate for a Berlin constituency, to use him in the common struggle against the Social Democrats and the Progressive Party (which was generally regarded as a Jewish political group). As for mass agitation engaged in by Stöcker, and in particular his appeal to the petty bourgeoisie, Bismarck declared himself indifferent as to whether or not the priest incited people against the Jews as such. The trouble, as Bismarck saw it, was that he also attacked wealthy Jews, including such men as his private banker, Gerson von Bleichröder, and it was only a step from such preaching to demagogic socialist propaganda against private property.

But Stöcker came to grief during one of his propaganda missions to England. His enemies disrupted a public meeting that he was to address in London. The incident suggested scandal to the court in Berlin, for it was unthinkable for a preacher of the Kaiser to be mixed up in an ugly incident with the rabble of a foreign capital. So when Stöcker also became involved in a court case and was convicted on a charge of perjury, his career came to an end.

One may warrant the generalization from this episode and from others like it in several European countries, particularly the attempted seizure of power by Boulanger in France, that the victory of extreme anti-Semitic mass movements becomes possible only after the traditional Right has been completely demoralized. This is borne out by the history of Germany between the two wars.

On the eve of Hitler's rise to power in Germany, right-wing politicians such as von Papen, Hugenberg, and some Rhineland industrialists toyed with the idea of championing the "Bohemian *Feldwebel*" (as Hindenburg called him) and using him as a puppet. Paradoxically and ironically, Hindenburg was persuaded to appoint Hitler as the only way of restoring the parliamentary constitution. A coalition of Nazis and conservative nationalists would be able, he was assured, to command a parliamentary majority, and thus put Germany back upon the road of constitutional legitimacy which had been so badly battered by the governments of Brüning, Papen, and Schleicher. These, for lack of majority support, were compelled to rule by presidential decrees designed for situations of national emergency. The Nazis were in fact a minority in the first government set up on January 31, 1933. It was humanity's disaster that Hitler was swept forward on the tide of an extremely cohesive movement based on a weltanschauung.

Hatred of the Jews by the traditional Right was rather a peripheral and empirical matter than a central point in a definite ideological system. We could even term it "defensive anti-Semitism." The traditional Right recoiled from contact with Jews and wanted to set a limit to their influence. But the rights accorded to Jews were, as we saw, considered by them as part and parcel of the law of the land. The state was duty-bound to protect the life, property, and safety of its citizens, and incitement that insulted a citizen's self-respect was considered vulgar and uncouth. Stöcker himself declared that though in principle he deplored the fact that "the Jews can vote and be elected, serve as civil servants and occupy commanding posts, sit on local councils and even in parliamentary bodies, and are permitted to teach in our schools," he could not avert his eyes from the fact that "emancipation is a fact of life that cannot be ignored. There is not a government or a parliament that would consider abolishing it." He went on to say that if a conservative government were one day to put an end to Jewish emancipation, their action would be undone as soon as a more liberal regime were returned to power at a later date. "We are a nation based on the rule of law," Stöcker declared, "and we wish to stay that way." When elected *Bürgermeister* of Vienna, Lueger dismissed Jewish officials from his municipal administration, but he took the trouble to find alternative employment for every Jew who had been deprived of his job; the world was no jungle, and people cannot be deprived of means to exist.

Treitschke may be looked upon as a watershed between the traditional hatred of Jews and modern theoretical anti-Semitism. He adopted the popular cry that "the Jews are our great misfortune." His immense prestige as national historian and prophet of the Second Reich lent respectability to the slogan. It was the mocking approach of Jewish writers to the sacred values of the Teutonic race and the Prussian tradition that aroused the ire of that poet of Prussianism. Börne and Heine represented in his view an alien influence, since they tried to nourish the Germans with Western ideas borrowed from the liberal tradition and revolutionary France. To Treitschke, as to German conservatives of all hues and the various radical Christian mass movements, "*Manchesterlum*" (in the sense of liberal laissez-faire) was interchangeable with "*Judentum*": both connoted selfish materialism, unconcerned with social welfare or national glory. Treitschke was shocked by a slip of the pen committed by Heinrich Graetz. Graetz had written that Gabriel Riesser, the German-Jewish politician, was *by chance* born on German soil. So, the enraged Treitschke commented, the place of birth of a Jew is merely a matter of chance! Graetz had also said that although Jews had been accorded recognition in Germany, Judaism as such had not been similarly recognized. In what capacity does Judaism seek recognition?—Treitschke asks in his polemic with Graetz. In its capacity as a nation within a nation? If that is so, the answer is a categorical "never"—"*Nie.*" If the Jews consider themselves to be a people, let them pack their bags and emigrate to the Land of Israel.

But Treitschke was not so extreme as to draw the conclusion that all Jews were foreigners and would never be able to form part of the German nation. On the contrary, he blamed the Jews for their stubborn refusal to assimilate. Yet it was only a short step from this opinion to the conclusion that the Jews would never be able to be absorbed by other peoples, and should therefore be denied the opportunity of mixing with the pure Germans. In order to arrive at so extreme a conclusion it was necessary to abandon certain restraints which neither conservatives nor anti-Semites of the type of Stöcker could easily break. It was necessary to question the fundamental assumptions of Christianity in respect of the unity of mankind, the brotherhood of men, each created in the image of God. The whole of the Judeo-Christian tradition had to be thrown overboard. There was indeed no escape from a denial of Christianity as such. Many of Stöcker's allies, such as Wilhelm Marr (who invented the term *anti-Semitism*), Karl Eugen Dühring, and others were bold enough to take this final leap.

IV

Richard Wagner inspired Houston Stewart Chamberlain, and Chamberlain became the oracle of Adolf Hitler and Alfred Rosenberg. Chamberlain, son of a British admiral, who fell in love with the Teutonic race, was the son-in-law of Richard Wagner, and the high priest of the cult of Wagnerism. In 1923 just before the death of Chamberlain, Hitler came to pay homage to the racist philosopher. After the meeting Chamberlain wrote: "My faith in the German people has never been shaken, yet I must confess that my hopes had sunk to a low ebb (in the last few years). But your visit has wrought a complete change in my mood." That was in 1923. Rosenberg's book *The Myth of the Twentieth Century* takes up the thread of Chamberlain's work *The Foundations of the Nineteenth Century*.

Alfred Bäumler, who was one of the first Nazi theoreticians in the Faculty of Philosophy at Berlin University, was advancing this set of ideas when he proclaimed that "when we shout 'Heil Hitler' to German youth, we are also hailing Friedrich Nietzsche"; he also asserted that "the theory of race was the Copernican revolution of modern times."

The theory of race is a compound of many and diverse elements: Ernest Renan's theory on the essential differences between Semitic and Aryan languages, revealing basic differences in the spirit and mentality of the two racial groups; the studies of Count Gobineau purporting to prove the inequality of the respective roles of different races on the stage of world history; the philosophy of history propounded by Chamberlain; biological evolutionism as taught by Darwin, which substitutes the principle of the struggle for existence for the older vision of a universe of natural harmony; Nietzsche's glorification of the strong natural man, impelled irresistibly by elemental forces and unhampered by pity or the whisper of conscience; Wagner's Gothic pagan Valhalla, the home of heroes larger than life.

Yet it seems questionable whether these diverse elements would ever have combined to produce such a destructive and demoniacal gospel, were it not for the fact that there were Jews in Europe whose presence made it possible to demonstrate what the word *Aryan* meant. As for the other non-Aryan races, they were far away. Negroes were out of sight, and Germany had not yet come into contact with the world of the Chinese and the Japanese. As for the Arabs, no one gave them a thought. The racial theory made possible the systematization of disparate anti-Jewish notions and anti-Semitic sentiments into a coherent pattern. It raised the status of anti-Semitism to the dignity of a comprehensive weltanschauung, based on the findings of science, providing a key to the understanding of history and offering a political program, armed with a ready-made guide to the art of political techniques. With the help of the theory of race, traditional dislike of the Jews on the part of those who wanted to preserve their historic national identity undiluted, and were concerned with nothing outside their own existence and purity, was transformed from a defensive reaction into a universal mission. The Jews were said to be a menace to all the peoples of the Aryan race, and the Teutonic peoples, who personified the noble virtues of the Aryan and Nordic races at their finest, were called upon to act as a spearhead in the struggle against the force which threatened to destroy the Aryan brotherhood.

Both branches of Western civilization, the Christian and the rationalist, despite other important differences, share the common premise of a direct relationship between man as an individual and humanity as a species. Differences of race, origin, language, and religion are of secondary importance in comparison with the primary fact of man's humanity. The Western tradition has always drawn a clear distinction between the human species, whose distinguishing attributes are soul and reason, and all other manifestations of creation. The destiny of man, in this view, is in the never-ceasing endeavor to gain clear knowledge of reality and achieve a social order based on harmony.

The doctrine of race negates the reality of man as man, as well as the conception of humanity as such. The oneness of humanity is regarded by the racial theory as an artificial abstraction. Such an abstraction has no real life. Life, that is to say reality, is possessed only by organic entities, in other words races.

For all its seemingly scientific basis, the doctrine of race gives rise to a kind of mysticism which expands into boundlessness. Blood becomes the real primary cause that determines the whole personality of its bearer. It is held to predetermine the character, the mentality, indeed the values and preferences, dispositions and modes of thought of everyone who has a share of that blood. Thinking is speaking with one's blood: man does not fashion his character out of his free will, with the help of his autonomous power of decision and clear reason. His place, role, actions are determined for him by the great organism of which he is part.

The universe appears in the race theory as the fullness of life, the totality of power in it. The destiny of man is not to learn and to know for its own sake, but to live, to fight, like all other creatures, for his share of that fullness of life and power—the universe. The fact of struggle is the highest reality, and the word *Kampf* is a key word in the vocabulary of Hitler and the Nazi party. The predetermined way on which every race struggles to express, assert, and realize itself, and the requirements of that strategy at the given hour and in the given circumstances, are seen as forming together the supreme and sole laws of the race. It follows therefore that it is foolish to confront any race with an objective test of validity applicable to all mankind.

In its cosmic struggle the race must be permanently on the alert, mobilized and fit for battle. Viewed from this angle, reason was not a quality that could be singled out or put above other faculties. When isolated, it was bound to become sterile, for exaggerated analytical intellectualism weakened the will and lessened the individual's instinctive self-assurance. Intellectualism was a sure sign of the weakening of the voice of the blood and man's elemental impulses. Not with ideas will the leader come to the masses— taught Hitler—nor to teach them to consider dispassionately the pros and cons of any issue. The intellect was in the service of those forces which reason had neither produced nor set in motion. Mobilization for a breakthrough demanded the coordination of all those faculties that influenced the fighting ability. The different areas of life and endeavor could not therefore be allowed to retain their autonomy, a thing impossible anyway in the light of the all-determining quality of the race. The different efforts had to be guided by one single and exclusive principle so as to respond to the common impulse with the same thrill and rhythm. Totalitarianism is the companion and function of the permanent war-readiness of the race in its struggle for power. It is, at the same time, the logical outcome of the idea of organic determinism.

In according supreme significance to race, nature invested in the race the right to use its strength to the full. There was no room therefore for any respect for each other's rights, for relations based on equality or mutual consent or numerical majority between races. And the same was true within the framework of the race. Dominion and government were not matters to be decided by elections and negotiations. The leader would grasp power because his qualities, his vital powers, and sense of destiny moved him with irresistible force. For he was the supreme personification of the race. Being the most perfect creation of the evolutionary process, overflowing with love for his race, he was endowed with the special powers of the visionary and prophet so that he was able to perceive the deeper meaning of his age, to hear the steps of the race's destiny, still hidden in a nebulous future. The leader's intuition was thus hailed as the highest law; the will of the supreme commander of the race in its life-and-death struggle was proclaimed the categorical imperative.

It is difficult to establish whether it was hatred for the Jews that led to this denial of Christianity, or whether the rejection of Christianity removed all limitations from hatred for the Jews. Christians may have disliked Jews, hated and persecuted them, treated them with contempt, and held them responsible for all manner of misdeeds. Yet, they could not but stand in awe before the mother-religion and the bearer of a divine mystery, the central figure in an enormously significant part of God's scheme of history. Furthermore, the Jewish element served to emphasize the universal side of Europe's history and culture: the unity of all believers in a church universal and the equality of all believers in the eyes of their Creator, race being wholly irrelevant.

Anti-Semites such as Bruno Bauer, Chamberlain, Julius Langbehn, and Paul Anton de Lagarde, joined forces in destroying the Christian image of Judaism and denied to it its historic role. Bauer did not try to deny that Christianity had developed out of Judaism and had been born in the land of Israel within a Jewish society. But Chamberlain sought to prove that Jesus did not belong to the same race as Abraham. He was sure that Jesus had fair hair and blue eyes, and laid great stress on the fact that Jesus was born in Galilee where a considerable section of the population was Greek. The most important of Chamberlain's arguments was the claim that Jesus and Christianity were born among Jews in order to demonstrate the tremendous difference between the irreligion of the Jews and real religion. Christianity came into being as a reaction to the caricature of religion that had its roots in materialistic Jewish racialism.

Bauer developed the historical thesis that from antiquity to the present day, the Jews had always acted as a solvent, a virus of disintegration. Modern Jewish universalism in the form of international capitalism or international Marxism was the same thing using two differing disguises, since both aimed at weakening the organic unity of the race and national solidarity.

The "stab in the back" explanation of Germany's defeat in 1918 was seized upon as conclusive proof of the correctness of the racial theory. The nationalist Right found it easy to fasten upon international Jewry its old obsession with encirclement plots by envious neighbors, especially since Jewish devotees of universal political messianism played so prominent a part in the mounting wave of the international revolution. It could be said that it was upon the corpse of the assassinated Jewish intellectual, Kurt Eisner, the ephemeral and ineffectual dictator of the Revolutionary Republic in Munich, that Adolf Hitler began, in that Bavarian capital, his climb to supreme power. Jewish international finance was also made to bear the odium of the ravages of inflation. The Jew thus became the target of the two most powerful resentments, nationalist rage and social protest. Instead of being at odds as they had previously been, the two passions were now fused to form an infinitely more dangerous dynamite than the anti-Semitic movements a generation earlier in France, Germany, or Austria-Hungary.

"The decline of civilizations is the most horrifying and most mysterious spectacle in history"—with these words Count de Gobineau opens his *Essay on the Inequality of the Human Races.* Oswald Spengler's influential book was entitled *The Decline of the West.* Edouard-Adolphe Drumont, author of *La France juive,* wrote in a similar vein: "There is nothing more instructive than the examination of the first signs of those diseases which slowly but relentlessly weaken, pervert, and finally destroy the body of . . . society." Extreme right-wing French authors whose writings abound with hatred and incitement, such as Maurice Barrès and Charles Maurras, reach the heights of lyricism in the description of the sadness of cemeteries, death of civilizations, the disintegration of traditional and stable forms of life in towns and villages, under the impact of the industrial revolution.

These writers' dread of some approaching end, the sense of decline and degeneration are accompanied by a morbid fear of
infection. Chamberlain remarked that one could be infected without coming into physical contact with the Jews. It sufficed to read
newspapers to which Jews contributed, or books they wrote, for
their poisonous influence to penetrate the human mind.

At the same time the writings, pamphlets, and papers of the
Nazis and various other groups of fascists are teeming with expressions such as "assault," "charge," and "break-out." It is strange
to note that baffling contradiction between the dread of Jews, and
the fierce desire to demonstrate strength and to assert superiority.

V

The disintegration of traditional and stable forms of life under the
impact of the Industrial Revolution and massive urbanization deprived man of the self-assurance of a creature of routine. The loss
of traditional stability makes man increasingly uncertain of his real
identity. Men have a feeling of impotence and frustration when
confronted with the terrible problems brought about by the development of technology—the fruit of man's genius and the glorious
vindication of his mastery over nature, and when faced with world
conflict often conducted by governments chosen by the common
man.

Reason has not succeeded in preventing or curing this mass
distress. There has been no single clear voice of reason in the
modern world. Reason has been employed to defend every possible
cause, and no evil action has ever lacked intellectuals to offer a
rational justification for it.

The mass movements of messianic totalitarianism came into
being as an expression of and response to the neurosis that has
held humanity in its grip throughout the modern age. It has been
pointed out many times that the secret of Hitler's extraordinary
success as a mob orator lay in his uncanny ability to strike the
most sensitive chords in the hearts of the masses. He knew how
to release the most hidden passions in the masses, to liberate them
from feelings of malaise and frustration, and to enable them to
take part in an ecstasy of anger, hatred, and fanatical enthusiasm.
There was a hypnotic effect in the permanent repetition of the

same themes, while the demonstrations of strength and acts of violence were intended to create the impression that here was a force that could not be resisted, that fate had already decided, and history had already pronounced and carried out its verdict. The masses were only too happy to be raped.

The Nazis had a preference for the *Jude* in the singular rather than for *Juden* in the plural, when speaking of the Jewish people. They refused to recognize differences, to discern individual faces or acknowledge different characteristics. One can detect in this the culmination of a long trend, whose dangerous potentialities were for the first time revealed in the French Revolution—the frame of mind that thinks of collective entities upon which history has pronounced a verdict of death. They are to be eliminated not for any crime committed by each of them or all of the members of the group together at that hour and in that place, but for the crime of having been born into that collective entity, be it aristocracy, the bourgeoisie, Kulaks, the Jews. The individual, his guilt or innocence, are irrelevant. The individuals are "they," specimens of a force which has to be destroyed, eliminated, annihilated.

Ironically, in the late stage of the war Goebbels would implore the Germans not to weaken, for they all shared the common responsibility, and the "Jews will never forgive us what we have done unto them and will never make any distinction between one German and another."

This frame of mind that is capable of ignoring fundamental moral distinctions was strongly enforced by those biological teachings which tend to abolish the barrier between human beings and the world of animals and plants. Formerly the bearer of an immortal soul, raised above all creation and creatures by his soul, reason, and consciousness, man has now, as it were, been integrated into the universal evolutionary process, and the fullness of life universal. As one of the protagonists, along with others in the struggle for existence, the human species, itself allegedly divided into struggling races, loses its uniqueness. Races emerge and races perish, and are wiped out from the surface of the earth. There are fine races and harmful species. And human life forfeits the sanctity that hallowed every individual soul for so long.

The absolute sanctification of the totality of life on earth in the spirit of universal pantheism is also conducive to an attitude of indifference to the life and dignity of man. For the difference between man and any other living creature has been blurred. Both are part of life universal, and the body of a man is only a temporary receptacle for that tiny fraction of life.

There is little doubt that the instinctive revulsion from taking away a human life had been greatly weakened in our day in comparison with the climate that has prevailed for some two centuries after the end of the wars of religion in the seventeenth century. If that be so, apocalyptic fears of an imminent Day of Judgment should not be lightly dismissed.

VI

The root cause of these mortally dangerous tendencies is the refusal, perhaps even inability, to take for granted the rights of man per se. Human rights, instead of being seen as natural and inalienable, are held to be a concession or a gift—to be bestowed by the masters among mankind on those others whose destiny it has been to serve the privileged, giving them a sense of higher dignity and that measure of communal cohesion which is cemented by the sight of the excluded outsiders. This assumption of a master-slave relationship is so deep-rooted that even at the historical hour of the apparent enthronement of the principles of the rights of man we see the simultaneous emergence of those rationalizations calculated to legitimate the denial of rights to entire groups without reference to any justifiable disqualification or personal guilt.

Often, of course, the outsiders, the "strangers in our midst," have been minorities and nonconformists, men of different religion or race or color. As the nonconformists par excellence, the Jews have epitomized the position of the outsider in Western societies. Yet, paradoxically, the stubborn retention of a separate identity has also been the source of their contribution to universalism throughout their history. Thus the Jews, though powerfully influenced by Hellenism, were not absorbed by the Graeco-Roman civilization. Conscious of being the only guardians of the tremendous message of the existence of a transcendental God, the source of all truth, the Jews successfully resisted assimilation. By remaining themselves alone, paradoxically, the Jews prepared the way for the universal message of Christianity. Nevertheless, despite its acknowledgment of Judaism as its source, Christianity denied legitimacy to the earlier religious tradition, and throughout the many centuries of Christendom's dominion over Western civilization, Jews were denied equality of rights. Consequently, the secular and universalist Enlightenment seemed to hold out to the Jews the promise of relief from religious intolerance. It soon emerged, however, that Jews were now exposed to attack from another direction, for the rationalist rejection of religion was incompatible with any religious reverance for the Jewish phenomenon, nor did its atomistic universalism allow for any raison d'être for a Jewish ethnic collectivity.

Notwithstanding their commitment to liberal individualism and their interest in social mobility, the majority of Jews neither would nor could disperse into human atoms. Nor, for that matter, was the majority community able to shed its historically conditioned view of the Jews as an indigestible collective entity. That view, moreover, had received a new stimulus from nationalism, especially its organicist and Darwinian variety. Lingering unwillingness to grant full legitimacy to Jews meant that any increased Jewish participation in the national life would be perceived as an alien invasion. And, as we have seen, that image of a compact alien force conjured up specters of an international Jewish plot to gain world mastery. The hatred and fear of the alien who had set out to dominate were now systematized and absolutized into the race theory which was to prove the fatal verdict for European Jewry.

Many Jews, especially in the poverty-stricken ghettoes of Eastern Europe, whose newly awakened sense of human and Jewish dignity was deeply offended by degrading czarist oppression and threatened by the hostility of nascent militant nationalisms, looked to the socialist revolution as the harbinger of universal equality and the liquidator of all types of oppression. In the light of the commitment and the contribution made by so many Jews to the cause of social revolution, it has come as a shock to behold the fatherland of socialism—which had originally taken a public stance against any form of anti-Semitism—now pursuing policies designed to eliminate all religious and cultural Jewish self-expression, barring to Jews the road to professional advancement, and giving free rein to defamatory public utterances. To many it must have seemed unbelievable that a Communist regime could, as did the Polish government a few years ago, resort to racist policies in the name of a "national self-respect which could not brook an undue influence by an ethnically foreign element." Should we see in this baffling volte face an example of the burden of history and of ineradicable prejudice? Is it another manifestation of the historic role of the Jews as nonconformists, dissidents? Or is it perhaps an expression of that ever-present opportunism which diverts social frustration in the direction of a vulnerable, always suspect, group of never quite fully recognized legitimacy?

The most recent, and not least baffling, episode in the long history of denial of rights to Jews centers on the embattled and isolated State of Israel. For centuries the curses of anti-Semites had been dispatching the unwanted Jews of all countries to Palestine. Finally, after almost two millennia in dispersion, the never-extinguished messianic dream of national restoration in the ancestral land, coinciding with a worldwide drive for national self-determination, combined into an irresistible resolve to create a Jewish national home in Palestine. The search for a refuge—whether from indignities, ambiguities, or ambivalences—by a people despairing of ever being accorded full status as men and as Jews was given burning urgency. The irreversible destruction of a Jewish civilization of well over a thousand years in Central Europe transformed the land of Israel into the sole repository and heir of that civilization.

Now, however, it almost seems a part of the curse pursuing the Jews to their Promised Land that their claims should there clash with the national aspirations of another people. The right of Jews to reclaim their ancient land has been uncompromisingly rejected by the modern Palestinian Arabs, notwithstanding the asymmetry between the exclusive significance of Israel to the Jewish people and the colossal arena upon which the Arab civilization is free to unfold. It has also been the singular misfortune of the Jews that their return to their ancestral home coincided with the withdrawal of the Western colonial presence from Asia and Africa. For while the Christian nations of the West, conscience-stricken by the Holocaust, have not allowed their commitment to the preservation of the Jewish state to be entirely overcome by political and economic self-interest, the newly emerged nations of Asia and Africa—whose record is free of anti-Semitism but also empty of Jews or of any association with Judaism—fail to comprehend the unique relationship between the Jewish people and the land of Israel. They can therefore be easily blandished into joining in the condemnation of the State of Israel as an outpost of "American imperialism" and the embodiment of "racist Zionism."

So, at the very hour and from the very forum of the apparent enshrinement of the universal principle of human rights we have heard the latest version of the denial of legitimacy and rights to the Jewish people.

The case of the Jews is that of a product and at the same time a victim of history. History has been its Archimedean point as well as its prison. Its uniqueness has been the secret of its universality, and simultaneously the justification for the enmity of its adversaries. Man's stand toward history should be likened to that of psychoanalysis, and indeed also to that of the fighters for human rights: to recognize the extreme potency of the determinations, deprivations, and compulsions created by the past, and to lay them bare, while endeavoring to liberate men from their thralldom.